Accounting for Changing Prices

WILEY/HAMILTON Series in
Management, Accounting, and Information Systems

Consulting Editor   John W. Buckley

Buckley and Buckley
The Accounting Profession

Buckley, Nagaraj, Sharp, and Schenk
Management Problem-Solving with APL

DeCoster, Ramanathan, and Sundem
Accounting for Managerial Decision Making

Estes
Accounting and Society

Estes
Corporate Social Accounting

Hill
Information Processing and Computer Programming: An Introduction

Kircher and Mason
Introduction to Enterprise: A Systems Approach

Largay and Livingstone
Accounting for Changing Prices

McCullers and Van Daniker
Introduction to Financial Accounting

McCullers and Van Daniker
Contemporary Business Environment: Readings in Financial Accounting

Mock and Vasarhelyi
APL for Management

Seidler
Social Accounting: Theory, Issues, and Cases

Sethi
The Unstable Ground: Corporate Social Policy in a Dynamic Society

Vazsonyi
Finite Mathematics/Quantitative Analysis for Management

Accounting for Changing Prices

Replacement Cost and
General Price Level Adjustments

James A. Largay III, Ph.D., CPA

Georgia Institute of Technology

John Leslie Livingstone, Ph.D., Chartered Accountant

Georgia Institute of Technology

A Wiley/Hamilton Publication
JOHN WILEY & SONS, INC
Santa Barbara   New York   London   Sydney   Toronto

This book was set by Typothetae in Illumna and Galaxy types
and printed and bound by Vail-Ballou Press. Joe Di Chiarro designed the book,
Barbara Phillips was the editor, and Charles Pendergast supervised production.

Library of Congress Cataloging in Publication Data

Largay, James A
    Accounting for changing prices.

    "A Wiley/Hamilton publication."
    Includes index.
    1.   Inflation (Finance) and accounting.
2.   Accounting and price fluctuations.   3.   Financial
statements.   I.   Livingston, John Leslie,
joint author.   II.   Title.
HF5657.L36   657   76-7491
ISBN 0-471-54210-5 (hard binding)
ISBN 0-471-02157-1 (soft binding)

Printed in the United States of America
10   9   8   7   6   5   4   3   2

About the authors

James A. Largay, III received his Ph.D. from Cornell University in 1971, and is a Certified Public Accountant in Colorado. Formerly on the faculty of Rice University, Dr. Largay has extensive public accounting experience and has written widely on direct costing and stock price behavior. He is currently Associate Professor in the College of Industrial Management at the Georgia Institute of Technology.

John Leslie Livingstone received his Ph.D. from Stanford University in 1965, and was previously the Arthur Young Distinguished Professor of Accounting at The Ohio State University. Dr. Livingstone is the writer of several books and numerous scholarly journal articles, and has served as a consultant to both the government and business sectors. He is presently Callaway Professor of Industrial Management at Georgia Institute of Technology.

Preface

Contemporary accounting practice is being subjected to the most significant criticism since the McKesson-Robbins fraud case, some forty years ago. Much of the criticism charges that contemporary financial reporting no longer adequately reflects the economic events underlying financial statements. Inflation is lessening the credibility of the accounting profession just as it is eroding the standard of living of people around the world. In short, many people argue that financial statements based on the assumption of a stable monetary unit are no longer realistic.

This book is designed to meet one aspect of inflation's challenge to contemporary accounting. It is a compact, self-contained explanation of how to adjust historical cost financial statements in order to reflect the impact of price changes. The concepts and techniques involved in this adjustment process are presented in an understandable and straightforward way. We hope that the book will contribute to a better understanding of the problem and its solution among students of accounting, professional accountants and others having a stake in the usefulness of financial statements. Of course, the other aspect of inflation's challenge to accounting refers to the profession's actual implementation of the proposals discussed herein. If the book helps the implementation process, the royalties we earn will be of secondary importance to us.

We have assumed that the reader has a solid working knowledge of basic financial accounting concepts and techniques. No sophisticated mathematics is employed; numerical examples are used throughout to illustrate and clarify points developed in the text. Exercises prepared to reinforce the text material are located at the conclusion of each chapter. This book should be adaptable to a wide variety of uses. For accounting students, it is tailor-made to serve as a supplementary text in intermediate and advanced financial accounting courses. It is equally suitable for professional accountants, whether in public practice, in corporate positions or elsewhere, who seek a practical treatment of this important subject.

We acknowledge a significant intellectual debt to Edgar O. Edwards and Philip W. Bell. Their classic work, *The Theory and Measurement of Business Income* (University of California Press), was first published in 1961. Much of the subject matter in this book is based on the principles and procedures developed by Edwards and Bell.

Professor Roman L. Weil of the Georgia Institute of Technology read the entire manuscript carefully and commented incisively. Many of his suggestions have been incorporated to improve the text. In addition, we are indebted to our students who struggled through earlier drafts of the manuscript and contributed helpful suggestions. We also thank Betty Jean Smith for efficient editorial and typing assistance and Sandra Mashburn and Kathy Jaye for their help in typing the manuscript. Finally, we gratefully acknowledge the professional performance of the editorial staff at Wiley/Hamilton at all stages of this project and particularly wish to recognize Barbara Phillips for a superb job of copyediting.

Despite the efforts of all those who played a role in this project, some errors undoubtedly remain. These are, of course, our responsibility.

Atlanta, Georgia   J.A.L.
January 1976   J.L.L.

Contents

1 Introduction: The Problem and Its Significance   1
  Questions and Problems   5

2 Accounting for Changes in the General Price-Level   7
  Introduction to General Price-Level Adjustments   8
    Restatement of the Income Statement   9
    Restatement of the Statement of Financial Position   10
  Illustrative Example 2.1   12
  Illustrative Example 2.2   21
    Restatement of the Statement of Changes in Financial
    Position   42
    Restatement when Intra-Year Price Changes are Large   44
  Proof of the Restatement Procedure   46
  Summary and Conclusion   47
  Appendix: Monetary and Nonmonetary Items   48
  Questions and Problems   52

3 Price Level Accounting: Some Further
  Considerations   59
  The Indiana Telephone Corporation Financial Statements   59
    Comments on the Indiana Telephone Corporation
    Statements   68
  Other Examples of Price Level Adjusted Financial
  Statements   72
  Other Issues Associated with General Price Level Adjustments   76
    The Income Tax Question   76
    Accounts Stated in Foreign Currency   79
    Lower of Cost or Market and Price Level Restatements   81
  The Nature of Price Level Indexes   83
  The Impact of Inflation Upon Financial Statements   84
  Summary and Evaluation of General Price Level Adjusted
  Financial Statements   88
  Appendix: "Inflation Accounting—What Will
  General Price Level Adjusted Statements Show?"   91

4 Accounting for Changes in Specific Prices   111

Introduction to Replacement Cost Accounting   113
Analysis of the Replacement Cost Income Statement   117
   Realizable Cost Savings   117
   Realized Cost Savings   119
   Unrealized Cost Savings   120
A Brief Analysis and Evaluation of Replacement Cost
Accounting   124
   Treatment of Cost Savings in Subsequent Periods   127
Summary   128
Questions and Problems   129

5 The Theory behind Replacement Cost Accounting   131

Net Income: Operating Income and Realizable Income   131
   Realized Income vs. Realizable Income   132
Alternative Bases for Valuation and Income Measurement   135
   Entry Prices   135
   Exit Prices   135
   Bases for Preferring a Replacement Cost Entry Price over
   an Opportunity Value Exit Price   140
Summary of the Components of Replacement Cost Income   142
Questions and Problems   143

6 Replacement Cost Treatment of Inventories   145

Review of Historical Cost Inventory Accounting   146
Replacement Cost Inventory Accounting   149
   Computation of Realized Cost Savings   150
   Computation of Realizable Cost Savings   150
   Effects when Inventories are Decreasing   160
   A Note on Perpetual Inventories   162
   Lower of Cost or Market and Replacement Cost
   Accounting   162
Replacement Costs, Inventory Profits, Operating Income
and Distributable Profits   163
Manufactured Inventories   166
LIFO Inventory Accounting and Inflation   167
Questions and Problems   171

7 Replacement Cost Treatment of Fixed Assets   173

Replacement Cost Accounting and Fixed Assets   173
   The "Revalorization" Problem   177

Other Issues in the Replacement Cost Treatment of Fixed
Assets   180
   Accelerated Depreciation: Sum-of-the-Years-Digits   180
   Accelerated Depreciation: Double-Declining Balance   181
   Replacement Cost Depreciation in Fixed Manufacturing
   Overhead Rates   184
Questions and Problems   187

8 Replacement Cost Treatment of Other Accounts   189
   Investments in Securities with No Fixed Return   189
   Securities with Fixed Return   191
   Questions and Problems   194

9 Illustration of Comprehensive Replacement Cost
   Financial Statements   196
   Comprehensive Replacement Cost Financial Statements   197
   Deferred Income Taxes on Unrealized Cost Savings/Holding
   Gains   204
     Disclosure on the Statement of Financial Position   207
   Summary   209
   Questions and Problems   210

10 Practical Determination of Replacement Costs   212
   Determination of Replacement Costs   212
     Valuation of Tobacco Leaf Inventory   214
     Buildings, Plant and Equipment   215
   Replacement versus Reproduction Cost   220
   Replacement Cost Estimation: Summary and Final Examples   221
     Illustrative Example 10.1: Barber-Ellis of Canada, Limited 222
   Summary   232
   Appendix A: Philips Lamp   233
   Appendix B: Sea Pines Company   246
   Questions and Problems   257

11 Integration of General Price-Level and Specific
   Price-Change Adjustments   259
   Importance of Measurement and Valuation Problems   259
   Introduction to Real Profit   262

General Procedure for the Preparation of Financial
Statements Reporting Price Level Adjusted Replacement
Cost Data   263
   Calculation of Fictional Realizable Gains   264
   Calculation of Fictional Realized Gains   265
   Calculation of Real Gains   268
   Calculation of the Change in Real Unrealized Gains 269
   Statement of Real Income   271
   Replacement Cost Statement of Financial Position
   Adjusted for Changes in the General Price Level   274
   Replacement Cost Statement of Changes in Financial
   Position Adjusted for Changes in the General Price Level 276
Keeping Track of Real Data in the Accounts   277
Replacement Costs and Price Level Adjustments—An
Evaluation   281
Questions and Problems   283

12 Summary and Conclusions   288
   The Major Problems of Historical Cost Accounting   294
      The Rubber Ruler   295
      Holding Gains and Operating Results Confused 296
      Outdated Asset Values   296
      Showing the Impact of Inflation on the Firm 297
   Other Factors   297
   The Final Choice   299

Index   300

Accounting for Changing Prices

Introduction: The Problem
and Its Significance

One of the fundamentals upon which accounting is based is the stability of the unit of measurement, the dollar. Changes in the value of the monetary unit are assumed either not to occur or to be unimportant. While this assumption has never been completely accurate, it has become more and more unrealistic. In the last few years, inflation has increased rapidly. The stable-dollar assumption is no longer tenable. In the face of widely fluctuating prices, financial statements based on historical dollar values lose much of their significance. Management and the public may be better served by financial statements based on current dollar values.

Current dollar information with regard to financial statements would greatly assist management in making and evaluating business decisions. As one important example, a firm's earning power in the current economic environment could be more realistically appraised. Management could also evaluate the current dollar equivalent of invested capital.

By supplementing historical cost statements with current dollar information the public and government too would be better informed. Statistics compiled by government would become increasingly relevant to current economic conditions. This would aid in the development of effective government policies in such areas as taxation and regulation of economic affairs.

In order to present several methods for supplementing historical accounting data with useful current dollar information, we must consider two types of price changes. First, changes in the general price level should be dealt with; otherwise, realistic financial statements cannot be prepared. In a period of changing prices, the dollars of one period are not the same as the dollars of another period. They do not have the same purchasing power. The monetary measuring unit becomes *elastic*, rather than remaining *fixed*.

A change in purchasing power means that a dollar now will not buy the same goods that a dollar did last year. If prices are assumed to be rising, a dollar today will buy less than a dollar did a year ago. Similarly, a dollar now will buy more than a dollar will one year from now, if prices continue to rise. Thus, financial statements which add assets, liabilities, expenses and revenues measured in dollars originating in several periods and having unequal purchasing power may, if price changes are large, be meaningless. To produce financial statements in this manner is like adding grapes and oranges; it will yield some "units of fruit" but the "units" are too different to be measured and combined in this way.

The objective of this first method, discussed in Chapters 2 and 3, is to provide financial statements in which all information is reported in dollars of the same purchasing power.

Second, changes in the prices of specific items in the accounts (e.g., inventories and fixed assets) should be considered. All individual prices do not change at the same rate as the general price level. Some items may increase more rapidly than the general price level; some may increase less rapidly or even decline during a period of generally rising prices. Therefore, to fully account for the effects of changing prices, we need to deal with the impact of individual price changes on a firm's asset, liability, revenue and expense accounts.

It is important to understand clearly the distinction between individual-item price changes and the movement of the general price level. To clarify that distinction, consider a swarm of bees. Individual bees are analogous to individual-item prices; they can move up or down, or speed up or slow down independently of the swarm. Each can change its place in the swarm at any time. The swarm as a whole is the composite of all individual bees, just as the general price level is the composite of many individual prices. The general price level is represented by a single index, such as the Consumer Price Index, based on a weighted average of many individual commodity prices. Changes in *individual* prices (or movements of individual bees), however, cannot normally be determined through reference to movements in the general price level (or movements of the swarm as a whole).

As an example, the average Consumer Price Index and prices of several individual commodities for the years 1969–1974 are given in Table 1.1. As you can see, the prices shown did not all move in the same way. This is an important point and must be recognized in the preparation of financial statements.

This second method, to be discussed in Chapters 4 through 10, is designed to provide financial statements in which all information reported is based on current *specific prices* rather than on the current *general price level*.

The third and final method reflects our belief that accounting for either of the two types of price changes alone is not sufficient. Therefore, we will integrate the method of accounting for general price-level changes within the framework of accounting for specific price changes in Chapter 11.

Table 1.1

PRICE INDEX DATA, 1969–1974

1967 = 100	1969	1970	Change*	1971	Change*	1972	Change*	1973	Change*	1974	Change*
Consumer Price Index	109.8	116.3	5.9%	121.3	4.3%	125.3	3.3%	133.1	6.2%	147.7	11.0%
Individual Commodities:											
Food	108.9	114.9	5.5%	118.4	3.0%	123.5	4.3%	141.4	14.5%	161.7	14.4%
Housing	110.8	118.9	7.3%	124.3	4.5%	129.2	3.9%	135.0	4.5%	150.6	11.6%
Fuel Oil and Coal	105.6	110.1	4.3%	117.5	6.7%	118.5	0.9%	136.0	14.8%	214.6	57.8%
Apparel and Upkeep	111.5	116.1	4.1%	119.8	3.2%	122.3	2.1%	126.8	3.7%	136.2	7.4%
Transportation	107.2	112.7	5.1%	118.6	5.2%	119.9	1.1%	123.8	3.3%	137.7	11.2%
Health and Recreation	110.3	116.2	5.3%	122.2	5.2%	126.1	3.2%	130.2	3.3%	140.3	7.8%
Wholesale Price Index:											
22 Commodities	110.3	113.4	2.8%	108.0	(4.8)%	120.0	11.1%	173.8	44.8%	228.0	31.2%
13 Raw Industrials	111.4	113.8	2.2%	107.1	(5.9)%	123.0	14.8%	173.1	40.7%	219.0	26.5%
All Commodities	106.5	110.4	3.7%	113.9	3.2%	119.1	4.6%	134.7	13.1%	160.1	18.9%
Farm Products	108.8	111.0	2.0%	112.9	1.7%	125.0	10.7%	176.3	41.0%	187.7	6.5%
Industrial Commodities	106.0	110.0	3.8%	114.0	3.6%	117.9	3.4%	125.9	6.8%	153.8	22.2%
Coal	112.5	150.0	33.3%	181.8	21.2%	193.8	6.6%	218.2	12.6%	332.4	52.3%
Electric Power	102.0	104.8	2.7%	113.6	8.4%	121.5	7.0%	129.3	6.4%	163.1	26.1%

SOURCE: *Survey of Current Business*, U.S. Department of Commerce, Office of Business Economics.

*The percentage increase (decrease) in the index from the previous year.

The methods presented will produce supplementary financial statements derived from the historical cost accounts without destroying the historical data, which must be preserved so that historical cost financial statements can be prepared. Although the information in the supplementary statements gives a more realistic picture of events, historical cost statements are still needed for other accounting purposes, one of the most important of which is the computation of income taxes. Even though current income tax regulations often prescribe treatments which differ from generally accepted accounting principles, the regulations rely on historical cost accounting data.

Questions and Problems

1.1. What is meant by a change in purchasing power?

1.2. What is a general price index and what is its role in determining whether purchasing power has changed?

1.3. Why does the text stress the difference between changes in the general price level and changes in specific prices?

1.4. Assume that the Consumer Price Index increased to 120 from 100 two years ago. What is the gain (loss) in purchasing power represented by that change? How many dollars are required today to purchase what $5,000 purchased two years ago?

1.5. General price indexes are said to adequately measure changes in the general price level. Would a given index, such as the CPI or GNP Deflator, adequately reflect the effects of changing prices on individual consumer units and firms? Explain.

1.6. Briefly discuss the implications of changing prices for financial statements based on historical costs.

1.7. The *change* in a price index from time t to time $t + n$ is generally defined as

$$\frac{P_{t+n} - P_t}{P_t}$$

where P is the value of the price index. If an item procured during period t is to be restated to reflect the price level at time $t + n$, the restatement factor would be

$$\frac{P_t + (P_{t+n} - P_t)}{P_t} = \frac{P_{t+n}}{P_t} \qquad (1)$$

Similarly, if one wished to restate a price paid in period $t + n$ to reflect the (past) price level in period t, the restatement factor would be

$$\frac{P_{t+n} - (P_{t+n} - P_t)}{P_{t+n}} = \frac{P_t}{P_{t+n}} \qquad (2)$$

In a period of rising prices, (1) *inflates* a past dollar amount to its current dollar equivalent and (2) *deflates* a current dollar amount to its past dollar equivalent.

a. A professor earned $10,000 several years ago when the CPI stood at 110.

If the CPI rises to 132, how much should the professor earn to stay even with the general level of inflation?

b. The professor currently pays $600 per month for consumption expenses. The CPI is 132. How much would have been spent on these expenses when the CPI stood at 100?

c. Ten years ago the professor purchased a color television set for $600, when the CPI stood at 80. With the CPI now at 132, such a television set would now probably cost

$$\frac{P_{t+n}}{P_t} \times \$600 = \frac{132}{80} \times \$600 = \$990$$

Do you agree? Explain.

d. Five years ago the professor paid $20 a month for electric power used in his home, when the CPI was at 105. Now the CPI is at 132, and thus his electric bill would be about

$$\frac{132}{105} \times \$20 = \$25 \text{ a month}$$

Do you agree? Explain.

Accounting for Changes in the General Price Level

Accounting for changes in the general price level has been under study, more or less continuously, since the 1920s and 1930s.* A relatively simple and inexpensive method to account for the effects of inflation, the method requires no change in existing accounting principles; the measurement unit is merely restated. In many respects, the adjustment procedure is similar to that used in translating foreign currency accounts and transactions: the accounts measured in foreign currency are translated to the domestic currency by means of an appropriate *exchange rate,* which expresses the equivalence between dollars and units of the foreign currency. Thus, the foreign account balances, based on one type of measurement, are restated in terms of the domestic currency, another type of measurement. This general notion of translation also holds for price-level adjustments, except that the *types* of measurement are dollar balances generated over *time.* The objective is to restate in *current* dollars those events measured in *past* dollars.

Accounting for changes in the general price level is currently being studied more vigorously than ever before. The accelerating inflation experienced in the late 1960s and early 1970s could not be ignored. Other countries have already responded to the effects of inflation on financial statements. Specifically, general price-level adjustment procedures have been recommended by the English Institute of Chartered Accountants and by the Canadian Institute of Chartered Accountants. In addition, several Latin American countries have been employing these procedures to adjust financial statements for the high rates of inflation which they have been experiencing.

---

*See, for instance, Henry W. Sweeney, *Stabilized Accounting* (Harper & Row, 1936). The 1963 publication of Accounting Research Study No. 6, *Reporting the Financial Effects of Price-Level Changes* by the AICPA motivated a heightened interest in the subject.

In the United States, we expect that definitive action will shortly be forthcoming.* In 1969 the Accounting Principles Board (APB) of the AICPA issued its Statement 3 entitled "Financial Statements Restated for General Price-Level Changes," and in December 1974 the Financial Accounting Standards Board (FASB) published "Financial Reporting in Units of General Purchasing Power," the Exposure Draft of a proposed statement of financial accounting standards. As this book was being written, public commentary on the Exposure Draft was being received and evaluated by the FASB. Although the contents of the Exposure Draft are unofficial, this book employs the procedures presented there; they are, in general, consistent with those published in APB Statement 3. Although we gently remind the reader that general price-level adjustments represent but one response to the effects of inflation, we are pleased that the accounting profession is making a real attempt to come to grips with the problem.

Introduction to General Price-Level Adjustments

In conventional accounting, based on historical dollars, the position statement** and the income statement are reported in dollars of varied purchasing power. As we have stated, items from one period cannot be added to items from another period to produce realistic statements. Consider the following example relative to fixed assets.

Assume that a firm purchased equipment as follows:

Date	Equipment Cost
1957	$1,000
1962	1,200
1968	1,700
1974	1,400

The normal accounting convention is to add these together and to report equipment as $5,300 (before depreciation). However, to add 1957, 1962, 1968 and 1974 dollars together is not appropriate. This would be comparable to adding grapes, oranges, cantaloupes and watermelons. It is clearly a violation of the most basic principles of aggregation.

In statements adjusted for general price-level changes, the unit of measure is a dollar with purchasing power at a specific date, usually that of the latest position statement. Only by adjusting all financial statement

---

*As this book goes to press, competing proposals are appearing. In August 1975, the U.S. Securities and Exchange Commission issued proposed rules for disclosure of certain replacement cost (rather than price-level) information. Shortly thereafter, the Sandilands Commission in Great Britain issued a report recommending that replacement cost accounting be employed. These proposals are briefly reviewed in Chapter 4.

**Throughout this text, we use *position statement* or *statement of financial position* in lieu of the more traditional term *balance sheet*.

items to the purchasing power as of the specified date can the statements be based on a standard unit of measure. Items of one period can then be added to items of another period.* Furthermore, general price-level statements of earlier periods should be updated to allow interperiod comparison in dollars of common purchasing power.

Except for the computation of the purchasing-power gain or loss on monetary items, to which we shall return shortly, restatement of the income statement is fairly straightforward. Each income statement item will be restated in end-of-period dollars by multiplying it by a *restatement factor* or *ratio to restate*.

Restatement of the Income Statement

$$\text{Ratio to Restate} = \frac{\text{Price Level at}}{\text{End of Period}} \Big/ \frac{\text{Price Level When}}{\text{Item Originated}}$$

For example, if sales of \$140,000 occurred at an average price level of 120 and the year-end price level is 132, restated sales equal \$154,000 [= \$140,000 × (132/120)].

Purchasing-Power Gain or Loss on Monetary Items.   General price-level restatements introduce a new item into the income statement—the purchasing-power gain or loss on monetary items. *Monetary items are those assets and liabilities having fixed dollar values, regardless of changes in prices.*

During a period of rising prices, a given quantity of money buys less and less over time. Thus, if cash or other monetary assets (with fixed dollar values) are held during a period of inflation, a loss in purchasing power occurs. Monetary liabilities, however, generate a gain in purchasing power because the money owed declines in value during inflation. It takes less purchasing power to pay off the debts.

Monetary assets and liabilities, then, bring about real losses or gains as a direct result of inflation (i.e., losses or gains in purchasing power). Examples of monetary assets include cash on hand, bank deposits and accounts receivable. Monetary liabilities include accounts and notes payable, dividends declared but not paid and long-term debt.

---

*It is important to understand that technological change detracts from comparability over time. For example, a 1966 Chevrolet is not the same piece of equipment as a 1976 Chevrolet. Even when prices are stable, accounting valuations do not reflect changing technologies. Adjusting for price-level changes does not overcome this problem either; it merely restates the dollars expended for the 1966 Chevrolet in terms of their general purchasing-power equivalent in 1976 dollars.

We define net monetary items as monetary assets less monetary liabilities. If net monetary items are positive during a period of inflation, there is a purchasing-power loss. The gain in purchasing power attributed to the monetary liabilities is more than offset by the loss in purchasing power of the monetary assets. The opposite will be true for a negative net monetary item position during a period of inflation. Furthermore, if the net monetary items *increase* during inflation, the purchasing-power loss will be greater (or the gain smaller).

The purchasing-power gain or loss is calculated by multiplying net monetary items and all changes in net monetary items by the appropriate restatement factors and then subtracting the historical monetary values.

$$\text{Purchasing-Power Gain or Loss} = \frac{\text{Historical Monetary Item or}}{\text{Change in Monetary Item}} \times$$
$$\left(\frac{\text{Price Level at}}{\text{End of Period}} \Big/ \frac{\text{Price Level When}}{\text{Item Originated}}\right) - \frac{\text{Historical Monetary Item}}{\text{or Change in Monetary Item}}$$

Positive net monetary items (i.e., monetary assets > monetary liabilities) and increases in net monetary items due to transactions such as sales will generate purchasing-power losses. Negative net monetary items (i.e., monetary liabilities > monetary assets) and decreases in net monetary items due to transactions such as merchandise purchases will generate purchasing-power gains. The purchasing-power gain or loss is the amount by which a monetary item *should have changed*, in the face of a changing price level, *to preserve the purchasing power inherent in the item.* Therefore, since the dollar value of monetary items is *fixed*, a rising price level will result in purchasing-power losses on positive monetary items and purchasing-power gains on negative monetary items.

For example, assume that the ending price level is 110. If sales of $2,000 were made when the price level stood at 100, at the end of the period the monetary assets generated by those sales would suffer a purchasing-power *loss* of $200 [= $2,000 × (110/100) − $2,000]. Similarly, if merchandise purchases of $1,500 were made on account when the price level was 100, the monetary liabilities generated by those purchases would provide a purchasing-power *gain* of $150 [= $1,500 × (110/100) − $1,500]. The dollars *owned* had *lost* purchasing power; the dollars *owed* had produced a *gain* in purchasing power because less purchasing power would be required to liquidate the fixed quantity of dollars owed.

Restatement of the
Statement of
Financial Position

Monetary items are those assets and liabilities having fixed dollar values, regardless of changes in prices. All other assets and liabilities are *nonmonetary,* that is, their money values can change as price levels fluctuate.

Whether there are purchasing-power gains or losses associated with non-monetary items depends on how their prices move *relative to* the general price level. For example, when the specific price of a nonmonetary asset rises faster than the general price level, a real gain occurs.* Typical nonmonetary assets are inventories and fixed assets.

On the statement of financial position, nonmonetary items will be restated in dollars of end-of-period purchasing power.

$$\text{Restated Nonmonetary Item} = \text{Historical Nonmonetary Item} \times \left(\frac{\text{Price Level at End of Period}}{\text{Price Level When Item Originated}} \right)$$

For example, if equipment was acquired for $10,000 when the price index was 110, its restated value when the price index is 143 is $13,000 [$= \$10,000 \times (143/110)$]. Monetary items, however, will not be restated because they represent fixed quantities of dollars. It should be observed, however, that the potential amount of restatement of monetary items will be reflected in the computation of the purchasing-power gain or loss. In subsequent years, of course, all of the prior period account balances, both monetary and nonmonetary, will be restated for comparative statement purposes.

Some items have both monetary and nonmonetary characteristics and should be classified according to the major purpose for which they are held. The appendix to this chapter lists common accounts, indicates the appropriate monetary/nonmonetary classification and provides some guidance for those accounts in which the monetary/nonmonetary distinction is not clear-cut.

Illustrative Example 2.1 shows how to prepare financial statements adjusted for changes in the general price level. The scenario involves a firm which has been in business for two years. At the end of the second year, it is decided that the historical cost financial statements for the two years are to be restated in dollars reflecting the general price level at the end of year two.

---

*Determination of such *real gains* on nonmonetary items is the subject of Chapter 11. The price-level restatement procedures discussed here are not designed to reveal real gains or losses on nonmonetary items.

**Illustrative
Example 2.1.***

The purpose of the following demonstration is to provide a simplified illustration of the essential features of price-level adjustments of financial statements, and to contribute to an understanding of the effect of price-level changes. It is not intended to provide a detailed technical guide for the use of an accountant in preparing a set of adjusted financial statements for an actual case. It will be followed by comments on certain variations and special problems not covered in the basic demonstration.

The illustration will include a two-year period, beginning with the opening of business. Adjusted income statements will be prepared for each of the two years, and adjusted balance sheets for the opening of business, the close of the first year, and the close of the second year.

The following price-level index numbers are assumed for use in the demonstration:

Opening of business	150	Second year—average	190
First year—average	160	Second year—end	200
First year—end	175		

The financial statements will be restated in terms of the *dollar at the end of the second year*, that is, in terms of the *"current dollar"* when the index is at 200.

Other assumptions are:

1. The inventory is priced on a first-in, first-out (Fifo) basis.

2. All revenue and expenses, except for depreciation and that portion of the cost of goods sold represented by the beginning inventory, are earned or incurred evenly throughout each year, i.e., in effect, the transactions occur at the average price level of the year.

3. Dividends are declared and paid at the end of each year.

4. At the beginning of the second year, $50,000 of the long-term liabilities are paid in cash, and $300,000 are converted to capital stock.

5. Acquisitions of plant and equipment take place at the opening of business and at the close of the first year. The land on which the plant is located is held under a lease, so all items of plant and equipment are subject to depreciation. The average depreciation rate is 10 per cent a year on the straight-line basis.

---

*Source: Accounting Research Study No. 6, *Reporting the Financial Effects of Price-Level Changes.* Copyright 1963. Reprinted with the permission of the American Institute of Certified Public Accountants, Inc.

Comparative Income Statement (Historical Basis)

	First Year	*Second Year*
SALES	$800,000	$1,000,000
OPERATING EXPENSES:		
Cost of goods sold	$470,000	$ 600,000
Depreciation	30,000	40,000
Other expenses (including income tax)	280,000	300,000
Total Operating Expenses	$780,000	$ 940,000
NET PROFIT FROM OPERATIONS	$ 20,000	$ 60,000

Comparative Statement of Retained Earnings (Historical Basis)

Retained Earnings, Beginning of Year	$ ——	$15,000
Net Profit from Operations	20,000	60,000
Total	$20,000	$75,000
Dividends to Stockholders	5,000	10,000
Retained Earnings, End of Year	$15,000	$65,000

Comparative Balance Sheet (Historical Basis)

	Opening of Business	*End of First Year*	*End of Second Year*
ASSETS			
Cash, Receivables, and Other Monetary Items	$200,000	$195,000	$235,000
Inventories	250,000	300,000	200,000
Plant and Equipment	300,000	400,000	400,000
Less: Accumulated Depreciation	——	(30,000)	(70,000)
Total Assets	$750,000	$865,000	$765,000
LIABILITIES			
Current Liabilities	$100,000	$200,000	$100,000
Long-term Liabilities	350,000	350,000	——
Total Liabilities	$450,000	$550,000	$100,000
STOCKHOLDERS' EQUITY			
Capital Stock	$300,000	$300,000	$600,000
Retained Earnings	——	15,000	65,000
Total Stockholders' Equity	$300,000	$315,000	$665,000
Total Liabilities and Stockholders' Equity	$750,000	$865,000	$765,000

Adjustment of Income and Retained Earnings Statements

Sales

Sales took place evenly throughout the year, so, in effect, they took place at the average dollar of the year, i.e., when the price index was at the average for the year. The adjustment of the sales amounts to the end-of-second-year dollar, or the current dollar, would be:

First year: $ 800,000 × 200/160 = $1,000,000
Second year: $1,000,000 × 200/190 = $1,052,632

Cost of Goods Sold*

Under the first-in, first-out (Fifo) method of inventory pricing, the cost of goods sold is measured by the beginning inventory plus a portion of the merchandise purchased during the period.

First year. The beginning inventory was acquired at the opening of business when the index number was 150. The merchandise purchases were made at the average price level of the year, or when the index number was 160. The adjustments to express the cost of goods sold in terms of the current dollar would be:

Beginning inventory	$250,000 × 200/150 =	$333,333
Portion of merchandise purchases	220,000 × 200/160 =	275,000
Cost of goods sold	$470,000	$608,333

The traditional calculation of cost of goods sold could have been used. (The merchandise purchases of $520,000 is derived from the other related figures.)

Beginning inventory	$250,000 × 200/150 =	$333,333
Merchandise purchases	520,000 × 200/160 =	650,000
	$770,000	$983,333
Ending inventory	300,000 × 200/160 =	375,000
Cost of goods sold	$470,000	$608,333

Second year. The beginning inventory of $300,000 at historical cost, or $375,000 as adjusted to the current dollar, is carried forward from the close of the first year. An additional $300,000 (historical cost) is a part of the merchandise purchased during the second year when the price index was at 190. The adjustments are:

Beginning inventory	$300,000 × 200/160 =	$375,000
Portion of merchandise purchases	300,000 × 200/190 =	315,789
Cost of goods sold	$600,000	$690,789

Depreciation

The most time-consuming step in the adjustment process is the "aging" of the depreciable property and the corresponding adjustment of the periodic depreciation. Strictly speaking, the date of acquisition of each item of property must be determined as well as its cost, and the corresponding depreciation must be adjusted to the current-dollar basis. Once the "aging" process has been carried out, however, it can be kept up to date with a relatively small amount of time and effort. Various simplifications can be introduced. All items acquired at approximately the same time, such as a month or a quarter, can be grouped together and treated as a single item, unless the depreciation charge to operations must be broken down for more detailed accounting purposes. An arbitrary cut-off point can sometimes be used

---

*The careful reader will observe that a strict application of FIFO is not being used here. Since inventory did not decline to zero during the year, the portion of merchandise purchases charged to cost of goods sold was not acquired at the average price level for the year. Under FIFO, the earliest merchandise purchases are charged to cost of goods sold. In this case, merchandise purchases acquired during the first half of the year (when the price level was *less than* 160) should enter cost of goods sold, resulting in a cost of goods sold *higher* than that shown in the example. It appears that, for restatement purposes, FIFO is being combined with the weighted average cost flow assumption.

for the older items of property, which are often a small proportion of the total, and all items acquired prior to a certain point of time can be treated as though they were all acquired at the cut-off point. Where a very large number of similar units of equipment are in use, statistical methods are available for the aging calculation. Survivorship tables, similar to the mortality tables used by insurance companies, may be employed to determine under rules of statistical probability how many items are in use, classified by date of acquisition.

Ordinarily the simplest way to revise the depreciation charges is to apply the normal depreciation rates to the adjusted cost amounts. In the demonstration, the $300,000 of plant and equipment used during the first year was acquired at the beginning of that year, and the addition of $100,000 was acquired at the close of the first year. The calculations are:

Plant and equipment, acquired at beginning of first year,	
$300,000 × 200/150	$400,000
Plant and equipment, acquired at end of first year,	
$100,000 × 200/175	114,286
Total adjusted cost of plant and equipment, beginning and end of second year	$514,286
Depreciation, first year— 10% of $400,000	$ 40,000
Depreciation, second year—10% of $514,286	51,429

Other Expenses

The other expenses, which include income tax expense, were incurred evenly throughout each year or at the average dollar of the year. The adjustments are:

First year,	$280,000 × 200/160 = $350,000
Second year,	$300,000 × 200/190 = $315,789

Dividends

Dividends to stockholders were declared and paid at the end of each year. The adjustments are:

First year,	$ 5,000 × 200/175 = $ 5,714
Second year,	$10,000 × 200/200 = $10,000

Gain or Loss on Monetary Items

A loss in purchasing power of monetary items arises from holding monetary assets during a period of rising prices or from maintaining liabilities during a period of falling prices. A gain is the reverse; it arises from holding monetary assets during a period of falling prices or from maintaining liabilities during a period of rising prices.

The purchasing-power gain or loss on monetary assets and liabilities appears only on adjusted financial statements. Differences of opinion exist as to the method of reporting these gains and losses, but for purposes of this demonstration, they will be treated in a statement of income and inflation gain or loss as separately disclosed elements immediately following the determination of net profit.

The amount of the accumulated net gain or loss on monetary items can be calculated by determining the amount needed to balance the financial statements after making all adjustments of the nonmonetary accounts. A more detailed analysis, however, is desirable as a verification of the net gain or loss and to analyze it as to types of monetary items. The calculation in the demonstration will be made in two parts: (1) the gain or loss on the net current monetary items, and (2) the gain or loss on the long-term liabilities.

There are several ways of computing the gain or loss from holding monetary items. The computations which follow are in more detail than would ordinarily be needed because in an actual case calculation could be facilitated by grouping together items to be adjusted by the same multiplier. Regardless of the method chosen, however, care must be used to insure consistency. That is, both sides of a transaction must be adjusted by the same index number. In our illustration, for example, the choice of the index number at the end of the first year to adjust the acquisition of plant and equipment dictates that the outlay of monetary assets for plant and equipment in that year be adjusted by the index at the same date.

Net Current Monetary Items

	Opening of Business	End of First Year	End of Second Year
Cash, receivables, and other monetary items	$200,000	$195,000	$235,000
Current liabilities	100,000	200,000	100,000
Net monetary assets (liabilities)	$100,000	($ 5,000)	$135,000

First Year	Unadjusted Amount	Multiplier	Adjusted Amount
Net monetary assets—beginning	$100,000	175/150	$116,667
add—			
Sales	800,000	175/160	875,000
	$900,000		$991,667
deduct—			
Purchases of merchandise	$520,000	175/160	$568,750
Other expenses	280,000	175/160	306,250
Dividends paid at end of year	5,000	175/175	5,000
Plant and equipment purchased at end of year	100,000	175/175	100,000
	$905,000		$980,000
Net monetary assets—end	($ 5,000)		$ 11,667
			(5,000)
Purchasing-power loss			$ 16,667

Since this loss is stated in terms of the dollar at the end of the first year, it must be converted into terms of the dollar at the end of the second year for inclusion in the adjusted statements:

$$\$16,667 \times 200/175 = \$19,047 \text{ (Loss)}$$

Second Year	Unadjusted Amount	Multiplier	Adjusted Amount
Net monetary assets—beginning	$ (5,000)	200/175	$ (5,714)
add—			
Sales	1,000,000	200/190	1,052,632
	$ 995,000		$1,046,918
deduct—			
Retirement of debt at beginning of year	$ 50,000	200/175	$ 57,144
Purchases of merchandise	500,000	200/190	526,316
Other expenses	300,000	200/190	315,789
Dividends paid at end of year	10,000	200/200	10,000
	$ 860,000		$ 909,249
Net monetary assets—end	$ 135,000		$ 137,669
			135,000
Purchasing-power loss			$ 2,669

Long-term Liabilities

	First Year	Second Year
Balance at beginning of year	$350,000	$350,000
Balance at end of year	350,000	——
Decrease during year	None	$350,000

First year. The $350,000 of long-term liabilities remained constant throughout the year. The calculation of the purchasing-power gain for the year, converted into terms of the dollar at the end of the second year is:

$$\$350,000 \times 175/150 = \$408,333;$$
$$\$408,333 - \$350,000 = \$ 58,333;$$
$$\$ 58,333 \times 200/175 = \$ 66,667 \text{ (gain).}$$

Second year. There is no gain or loss of purchasing power because the decrease took place at the beginning of the year.

Summary

	First Year	Second Year
Loss on net current monetary assets	$19,047	$2,669
Gain on long-term liabilities	66,667	——
Net gain or loss	$47,620 (Gain)	$2,669 (Loss)

The adjusted comparative income statement can now be prepared in terms of "end-of-second-year" dollars and appears as follows:

**Adjusted Comparative Statement of Income and
Inflation Gain (Loss)**

	First Year	*Second Year*
SALES	$1,000,000	$1,052,632
OPERATING EXPENSES:		
Cost of goods sold	$ 608,333	$ 690,789
Depreciation	40,000	51,429
Other expenses (including income tax)	350,000	315,789
Total Operating Expenses	$ 998,333	$1,058,007
Net Profit (Loss) From Operations	$ 1,667	$ (5,375)
INFLATION GAINS OR LOSSES		
Gain (loss) on short-term monetary items	$ (19,047)	$ (2,669)
Gain (loss) on long-term debt	66,667	—
Net Inflation Gain (Loss)	$ 47,620	$ (2,669)
NET PROFIT AND NET INFLATION GAIN (LOSS)	$ 49,287	$ (8,044)

Adjusted Comparative Statement of Retained Earnings

Retained Earnings, Beginning of Year	$ —	$43,573
Net Profit and Net Inflation Gain (Loss)	49,287	(8,044)
Total	$49,287	$35,529
Dividends to Stockholders	5,714	10,000
Retained Earnings, End of Year	$43,573	$25,529

Adjustment of the Balance Sheet

Monetary Items

The amounts of the monetary items at the end of the second year require no adjustment since they are, as legal tender, or by agreement with the debtors and creditors, receivable or payable in current dollars. The amounts at the opening of business and at the end of the first year, however, must be restated in order to express them in terms of the purchasing power of the dollar at the end of the second year.

Cash, Receivables, and Other Monetary Items:

Opening of business,	$200,000 × 200/150 = $266,667
End of first year,	$195,000 × 200/175 = $222,857
End of second year,	$235,000 × 200/200 = $235,000

Current Liabilities:

Opening of business,	$100,000 × 200/150 = $133,333
End of first year,	$200,000 × 200/175 = $228,570
End of second year,	$100,000 × 200/200 = $100,000

Long-term Liabilities:

Opening of business,	$350,000 × 200/150 = $466,667
End of first year,	$350,000 × 200/175 = $400,000
End of second year,	None

Inventories

The merchandise inventory at the opening of business was acquired at the price level of that date. The inventories at the end of the first and second years were, under the Fifo pricing method, assumed to have been acquired at the average price level of each of the respective years. The adjustments to the current-dollar basis, therefore, are:

Opening of business,	$250,000 \times 200/150 = $333,333
End of first year,	$300,000 \times 200/160 = $375,000
End of second year,	$200,000 \times 200/190 = $210,526

Plant and Equipment

The adjustment of the plant and equipment was demonstrated in the previous section, "Adjustment of the Income Statement." The adjusted amounts for the plant and equipment were:

Opening of business,	$400,000*
End of first year,	$514,286*
End of second year,	$514,286

The adjusted amount of accumulated depreciation can be derived from the adjusted annual depreciation, as follows:

End of first year, 10% of $400,000*	$40,000
Depreciation during second year, 10% of $514,286	51,429
Accumulated depreciation, end of second year	$91,429

Capital Stock

The first $300,000 was issued at the opening of business. The next $300,000 was issued by conversion of long-term liabilities at the beginning of the second year. Expressed in terms of the current dollar, the adjusted capital stock appears as follows:

Issued at opening of business,	$300,000 \times 200/150 = $400,000
Issued at beginning of second year,	$300,000 \times 200/175 = 342,854
Total, end of second year	$742,854

Retained Earnings

The adjusted retained earnings are derived from the series of adjusted income statements. As a matter of informative disclosure for purposes of this demonstration, the retained earnings from ordinary operations will be shown separately from the accumulated gain or loss on monetary items:

Retained earnings from operations:

---

*Recall that $400,000 of plant and equipment was held throughout the first year. The additional plant and equipment were acquired at the *end* of the first year. No depreciation was allocated on this additional amount during the first year.

	First Year	Second Year
Carried over from previous year	$ —	($4,047)
Net profit or (loss) from operations	1,667	(5,375)
	$1,667	($9,422)
Adjusted dividends	5,714	10,000
Retained earnings from operations	($4,047)	($19,422)

Accumulated gain or loss on net monetary items:

Gain on net monetary items, first year	$47,620
Loss on net monetary items, second year	2,669
Accumulated gain on net monetary items	$44,951

Adjusted Comparative Balance Sheet

	Opening of Business	End of First year	End of Second year
ASSETS			
Cash, Receivables, and Other Monetary Items	$ 266,667	$ 222,857	$235,000
Inventories	333,333	375,000	210,526
Plant and Equipment	400,000	514,286	514,286
Less Accumulated Depreciation	—	(40,000)	(91,429)
Total Assets	$1,000,000	$1,072,143	$868,383
LIABILITIES			
Current Liabilities	$ 133,333	$ 228,570	$100,000
Long-term Liabilities	466,667	400,000	—
	$ 600,000	$ 628,570	$100,000
STOCKHOLDERS' EQUITY			
Capital Stock	$ 400,000	$ 400,000	$742,854
Retained Earnings:			
From Operations (after dividends)	—	(4,047)	(19,422)
Accumulated Gain or (Loss) on Net Monetary Items	—	47,620	44,951
Total Stockholders' Equity	$ 400,000	$ 443,573	$768,383
Total Liabilities and Stockholders' Equity	$1,000,000	$1,072,143	$868,383

Additional Comments

The demonstration assumed that no adjustment of the financial statements had been made prior to the end of the second year. This required the restatement of the historical income statement for the first year and of the historical balance sheets at the beginning and end of the first year in terms of the current dollar in order to make them comparable with the adjusted financial statements for the second year. If adjustments had been made at the end of the first year, the results at the end of the second year would have been the same, but the procedure would have been somewhat different. Each amount in the adjusted statements prepared at the close of the first year would have been multiplied by the fraction 200/175 in order to restate them for use in the comparative financial statements prepared at the close of the second year. Other calculations involving items carried over from the first to the second year would correspondingly be modified.

It was assumed in the demonstration that the inventory was priced on a first-in, first out (Fifo) basis. Other pricing methods would require variations in the computations. For example, if the last-in, first-out (Lifo) method had been used, the inventory at the end of the first year would have consisted of $250,000 acquired at the opening of business when the price-level index was 150, and $50,000 acquired during the first year when the average price-level index was 160. The calculation for the adjustment to the current dollar would have been:

$$\begin{array}{ll} \$250,000 \times 200/150 = & \$333,333 \\ \underline{50,000} \times 200/160 = & \underline{62,500} \\ \underline{\$300,000} & \underline{\$395,833} \end{array}$$

The corresponding amount of goods sold would have been acquired entirely from the first year's purchases of merchandise and the adjustment calculation of the cost of goods sold for the first year would have been

$$\$470,000 \times 200/160 = \$587,500$$

For the purposes of the demonstration, price-level index numbers were available only for the beginning, the end, and the average of each year. Index number series are usually available at monthly or quarterly intervals and should be used if greater refinement of the restated amounts is considered desirable. On the other hand, a still greater simplification than the one used in the demonstration could be employed when the movement of the price level is relatively slow by assuming that the index number at the beginning of each year applied to all transactions during the year. The results might be sufficiently accurate for most purposes.

In the demonstration, the accumulated gain or loss on monetary items and the accumulated undistributed earnings from ordinary operations were shown as separate portions of the retained earnings. This was possible because the illustration started with the opening of business and the accumulations could readily be computed over the two-year period. Where the price-level adjustment technique is put into effect for a company which has been in existence for a great many years, the accumulated adjusted retained earnings is obtained as a balancing figure in the first set of financial statements. To isolate the accumulated gain or loss on monetary items would not be feasible since it would require calculating the purchasing-power gain or loss on monetary items back to the date of origin of the company. Either the accumulated amount must be left as an undivided and unidentified portion of the retained earnings, or a practical compromise must be adopted such as starting the accumulation at a practicable date and disclosing this limitation of the accumulated amount by means of a footnote.

This discussion concerns the preparation of financial statements restated for general price-level changes and provides a more complex example of the restatement process. In the example, the historical cost records of a firm in existence for several years are the basis for preparing current year price-level adjusted statements. All accounts reflecting transactions which occurred in

Illustrative Example 2.2

different time periods must be aged in order that the proper restatement factors can be applied to the dollar amounts associated with the various time periods. As a result, the example shows how existing historical cost data can be converted to generate price-level adjusted financial statements without destroying the historical cost data base. The historical cost financial statements are presented in Exhibits 2.1 through 2.3.

In order to make the necessary adjustments for general price-level changes, we need an index of price levels. Such indexes measure changes in purchasing power by expressing the current price level relative to the price level at some base year. For example, if a price index stands at 195 today and 1958 was the base year (i.e., in 1958, the index stood at 100), the interpretation is that prices are 95 percent higher today than they were in 1958. This would be true on the average for the goods and services whose prices are tracked in the index.

There is, however, some controversy over which of the two major indexes of general purchasing power should be used—the Consumer Price Index (CPI) or the Gross National Product (GNP) Implicit Price Deflator. The CPI reflects only consumer prices, not prices associated with wholesale, industrial and other nonconsumer transactions. Since the end result of all economic activity is consumption, some individuals believe that the CPI is the ultimate measure of value. On the other hand, the GNP Implicit Price Deflator reflects a sample of prices of *all* economic activities that enter into computation of the Gross National Product. Its supporters argue that it is therefore the more comprehensive index, and that it reflects more actual transactions—not just the hypothetical "market basket" of the CPI.

These indexes, however, move in fairly close harmony. In fact, the CPI is included in the GNP Implicit Price Deflator. They are highly correlated and, as a practical matter, it will normally make little difference which is chosen for use. Both will give similar results for our purposes. There is a further discussion of price indexes in Chapter 3.

In selecting the index to be used in our illustration, we followed the recommendations of the APB and the FASB that the GNP Implicit Price Deflator be used, as it "is the most comprehensive indicator of the general price level in the United States." This recommendation was first made in APB Statement 3 (June 1969) and reaffirmed in December 1974 by the FASB in its Exposure Draft. Exhibit 2.4 presents the average annual values of the GNP Implicit Price Deflator for the years 1963–1973 and quarterly values for 1965–1973.* These values will be used in our example.

---

*A similar, but more complete, table of GNP Deflator values for 1947–1974 is reproduced in Exhibit 3.1. This table is taken from the FASB Exposure Draft. Its values differ slightly from those in Exhibit 2.4. These differences reflect periodic revisions which are made to the GNP Deflator series. Such revisions occur quite frequently, and can affect figures going back to earlier years as well as more recent periods.

The firm in our example has been in business for eleven years. Restated financial statements are first prepared for year eleven. For purposes of this illustration, we assume that the values of the GNP Deflator for years one through eleven are those in Exhibit 2.4 for 1963–1973. Thus, the value of the GNP Deflator at the end of year eleven corresponds to the value for the fourth quarter of 1973, and so forth.

Most of the difficulties associated with the preparation of financial statements restated for changes in the general price level occur in the first year for which restated statements are prepared. Once the initial restatement is complete, preparation of the subsequent years' restated financial statements should be fairly routine. Our approach to the restatement process is from a "first time through" point of view. The restatement process is readily accomplished in the following steps.

a. Identify the monetary items in the statement of financial position and calculate the net monetary items (monetary assets less monetary liabilities) at the beginning of the period (i.e., using the 12/31/10 statement of financial position).

b. Convert the 1/1/11 (i.e., 12/31/10) net monetary items into 12/31/11 dollars by multiplying by the ratio of the GNP Deflator on 12/31/11 over the GNP Deflator on 12/31/10. (See Exhibit 2.5.)

c. Convert to 12/31/11 dollars the increases and decreases to net monetary items which occurred during year 11. Prepare a schedule of sources and applications of monetary items* during year 11. Multiply each source and use by the ratio of the GNP Deflator on 12/31/11 over the GNP Deflator for the date of the increase or decrease. Increases (such as sales) and decreases (such as merchandise purchases) which occur uniformly throughout the year are assumed to have taken place at the average value of the GNP Deflator for the year. On the other hand, the sale of equipment in December, year 11, is assumed to have taken place at the value of the GNP Deflator during the fourth quarter of year 11.** (See Exhibit 2.6.)

---

*This is similar to the Sources and Applications of Working Capital section in the statement of changes in financial position. The basic difference is that our schedule uses only sources and applications of monetary items. *Nonworking capital items* represent sources and applications of working capital and *nonmonetary items* represent sources and applications of monetary items.

**Note that application of the FASB restatement procedure has the effect of restating items assumed to have taken place at the average price level for the year for only four and one-half months of price change. The reason is that the published GNP Deflator values are *annual* and *quarterly averages*. Thus, the annual average relates approximately to the end of June and the fourth-quarter average relates approximately to the middle of November. The elapsed time between them is approximately four and one-half months.

d. Determine the real gain or loss in purchasing power caused by the impact of the dollar's changing value on monetary items. Subtract the historical amount of net monetary items at 12/31/11 from the total of the beginning net monetary items and the year 11 increases and decreases, all of which have now been restated in 12/31/11 dollars. If the result is positive, there is a real loss; if it is negative, there is a real gain.* (See Exhibit 2.6.) Note that the same result is achieved by summing the differences between the historical and restated amounts of the net monetary items at 12/31/10 and the changes during year 11. This is also shown in Exhibit 2.6.

e. Convert all historical basis income statement accounts to 12/31/11 dollars using the appropriate adjustment factors. These calculations are shown in Exhibits 2.7 through 2.12.

f. Convert the nonmonetary items in the statement of financial position to 12/31/11 dollars (the monetary items are already so stated). Prepare an aging schedule for each category of nonmonetary items showing when they originated. Restate each individual item in 12/31/11 dollars using the ratio of the GNP Deflator on 12/31/11 over the GNP Deflator for the date the item originated. Items occurring fairly evenly during the year are assumed to have originated at the average general price level for the year. These calculations are shown in Exhibits 2.13 through 2.21.

g. Apply the "lower of cost or market" rule to restated assets and liabilities when that rule is applied in historical cost statements. (See Chapter 3 for discussion of this rule in the context of price-level restatements.)

h. Using the data developed in the previous steps, prepare the year 11 price-level adjusted financial statements. These are shown in Exhibits 2.23, 2.24 and 2.25.

i. In subsequent years, "roll forward" previous years' restated financial statements by multiplying each item by the ratio of the price index at the end of the subsequent period over the price index at the end of the previous period.

---

*As previously stated, in a period of rising prices monetary assets generate purchasing-power losses while monetary liabilities generate purchasing-power gains. Steps *a* through *d* show the improvement or deterioration in purchasing power associated with the monetary items during year 11.

Exhibit 2.1

ABC CORPORATION

Comparative Statements of Financial Position
December 31, Year 11 and Year 10 (Historical Cost)

ASSETS		Year 11	Year 10
(Monetary)	Cash	$ 5,100,000	$ 2,430,000
(Nonmonetary)	Marketable Securities*	4,500,000	4,410,000
(Monetary)	Receivables—Net	15,150,000	5,700,000
	Inventories, at Lower of Cost or Market, First-in, First-out:		
(Nonmonetary)	Raw Materials	8,430,000	8,040,000
(Nonmonetary)	Finished Goods	7,680,000	7,350,000
(Nonmonetary)	Parts and Supplies	1,710,000	2,100,000
(Nonmonetary)	Prepayments	144,000	150,000
	Total Current Assets	$42,714,000	$30,180,000
(Nonmonetary)	Property, Plant and Equipment	$77,700,000	$76,200,000
(Nonmonetary)	Less: Accumulated Depreciation	54,780,000	49,050,000
		$22,920,000	$27,150,000
	Total Assets	$65,634,000	$57,330,000
LIABILITIES			
(Monetary)	Current Liabilities	$14,310,000	$ 8,850,000
(Nonmonetary)	Deferred Income—Payments Received in Advance	300,000	360,000
(Monetary)	Long-Term Debt	15,000,000	15,900,000
	Total Liabilities	$29,610,000	$25,110,000
STOCKHOLDERS' EQUITY			
(Nonmonetary)	Capital Stock—Common	$ 5,280,000	$ 5,280,000
(Nonmonetary)	Additional Paid-in Capital	9,450,000	9,450,000
(Nonmonetary)	Retained Earnings	21,294,000	17,490,000
	Total Stockholders' Equity	$36,024,000	$32,220,000
	Total Liabilities and Stockholders' Equity	$65,634,000	$57,330,000

*These items are investments in equities rather than bills or notes. Consequently, they are nonmonetary items.

Exhibit 2.2

ABC CORPORATION

Statement of Income and Retained Earnings
For the Year Ended December 31, Year 11 (Historical Cost)

SALES:

Current		$89,430,000
Deferred Income Realized:		
Balance, 12/31/10		360,000
Plus Additions in Year 11		510,000
Total	$	870,000
Less Balance 12/31/11		300,000
Deferred Income Realized in Year 11	$	570,000
Total Sales		$90,000,000

OPERATING EXPENSES:

Cost of Goods Sold		$68,205,000
Depreciation Expense		6,930,000
Total Operating Expenses		$75,135,000
Selling and Administrative Expenses:		
Amortization of Prepayments:		
Balance, 12/31/10	$	150,000
Plus Additions in Year 11		135,000
Total	$	285,000
Less Balance, 12/31/11		144,000
Amortization of Prepayments in Year 11	$	141,000
Other Selling and Administrative Expenses		7,590,000
Total Selling and Administrative Expenses		$ 7,731,000
Total Expenses		$82,866,000
Income before Federal Income Taxes		$ 7,134,000
Federal Income Taxes		2,730,000
NET INCOME		$ 4,404,000
Retained Earnings, December 31, Year 10		17,490,000
		$21,894,000
Less: Dividends Paid		600,000
Retained Earnings, December 31, Year 11		$21,294,000

Exhibit 2.3

ABC CORPORATION

Statement of Changes in Financial Position
For the Year Ended December 31, Year 11 (Historical Cost)

SOURCES OF WORKING CAPITAL:

Net Income after Taxes	$ 4,404,000
Add: Charge to Income Not	
Requiring the Outlay of Working Capital:	
Depreciation	6,930,000
Total Sources from Operations	$11,334,000
Proceeds from Sale of Equipment	300,000
Total Sources	$11,634,000

APPLICATIONS OF WORKING CAPITAL:

Dividends. . . . .$	600,000
Purchase of Property, Plant and Equipment	3,000,000
Retirement of Long-Term Debt	900,000
Total Applications. . . . .$	4,500,000
INCREASE IN WORKING CAPITAL . . . .$	7,134,000

Increase (Decrease) in Working Capital Accounts*

	Year 11	Year 10	Increase	Decrease
Cash	$ 5,100,000	$ 2,430,000	$ 2,670,000	
Receivables	15,150,000	5,700,000	9,450,000	
Marketable Securities.	4,500,000	4,410,000	90,000	
Inventory.	17,820,000	17,490,000	330,000	
Prepayments	144,000	150,000		$ 6,000
Current Liabilities	14,310,000	8,850,000		5,460,000
Deferred Income	300,000	360,000	60,000	
			$12,600,000	$5,466,000
			5,466,000	
Increase in Working Capital			$ 7,134,000	

*This analysis of increases and decreases in working capital accounts is not in accordance with conventional format and is provided for instructional purposes only.

Exhibit 2.4*

Gross National Product Implicit Price Deflator

Year		GNP Deflator (Annual Average)
1	1963	107.1
2	1964	108.9
3	1965	110.9
4	1966	113.9
5	1967	117.3
6	1968	121.8
7	1969	128.1
8	1970	135.3
9	1971	141.6
10	1972	146.1
11	1973	153.9

Year		Quarter	GNP Deflator (Quarterly Average)	Year		Quarter	GNP Deflator (Quarterly Average)
3	1965	1st	110.0	8	1970	1st	132.6
		2d	110.7			2d	134.3
		3d	111.0			3d	136.0
		4th	111.6			4th	138.1
4	1966	1st	112.5	9	1971	1st	139.9
		2d	113.5			2d	141.3
		3d	114.4			3d	142.4
		4th	115.3			4th	142.9
5	1967	1st	116.0	10	1972	1st	144.7
		2d	116.6			2d	145.3
		3d	117.7			3d	146.2
		4th	118.9			4th	147.6
6	1968	1st	120.0	11	1973	1st	149.8
		2d	121.7			2d	152.5
		3d	122.9			3d	155.1
		4th	124.2			4th	158.4
7	1969	1st	125.7				
		2d	127.2				
		3d	129.0				
		4th	130.5				

*Source: *Survey of Current Business*, U.S. Department of Commerce, Office of Business Economics.

Exhibit 2.5

Restatement of 12/31/10 Monetary Items

Monetary Items, 12/31/10	Historical	Ratio to Restate*	Restated in 12/31/11 $
Monetary Assets:			
Cash	$ 2,430,000	158.4/147.6	$ 2,607,390
Receivables	5,700,000	158.4/147.6	6,116,100
	$ 8,130,000		$ 8,723,490
Less Monetary Liabilities:			
Current Liabilities	$ 8,850,000	158.4/147.6	$ 9,496,050
Long-Term Debt.	15,900,000	158.4/147.6	17,060,700
	$ 24,750,000		$ 26,556,750
Net Monetary Items . .	$(16,620,000)		$(17,833,260)

*All ratios are rounded to three decimal places (e.g., 158.4/147.6 = 1.073).

Monetary Items, 12/31/11	Year 11
Monetary Assets:	
Cash	$ 5,100,000
Receivables	15,150,000
	$ 20,250,000
Less Monetary Liabilities:	
Current Liabilities	$ 14,310,000
Long-Term Debt.	15,000,000
	$ 29,310,000
Net Monetary Items (12/31/11)	$ (9,060,000)

Exhibit 2.6

Computation of Purchasing-Power Gain or Loss on Monetary Items

	Historical Amount	Ratio to Restate	Restated in 12/31/11 $	Difference between Historical and Restated
Net Monetary Items, 12/31/10	$(16,620,000)	158.4/147.6	$(17,833,260)	$(1,213,260)
Add:				
Current Sales	89,430,000	158.4/153.9	92,023,470	2,593,470
Additions to Deferred Income in Year 11	510,000	158.4/153.9	524,790	14,790
Retirement of Long-Term Debt,* 12/11	900,000	158.4/158.4	900,000	—
Proceeds from Sale of Equipment, December, Year 11	300,000	158.4/158.4	300,000	—
	$ 74,520,000		$ 75,915,000	$ 1,395,000
Deduct:				
Purchases	$ 68,535,000	158.4/153.9	$ 70,522,515	$ 1,987,515
Other Selling and Administrative Expenses	7,590,000	158.4/153.9	7,810,110	220,110
Federal Income Taxes	2,730,000	158.4/153.9	2,809,170	79,170
Dividends	600,000	158.4/153.9	617,400	17,400
Purchase of Marketable Securities	90,000	158.4/153.9	92,610	2,610
Purchase of Property, Plant and Equipment	3,000,000	158.4/153.9	3,087,000	87,000
Additions to Prepayments	135,000	158.4/153.9	138,915	3,915
Retirement of Long-Term Debt,* 12/11	900,000	158.4/158.4	900,000	—
	$ 83,580,000		$ 85,977,720	$ 2,397,720
Net Monetary Items, 12/31/11	$ (9,060,000)		$(10,062,720)	
			— (9,060,000)	
Purchasing-Power Gain on Monetary Items			$ (1,002,720)	$(1,002,720)

*A source *and* application of monetary items.

Exhibit 2.6, Postscript. It is often useful to calculate separately the purchasing-power gain or loss on *current* monetary items and *noncurrent* monetary items, particularly in preparing general price-level statements of changes in financial position (Exhibit 2.25). The only noncurrent monetary item in our example is long-term debt. The calculation of the purchasing power-gain on long-term debt is:

	Historical Amount	Ratio to Restate	Restated in 12/31/11 $	Difference between Historical and Restated
Long-Term Debt 12/31/10	$15,900,000	158.4/147.6	$17,060,700	$1,160,700
Retirement of Long-Term Debt. 12/11	(900,000)	158.4/158.4	(900,000)	—
Long-Term Debt. 12/31/11	$15,000,000		$16,160,700 15,000,000	
Purchasing-Power Gain on Long-Term Debt.			$ 1,160,700	$1,160,700

Since the purchasing-power gain on long-term debt ($1,160,700) exceeds the purchasing-power gain on all monetary items ($1,002,720), there is a purchasing-power *loss* of $157,980 [= $1,160,700 − $1,002,720] on the current monetary items. As an alternative, the procedure employed in Illustrative Example 2.1 could be used. In that case, purchasing-power gain (loss) was computed separately on the current and the noncurrent monetary items.

Exhibit 2.7

Sales

	Historical	Ratio to Restate	Restated in 12/31/11 $
Current Sales	$89,430,000	158.4/153.9	$92,023,470
Deferred Income Realized from:			
Year 10	360,000	158.4/146.1	390,240
Year 11	210,000	158.4/153.9	216,090
Total Sales	$90,000,000		$92,629,800

Exhibit 2.8

Cost of Goods Sold

	Historical	Ratio to Restate	Restated in 12/31/11 $
Inventories, 12/31/10:			
Raw Materials	$ 8,040,000	158.4/146.1	$ 8,715,360
Finished Goods	7,350,000	158.4/147.6	7,886,550
Parts and Supplies . . .	2,100,000	158.4/146.1	2,276,400
	$17,490,000		$18,878,310
Plus Purchases	68,535,000	158.4/153.9	70,522,515
	$86,025,000		$89,400,825
Less:			
Inventories, 12/31/11:			
Raw Materials	8,430,000	158.4/153.9	8,674,470
Finished Goods	7,680,000	158.4/158.4	7,680,000
Parts and Supplies . . .	1,710,000	158.4/153.9	1,759,590
	$17,820,000		$18,114,060
Cost of Sales	$68,205,000		$71,286,765

NOTE: Raw Materials and Parts and Supplies are assumed to be acquired fairly evenly throughout the year. Finished Goods are assumed to have accumulated during the last quarter.

Exhibit 2.9

Depreciation

Year	Accumulated Depreciation Beginning Balance	Depreciation	Retirements	Accumulated Depreciation Ending Balance	Ratio to Restate	Accumulated Depreciation Beginning Balance Restated in 12/31/11 $	Depreciation Restated in 12/31/11 $	Retirements Restated in 12/31/11 $	Accumulated Depreciation Ending Balance Restated in 12/31/11 $
1	$ 9,000,000		$ 600,000	$ 8,400,000	158.4/107.1	$13,311,000		$ 887,400	$12,423,600
2	8,100,000	$ 870,000	270,000	8,700,000	158.4/108.9	11,785,500	$1,265,850	392,850	12,658,500
3	9,600,000	1,170,000	240,000	10,530,000	158.4/110.9	13,708,800	1,670,760	342,720	15,036,840
4	7,560,000	1,080,000		8,640,000	158.4/113.9	10,515,960	1,502,280		12,018,240
5	1,440,000	240,000		1,680,000	158.4/117.3	1,944,000	324,000		2,268,000
6	7,500,000	1,500,000		9,000,000	158.4/121.8	9,750,000	1,950,000		11,700,000
7	3,600,000	900,000		4,500,000	158.4/128.1	4,453,200	1,113,300		5,566,500
8	1,800,000	570,000	90,000	2,280,000	158.4/135.3	2,107,800	667,470	105,390	2,669,880
9	300,000	150,000		450,000	158.4/141.6	335,700	167,850		503,550
10	300,000	150,000		300,000	158.4/146.1	162,600	162,600		325,200
11		300,000		300,000	158.4/153.9		308,700		308,700
Total	$49,050,000	$6,930,000	$1,200,000	$54,780,000		$68,074,560	$9,132,810	$1,728,360	$75,479,010

NOTE: Depreciation is computed on a straight-line basis over a 10-year life with no salvage values. Assume a full year's depreciation in the year of acquisition and no depreciation in the year of disposition.

Exhibit 2.10

Selling and Administrative Expenses

	Historical	Ratio to Restate	Restated in 12/31/11 $
Amortization of Prepayments			
Year 8	$ 15,000	158.4/135.3	$ 17,565
Year 9	21,000	158.4/141.6	23,499
Year 10	75,000	158.4/146.1	81,300
Year 11	30,000	158.4/153.9	30,870
	$ 141,000		$ 153,234
Other Selling and Administrative Expenses. . . .	$7,590,000	158.4/153.9	$7,810,110
Total	$7,731,000		$7,963,344

Exhibit 2.11

Federal Income Taxes and Dividends

These figures, computed in the purchasing-power gain on monetary items, were:

	Historical	Ratio to Restate	Restated in 12/31/11 $
Federal Income Taxes	$2,730,000	158.4/153.9	$2,809,170
Dividends.	600,000	158.4/153.9	617,400

Exhibit 2.12

Loss on Equipment Retired and Sold, Year 11

	Year	Historical	Ratio to Restate	Restated in 12/31/11 $
Original Cost of	1	$ 600,000	158.4/107.1	$ 887,400
Equipment Retired	2	300,000	158.4/108.9	436,500
and Sold	3	300,000	158.4/110.9	428,400
	8	300,000	158.4/135.3	351,300
		$1,500,000		$2,103,600
Less: Accumulated	1	$ 600,000	158.4/107.1	$ 887,400
Depreciation	2	270,000	158.4/108.9	392,850
	3	240,000	158.4/110.9	342,720
	8	90,000	158.4/135.3	105,390
		$1,200,000		$1,728,360
Net Book Value		$ 300,000		$ 375,240
Less: Proceeds from Sales in December	11	300,000	158.4/158.4	300,000
Loss	11	$ ——		$ 75,240

NOTE: This will be a loss on the restated income statement only because the restated book value of the equipment exceeded the sale proceeds by $75,240, thereby generating the loss.

Exhibit 2.13

Marketable Securities

Year	Historical	Ratio to Restate	Restated in 12/31/11 $
5	$1,500,000	158.4/117.3	$2,025,000
8	2,250,000	158.4/135.3	2,634,750
9	660,000	158.4/141.6	738,540
11	90,000	158.4/153.9	92,610
Total	$4,500,000		$5,490,900

Exhibit 2.14

Inventories

The restated amounts for inventories have already been computed (see Exhibit 2.8). The amounts of ending inventories on December 31, year 11, were:

	Historical	Ratio to Restate	Restated in 12/31/11 $
Raw Materials	$ 8,430,000	158.4/153.9	$ 8,674,470
Finished Goods	7,680,000	158.4/158.4	7,680,000
Parts and Supplies	1,710,000	158.4/153.9	1,759,590
Total	$17,820,000		$18,114,060

Exhibit 2.15

Prepayments

Year	Historical Prepayments	Historical Amortization	Balance 12/31/11	Ratio to Restate	Prepayments Restated in 12/31/11 $	Amortization Restated in 12/31/11 $	Balance Restated in 12/31/11 $
8	$ 15,000	$ 15,000	$ —	158.4/135.3	$ 17,565	$ 17,565	$ —
9	30,000	21,000	9,000	158.4/141.6	33,570	23,499	10,071
10	105,000	75,000	30,000	158.4/146.1	113,820	81,300	32,520
11	135,000	30,000	105,000	158.4/153.9	138,915	30,870	108,045
Total	$285,000	$141,000	$144,000		$303,870	$153,234	$150,636

Exhibit 2.16

Property, Plant and Equipment

In order to compute the restated values for these fixed assets, purchase and retirement dates must be known. In our example, purchases and retirements of property, plant and equipment were assumed to occur evenly throughout the year.

Year	Historical Cost	Historical Retirements	Historical Balance	Ratio to Restate	Cost Restated in 12/31/11 $	Retirements Restated in 12/31/11 $	Balance Restated in 12/21/11 $
1	$ 9,000,000	$ 600,000	$ 8,400,000	158.4/107.1	$ 13,311,000	$ 887,400	$ 12,423,600
2	9,000,000	300,000	8,700,000	158.4/108.9	13,095,000	436,500	12,658,500
3	12,000,000	300,000	11,700,000	158.4/110.9	17,136,000	428,400	16,707,600
4	10,800,000	—	10,800,000	158.4/113.9	15,022,800	—	15,022,800
5	2,400,000	—	2,400,000	158.4/117.3	3,240,000	—	3,240,000
6	15,000,000	—	15,000,000	158.4/121.8	19,500,000	—	19,500,000
7	9,000,000	—	9,000,000	158.4/128.1	11,133,000	—	11,133,000
8	6,000,000	300,000	5,700,000	158.4/135.3	7,026,000	351,300	6,674,700
9	1,500,000	—	1,500,000	158.4/141.6	1,678,500	—	1,678,500
10	1,500,000	—	1,500,000	158.4/146.1	1,626,000	—	1,626,000
11	3,000,000	—	3,000,000	158.4/153.9	3,087,000	—	3,087,000
Total	$79,200,000	$1,500,000	$77,700,000		$105,855,300	$2,103,600	$103,751,700

Exhibit 2.17

Accumulated Depreciation

Accumulated depreciation figures have already been computed (see Exhibit 2.9). The totals were as follows:

	Historical	Ratio to Restate	Restated in 12/31/11 $
Total, 12/31/11	$54,780,000	(Various)	$75,479,010

Exhibit 2.18

Deferred Income — Payments Received in Advance

Year	Historical Deferred Income	Historical Amount Realized	Historical Balance	Ratio to Restate	Deferred Income Restated in 12/31/11 $	Amount Realized Restated in 12/31/11 $	Balance Restated in 12/31/11 $
10	$360,000	$360,000	$ ——	158.4/146.1	$390,240	$390,240	$ ——
11	510,000	210,000	300,000	158.4/153.9	524,790	216,090	308,700
Total	$870,000	$570,000	$300,000		$915,030	$606,330	$308,700

Exhibit 2.19

Capital Stock — Common

Year	Historical	Ratio to Restate	Capital Stock Restated in 12/31/11 $
1	$3,000,000	158.4/107.1	$4,437,000
2	1,500,000	158.4/108.9	2,182,500
5	780,000	158.4/117.3	1,053,000
Total	$5,280,000		$7,672,500

Exhibit 2.20

Additional Paid-in Capital

Year	Historical	Ratio to Restate	Additional Paid-in Capital Restated in 12/31/11 $
1	$6,000,000	158.4/107.1	$ 8,874,000
2	2,250,000	158.4/108.9	3,273,750
5	1,200,000	158.4/117.3	1,620,000
Total	$9,450,000		$13,767,750

Exhibit 2.21

Retained Earnings

Retained earnings can be restated in the same manner as were the other nonmonetary accounts. This, however, would involve a restatement of all previous income and retained earnings statements. Since retained earnings is a residual, there is a simpler way to restate this account for the first time through.

To get the restated beginning balance, restate the previous year's statement of financial position (12/31/10), except for retained earnings, in current (12/31/11) dollars. The restated beginning balance in retained earnings is simply the residual amount needed to balance the restated 12/31/10 statement of financial position. This procedure is shown below.

MONETARY ITEMS (see Exhibit 2.5):	Historical	Restated in 12/31/11 $
Cash, 12/31/10	$ 2,430,000	$ 2,607,390
Receivables—Net, 12/31/10	5,700,000	6,116,100
Current Liabilities, 12/31/10	8,850,000	9,496,050
Long-term Debt, 12/31/10	15,900,000	17,060,700

MARKETABLE SECURITIES (see Exhibits 2.13, 2.15)	Historical	Restated in 12/31/11 $
Balance, 12/31/11	$ 4,500,000	$ 5,490,900
Less Year 11 Transactions	90,000	92,610
Balance, 12/31/10	$ 4,410,000	$ 5,398,290

INVENTORIES (see Exhibit 2.8):	Historical	Restated in 12/31/11 $
Raw Materials, 12/31/10	$ 8,040,000	$ 8,715,360
Finished Goods, 12/31/10	7,350,000	7,886,550
Parts and Supplies, 12/31/10	2,100,000	2,276,400
	$17,490,000	$18,878,310

PREPAYMENTS (see Exhibit 2.15)	Historical	Restated in 12/31/11 $
Balance, 12/31/11	$ 285,000	$ 303,870
Less Year 11 Transactions	135,000	138,915
Balance, 12/31/10	$ 150,000	$ 164,955

PROPERTY, PLANT AND EQUIPMENT (see Exhibit 2.16)	Historical	Restated in 12/31/11 $
Balance, 12/31/11	$79,200,000	$105,855,300
Less Year 11 Transactions	3,000,000	3,087,000
Balance, 12/31/10	$76,200,000	$102,768,300

ACCUMULATED DEPRECIATION (see Exhibit 2.9)	Historical	Restated in 12/31/11 $
Balance, 12/31/10	$49,050,000	$68,074,560

DEFERRED INCOME—PAYMENTS RECEIVED IN ADVANCE (see Exhibit 2.18)	Historical	Restated in 12/31/11 $
Balance, 12/31/10	$ 360,000	$ 390,240

CAPITAL STOCK—COMMON (see Exhibit 2.19)	Historical	Restated in 12/31/11 $
Balance, 12/31/10	$ 5,280,000	$ 7,672,500

ADDITIONAL PAID-IN CAPITAL (see Exhibit 2.20)	Historical	Restated in 12/31/11 $
Balance, 12/31/10	$ 9,450,000	$13,767,750

The 12/31/10 restated balance of retained earnings can now be determined. We use a "T-account" format in which asset balances are on the left side and liabilities and stockholders' equity balances are on the right side. Each of the restated 12/31/10 balances is posted to this T-account. The amount needed to equate both sides of the T-account will be the restated 12/31/10 retained earnings, the only account not directly restated above.

12/31/10 Account Balances Restated in 12/31/11 $ (Assets = Liabilities + Stockholders' Equity)			
Cash	$ 2,607,390	Current Liabilities	$ 9,496,050
Receivables—Net	6,116,100	Long-Term Debt	17,060,700
Marketable		Accumulated	
Securities	5,398,290	Depreciation	68,074,560
Inventories	18,878,310	Deferred Income	390,240
Prepayments	164,955	Capital Stock—Common	7,672,500
Property, Plant and		Additional Paid-in	
Equipment	102,768,300	Capital	13,767,750
			$116,461,800
		Retained Earnings	19,471,545
	$135,933,345		$135,933,345

The 12/31/10 statement of financial position restated in 12/31/11 dollars can now be prepared; it is presented in Exhibit 2.22. The financial statements for year 11 follow in Exhibits 2.23, 2.24, and 2.25.

Exhibit 2.22

ABC CORPORATION
General Price-Level Statement of Financial Position
December 31, Year 10
(Restated in 12/31/11 dollars)

ASSETS

Cash	$ 2,607,390
Marketable Securities	5,398,290
Receivables—Net	6,116,100
Inventories, at Lower of Cost or Market, First-in, First-out:	
Raw Materials	8,715,360
Finished Goods	7,886,550
Parts and Supplies	2,276,400
Prepayments	164,955
Total Current Assets	$ 33,165,045
Property, Plant and Equipment	$102,768,300
Less: Accumulated Depreciation	68,074,560
	$ 34,693,740
Total Assets	$ 67,858,785

Exhibit 2.23

ABC CORPORATION
General Price-Level Statement
of Income and Retained Earnings
For the Year Ended December 31, Year 11
(Restated in 12/31/11 dollars)

SALES	$92,629,800
Less: Cost of Goods Sold	$71,286,765
Depreciation Expense	9,132,810
Selling and Administrative Expenses	7,963,344
	$88,382,919
OPERATING PROFIT	$ 4,246,881
Loss on Sale of Equipment	(75,240)
Purchasing-Power Gain on Monetary Items	1,002,720
	$ 927,480
Income before Federal Income Taxes	$ 5,174,361
Federal Income Taxes	2,809,170
NET INCOME	$ 2,365,191
Retained Earnings, December 31, Year 10	19,471,545
	$21,836,736
Less: Dividends Paid	617,400
Retained Earnings, December 31, Year 11	$21,219,336

Exhibit 2.22 (continued)

LIABILITIES

Current Liabilities	$ 9,496,050
Deferred Income—Payments Received in Advance	390,240
Long-Term Debt	17,060,700
Total Liabilities	$ 26,946,990

STOCKHOLDERS' EQUITY

Capital Stock—Common	$ 7,672,500
Additional Paid-in Capital	13,767,750
Retained Earnings	19,471,545
Total Stockholders' Equity	$ 40,911,795
Total Liabilities and Stockholders' Equity	$ 67,858,785

Exhibit 2.24

ABC CORPORATION
General Price-Level Statement of Financial Position
December 31, Year 11
(Restated in 12/31/11 dollars)

ASSETS

Cash	$ 5,100,000
Marketable Securities	5,490,900
Receivables—Net	15,150,000
Inventories:	
Raw Materials	8,674,470
Finished Goods	7,680,000
Parts and Supplies	1,759,590
Prepayments	150,636
Total Current Assets	$ 44,005,596
Property, Plant and Equipment	$103,751,700
Less: Accumulated Depreciation	75,479,010
	$ 28,272,690
Total Assets	$ 72,278,286

LIABILITIES

Current Liabilities	$ 14,310,000
Deferred Income—Payments Received in Advance	308,700
Long-Term Debt	15,000,000
Total Liabilities	$ 29,618,700

STOCKHOLDERS' EQUITY

Capital Stock—Common	$ 7,672,500
Additional Paid-in Capital	13,767,750
Retained Earnings	21,219,336
Total Stockholders' Equity	$ 42,659,586
Total Liabilities and Stockholders' Equity	$ 72,278,286

Exhibit 2.25

ABC CORPORATION

General Price-Level Statement of Changes in Financial Position
For the Year Ended December 31, Year 11
(Restated in 12/31/11 dollars)

SOURCES OF WORKING CAPITAL:

Net Income after Taxes	$ 2,365,191
Add: Charge to Income Not Requiring the Outlay of Working Capital:	
Depreciation	9,132,810
Loss on Sale of Equipment	75,240
	$ 9,208,050
	$11,573,241
Subtract: Credit to Income Not Providing Working Capital:	
Purchasing-Power Gain on Long-Term Debt	(1,160,700)
Total Sources from Operations	$10,412,541
Proceeds from Sale of Equipment	300,000
Total Sources	$10,712,541

APPLICATIONS OF WORKING CAPITAL:

Dividends	617,400
Purchase of Property, Plant and Equipment	3,087,000
Retirement of Long-Term Debt	900,000
Total Applications	$ 4,604,400
INCREASE IN WORKING CAPITAL	$ 6,108,141

Increase (Decrease) in Working Capital Accounts*

	Year 11	Year 10	Increase	Decrease
Cash	$ 5,100,000	$ 2,607,390	$ 2,492,610	
Receivables	15,150,000	6,116,100	9,033,900	
Marketable Securities	5,490,900	5,398,290	92,610	
Inventory	18,114,060	18,878,310		764,250
Prepayments	150,636	164,955		14,319
Current Liabilities	14,310,000	9,496,050		4,813,950
Deferred Income	308,700	390,240	81,540	
			$11,700,660	$5,592,519
			5,592,519	
Increase in Working Capital			$ 6,108,141	

*This analysis of increases and decreases in working capital accounts is not in accordance with conventional format and is provided for instructional purposes only.

Restatement of the Statement of Changes in Financial Position

A quick comparison of the historical and restated statements of changes in financial position suggests that the latter is more than a mere restatement of the former. The items that are restatements include: (1) Net Income after Taxes; (2) Depreciation; (3) Proceeds from Sale of Equipment (received in December, year 11; ratio to restate is 158.4/158.4); (4) Dividends and (5) Purchase of Property, Plant and Equipment.

The *loss on sale of equipment* is a result of the restatement process. Recall that equipment having a historical cost book value of $300,000 was sold for $300,000. In the restatement process, however, the book value of the equipment rose to $375,240 (see Exhibit 2.12). The loss results from the fact that the cash proceeds fell short of the restated book value by $75,240. Since this loss has no effect on working capital, it must be added back to restated net income. If there had been a loss on sale of equipment in historical dollars, it would have been added back to net income on the historical cost statement of changes in financial position.

The *purchasing-power gain on long-term debt* is included in net income as part of the purchasing-power gain on monetary items. Unlike the purchasing-power gain or loss on the other monetary items in our example (cash, receivables and current liabilities), however, the purchasing-power gain on long-term debt has no effect on working capital. Hence, the purchasing-power gain on long-term debt must be *subtracted* from restated net income on the statement of changes in financial position. Referring to Exhibit 2.6, we observe that $900,000 of long-term debt was retired in December, year 11. This means that the beginning long-term debt of $15,900,000 was, in effect, held for the entire year. The purchasing-power gain on this debt, as previously calculated, was $1,160,700 [= $15,900,000 × (158.4/147.6) − $15,900,000].

The payment of $900,000 used to retire the debt requires no restatement because it was made at the end of year 11. Note that the retirement of debt has no effect on net monetary items. The reduction in debt was a *source* of net monetary items, while the cash outlay used to retire the debt was an *application* of net monetary items. Since long-term debt is not a working capital item, the payment used to retire it must be shown as an application of working capital on the statement of changes in financial position.

If the debt had been retired at any other time during the year, the payment to retire the debt would be shown at its restated value. For example, suppose that the debt was retired at mid-year. The retirement would be shown on the statement of changes in financial position at $926,100 [= 158.4/153.9 × $900,000]. At the same time, the gain on long-term debt would be reduced by $26,100 because $900,000 of it was only held for half of the year. Similarly, the loss on current monetary items would be decreased by $26,100, since the cash used to retire the debt was held for six months rather than for the entire year. The net effect of all of this on the statement of changes in financial position is zero. Net income will be unchanged because the total gain or loss on monetary items is unchanged—the decline in gain on the long-term debt is exactly offset by the decline in loss on current monetary items. Furthermore, the amount subtracted under gain on long-term debt will be *reduced* (an increase to working capital) and the amount deducted to retire the debt will be *increased* (a decrease in working capital), both by $26,100.

In the preceding Illustrative Examples, historical dollar information was scheduled for restatement purposes according to the years in which the various items originated. This is adequate for years in which there was no significant change in the price level or for years in which transactions occurred uniformly. For years in which the price level increased rapidly and transactions did not occur uniformly, it may become necessary to further break down the historical dollar information. Transactions should then be scheduled by quarters or, under extreme inflation, by months.*

To illustrate the effects of restatement when items are scheduled quarterly rather than annually, we employ some of the data from Illustrative Example 2.2 in the following three sample cases.

1. *Deferred Income Realized*

Assume that the firm had the following transactions.

	Date of Origin	Amount
Deferred Income, year 10*:	3d quarter, year 10	$200,000
	4th quarter, year 10	160,000
Total on 12/31/10 Statement of Financial Position		$360,000
Deferred Income, year 11:	1st quarter, year 11	$120,000
	2d quarter, year 11	90,000
	3d quarter, year 11	200,000
	4th quarter, year 11	100,000
Total Deferred Income, year 11		$510,000
Total for years 10 and 11		$870,000
Less: Amounts realized in year 11 from:	3d quarter, year 10	$200,000
	4th quarter, year 10	160,000
	1st quarter, year 11	120,000
	2d quarter, year 11	90,000
		$570,000
Total on 12/31/11 Statement of Financial Position (amount yet to be realized)		$300,000

*Amounts originating before this date have already been realized.

The restatements would be as follows.

	Historical	Ratio to Restate	Restated in 12/31/11 $
Deferred Income Realized in year 11 from:			
3d quarter, year 10	$200,000	158.4/146.2	$216,600
4th quarter, year 10	160,000	158.4/147.6	171,680
1st quarter, year 11	120,000	158.4/149.8	126,840
2d quarter, year 11	90,000	158.4/152.5	93,510
	$570,000		$608,630

*Restatement of monthly transactions may make use of the GNP Deflator inappropriate, as only quarterly values are published. It may then become necessary to use the Consumer Price Index for restatement purposes, as it is published monthly.

We now add this figure to restated current sales and compare the result with restated sales including realized deferred income scheduled by years, not quarters.

	Restated in 12/31/11 $
Current Sales	$92,023,470
Deferred Income Realized (by quarters)	608,630
Total Sales	$92,632,100
Total Sales (Deferred Income scheduled by years only)	92,629,800
Difference	$ 2,300

2. *Additional Paid-in Capital*

Instead of assuming that the additional paid-in capital for year 5 occurred evenly throughout that year, assume that it arose in the first quarter of year 5. (We disregard the related intra-year effect on Capital Stock—Common.)

Year	Additional Paid-in Capital	Ratio to Restate	Restated in 12/31/11 $
1	$6,000,000	158.4/107.1	$ 8,874,000
2	2,250,000	158.4/108.9	3,273,750
5 (1st quarter)	1,200,000	158.4/116.0	1,639,200
	$9,450,000		$13,786,950
Additional Paid-in Capital (scheduled by years only)			13,767,750
Difference			$ 19,200

3. *Marketable Securities*

Assume that marketable securities were purchased in the first quarter of each year shown, rather than uniformly throughout each year.

1st Quarter of Year	Historical	Ratio to Restate	Restated in 12/31/11 $
5	$1,500,000	158.4/116.0	$2,049,000
8	2,250,000	158.4/132.6	2,688,750
9	660,000	158.4/139.9	747,120
11	90,000	158.4/149.8	95,130
	$4,500,000		$5,580,000
Marketable Securities (scheduled by years only)			5,490,900
Difference			$ 89,100

It is obvious that scheduling items by quarters rather than years can make a difference in the restated financial statements. However, in double-entry accounting, all transactions have two sides. We have emphasized only one side of each transaction. That is, the increased credits associated with quarterly restatement of the deferred income realized and additional paid-in capital must be balanced by increased debits. Similarly, the increased debits caused by quarterly restatement of the marketable securities must be balanced by increased credits. Therefore, the receipt of cash relating to the payments received in advance (deferred income) and the additional paid-in capital must also be scheduled by quarters, as must the expenditure of cash for the marketable securities. Consequently, the quarterly scheduling of these increases and decreases in cash would affect the amount of the purchasing-power gain or loss on monetary items. Since deferred income and additional paid-in capital would be *sources* of net monetary items, quarterly scheduling would increase the purchasing-power losses (debits) attributable to these sources, an increase equal to the additional restated credits to sales and additional paid-in capital. On the other hand, purchases of marketable securities are *applications* of net monetary items, so quarterly scheduling would increase the purchasing-power gains (credits) attributable to these applications. This increase would be equal to the additional restated debits to marketable securities.

Consider, for example, the deferred income which originated and was realized in year 11. The historical amount was $210,000; with quarterly scheduling, the restated amount is $220,350 [= $126,840 + $93,510]. With annual scheduling, the restated amount is $216,090 [= $210,000 × (158.4/153.9)]; the difference is $4,260 [= $220,350 − $216,090]. Now, if quarterly scheduling had been employed in computing the purchasing-power gain or loss on monetary items, identical but opposite effects would be observed. In Exhibit 2.6, additions to deferred income of $510,000 (including the $210,000 realized in year 11) were restated as $524,790, of which $216,090 [= $524,790 × ($210,000/$510,000)] relates to deferred income realized in year 11. Quarterly scheduling would increase this amount to $220,350 and create additional purchasing-power losses of $4,260 [= $220,350 − $216,090]. Thus the debit-credit equality would be preserved.

Proof of the Restatement Procedure

It is now appropriate to discuss *why* the procedure for restating financial statements in end-of-period dollars works. The reader will observe that the restated financial statements articulate in the same way as the historical cost statements. This result is not a chance happening: the debit-credit equality in conventional accounting is preserved in the restatement process. Although the residual calculation of the beginning restated retained earnings may cloud the issue, let us see how the debit and credit sides of some typical year 11 transactions are restated by equal amounts.

Consider the current year's sales. Assumed to occur evenly throughout the year, historical sales of $89,430,000 were restated as $92,023,470 (see Exhibit 2.7). This generated additional income statement *credits* of $2,593,470 [= $92,023,470 − $89,430,000]. The monetary assets accompanying those sales generated additional income statement *debits* of $2,593,470 through their effect on the purchasing-power gain or loss on monetary items (see Exhibit 2.6).

The current year's depreciation expense on fixed assets acquired in year 11 also contributed equal amounts of additional debits and credits in the restatement process. In Exhibit 2.9, year 11 historical depreciation expense of $300,000 on current acquisitions increased the restated depreciation expense (debit) *and* the restated accumulated depreciation (credit) by $8,700 [= $308,700 − $300,000].

Current year amortization of prepayments increased current year expenses (debit) and decreased the related nonmonetary assets (credit) by the identical amount of $12,234 [= $153,234 − $141,000]. See Exhibits 2.10 and 2.15.

Clearly, then, restatement of the current year's transactions must generate equal amounts of debits and credits if these transactions are restated properly (i.e., if *both sides* are restated by the same restatement factor). Therefore, if all prior year transactions (except retained earnings) are restated properly, it follows that (1) equal debits and credits are generated in those prior years, and (2) the residually determined restated retained earnings reflects the net effect of the restatement of all those transactions. The debit-credit equality is therefore preserved.

Once the basic techniques of price-level accounting are understood, preparation of price-level adjusted financial statements in subsequent years should create no major technical problems. Prior years' restated financial statements will be "rolled forward" by multiplying items in those statements by the ratio of the price index at the end of the subsequent period over the price index at the end of the prior periods. The several "aging" schedules will have to be updated and the purchasing-power gain or loss on monetary items must be calculated anew.

Summary and Conclusion

We anticipate that various short-cut approximating methods will be employed to simplify the restatement process. In the next chapter, one of these approximating methods will be considered as we discuss some further aspects of price-level accounting.

Appendix

Monetary and Nonmonetary Items*

37. *The following balance sheet items shall be classified as monetary items:*

    a) *Assets.* Cash and claims to cash that are fixed in terms of numbers of dollars regardless of changes in prices.

    b) *Liabilities.* Liabilities for which the amount owed is fixed in terms of numbers of dollars regardless of changes in prices.

    c) *Stockholders' equity.* Those stockholders' equity items that are fixed in terms of numbers of dollars, such as preferred stock that is carried in the balance sheet at an amount equal to its fixed liquidation or redemption price.

38. *Balance sheet items other than those classified as monetary items in accordance with paragraph 37 shall be classified as nonmonetary items.*

Appendix C
MONETARY AND NONMONETARY ITEMS

85. Paragraphs 37–38 distinguish between monetary and nonmonetary items for purposes of financial reporting in units of general purchasing power. This appendix provides examples of the classification of common individual balance sheet items as monetary or nonmonetary. It should be recognized that the fact that an item is nonmonetary does not necessarily mean that it will be reported at different numbers in terms of units of general purchasing power and units of money.

ASSETS	Monetary	Nonmonetary
Cash on hand and demand bank deposits (U.S. dollars)	x	
Time deposits (U.S. dollars)	x	
Foreign currency on hand and claims to foreign currency Because foreign currency exchange rates fluctuate, foreign currency items are not fixed in terms of numbers of U.S. dollars.		x
Marketable securities:		
Stocks Stocks are nonmonetary because their prices fluctuate.		x

*Source: Financial Accounting Standards Board, "Financial Reporting in Units of General Purchasing Power," Exposure Draft (December 31, 1974), pp. 9, 27–32.

	Monetary	Nonmonetary
Bonds		(See Discussion)

Bonds
    Bonds that are expected to be held to maturity and redeemed at a fixed number of dollars are monetary; others are nonmonetary because their prices can fluctuate and receipt of a fixed number of dollars is not assured.

Convertible bonds   (See discussion)
    If a convertible bond is expected to be converted or sold, it is nonmonetary. If it is expected to be held to maturity and redeemed at a fixed number of dollars it is monetary.

Accounts and notes receivable   x

Allowance for doubtful accounts and notes receivable   x

Inventories produced under fixed price contracts accounted for at the contract price   x
    Monetary because they are, in substance, accounts receivable in a fixed number of dollars.

Inventories (other than inventories produced under fixed price contracts)   x

Loans to employees   x

Prepaid insurance, advertising, rent, and other prepayments   x
    Prepayments represent claims to future services, not claims to a fixed number of dollars. The prices of identical services may fluctuate in a period of inflation or deflation. Thus, prepayments are nonmonetary.

Long-term receivables   x

Refundable deposits   x

Advances to unconsolidated subsidiaries   x
    Although advances to unconsolidated subsidiaries are often reported together with investments in those subsidiaries as a single amount, the advances are monetary because they are fixed in terms of numbers of dollars.

Investments in unconsolidated subsidiaries or other investees   (See discussion)
    If an investment is carried at cost, it is nonmonetary. If an investment is carried by the equity method, the financial statements of the investee shall be restated in terms of units of general purchasing power and the equity method should then be applied.

	Monetary	Nonmonetary
Pension, sinking, and other funds under an enterprise's control		(See discussion)
Classification of a fund as monetary or nonmonetary depends on the asset composition of the fund (see discussion under marketable securities above).		
Property, plant and equipment		x
Accumulated depreciation of property, plant, and equipment		x
Cash surrender value of life insurance	x	
Advances paid on purchase contracts		x
The prices of the goods to be received may fluctuate; consequently, the advances are not claims to a fixed number of dollars.		
Deferred income tax charges		x
Deferred income taxes are nonmonetary because they represent a deferred past cost that will be amortized to expense in future periods.		
Patents, trademarks, licenses, formulas		x
Goodwill		x
Other intangible assets and deferred charges		x

LIABILITIES

	Monetary	Nonmonetary
Accounts and notes payable	x	
Accrued expenses payable (salaries, wages, etc.)	x	
Similar to accounts payable because the obligation will be settled in a fixed number of dollars.		
Accrued vacation pay	(See discussion)	
Accrued vacation pay is monetary if it is based on a fixed contract. It is nonmonetary if it is payable based on wage or salary rates that may change after the balance sheet date.		
Cash dividends payable	x	
Debts payable in foreign currency		x
Because foreign currency exchange rates fluctuate, foreign currency debt is not fixed in terms of numbers of U.S. dollars.		
Advances received on sales contracts		x
The obligation will be satisfied by delivery of goods or services that are nonmonetary because their prices can fluctuate.		

	Monetary	Nonmonetary
Accrued losses on firm purchase commitments	x	
In essence, these are accounts payable and, therefore, are monetary.		
Deferred income		x
Payable in goods or services whose prices may fluctuate.		
Refundable deposits	x	
Bonds payable and other long-term debt	x	
Unamortized premium or discount and prepaid interest on bonds or notes payable	x	
Inseparable from the debt to which it relates, a monetary item.		
Convertible bonds payable	x	
Until converted, these are obligations to pay a fixed number of dollars.		
Accrued pension obligations	(See discussion)	
Fixed amounts payable to a fund are monetary; all other amounts are nonmonetary.		
Obligations under warranties		x
These are nonmonetary because they are liabilities to provide nonmonetary goods or services whose prices may fluctuate.		
Deferred income tax credits		x
Deferred income taxes are nonmonetary because they represent a past cost saving that will be amortized to income in future periods as a reduction of expenses. Moreover, amounts of income taxes that will ultimately be paid when the timing differences related to the tax credits reverse can change as a result of changes in tax rates or tax laws and depend on future taxable income.		
Deferred investment tax credits		x
Minority interest	(See discussion)	
The restated amount of minority interest reported in the consolidated general purchasing power financial statements would be based on the restated financial statements of the subsidiary in which there is a minority interest.		

Questions and Problems

2.1. Define monetary assets and monetary liabilities.

2.2. Define nonmonetary assets and nonmonetary liabilities.

2.3. Define net monetary items.

2.4. Briefly discuss the relationship between net monetary items and purchasing-power gains and losses.

2.5. Why is it desirable to distinguish between current and noncurrent monetary items?

2.6. Assume that at the beginning of the year, net monetary items amounted to $500,000 (i.e., net monetary *assets* of $500,000). At year end, net monetary items were −$100,000 (i.e., net monetary *liabilities* of $100,000). Assume that the change in net monetary items took place evenly over the year and that a general price index had the following values.

Beginning of the year	95
Average for the year	100
End of the year	105

a. Compute the purchasing-power gain or loss during the year.

b. Suppose that, on July 1, long-term debt of $500,000 was retired by a distribution of inventory. This is reflected in the above totals. If this debt has been the only noncurrent monetary item, calculate separately the purchasing-power gain or loss on current monetary items and on noncurrent monetary items.

c. Suppose that the above totals reflect the purchase of $200,000 worth of equipment on January 5 (all other changes in net monetary items occurred evenly during the year). Compute the purchasing-power gain or loss during the year.

d. Same suppositions as in c, except that the equipment was purchased on December 28.

2.7. Clever Corp. has experienced rapid growth in earnings in recent years. As a securities analyst, you observe that Clever is very capital intensive. Indeed, 90 percent of its assets are property, plant and equipment. You analyze the property, plant and equipment account and find the following entries, net of depreciation.

Date	Item	Net Book Value
March 1935	Factories	$50,000,000
October 1957	Machinery	20,000,000
1965–1975	(Various)	10,000,000
Total Property, Plant and Equipment, Net		$80,000,000

Based on the information given, comment on (a) the earning power of
Clever and (b) the usefulness of its statement of financial position.

2.8. What short-cut method is available for the determination of the restated
balance in retained earnings when a firm first adopts general price-level
accounting?

2.9. Using the data in Illustrative Example 2.1, prepare: (a) historical comparative statements of changes in financial position for the first and second
years, and (b) general price-level comparative statements of changes in
financial position for the first and second years restated in end-of-second-
year dollars.

2.10. The following case was prepared by David Clark, MBA student, under the
supervision of Associate Professor John K. Shank of the Harvard Business
School. It is reprinted here with the permission of the President and Fel-
lows of Harvard College. The requirements listed at the end of the case
are not part of the text of the case itself.

Forever Stores, Inc.

Karl Stone, president and principal stockholder of Forever Stores, Inc., sat
at his desk reflecting on the condition of his business in general, and on the
1973 results (see Exhibits 1 and 2) in particular. It hadn't been a great year,
he mused, but it hadn't been a disaster either. At least he didn't have to
worry about the energy crisis; his 94 jewelry stores were all located in high
pedestrian-traffic areas of major metropolitan areas, and he had recently
been assured by his regional managers that there had been no noticeable
slump in sales. Still, Stone felt mildly uncomfortable about another problem
in the U.S. economy that didn't seem to want to go away: inflation. He felt
that if he could only get some feel for the parameters of the situation as it
affected Forever, he would be better able to deal with it. With this in mind
he called his assistant, a recent graduate of a well-known eastern business
school, into his office.

"Carole," he began, "I have the feeling that we're getting clobbered by
rising prices, but these statements look as healthy as ever. Since it looks as
though inflation is here to stay, at least for a while, I think that this might
be a good time to review some of our financial policies: capital structure,
dividend policy, credit policies, things of that sort. But I have to be able to
see what I'm fighting first; I need *information*. Do you see what I'm driving
at?

Carole Schultz shifted in her chair. "Yes, I believe I do," she replied.
"What you're referring to are price-level adjusted financial statements; the
techniques involved here have been part of GAAP for years, but have been
largely ignored in practice. They relate a company's reported results to
general price-level changes in the economy."

Stone leaned back, looking slightly relieved. "Excellent. What do you
need to construct these statements?"

"First, I'll need a table of the Gross National Product Implicit Price Deflator (GNPI) going back to 1963, the year the company was formed," she responded, "but I can get that at the library [see Exhibit 3]. Then, in addition to the basic financial statements, I'll need schedules that show the age of individual items in our 'non-monetary' accounts: Plant and Equipment, Other Current Assets, Other Assets, Other Liabilities, and Common Stock and Surplus [Exhibit 4]. I'll get on it right away."

"Fine," replied Stone. "While you're at it, I'd like you to think about the implications of the figures you come up with. I'd like to know what kinds of decisions the price-level adjusted data will help us make, and I'd also like to get your ideas on some of the weaknesses or pitfalls that we should watch out for. I have a meeting with another director later today, so I'd like to go over your results with you before then. I'll see you at three."

Carole got up and turned to leave. Before she reached the door Stone called out, "Oh, and don't worry about lunch; I'll send one of the boys out for sandwiches."

Exhibit 1

FOREVER STORES, INC.

Comparative Balance Sheets

at 12/31/73 and 12/31/72 ($000,000)

	December 31	
	1973	1972
ASSETS		
Cash	$ 2.4	$ 2.3
Accounts Receivable	56.3	53.7
Inventories	34.3	32.7
Other Current Assets	0.6	0.6
Total Current Assets	93.6	89.3
Plant and Equipment	10.6	10.6
Less Accumulated Depreciation	3.9	3.4
	6.7	7.2
Other Assets	3.4	3.5
	$103.7	$100.0
LIABILITIES		
Accounts Payable	$ 31.5	$ 29.9
Accruals	4.4	4.2
Other Current Liabilities	1.4	1.3
Total Current Liabilities	37.3	35.4
Long-term Debt	15.3	14.9
Other liabilities	10.5	10.1
Common Stock and Surplus	33.6	33.6
Retained Earnings	7.0	6.0
	40.6	39.6
	$103.7	$100.0

Exhibit 2

FOREVER STORES, INC.

Statement of Income and Retained Earnings
for year ended December 31, 1973 ($000,000)

Sales		$100.0
Cost of Goods Sold		
Opening Inventory	$32.7	
Purchases	81.6	
Closing Inventory	34.3	80.0
Gross Margin		20.0
Depreciation		0.5
Other Expenses		13.8
Operating Profit		5.7
Interest (@ 7.5%)		1.7
Profit Before Tax		4.0
Profit After Tax		2.0
Retained Earnings, 12/31/72		$ 6.0
		8.0
Less: Dividends paid, 1973		1.0
Retained Earnings, 12/31/73		$ 7.0

Exhibit 3

FOREVER STORES, INC.

Implicit Price Deflators for Gross National Product
for years 1963–1973* (1958 = 100)

Year	GNPI	GNPI as % of index (12/31/73)
1963	107.2	1.478
1964	108.8	1.456
1965	110.9	1.428
1966	113.94	1.390
1967	117.59	1.347
1968	122.30	1.294
1969	128.20	1.235
1970	135.24	1.171
1971	141.60	1.118
1972	146.10	1.084
1973	153.94	1.029

Quarterly Averages

	1972		1973	
I	144.85	1.093	149.81	1.057
II	145.42	1.089	152.46	1.039
III	146.42	1.082	155.06	1.021
IV	147.63	1.073	158.36	1.000

*Source: U.S. Department of Commerce, Bureau of Economic Analysis: *Survey of Current Business*, February 1974, for 1973 data; 1972 *Business Statistics* for all other data.

Exhibit 4

FOREVER STORES, INC.

Chronological Analysis of Selected Accounts ($000,000)

Plant and Equipment

Year Acquired	Gross Investment	Accumulated Depreciation* 12/31/72	Net Amount 12/31/72	12/31/73
1963	$ 3.6	$1.8	$1.8	$1.6
1965	1.5	0.6	0.9	0.8
1968	2.4	0.6	1.8	1.7
1970	2.1	0.3	1.8	1.7
1971	1.0	0.1	0.9	0.8
	$10.6	$3.4	$7.2	$6.7

(All Plant and Equipment depreciated straight-line over 20 years.

Common Stock and Surplus

Year Acquired	Amount
1963	$16.8
1966	8.4
1970	8.4
	$33.6

Other Current Assets, Other Assets and Other Liabilities

For simplicity, assume that entire amounts appearing on 1972 statements were acquired in 1968.

Required:

a. Compute the purchasing-power gain or loss on monetary items for 1973. Assume all changes in monetary items occurred evenly throughout the year.

b. Prepare schedules to restate property, plant and equipment, accumulated depreciation, depreciation expense and capital stock and surplus. Assume all items occurred at the average price level in the various years.

c. Prepare a price-level adjusted statement of income and retained earnings for 1973. Assume sales, purchases, other expenses, interest, taxes and dividends occurred evenly throughout the year. Beginning restated retained earnings must be taken from part d (below).

d. Prepare price-level adjusted statements of financial position at 12/31/73 and 12/31/72 in 12/31/73 dollars.

e. Prepare historical cost and restated statements of changes in financial position for 1973. Assume all changes in noncurrent accounts occurred at the average price level for 1973.

f. Comment on the historical and restated financial statements in terms of Karl Stone's concerns over the impact of inflation on Forever Stores, Inc.

2.11. The following data relate to the Hale Corporation.*

HALE CORPORATION
Post-Closing Trial Balance, December 31, 19x5 (Historical Cost)

	Dr.	Cr.
Cash	$ 600,000	
Accounts Receivable, Net	900,000	
Inventories	1,800,000	
Land	300,000	
Buildings and Equipment (A)	1,000,000	
Accumulated Depreciation (A)		$ 400,000
Buildings and Equipment (B)	800,000	
Accumulated Depreciation (B)		160,000
Accounts Payable		750,000
Long-Term Note Payable		500,000
Paid-in Capital		2,000,000
Retained Earnings		1,590,000
	$5,400,000	$5,400,000

NOTES:

(1) The Company was organized early in 19x2, at which time all capital stock was issued, the land was purchased and the buildings and equipment (A) were purchased.

(2) Late in 19x3, buildings and equipment (B) were purchased.

(3) All buildings and equipment are being depreciated at an annual rate of 10 percent; no salvage values.

(4) The long-term note payable was issued at the end of 19x4.

(5) The inventory, which is accounted for under the FIFO cost flow assumption, represents purchases made in the last quarter of the year.

(6) The following income statement data were generated by transactions occurring evenly throughout the year.

Sales	$8,000,000
Merchandise Purchases	6,350,000
Cost of Goods Sold	5,800,000
Selling and Administrative Expenses	1,260,000
Interest Expense	40,000
Income Taxes	300,000

(7) Cash dividends of $200,000 were paid on December 31, 19x5.

(8) Historical cost depreciation expense was $180,000.

(9) The GNP Deflator had the following recent values.

Time Period	Index Value
Fourth quarter, 19x5	110
Average for 19x5	105
Fourth quarter, 19x4	100
Fourth quarter, 19x3	90
First quarter, 19x2	80

---

*For a more complete study of the case from which this problem is adapted, see the article by John R. O'Donnell in the July 1974 issue of the *Arthur Andersen Chronicle.*

Required:

a. Restate the Hale Corporation's 12/31/x5 statement of financial position using a worksheet with the following columnar headings.

Account	Historical Balance per Books		Ratio to Restate	Historical Balance Restated in 12/31/x5 $	
	Dr.	Cr.		Dr.	Cr.

b. Compute the purchasing-power gain or loss on monetary items during 19x5. Net monetary items at 12/31/x4 were $400,000.

c. Restate the Hale Corporation's statement of income and retained earnings in 19x5. Be sure to include the purchasing-power gain or loss on monetary items.

d. Compute separately the purchasing-power gain on the long-term note payable. How would this be treated on the restated statement of changes in financial position? Why?

Price Level Accounting: Some Further Considerations **3**

The different aspects of price-level accounting discussed in this chapter range from the nature and limitations of price indexes to the impact of inflation, through price-level adjustments, on the financial statements of various companies. We will also deal with the major controversial areas in price-level accounting.

As an example of price-level adjusted financial statments from the real world, we include the actual financial statements of Indiana Telephone Corporation (ITC), a firm which has pioneered the use of price-level adjustments in the United States. It should be noted that ITC does not follow the FASB procedure with respect to purchasing-power gain (loss) on long-term monetary items. Purchasing-power gains on long-term debt and preferred stock are not included in income until the debt or preferred stock is retired and not refinanced. At the time this book was written, however, the ITC statements were the only *complete* set of price-level adjusted financial statements which had been audited and published. We will return to the ITC treatment of purchasing-power gains on long-term monetary items later in this chapter.

The Indiana Telephone Corporation Financial Statements

As of December 31, 1974, Indiana Telephone Corporation acquired 100 percent of the common stock of Public Telephone Corporation. Since this acquisition took place on the last day of the year and was treated as a purchase, the Indiana Telephone Corporation *corporate* statements of income, retained earnings and changes in financial position are the same as the *consolidated* statements of income, retained earnings and changes in financial position for 1974. The *consolidated* statement of financial position, however, differs from the *corporate* statement of financial position. To facilitate comparisons with 1973, we have chosen to reproduce the *corporate* rather than the *consolidated* statement of financial position along with the other comparative statements for 1974 and 1973 — a portion of ITC's 1974 annual report. Included are the statement of financial position (i.e., the statement of assets and the statement of capital), statement of income, statement of changes in financial position, statement of retained earnings, portions of the notes from the report and some corporate comparative data for the years 1970–1974.

INDIANA TELEPHONE CORPORATION

Corporate Statements of Assets
December 31, 1974 and 1973

	Column A Historical Cost		Column B Historical Cost Restated to Reflect Purchasing Power of 1974 Dollar	
	1974	1973	1974	1973
TELEPHONE PLANT, at original cost, Note 1(a):				
In service	$47,463,697	$41,273,210	$66,887,274	$61,088,399
Less—Accumulated depreciation	15,076,603	13,461,070	23,039,987	21,283,673
	32,387,094	27,812,140	43,847,287	39,804,726
Plant under construction	2,466,514	1,167,500	2,579,134	1,350,221
	34,853,608	28,979,640	46,426,421	41,154,947
WORKING CAPITAL:				
Current assets—				
Cash and special deposits	536,855	528,784	536,855	595,367
Temporary cash investments, at cost, which approximates market	2,472,888	5,413,126	2,472,888	6,094,731
Accounts receivable, less reserve	1,615,895	1,586,033	1,615,895	1,785,741
Materials and supplies	1,263,919	1,133,017	1,345,434	1,315,054
Prepayments	83,342	114,133	87,147	131,996
	5,972,899	8,775,093	6,058,219	9,922,889
Current liabilities—				
Sinking funds and current maturities of long-term debt, Note 3	220,795	121,000	220,795	136,236
Accounts payable, Note 6	3,595,424	2,815,240	3,595,424	3,169,727
Advance billings	391,751	366,458	391,751	412,601
Dividends payable	167,463	84,177	167,463	94,776
Federal income taxes, Note 1 (b)	295,177	471,867	295,177	531,283
Other accrued taxes	647,138	591,810	647,138	666,329
Other current liabilities	1,138,275	708,804	1,138,275	798,055
	6,456,023	5,159,356	6,456,023	5,809,007
Net working capital	(483,124)	3,615,737	(397,804)	4,113,882
OTHER:				
Investment in common stock of Public Telephone Corporation, at cost, Note 2	3,320,000	—	3,320,000	—
Debt expense being amortized, Note 1(c)	194,723	202,054	298,452	309,752
Deferred charges	118,344	68,485	124,652	79,801
Deferred Federal income taxes, Note 1(b)	(2,871,302)	(2,090,144)	(3,605,034)	(2,739,180)
Unamortized investment tax credit, Note 1(e)	(885,857)	(689,647)	(1,103,103)	(919,459)
	(124,092)	(2,509,252)	(965,033)	(3,269,086)
TOTAL INVESTMENT IN TELEPHONE BUSINESS	$34,246,392	$30,086,125	$45,063,584	$41,999,743

The accompanying notes are an integral part of these statements.

INDIANA TELEPHONE CORPORATION

Corporate Statements of Capital
December 31, 1974 and 1973

| | Column A Historical Cost | | | | Column B Historical Cost Restated to Reflect Purchasing Power of 1974 Dollar | | | |
| | 1974 | | 1973 | | 1974 | | 1973 | |
	Amount	Ratio	Amount	Ratio	Amount	Ratio	Amount	Ratio
LONG-TERM DEBT:								
First mortgage sinking fund bonds—								
Series 6, 5⅜%, due September 1, 1991	$ 1,780,000		$ 1,800,000		$ 1,780,000		$ 2,026,651	
Series 7, 4¾%, due May 1, 1994	1,932,000		1,953,000		1,932,000		2,198,916	
Series 8, 4¾%, due July 1, 2005	2,771,000		2,823,000		2,771,000		3,178,464	
Series 9, 6½%, due October 1, 2007	2,850,000		2,880,000		2,850,000		3,242,641	
Series 10, 7¾%, due June 1, 2008	4,875,000		4,875,000		4,875,000		5,488,845	
Less—Current sinking funds, Note 3	(149,750)		(101,000)		(149,750)		(113,718)	
Total first mortgage sinking fund bonds	14,058,250		14,230,000		14,058,250		16,021,799	
Unsecured variable interest rate notes payable, due semi-annually from June 30, 1975 to December 31, 1989, Note 2	2,988,000		—		2,988,000		—	
Less—Current maturities, Note 3	(51,045)		—		(51,045)		—	
	2,936,955		—		2,936,955		—	
Total long-term debt	16,995,205	50%	14,230,000	47%	16,995,205	38%	16,021,799	38%
PREFERRED STOCK:								
Cumulative, 1% sinking fund, par value $100 per share, 30,000 shares authorized of which 10,000 are unissued—								
1950 Series 4.80%	226,400		229,900		226,400		258,848	
1951 Series 4.80%	230,400		235,400		230,400		265,041	
1954 Series 5¼%	315,800		322,100		315,800		362,658	
1956 Series 5%	243,100		248,600		243,100		279,903	
1967 Series 6⅛%	665,000		672,000		665,000		756,616	
Less—Current sinking funds, Note 3	(20,000)		(20,000)		(20,000)		(22,518)	
Total preferred stock	1,660,700	5	1,688,000	6	1,660,700	4	1,900,548	4
COMMON SHAREHOLDERS' INTEREST:								
Common stock, no par value, authorized 500,000 shares, issued 492,086 shares, Note 5	9,841,720		4,251,785		13,918,691		8,073,515	
Retained earnings	5,827,906		9,996,665		1,632,655		7,070,428	
Treasury stock, 4,336 shares, at cost	(5,192)		(5,192)		(9,828)		(9,828)	
Stock discount and expense	(73,947)		(75,133)		(144,288)		(146,646)	
Total common shareholders' interest	15,590,487	45	14,168,125	47	15,397,230	34	14,987,469	36
UNREALIZED EFFECTS OF PRICE-LEVEL CHANGES, Note 1(a)	—	—	—	—	11,010,449	24	9,089,927	22
TOTAL INVESTMENT IN TELEPHONE BUSINESS	$34,246,392	100%	$30,086,125	100%	$45,063,584	100%	$41,999,743	100%

The accompanying notes are an integral part of these statements.

Consolidated and Corporate Statements of Income

	Column A Historical Cost		Column B Historical Cost Restated to Reflect Purchasing Power of 1974 Dollar	
	1974	1973	1974	1973
OPERATING REVENUES:				
Local service	$ 7,050,010	$ 6,459,323	$ 7,371,913	$ 7,470,245
Toll service	6,050,463	5,623,163	6,326,727	6,503,221
Miscellaneous	405,894	412,199	424,427	476,711
Total operating revenues	13,506,367	12,494,685	14,123,067	14,450,177
OPERATING EXPENSES:				
Depreciation provision, Note 1(b)	2,631,584	2,295,252	3,782,992	3,414,966
Maintenance	2,132,419	1,699,037	2,229,785	1,964,946
Total depreciation and maintenance	4,764,003	3,994,289	6,012,777	5,379,912
Traffic	1,026,379	973,906	1,073,243	1,126,328
Commercial	700,958	651,606	732,964	753,586
General and administrative	1,524,482	1,096,568	1,613,204	1,278,797
State, local and miscellaneous Federal taxes	1,057,394	989,689	1,105,675	1,144,581
Federal income taxes, Note 1(b) —				
Currently payable	1,056,701	1,395,145	1,104,950	1,613,493
Deferred until future years	391,000	300,900	408,853	347,993
Deferred investment tax credit (net)	210,588	145,251	200,862	154,877
Total operating expenses	10,731,505	9,547,354	12,252,528	11,799,567
OPERATING INCOME	2,774,862	2,947,331	1,870,539	2,650,610
INCOME DEDUCTIONS:				
Interest on long-term debt	885,995	892,598	926,450	1,032,295
Other deductions	345,919	23,345	366,454	30,483
Allowance for funds used during construction (credit), Note 1(d)	(100,507)	(48,777)	(105,096)	(56,411)
Other income (credit)	(369,522)	(380,918)	(386,394)	(440,534)
Nonoperating Federal income taxes	19,267	171,600	20,147	198,456
Gain from retirement of long-term debt through operation of sinking funds (credit)	(22,627)	(16,303)	(23,660)	(18,855)
Price-level gain from retirement of long-term debt (credit), Note 1(a)	—	—	(74,195)	(55,835)
Gain from retirement of preferred stock through operation of sinking funds (credit)	(7,381)	(6,383)	(7,718)	(7,382)
Price-level gain from retirement of preferred stock (credit), Note 1(a)	—	—	(24,373)	(20,676)
Price-level loss from monetary items, Note 1(a)	—	—	141,472	235,407
Total income deductions	751,144	635,162	833,087	896,948
NET INCOME, Note 1(a)	2,023,718	2,312,169	1,037,452	1,753,662
Preferred stock dividends applicable to the periods	92,029	93,534	96,231	108,173
EARNINGS APPLICABLE TO COMMON STOCK	$ 1,931,689	$ 2,218,635	$ 941,221	$ 1,645,489
EARNINGS PER COMMON SHARE	$ 3.96	$ 4.55	$ 1.93	$ 3.37

The accompanying notes are an integral part of these statements.

INDIANA TELEPHONE CORPORATION

Consolidated and Corporate Statements of Changes in Financial Position

	Column A Historical Cost		Column B Historical Cost Restated to Reflect Purchasing Power of 1974 Dollar	
	1974	1973	1974	1973
FUNDS WERE PROVIDED BY:				
Operations—				
Net income	$ 2,023,718	$ 2,312,169	$ 1,037,452	$ 1,753,662
Items which did not require (provide) funds—				
Depreciation provision—				
Charged to income	2,631,584	2,295,252	3,782,992	3,414,966
Charged to clearing accounts	50,621	48,409	72,771	72,024
Deferred Federal income taxes	781,158	490,690	865,854	605,345
Deferred investment tax credit (net)	196,210	145,251	183,644	154,578
Allowance for funds used during Construction	(100,507)	(48,777)	(105,096)	(56,411)
Realized effects of price-level changes, Note 1(a)	—	—	(98,568)	(76,511)
Issuance of unsecured notes payable	2,988,000	—	2,988,000	—
Net salvage on plant retirements	403,821	389,976	380,699	441,559
	8,974,605	5,632,970	9,107,748	6,309,212
FUNDS WERE EXPENDED FOR:				
Gross additions to telephone plant	8,859,487	5,454,209	9,402,840	6,360,116
Purchase of Public Telephone Corporation, Note 2—				
Telephone plant (net)	6,249,376	—	8,369,285	—
Cost in excess of underlying book value	140,431	—	(219,271)	—
Long-term debt	(4,237,283)	—	(4,237,283)	—
Preferred stock	(97,700)	—	(97,700)	—
Other assets and liabilities (net)	709,886	—	665,892	—
Unrealized effects of price-level changes	—	—	(1,807,932)	—
Cash dividends declared—Common stock	487,750	182,906	510,021	211,532
—Preferred stock	114,792	69,918	120,033	80,861
Provision for and redemption of long-term debt and preferred stock, less unrealized effects of price-level changes	250,095	143,500	234,859	151,553
Miscellaneous (net)	41,342	83,053	31,681	139,244
	12,518,176	5,933,586	12,972,425	6,943,306
(DECREASE) IN NET WORKING CAPITAL	$ (3,543,571)	$ (300,616)	$ (3,864,677)	$ (634,094)
(DECREASE) IN NET WORKING CAPITAL				
REPRESENTED BY CHANGES IN:				
Cash and special deposits	$ 8,071	$ (267,187)	$ (58,512)	$ (366,828)
Temporary cash investments	(2,940,238)	930,576	(3,621,843)	676,081
Accounts receivable, less reserve	29,862	87,344	(169,846)	(25,923)
Materials and supplies and prepayments	100,111	500,391	(14,469)	530,580
Sinking funds and current maturities of long-term debt	(99,795)	—	(84,559)	10,033
Accounts payable and advance billings	(805,477)	(2,022,960)	(404,847)	(2,181,608)
Dividends payable	(83,286)	84,727	(72,687)	109,401
Accrued Federal and other taxes	121,362	108,356	255,297	219,179
Other current liabilities	(429,471)	278,137	(340,220)	394,991
Working capital acquired upon purchase of Public Telephone Corporation	555,290	—	647,009	—
(DECREASE) IN NET WORKING CAPITAL	$ (3,543,571)	$ (300,616)	$ (3,864,677)	$ (634,094)

The accompanying notes are an integral part of these statements.

INDIANA TELEPHONE CORPORATION

Consolidated and Corporate
Statements of Retained Earnings
for the Years ended December 31, 1974 and 1973

	Column A Historical Cost		Column B Historical Cost Restated to Reflect Purchasing Power of 1974 Dollar	
	1974	1973	1974	1973
BALANCE, beginning of year	$ 9,996,665	$ 7,937,320	$7,070,428	$5,609,159
NET INCOME	2,023,718	2,312,169	1,037,452	1,753,662
	12,020,383	10,249,489	8,107,880	7,362,821
DEDUCT:				
Cash dividends declared—				
Common stock, annual rate—$1.00 per share in 1974 and $.50 per share in 1973	487,750	182,906	510,021	211,532
Preferred stock	114,792	69,918	120,033	80,861
	602,542	252,824	630,054	292,393
Transfer to common stock, Note 5	5,589,935	—	5,845,171	—
BALANCE, end of year	$ 5,827,906	$ 9,996,665	$1,632,655	$7,070,428

The accompanying notes are an integral part of these statements.

AUDITORS' REPORT

To the Shareholders of Indiana Telephone Corporation:

We have examined the consolidated statements of assets and capital of INDIANA TELEPHONE CORPORATION (an Indiana corporation) and subsidiary and the statements of assets and capital of INDIANA TELEPHONE CORPORATION as of December 31, 1974 and 1973, and the related consolidated and corporate statements of income, retained earnings and changes in financial position for the years then ended. Our examination was made in accordance with generally accepted auditing standards, and accordingly included such tests of the accounting records and such other auditing procedures as we considered necessary in the circumstances.

In our opinion, the accompanying financial statements shown under Column A present fairly the financial positions of Indiana Telephone Corporation and subsidiary and of Indiana Telephone Corporation as of December 31, 1974 and 1973, and the results of their operations and the changes in their financial position for the years then ended, in conformity with generally accepted accounting principles consistently applied during the periods.

In our opinion, however, the accompanying financial statements shown under Column B more fairly present the financial positions of Indiana Telephone Corporation and subsidiary and of Indiana Telephone Corporation as of December 31, 1974 and 1973, and the results of their operations and the changes in their financial position for the years then ended, as recognition has been given to changes in the purchasing power of the dollar, on the basis explained in Note 1(a).

Indianapolis, Indiana,   ARTHUR ANDERSEN & CO.
February 27, 1975.

INDIANA TELEPHONE CORPORATION

Notes to Consolidated and Corporate Financial Statements

1. SUMMARY OF SIGNIFICANT ACCOUNTING POLICIES

(a) EXPLANATION OF FINANCIAL STATEMENTS

In the accompanying financial statements, costs measured by the dollars disbursed at the time of the expenditure are shown in "Column A—Historical Cost." In "Column B—Historical Cost Restated to Reflect Purchasing Power of 1974 Dollar" (where the amounts in A and B differ), these dollars of cost have been restated in terms of the price level at December 31, 1974, as measured by the Gross National Product Implicit Price Deflator. Since 1954, the Corporation has presented supplemental financial information recognizing the effect of the changes in the purchasing power of the dollar relating to telephone plant and depreciation expense in the annual report to shareholders.

As explained more fully in Note 2, as of December 31, 1974, the Corporation acquired all of the outstanding common stock of Public Telephone Corporation, which since 1954 has also presented supplemental financial information to shareholders recognizing the effect of the changes in the purchasing power of the dollar. Since the acquisition has been treated as a purchase for accounting purposes, the Consolidated Statements of Assets and Capital for December 31, 1974, include the accounts of Public Telephone Corporation in both Columns A and B. The amounts included in Column B have been computed for each Corporation in accordance with the methods described below. There are no amounts relating to Public Telephone Corporation included in the Consolidated Statements of Income for 1974 or 1973 in either Column A or B.

The Corporation has followed the methods set forth in Statement No. 3, of the Accounting Principles Board of the American Institute of Certified Accountants in determining the amounts set forth in Column B of the accompanying financial statements, except that, contrary to Statement No. 3, the effects of price-level changes on long-term debt and preferred stock have been reflected as income in the year in which the debt and preferred stock are retired (as required by the specific instruments under which they were issued) and not refinanced. The Accounting Principles Board took the position that all such amounts should be taken into income in the year of price-level change. The Corporation's management believes that the position of the Accounting Principles Board does not result in a proper determination of income for the period. "Unrealized Effects of Price-Level Changes" recognizes the excess of adjustments on the Statements of Assets over the adjustments of Common Shareholders' Interest.

The Financial Accounting Standards Board has recently issued an exposure draft of a proposed Statement of Financial Accounting Standards, "Financial Reporting in Units of General Purchasing Power," which closely parallels Statement No. 3 and endorses the concept of Column B financial statement reporting, except that, as in Statement No. 3, the annual effects of price-level changes on long-term debt would be included in income currently.

Dollars are a means of expressing purchasing power at the time of their use. Conversion or restatement of dollars of differing purchasing power to the purchasing power of the dollar at the date of conversion results in all dollars being treated as mathematical likes for the purpose of significant data. The resulting financial statements recognize the changes in price levels between the periods of expenditure of funds and the periods of use of property. Accordingly, the earnings, results of operations, assets and other data available for use by management and other readers of financial statements provide important information and comparisons not otherwise available.

No one would attempt to add, subtract, multiply, or divide marks, dollars and pounds. The failure to change the title of the monetary unit may be partially responsible for this violation of mathematical principle. This conceals the fact that mathematical unlikes are being used, and therefore unfortunate results have been produced by present generally accepted accounting principles.

INDIANA TELEPHONE CORPORATION

Corporate Comparative Data

	Historical Cost				
	1974	1973	1972	1971	1970
REVENUES, EXPENSES, AND EARNINGS:					
Operating revenues	$13,506,367	$12,494,685	$11,732,962	$10,901,034	$ 9,969,629
Operating expenses—					
Depreciation	2,631,584	2,295,252	2,053,700	1,943,551	1,541,560
Other	5,384,238	4,421,117	4,235,777	4,280,380	4,204,354
Operating taxes	2,715,683	2,830,985	2,748,174	2,370,609	2,161,086
Operating income	2,774,862	2,947,331	2,695,311	2,306,494	2,062,629
Net income	2,023,718	2,312,169	2,126,274	1,798,597	1,637,288
FINANCIAL RATIOS:					
Earnings per common share.	$ 3.96	$ 4.55	$ 4.16	$ 3.49	$ 3.16
Book value per share	$ 31.96	$ 29.05	$ 24.82	$ 21.45	$ 18.29
Return on average common equity	12.98%	16.89%	18.00%	17.56%	18.68%
Return on average total capital	9.07%	11.03%	11.04%	10.07%	9.95%
Proportion of debt in total capital	50%	47%	51%	51%	55%
Ratio of earnings after taxes to fixed charges	3.27	3.57	3.61	3.72	3.45
Annual depreciation rate per dollar of plant.	6.3%	6.2%	6.1%	6.3%	5.4%
Percent of earnings reinvested in telephone business	75%	89%	88%	86%	84%
TELEPHONE PLANT:					
Construction expenditures.	$ 8,859,487	$ 5,454,209	$ 4,586,237	$ 3,411,941	$ 3,315,190
Plant in service at end of year.	47,463,697	41,273,210	37,084,382	32,681,923	30,292,769
Investment per main station.	804	716	667	609	577
Investment per employee .	111,156	102,926	92,480	77,080	67,019
SERVICE AND EMPLOYEES:					
Total stations in service. . .	87,563	84,014	80,439	75,015	72,569
Total main stations	59,004	57,681	55,596	53,700	52,533
Long distance messages . .	7,305,913	6,985,343	6,176,327	5,252,988	5,283,657
Toll revenue per main station.	$ 103	$ 97	$ 94	$ 90	$ 84
Employees.	427	401	401	424	452
INDEXES:					
GNP—Implicit Price Deflator (1958 = 100)	170.2	153.9	146.1	141.6	135.3
Consumer Price Index (1957–1959 = 100) .	172.0	154.7	145.7	141.0	135.3

	Historical Cost Restated to Reflect Purchasing Power of 1974 Dollar				
	1974	1973	1972	1971	1970
REVENUES, EXPENSES, AND EARNINGS:					
Operating revenues	$14,123,067	$14,450,177	$14,311,518	$13,698,682	$13,150,034
Operating expenses—					
Depreciation	3,782,992	3,414,966	3,167,670	3,113,736	2,526,595
Other	5,649,196	5,123,657	5,169,288	5,395,454	5,612,830
Operating taxes	2,820,340	3,260,944	3,341,896	2,970,872	2,844,067
Operating income	1,870,539	2,650,610	2,632,664	2,218,620	2,166,542
Net income	1,037,452	1,753,662	1,883,624	1,559,705	1,539,529
FINANCIAL RATIOS:					
Earnings per common share	$ 1.93	$ 3.37	$ 3.62	$ 2.95	$ 2.89
Book value per share	$ 31.57	$ 30.73	$ 27.81	$ 25.17	$ 22.63
Return on average common equity	6.20%	11.53%	13.68%	12.34%	13.50%
Return on average total capital	4.54%	6.75%	7.35% ·	6.40%	6.64%
Proportion of debt in total capital	38%	38%	42%	43%	46%
Ratio of earnings after taxes to fixed charges . .	2.11	2.68	2.87	2.86	2.74
Annual depreciation rate per dollar of plant.	6.3%	6.2%	6.1%	6.3%	5.4%
Percent of earnings reinvested in telephone business	46%	83%	83%	79%	77%
TELEPHONE PLANT:					
Construction expenditures .	$ 9,402,840	$ 6,360,116	$ 5,586,492	$ 4,288,482	$ 4,362,234
Plant in service at end of year.	66,887,274	61,088,399	56,876,485	52,112,338	49,225,042
Investment per main station.	1,134	1,059	1,023	970	937
Investment per employee .	156,645	152,340	141,837	122,906	108,905
SERVICE AND EMPLOYEES:					
Total stations in service. . .	87,563	84,014	80,439	75,015	72,569
Total main stations	59,004	57,681	55,596	53,700	52,533
Long distance messages . .	7,305,913	6,985,343	6,176,327	5,252,988	5,283,657
Toll revenue per main station.	$ 107	$ 113	$ 114	$ 114	$ 111
Employees.	427	401	401	424	452
INDEXES:					
GNP—Implicit Price Deflator (1958 = 100)	170.2	153.9	146.1	141.6	135.3
Consumer Price Index (1957–1959 = 100)	172.0	154.7	145.7	141.0	135.3

This firm has been following the same basic procedures that we outlined, with two major exceptions. They do not recognize the purchasing-power gain on their bond and preferred stock accounts as realized in the year of price-level change. Their reasons for not doing so are stated in Note 1(a). They compensate for this by adding to the statement of capital an account entitled "Unrealized Effects of Price-Level Changes."

Let us briefly analyze and evaluate the position of Indiana Telephone on this matter of nonrecognition of purchasing-power gains on long-term debt and preferred stock. Although there is some disagreement over whether *preferred stock* is a monetary liability, the FASB and APB recommend that purchasing-power gains on preferred stock and long-term debt be included in income as they occur. Which position has more merit?

Indiana Telephone has adopted a conservative position in their non-symmetric treatment of monetary assets and liabilities. They have recognized the purchasing-power losses on their monetary assets (all current assets) and purchasing-power gains on their current monetary liabilities. They fail, however, to currently recognize purchasing-power gains on long-term debt and preferred stock as income *unless* the debt or stock is retired and not refinanced. Thus, there exists a bias in favor of continually reporting net purchasing-power losses on monetary items.

It seems that Indiana Telephone is relying on a cash-basis realization criterion to signal recognition of purchasing-power gains and losses. Since current monetary assets and liabilities tend to turn over during the course of a year, it can be argued that the purchasing-power gains and losses attributable to those items have been realized through collection and disbursement of cash. In dealing with the long-term debt and preferred stock, Indiana Telephone is at least consistent with respect to the cash-basis realization criterion: purchasing-power gains are recognized only when these liabilities are liquidated and not refinanced. Only at this point do these long-term liabilities "flow through" the cash account and the purchasing-power gains are deemed to be realized.

The FASB and APB have tentatively adopted the opposite view that *all* monetary assets and liabilities generate purchasing-power gains and losses during a period of inflation. Such gains and losses *accrue* with the passage of time and hence are deemed to be realized under accrual-basis accounting. Recall that monetary assets and liabilities represent fixed quantities of dollars. As the price level changes, the purchasing-power of a dollar changes. Thus, the purchasing power of a fixed quantity of dollars *owned* declines and the sacrifice in purchasing power attributable power is associated with the *holding* of monetary assets and liabilities and not with their *liquidation*. The accrual basis is just as valid for realizing these gains and losses as it is for sales and purchases on account.

We concur with the FASB and APB in this issue on the grounds that cash-basis realization (i.e., liquidation of the monetary items) is irrelevant here. Indeed, it is the *holding* or *nonliquidation* of these items that generates the gains and losses in purchasing power.

The Auditors' Report. The ITC financial statements received a clean opinion from the auditors. What is interesting, however, is that the auditors' report asserts that the financial statements restated in 1974 dollars are a *more fair* presentation than are the historical cost financial statements. Since detailed standards of reporting have not yet been developed for price-level adjusted financial statements, we cannot really criticize the report. Rather, ITC and its auditors should, in our opinion, be commended for their pioneering work in this area. Nevertheless, we question the meaning of "more fairly present" and wonder what "most fairly present" would imply. We will contrast the wording of the ITC auditors' report with that of the Shell Oil Company supplementary financial statements presented later in this chapter.

The "Funds" Statement. The 1974 ITC annual report represents the first year for which a restated statement of changes in financial position has been published. Prior annual reports did not include a restated funds statement. One of the present authors raised this point with ITC in some correspondence during 1974. We are pleased to observe that the ITC funds statement for 1974 has been restated. It is the only published restated funds statement of which we are aware.

The Indiana Telephone Company funds statement differs from the funds statement example of Chapter 2 in the following ways. Indiana Telephone Company does not follow the FASB recommended practice of recognizing as immediately realized the price-level gain on long-term monetary items. Essentially, ITC treats this item as unrealized until the relevant long-term debt or preferred stock is retired and not refinanced. Thus, the ITC funds statement adds back to net income only the *realized* price-level gain and not the entire price-level gain on long-term monetary items as in our example.

A further difference, due basically to the same reason, concerns the item in the ITC statement titled "Purchase of Public Telephone Corporation: Unrealized Effects of Price-Level Changes." Clearly, ITC regards this item not only as unrealized but also as not forming part of the common shareholders' interest (see reproduced portion of Note 2 to the Indiana Telephone statements given below). Under our treatment—and that of the FASB Exposure Draft—this item would not appear in the funds statement. It would already be included in retained earnings, via net income, and hence would be part of the common shareholders' interest.

INDIANA TELEPHONE CORPORATION

2. PURCHASE OF COMMON STOCK OF PUBLIC TELEPHONE CORPORATION

As of December 31, 1974, the Corporation purchased all of the 41,500 shares of outstanding common stock of Public Telephone Corporation (Public) for $3,320,000. The transfer of the Public common stock to the Corporation, currently held in escrow, will occur upon receipt of approval by the Federal Communications Commission to transfer control of Public, which owns microwave operating permits, to the Corporation. The purchase price includes a cash payment of $332,000 and the issuance of long-term, unsecured, variable interest rate notes totaling $2,988,000. Interest on the unpaid principal balance of the notes is to be paid semi-annually on June 20 and December 31 of each year, commencing June 30, 1975, at a rate 1% above the so-called "floating interest rate" to be paid by Citicorp (parent of First National City Bank of New York) on its $650,000,000 notes due in 1989, as more particularly described in Citicorp's prospectus dated July 24, 1974.

The acquisition has been treated as a purchase for accounting purposes. As a result, earnings of Public are not included in income for the year ended December 31, 1974, or prior. The cost in excess of underlying book value at data of acquisition totaling $140,431 has been shown as a separate component of telephone plant since no specific recognition of this amount is given in rate determinations. The Corporation intends to amortize this balance over a ten year period beginning in 1975. Other assets and liabilities acquired have been included in the consolidated financial statements at recorded book values as required for regulatory purposes.

Indiana Telephone Corporation and Public Telephone Corporation are each separate, legal entities and continue to be regulated individually by the Public Service Commission of Indiana. Since the Individual identities of the two corporations are not readily apparent in the Consolidated Statements of Assets and Capital, consolidating financial data of assets and capital for December 31, 1974, is presented as follows:

	Indiana Telephone Corporation	Public Telephone Corporation	Eliminations	Consolidated
Column A—Historical Cost				
Net telephone plant	$34,853,608	$6,249,376	$ 140,431	$41,243,415
Net working capital	(483,124)	555,290	—	72,166
Other assets and liabilities (net)	(124,092)	709,886	(3,320,000)	(2,734,206)
	$34,246,392	$7,514,552	$(3,179,569)	$38,581,375
Long-term debt	$16,995,205	$4,237,283	$ —	$21,232,488
Preferred stock	1,660,700	97,700	—	1,758,400
Common shareholders' interest	15,590,487	3,179,569	(3,179,569)	15,590,487
	$34,246,392	$7,514,552	$(3,179,569)	$38,581,375
Column B—Historical Cost Restated to Reflect Purchasing Power of 1974 Dollar				
Net telephone plant	$46,426,421	$8,369,285	$ (219,271)	$54,576,435
Net working capital	(397,804)	647,009	—	249,205
Other assets and liabilities (net)	(965,033)	665,892	(3,320,000)	(3,619,141)
	$45,063,584	$9,682,186	$(3,539,271)	$51,206,499
Long-term debt	$16,995,205	$4,237,283	$ —	$21,232,488
Preferred stock	1,660,700	97,700	—	1,758,400
Common shareholders' interest	15,397,230	3,539,271	(3,539,271)	15,397,230
Unrealized effects of price-level changes	11,010,449	1,807,932	—	12,818,381
	$45,063,584	$9,682,186	$(3,539,271)	$51,206,499

It seems likely that the treatment of the gain on long-term monetary items will be a major source of difference between the FASB and reporting companies.* The treatment of this important category can have a large impact on not only the statements of income and financial position but also on the funds statement.

Highlights of the Indiana Telephone Restatement. The results of this restatement are significant. We briefly highlight some of these effects.

1974

	Historical	Restated in 12/31/74 $
Telephone Plant	$34,853,608	$46,426,421
Total Investment	$34,246,392	$45,063,584
Common Shareholders' Interest	45%	34% ⎧Unrealized
		24% ⎨ effects of price-
	45%	58% ⎩level changes
Net Income	$ 2,023,718	$ 1,037,452
Earnings Applicable to Common Stock	$ 1,931,689	$ 941,221
Earnings per Share	$ 3.96	$ 1.93

The dividend payout ratio (cash dividends declared/earnings available to common shareholders) for 1974 was about 25 percent [=$487,750/ $1,931,689] on the historical cost basis; on the restated basis, it amounted to over 54 percent [=$510,021/$941,221].

For each of the above items the restated amounts are quite different from the historical amounts. Since this is a real-world example, these are real differences; they can be seen in the price-level adjusted statements.

Perusal of the ITC corporate comparative data permits some additional interesting observations.

1. On the historical cost basis, operating revenues grew to $13,506,367 in 1974 from $9,969,629 in 1970, an increase of about 35 percent. In terms of 1974 dollars, however, operating revenues grew to $14,123,067 in 1974 from $13,150,034 in 1970, an increase of only 7 percent.

2. On the historical cost basis, net income grew to $2,023,718 in 1974 from $1,637,288 in 1970, an *increase* of almost 24 percent. During the same period, net income, restated in 1974 dollars, declined to $1,037,452 from $1,539,529, a *decrease* of almost 33 percent.

---

*As a further example, Toledo Edison Company, which published supplementary general price-level adjusted financial statements for 1974, did not treat the gain on long-term monetary items as realized.

3. Other striking comparisons can be made between the historical cost and restated data for such items as earnings per common share, telephone plant in service at end of year, and so forth.

Other Examples of Price-Level Adjusted Financial Statements

A further example of the use of price-level accounting is furnished by the Shell Oil Company. Here are their 1974 financial statements in both historical and restated dollars, together with the auditors' report thereon. An explanatory note follows.

SHELL OIL COMPANY

Supplementary Price Level Adjusted Financial Information

	Current Dollars*			Historical Dollars		
	1974	1973	1972	1974	1973	1972
(Millions of dollars except per share amounts)						
Summary Statement of Income						
Revenues	$8,866.7	$6,614.4	$5,876.1	$8,493.0	$5,749.6	$4,849.8
Costs and expenses:						
Depreciation, depletion, etc.	654.2	626.5	585.4	502.9	441.7	396.8
Income, operating and consumer taxes	1,320.2	1,236.2	1,163.6	1,264.5	1,074.6	960.4
Interest & discount amortization on indebtedness	63.5	69.9	72.0	60.8	60.8	59.4
Other costs & expenses	6,317.3	4,426.2	3,866.1	6,044.3	3,839.8	3,172.7
Income before purchasing power gain or loss on monetary items	$ 511.5	$ 255.6	$ 189.0	$ 620.5	$ 332.7	$ 260.5
Purchasing power gain (loss) on:						
Long term debt	117.0	82.9	36.4	—	—	—
Other monetary items	(5.1)	(4.8)	2.2	—	—	—
Net income	$ 623.4	$ 333.7	$ 227.6	$ 620.5	$ 332.7	$ 260.5
Summary Balance Sheet						
Current assets	$2,161.7	$1,953.4	$1,925.2	$2,072.2	$1,713.1	$1,596.1
Investments & long term receivables	129.5	110.3	106.1	116.0	91.7	84.1
Properties, plant & equipment (net)	5,146.6	4,906.7	4,923.3	3,905.3	3,526.9	3,438.9
Deferred charges	42.3	61.4	67.5	35.4	49.5	52.5
Current liabilities	1,272.6	1,097.4	1,113.4	1,272.6	981.6	928.2
Long term debt	976.6	1,119.0	1,230.3	976.6	1,000.9	1,025.6
Deferred credits—federal income taxes	320.0	339.5	351.4	320.0	303.6	292.8
Shareholders' equity	$4,910.9	$4,475.9	$4,327.0	$3,559.7	$3,095.1	$2,925.0
Per Share Data†						
Net income	$ 9.25	$ 4.95	$ 3.38	$ 9.21	$ 4.94	$ 3.86
Cash dividends	$ 2.56	$ 2.76	$ 2.91	$ 2.45	$ 2.40	$ 2.40

Ratios

Return on shareholders' equity	13.9%	7.7%	5.3%	20.0%	11.4%	9.2%
Return on total capital	11.7%	6.6%	5.0%	16.0%	9.2%	8.0%
Net income: revenues**	7.7%	5.9%	4.6%	8.1%	6.7%	6.3%
Dividends: net income	27.7%	55.7%	86.1%	26.6%	48.6%	62.1%
Debt: total capital	16.6%	20.0%	22.1%	21.5%	24.4%	26.0%

*Based on purchasing power dollars at December 31, 1974.
†Per weighted average share outstanding each year.
**Excluding consumer excise and sales taxes.

REPORT OF INDEPENDENT ACCOUNTANTS

To the Board of Directors and Shareholders of Shell Oil Company:

We have examined the financial statements of Shell Oil Company appearing in the Annual Reports to Shareholders for the years 1974, 1973 and 1972, which are covered by our reports dated February 4, 1975 and February 4, 1974. Those financial statements do not reflect the changes in the general purchasing power of the U.S. dollar from the time transactions took place. We have also examined the supplementary information for the years 1974, 1973 and 1972 restated for effects of changes in the general price level as described in the Explanatory Note on page 4. In our opinion, the supplementary Summary Statement of Income, Summary Balance Sheet and Per Share Data shown above present fairly the historical financial information restated in terms of the general purchasing power of the U.S. dollar at December 31, 1974 in accordance with guidelines, consistently applied, recommended in Accounting Principles Board Statement No. 3 and a Proposed Statement of Financial Accounting Standards, except for the treatment, with which we concur, of deferred income taxes as monetary items.

1200 Milam Street
Houston, Texas 77002
February 4, 1975

Price Waterhouse & Co.

Explanatory Note

The accompanying supplementary price level adjusted financial information, expressed in terms of December 31, 1974 dollars, is based on the historical dollar financial information which is also presented in adjoining columns for comparative purposes. Both the supplementary and historical financial information presented here should be read in conjunction with the notes and other financial statement information in the Annual Report. The supplementary price level information reflects adjustments only for changes that have occurred in the general purchasing power of the dollar as measured by the Gross National Product Implicit Price Deflator. The amounts shown, therefore, do not purport to represent appraised value, replacement cost, or any other measure of the current value of assets. The Accounting Principles Board Statement No. 3 and a Proposed Statement of Financial Accounting Standards, which give general guidance on how to prepare and present price level financial statements, reflect deferred income taxes as nonmonetary items. For purposes of Shell's general price level restatement, such balances were classified as monetary items because Shell believes that when reversals of such tax differences take place, they give rise immediately to taxable income and to additional taxes payable in current dollars at that time. Had Shell followed the nonmonetary treatment for deferred income taxes, restated net income would have been $23.5, $12.5, and $1.2 million less in 1974, 1973 and 1972 and restated shareholders' equity would have been $102.1, $78.6 and $66.1 million less for these years.

Our final example for this section is part of a 1974 report of Toledo Edison Company entitled "General Price Level Financial Statement Study," published separately from its regular annual report.

TOLEDO EDISON COMPANY

	Method of Reporting	
	Traditional Accounting (Per 1974 Annual Report)	Price-Level Accounting (Current Purchasing Power)
	(in thousands of dollars)	
Investment in Net Plant in Service	$322,577	$544,636
Shareowners Equity	177,296	295,577
Operating Income	29,281	26,723
Earnings on Common Stock	19,686	16,600
Return on Net Plant Investment	9%	5%
Return on Common Equity (year-end basis)	11%	6%

It is instructive to compare the general purchasing-power statements of Indiana Telephone, Shell and Toledo Edison. One major difference is the treatment of the purchasing power gain on long-term monetary items. ITC does not recognize this item as income until it is realized through the retirement (without refinancing) of the relevant issue of long-term debt or preferred stock. The unrealized gain is shown on the ITC statement of capital, but not as part of common shareholders' interest. Shell, on the other hand, follows the FASB-recommended practice of taking this gain into income as it arises. Toledo Edison has its own method, described in the following notes which appear in this company's "General Price Level Financial Statement Study."

Accumulated Inflation Effect from Financing
Sources Other Than Common Stock Equity

Debt financing through the issuance of first mortgage bonds, short-term notes and other obligations; and funds secured through the issuance of preferred stock have been identified as "monetary" items. However, since these items comprise some of the sources of funds invested in property, plant and equipment, they have been treated on a basis consistent with the property financed. The approach used was to restate the historical cost amounts for these sources, based on the year of investment, to year-end 1974 purchasing power. The excess amounts over historical cost are identified as the "accumulated inflation effect from financing sources other than common stock equity." A portion of this accumulated inflation effect, equivalent to the percentage of reserve for depreciation to the plant-in-service, was credited to earnings reinvested at the beginning of the year. (See Note 1 for current year amortization.)

The part of Note 1 referred to above is as follows.

Amortization of Inflation Effect from Financing
Sources Other Than Common Stock Equity

Partially offsetting the impact of inflation on current depreciation, the "accumulated inflation effect from financing sources other than common stock equity" is being amortized into income at the same rate as the overall composite rate (3.3%) being used to determine the annual depreciation provision for property, plant and equipment. In our opinion, treating the sources of property investment on the same basis as the property it finances results in a realistic presentation for evaluating the overall impact of inflation.

We do not agree with the ITC or the Toledo Edison treatment. We feel that the gain should be recognized as it arises, and that the fact that it is not realized should not be a consideration for income statement purposes. However, a statement of changes in financial position would reflect the unrealized nature of this item. Therefore there is an additional and important reason for requiring the publication of a funds statement along with the income statement and the statement of financial position when general price-level statements are issued. If a funds statement is required under present generally accepted accounting principles (as is the case), its publication is even more essential in the case of general price-level adjusted statements.

Another aspect of the three companies' statements worthy of comment is the report of the auditors. For ITC, the auditors state that the conventional statements "fairly present," as is customary. However, this report is well known for stating that the general price-level adjusted statements "more fairly present." We may question the actual meaning of "fairly" or "more fairly." Can something be "more fair"? Or, as the conventional auditor's report implies, is not something simply fair or not fair, as the case may be?

For Shell, the auditors' report is more precise, but less indicative of the auditors' own opinion of the merits of general price-level adjusted statements. The precision is obtained by identifying the actual standards with which the supplementary price-level adjusted statements are in conformity. Within the context of these standards, APB Statement 3 and the FASB Exposure Draft, the supplementary statements "present fairly" the price-level adjusted information. However, the lack of a "*more* fairly" means that the auditors express no preference for either conventional or price-level adjusted statements.

For Toledo Edison, the price-level adjusted statements were not reported on by the auditors. These statements were not part of the annual report, but were published separately under the title of "General Price Level Financial Statement Study." Therefore, there was no requirement for an audit report on these statements.

Finally, note that ITC and Toledo Edison follow the FASB Exposure Draft in treating deferred income taxes as nonmonetary. However, Shell, with their auditors' concurrence, treat deferred taxes as a monetary item, in keeping with the "liability" view of deferred income taxes.

Other Issues Associated with General Price-Level Adjustments

Three other technical issues about which there has been some controversy should be discussed. The first involves the question of the impact of price-level adjustments on the reported income tax expense. The second deals with the treatment and restatement of accounts whose balances are measured in units of a foreign currency. The third refers to the "lower of cost or market" rule.

The Income Tax Question

In the conventional situation, the reported income tax expense must reflect the applicable relationship between the existing tax rates and the firm's reported net income, once the effects of "permanent" differences are removed. Certain income items such as interest on state bonds and certain expense items such as premiums on officers' life insurance are *permanently excluded* from the determination of taxable income.

However, many items can enter into the determination of reported net income and taxable income in *different time periods*. When these "timing" differences exist, the income tax expense based on reported net income will not be the same as the income tax assessed on the tax return in a particular year. They will increase or decrease the income tax payable in some subsequent period. Typically, when permitted by income tax regulations, certain income items recorded in the accounts for this period will be deferred for tax purposes as long as possible. For example, revenue on installment sales, totally recognized in conventional historical accounts in the year of the sale, may be deferred and recognized for tax purposes only as cash is collected in the future. On the other hand, when tax deductions can be claimed in advance of their recognition in conventional historical accounts, this is also typically done. A classic example is the practice of recording depreciation of fixed assets in the accounts on the straight-line basis while deducting accelerated depreciation (perhaps based on double-declining balance) on the tax return. The reason for deferring income and accelerating deductions for tax purposes is to minimize the present value of income tax payments. Whenever these timing differences exist in a particular year, reported income tax expense will differ from the income tax assessed on the tax return. The difference is recorded in the accounts as a deferred credit when the reported income tax expense exceeds the income tax payable and as a deferred charge when income tax payable exceeds reported income tax expense.

The adjustment of the historical cost income statement for general price-level changes generates yet another reason for reported net income (now adjusted for price-level changes) to differ from taxable income. The FASB Exposure Draft argues that income differences caused by price-level adjustments should have no effect on the amount of deferred taxes. Some accountants, however, have argued that the "timing" difference reasoning mentioned above should apply here also. These accountants support deferring the difference between income tax expense based on the price-level adjusted net income (not the restated historical cost income tax expense) and the income tax on the tax return. An example will be helpful in illustrating this issue.

The following condensed income statements were prepared according to (1) historical cost accounting; (2) historical cost accounting adjusted for general price-level changes (assumed average restatement ratios are shown); and (3) current income tax regulations (i.e., the tax return; price-level adjustments are not permitted). We assume no conventional permanent differences and a tax rate of 40 percent.

	Books			Tax Return
	Historical Cost	Ratio to Restate	Restated	Historical Cost
Sales	$10,000	1.1	$11,000	$10,000
Operating Expenses	8,000	1.2	9,600	8,500
Net Income before Taxes	2,000		1,400	1,500
Federal Income Tax	800	1.1	880	600
Net Income after Taxes	$ 1,200		$ 520	$ 900

In the conventional comparison of historical cost book and taxable income, tax deductions exceed book expenses (and book income before taxes exceeds taxable income) as a result of timing differences equal to $500. The journal entry made to record the income tax expense appears below.

    Dr. Income Tax Expense 800
        Cr. Income Tax Payable 600
        Cr. Deferred Income Tax. 200

To recognize current income tax expense and to record those portions currently payable and deferred.

Notice that another difference between net income per books and net income per tax return is created by the price-level restatement. It is important to understand, however, that the difference attributable to the price-level restatement is *not* a *timing* difference.* The Internal Revenue Code does not recognize such price-level adjustments; hence, under current regulations, the adjustments have no effect on the income tax payable in this or any subsequent period, and therefore lead to *permanent* differences.

To complete this example, it will be useful to show that the restatement process maintains the debit-credit equality. Deferred taxes is treated as a nonmonetary item in the FASB Exposure Draft; as income tax expense is restated to $880, deferred taxes would be restated to $220. The actual income tax liability of $600, a monetary item, would generate a purchasing-power gain of $60 (ratio to restate is 1.1). Thus, the debits will equal the credits, as shown below.

	Historical		Restated	
	Dr	Cr	Dr	Cr
Income Tax Expense	800		880	
Deferred Income Taxes		200		220
Income Tax Payable		600		600
Purchasing-Power Gain on Income Tax Payable . .				60
	800	800	880	880

Therefore, we agree with the position of the FASB and APB that for purposes of deferred income taxes, general price-level restatements result in *permanent* rather than *timing* differences between restated historical cost net income and taxable income. In addition, however, we will briefly comment on the FASB's determination that deferred income tax charges and credits will be treated as *nonmonetary* items for restatement purposes.

In many cases, particularly where growing firms are involved, deferral of income tax liabilities becomes indefinite; the periodic increases in deferred income taxes are at least as great as the periodic decreases. Thus there is a net increase on a "roll-over" basis. Treatment of deferred income taxes as a nonmonetary item in cases such as these certainly seems justified. On the other hand, in cases where deferred income taxes are in fact liquidated over time (i.e., the timing differences reverse themselves), deferred income taxes should be treated as a monetary item for restatement purposes. In this latter case, the deferred income tax liability will normally have to be paid. On this point, the FASB Exposure Draft argues:

Moreover, amounts of income taxes that will ultimately be paid when the

---

*See Accounting Principles Board Opinion 11, *Accounting for Income Taxes*, December 1967, for a further discussion of the nature of timing differences.

timing differences related to the tax credits reverse can change as a result of changes in tax rates or tax laws and depend on future taxable income.*

We do not, however, find this argument compelling. We believe that the treatment of deferred income taxes as monetary or nonmonetary should depend primarily on an evaluation of the facts and other circumstances faced by each firm.

Accounts Stated in Foreign Currency

In order to report on operations in foreign countries, domestic firms must *translate* accounts stated in foreign currency into dollars. For example, a wholly owned subsidiary doing business in West Germany would normally keep its books in the West German currency (marks). Fortunately, there are *foreign exchange rates* which express the value of one currency (e.g., marks) in terms of another (e.g., dollars). Once the foreign accounts are translated into dollars, the issue becomes how to treat the translated balances for purposes of general price-level restatement*—that is, whether they are *monetary* or *nonmonetary*. Once this decision has been made, the translated balances are treated like any other monetary or nonmonetary items in the restatement process. The issue is whether *all* foreign account balances are nonmonetary or only *some* are nonmonetary.

Do accounts which are monetary in the foreign country, such as foreign currency or cash and accounts receivable and payable in foreign currency, become nonmonetary as a result of the translation process? The APB in Statement 3 and the FASB in its Exposure Draft believe that they do. Recall that monetary items are those items stated in a fixed quantity of dollars, regardless of changes in the price level. The APB argues in Statement 3 that since the *price* of foreign currency (i.e., the foreign exchange rate) can and does *change*, foreign currency balances are subject to changing prices *independent* of changes in the general price level. "Therefore, the holder of foreign currency does not gain or lose general purchasing power simply as a result of general price level changes." However, State-

---

*See FASB Exposure Draft, Appendix C, reproduced here in Chapter 2, "Appendix: Monetary and Nonmonetary Items."

*At the time this book was being written, the FASB had issued an exposure draft entitled *Accounting for the Translation of Foreign Currency Transactions and Foreign Currency Financial Statements*. This draft expressed the opinion that such translation should be performed in accordance with the *temporal* method, explained in both the exposure draft and in Accounting Research Study No. 12, *Reporting Foreign Operations of U.S. Companies in U.S. Dollars* (1972). In short, under the temporal method, accounts stated in a foreign currency will be translated at exchange rates which do not change the basis of measurement employed in the accounts. The Exposure Draft summarizes the essentials of the temporal method as follows: accounts carried at prices in past exchanges (past prices) shall be translated at *historical rates*; accounts carried at prices in current purchase or sale exchanges (current prices) or future exchanges (future prices) shall be translated at the current rate.

ment 3 concludes that "even though foreign currency items are non-monetary, they may be stated at the current foreign exchange rate in general price level financial statements. Under these circumstances they would be treated as nonmonetary items carried at current market value."

The opposing view "is that foreign currency, accounts receivable and payable in foreign currency, and similar foreign currency items are similar to domestic monetary items." This is based on the contention that the holder of such items is subject to foreign exchange gains or losses due to changes in the foreign exchange rate *and* to purchasing-power gains or losses resulting from price-level changes in the United States. Since both components of total gain or loss can be measured, they should be disclosed and reported as foreign exchange gains or losses and as gains or losses on monetary items in the general price-level income statement.

In this case, we lean toward the latter (opposing) view. Although the dollar value of foreign currency balances clearly changes as the foreign exchange rate changes, whatever dollar balances are eventually derived in the translation process encounter the same exposure to domestic inflation as dollar balances originating domestically. In other words, the risk of changes in purchasing power is compounded by the risk of changes in the exchange rate. But changes in the exchange rate generate a different kind of gain or loss than do changes in the domestic price level. It is difficult to see how exposure to foreign exchange fluctuations negates the very real exposure to price-level fluctuations faced by liquid foreign currency balances. The following example will illustrate our position.

Consider a note receivable from a West German customer for 100,000 DM which was acquired by a domestic firm's West German branch on 1/1/x5. The note was collected on 12/31/x5 after both the foreign exchange rate and the U.S. general price level changed. Using the facts below, we will calculate the effect of these changes on the firm's general price-level adjusted income.

		Foreign Exchange Rate (DM / $)	Translated Dollar Balance	GNP Deflator
Foreign monetary item, 1/1/x5	100,000 DM	2	$50,000	100
Foreign monetary item, 12/31/x5	100,000 DM	1.6	$62,500	110

1. Foreign exchange gain (loss). During the year, the foreign exchange rate moved against the dollar and in favor of the mark. The dollar that could buy 2 marks at the beginning of the year could buy only 1.6 marks at the end of the year. Conversely, the mark which could buy $.50 at the beginning of the year could buy $.625 at year end.

Hence, the foreign currency balance is now worth more in dollars, so we have a foreign exchange *gain* of $12,500 [=$62,500 − $50,000].

2. Purchasing-power gain (loss). The price level rose by 10 percent during 19x5. It takes $1.10 at year end to purchase what $1.00 purchased at the beginning of the year. If we abstract from the foreign exchange gain, the $50,000 note at 1/1/x5 was collected on 12/31/x5, when $55,000 would have been required to keep pace with the rising price level. Hence, we have a purchasing-power *loss* of $5,000 [=$55,000 − $50,000].

Under the APB-FASB interpretation, only the $12,500 foreign exchange gain would be recognized as an income item. We believe that such a procedure is misleading and fails to disclose the total impact of changes in purchasing power.

Current practice requires that some nonmonetary assets (such as inventories and marketable securities) and liabilities (such as estimated warranty obligations) be carried and reported at the *lower of cost or market*. Such items are normally carried at acquisition cost (or, in the case of some nonmonetary liabilities, at an estimated amount) unless market value declines below cost. When market is less than cost, accepted practice is to write-down the carrying value of those assets and liabilities to their market values. These principles raise two important questions within the context of general price-level restatements.

Lower of Cost or Market and Price-Level Restatements

1. How should assets and liabilities written down to market on the historical dollar financial statements be treated for restated statement purposes?

2. How should items having a *restated cost* in excess of their market value be treated?

The FASB Exposure Draft recommended that the restatement procedures should not affect the basic rule of lower of cost or market. However, when price-level restatements are applied, the rule becomes "lower of *restated* cost or market." The determination of market is unaffected by the restatement process. Therefore, when restated cost exceeds market, the restated cost figure must be reduced to market and the amount of the reduction enters into the determination of restated net income as it would in historical dollar statements. The following series of short examples will illustrate the application of the lower of cost or market rule within the context of price-level adjustments. We assume that the price level stood at 120 on January 1 and at 132 on December 31. The increase is 10 percent and the average price level for the year was 126.

The first example deals with market below historical cost. Inventory purchased for $2,500 on July 1 was worth only $2,000 on December 31. The historical dollar financial statements reflect the write-down to $2,000.

Treatment. Restate the historical cost in end-of-period dollars; i.e., $2,619 = $2,500 × 132/126 and then write down to market using the following journal entry for restated statement purposes only.

Dr. Loss from Decline in Inventory Value   619
　Cr. Inventories 619

To write-down the restated cost of inventories to market.

In the second example, market is below restated cost but above historical cost. Inventory purchased in January for $5,000 was worth $5,200 on December 31. The inventory is carried at $5,000 on the historical dollar statements.

Treatment. Restate the historical cost in end-of-period dollars; i.e., $5,500 = $5,000 × 132/120 and then write down to market using the following journal entry for restated statement purposes only.

Dr. Loss from Decline in Inventory Value   300
　Cr. Inventories 300

To write-down the restated cost of inventories to market.

Note that the treatment is the same, regardless of whether a write-down was made on the historical dollar statements and regardless of whether market is less than acquisition cost or restated acquisition cost.

For the third example, estimated warranty obligations of $1,000 were accrued in last year's financial statements and remain unliquidated at December 31 of the current year. Management believes that the cost of performing these services moves more or less parallel to the general price level.

Treatment. The unliquidated warranty obligation is a nonmonetary liability. Restate it in end-of-period dollars; i.e., $1,100 = $1,000 × 132/120.

Fourth, management believes that the current cost of performing these warranty services has declined to $950 and the liability has been reduced accordingly in the historical dollar statements.

Treatment. Restate the historical dollar liability in end-of-period dollars ($1,100) and write down to market using the following journal entry for restated statement purposes only.

Dr. Estimated Warranty Obligations   150
　Cr. Gain from Reduction of Warranty Obligation 150

To reduce the restated estimated warranty obligation to the end-of-period cost (i.e., "market") of providing the services.

Note that in all cases the historical dollar number must first be restated and then written down to market as necessary. Restating the historical dollar gain or loss from reduction to market is not sufficient. In the case above, the restated historical dollar gain would be but $55 [=$50 × 132/120], which does not adequately reflect the facts.

Since a general index is essential in purchasing-power accounting, it is desirable to be familiar with the nature and limitations of the major, currently available general price indexes.

The Nature of Price-Level Indexes

The well-known *Consumer Price Index* is prepared monthly by the Bureau of Labor Statistics of the U.S. Department of Labor. It measures the average change in the retail prices of approximately 300 goods and services purchased by wage-earner and clerical-worker families in 46 U.S. cities. These goods and services include food, clothing, fuel, house furnishings, doctor and dentist fees, rents, utilities and the like. The 300-item "market basket" represents the standard of living of the subject families; it therefore does not measure price changes for families of different purchasing habits (due possibly to different levels of income as well as to different needs and tastes). Therefore, the popular title "Consumer Price Index" indicates a broader scope than the index actually reflects.

The market basket has been revised less than once every ten years, probably too infrequently to capture the rate of improvements, changes or replacements in the goods and services widely purchased in our economy. These and other limitations of the CPI do not invalidate its obvious usefulness. However, they do emphasize the caution with which it should be interpreted and used.

The *Wholesale Price Index* (WPI) is also prepared by the Bureau of Labor Statistics and is issued monthly. It covers approximately 2,200 commodities sold in large lots in primary markets in the U.S. Thus it is not, as its title suggests, an index of prices paid to wholesalers, distributors or jobbers. The index is a fixed weight, or "market basket" type, but the quantities of respective commodities are periodically updated using weights derived from the Census of Manufacturers.

The WPI is based on a relatively small sample of commodities, and does not include real estate, services, construction or transportation. In some cases, the index uses list or quoted prices which may not accurately reflect actual prices paid. However, the consistent use of such prices normally will not distort this index, since it attempts to measure relative price movements rather than the absolute level of prices.

The WPI should not be used to forecast movements in the CPI, especially in the short run. Many components of the WPI never directly enter retail markets (e.g., industrial machinery); similarly, many components of the CPI (such as services and rents) are not included in the WPI.

The *GNP Implicit Price Deflator* is prepared by the U.S. Department of Commerce, Bureau of Economic Analysis. The Deflator is issued quarterly, about 45 days after the end of each calendar quarter. The quarterly figures represent an average price for the entire quarter rather than for a single point of time. Therefore the Deflator does not exist as of any particular position statement date, but it probably reflects prices closer to mid-quarter than to any other point. The most recently published quarterly GNP Deflator should be used as an acceptable approximation of an index at the position statement date, according to the FASB Exposure Draft.

The Deflator is the most comprehensive index of the prices of all goods and services purchased and sold in all segments of our economy. It is derived from the relationship between (1) the total value of all goods and services produced in a given year expressed in dollars of current purchasing power (i.e., GNP in current dollars) and (2) the total value of the same goods and services expressed in prices of a base year (i.e., GNP in constant dollars). The base year presently used is 1958. For example, 1973 GNP was $1,294.9 billion in current dollars and $839.2 billion in constant (1958) dollars. Thus the 1973 GNP Deflator was $1,294.9 / $839.2 or 154.3.

The subindexes of the CPI, the WPI and of other indexes are used to deflate or convert the portions of GNP to which they apply from current to constant dollars. Therefore they enter into the computation of the GNP Deflator, which thus incorporates both their strengths and their weaknesses. Despite the limitations from which the Deflator (like all indexes) suffers, it is generally regarded as sufficiently reliable and comprehensive to serve the purposes of purchasing-power accounting.

Any measure of purchasing power loses precision over time because the impact of technological change is widespread and long-lived. The FASB has therefore selected 1945 as the earliest year that still offers meaningful current comparability. All assets, liabilities or stockholders' equity dating back prior to 1945 should generally be treated as if they had originated in 1945.

For reference purposes, Exhibit 3.1 shows the GNP Deflator, annually and quarterly for the years 1947–1974. This table is taken from the FASB Exposure Draft. Note that the values here differ slightly from those in Illustrative Example 2.1. These differences reflect periodic revisions frequently made in the GNP Deflator series; such revisions can affect figures from earlier years as well as more recent periods.

The Impact of Inflation upon Financial Statements

If we know the rate of change in general purchasing power, can we easily anticipate its impact on financial statements? Clearly, we cannot anticipate perfectly—otherwise there would be little need for the price-level accounting techniques with which we have dealt. On the other hand, some of the impact can be anticipated to a degree, and some general tendencies can be derived.

Exhibit 3.1

GNP DEFLATORS
Annual Averages 1947—1974
Quarterly Averages 1947—Fourth Quarter 1974 (1958 = 100)

Year	Annual Average Deflator	Percent Increase (Decrease) from Previous Year	First Quarter	Second Quarter	Third Quarter	Fourth Quarter
1947	74.6	11.9	73.0	73.7	74.9	77.0
1948	79.6	6.6	78.2	79.2	80.6	80.3
1949	79.1	(.6)	79.7	79.1	78.8	78.9
1950	80.2	1.3	78.3	79.0	80.8	82.3
1951	85.6	6.8	84.8	85.4	85.6	86.7
1952	87.5	2.1	86.7	87.1	87.7	88.3
1953	88.3	1.0	88.4	88.3	88.4	88.4
1954	89.6	1.5	89.5	89.6	89.5	89.8
1955	90.9	1.4	90.2	90.6	91.0	91.6
1956	94.0	3.4	92.6	93.4	94.6	95.4
1957	97.5	3.7	96.4	97.1	98.0	98.5
1958	100.0	2.5	99.3	99.7	100.1	100.6
1959	101.6	1.7	101.1	101.5	101.9	102.1
1960	103.3	1.6	102.6	103.1	103.5	104.0
1961	104.6	1.3	104.3	104.5	104.5	105.1
1962	105.8	1.1	105.5	105.6	105.8	106.3
1963	107.2	1.3	106.7	107.0	107.2	107.8
1964	108.8	1.6	108.2	108.5	109.1	109.6
1965	110.9	1.8	110.2	110.7	111.0	111.5
1966	113.9	2.8	112.4	113.5	114.5	115.4
1967	117.6	3.2	116.2	116.8	118.0	119.4
1968	122.3	4.0	120.4	121.6	122.9	124.3
1969	128.2	4.8	125.6	127.2	129.1	130.9
1970	135.2	5.5	132.9	134.4	135.8	137.9
1971	141.4	4.5	139.5	141.1	142.0	142.7
1972	146.1	3.4	144.6	145.3	146.5	148.0
1973	154.3	5.6	150.0	152.6	155.7	158.9
1974	170.2*	10.3*	163.6	167.3	171.9	178.0*

*These data became available subsequent to the publication of the FASB Exposure Draft and have been inserted by the authors.

SOURCE: United States Department of Commerce, Bureau of Economic Analysis. Reproduced in FASB Exposure Draft, "Financial Reporting in Units of General Purchasing Power" (December 31, 1974), pp. 34—35.

Exhibit 3.2, a partial reproduction of a study by Richard Vancil and James Kelly,* shows a five-year profit plan for a company that has characteristics and financial ratios which are at approximately the median for a *Fortune* 500 company.

Exhibit 3.2

Contrasting Projected Income Statements

A   HISTORICAL COST METHOD

ITEM	1974	1975	1976	1977	1978
Sales	73,054	82,770	93,778	106,251	120,382
Cost of sales	45,182	50,702	57,092	64,313	72,522
Period costs	19,227	21,700	24,488	27,627	31,182
% operating margin	11.83	12.53	13.01	13.47	13.85
Interest expense (net)	920	1,126	1,342	1,642	1,920
Tax expense	3,708	4,436	5,211	6,081	7,083
Profit after taxes	4,017	4,806	5,646	6,588	7,674
% PAT to sales	5.50	5.81	6.02	6.20	6.37
Earnings per share	2.01	2.40	2.82	3.29	3.84

B   PRICE-LEVEL-ADJUSTED METHOD (IN 1973 DOLLARS)

ITEM	1974	1975	1976	1977	1978
Sales	68,789	70,853	72,979	75,168	77,423
Cost of sales	44,598	45,756	47,012	48,272	49,603
Working capital loss	553	574	589	606	629
Period costs	18,101	18,576	19,053	19,543	20,051
% operating margin	8.05	8.39	8.67	8.97	9.22

*Richard F. Vancil and James N. Kelly, "Get Ready for Price-Level-Adjusted Accounting," *Harvard Business Review* (March-April 1975).

Exhibit 3.2 (continued)

Interest expense (net)	865	964	1,043	1,161	1,236
Financial liability gain	869	979	1,046	1,152	1,247
Tax expense	3,452	3,797	4,057	4,302	4,556
Profit after taxes	2,089	2,166	2,270	2,434	2,595
% PAT to sales	3.04	3.06	3.11	3.24	3.35
Earnings per share	1.04	1.08	1.14	1.22	1.30

NOTE: The projections assume 10% annual inflation in the cost of purchased materials and services, 10% increase in selling prices, 3% real growth per year, no productivity gains, and dividends that increase 13% per year (10% for inflation and 3% for growth). The company uses FIFO inventory costing, accelerated depreciation for tax purposes, and straight-line depreciation for book purposes. Normal operating policies are to hold operating cash equal to 50% of accounts payable, collect receivables in 45 days, hold 120 days of inventory, and pay vendors in 30 days. The company is moderately capital-intensive (net plant turnover through sales is about 3½ times per year, but the plant is rather short-lived (it has a 10-year depreciable life). Using debt not to exceed 40% of equity, the company has a return on equity historically of about 11% after taxes. Net profit on sales has been just under 5%.

SOURCE: From Richard F. Vancil and James N. Kelly, "Get Ready for Price-Level-Adjusted Accounting." *Harvard Business Review* (March-April 1975): 7. Reproduced by permission.

Exhibit 3.2, for the years 1974–1978, reflects management projections of annual growth in physical volume of 3 percent a year and a grim 10 percent annual inflation. On a conventional basis, the projection appears to be excellent. Sales increase 70 percent over the 1973 level of $70,000 and net income increases at an annual rate of almost 19 percent compounded.

However, when adjusted to 1973 dollars, the plan loses much of its luster. Sales increase only 3 percent a year, close to the rate of earnings growth. Note that earnings include a gain on net monetary items, which provides a substantial portion of the 3 percent annual earnings growth. Furthermore, the effective tax rate on restated income before taxes becomes 64 percent versus the 48 percent on the historical cost basis. Clearly, the picture has changed dramatically.

Some of the effects of purchasing-power adjustments on individual companies are detailed in the Appendix to this chapter, which reproduces portions of a most useful study by Professors Sidney Davidson and Roman Weil.* Their results clearly show that the effects of restatement can and do differ significantly from one firm to another. For example, in

---

*Sidney Davidson and Roman L. Weil, "Inflation Accounting: What Will General Price Level Adjusted Income Statements Show?" *Financial Analysts Journal* (January-February 1975).

Davidson and Weil's Table 1, using the 30 Dow Jones Industrial companies, 1973 adjusted net income before gain on net monetary items varied from 10 percent (for International Harvester) to 87 percent (for Procter & Gamble) of reported net income. Adjusted net income after gain on net monetary items ranged from 18 percent to 153 percent of reported net income.

What major factors cause these differential results? Clearly, the more capital-intensive companies are relatively likely to look worse on restatement because of their greater proportion of depreciation expense. This effect is compounded as assets are longer-lived.

First, as Davidson and Weil indicate, rapidly growing companies are affected less by restatement. They have, on the average, newer plants and thus the upward adjustment of depreciation is lower than for slow-growth (older plant) companies.

Second, purchasing power gains are a significant factor. For the Dow Jones Industrial companies, purchasing power gains raised the restated median firm from 69 percent to 92 percent of reported net income. Clearly, higher debt ratios produce higher purchasing power gains. However, purchasing power gains are not realized cash inflows, and with sufficient debt outstanding, a firm can report large restated profits right up to the time it goes bankrupt.

Third, the above conclusions become stronger in effect with more rapid rates of inflation.

Davidson and Weil have developed a shortcut estimating procedure for purchasing-power restatement of financial reports. Their procedure is quite accurate, and may be rapidly applied. We believe that this is a valuable set of techniques. Concentration on the essentials of the adjustment procedure aids clear understanding. The user can thus keep sight of the forest and not get lost in the trees. And with either manual or computerized methods, the estimated restatement can be done in very little time — about one hour by the manual method once it has been thoroughly learned.

The relevant portion of the Davidson and Weil article is reproduced in the Appendix to this chapter.

Summary and Evaluation of General Price-Level Adjusted Financial Statements

General price-level adjusted financial statements have a number of characteristics which recommend them to many accountants.

First, general price-level adjustments involve only a change in the measuring unit. They require no changes in accounting principles and will be objective and unambiguous.

Second, gains and losses in purchasing power resulting from the effect of the changing price level on the firm's monetary assets and liabilities are measured and disclosed.

Third, the restatement of *prior period* financial statements in current dollars enhances the comparability of accounting information over time.

Fourth, the AICPA's Accounting Standards Division believes that the cost of implementing general price-level adjustments should not be prohibitive, especially if reasonable approximations are permitted. The major cost should be incurred when the initial restatement is performed because of the necessity of "aging" many accounts. However, maintaining and updating the system should not be particularly burdensome.

On the other side, there are many, including the authors, who believe that general price-level adjusted financial statements deal adequately with but one part of the problem created by inflation, the purchasing-power gains and losses on monetary items. Disclosure of these gains and losses is indeed desirable. Let us now consider two major objections dealing with the inadequacy of general price-level adjusted financial statements.

First, the use of an index of general price levels fails to account for the fact that movements of prices of specific items will often differ from the movements of the index. An *implication* of general price-level adjusted accounts is that they represent current economic values; this would normally be true only by coincidence. When the price of motor vehicles has risen 25 to 30 percent, applying a general price-level change of 10 percent instead seems unrealistic and could give rise to misleading financial statements.

Second, imbedded in conventional historical cost accounting is the *realization criterion* for the recognition of income. In short, income is generally not deemed to be realized until a completed market transaction has taken place. General price-level adjustments leave the realization criterion unchanged. Thus, the gains and losses associated with changes in the value of items that have not been sold (and are still being held) are not recognized as such. Although general price-level restatements in a period of inflation raise the dollar value of nonmonetary assets which are being held, these adjustments are to the historical cost of the asset and do not reflect subsequent cost changes. These "holding gains" (to be defined more precisely in the next chapter) are thus not identified.

In summary, one needs to ask whether general price-level adjustments applied to a historical cost data base are sufficient to restore the usefulness of accounting information. Our response to this query is negative and is based on the above objections. We do not, however, reject the entire procedure, as we believe that the gains and losses on monetary items represent useful information and should be disclosed. The remaining aspects of general price-level adjustments seem, in our opinion, to be of doubtful usefulness.

In practice, the general price-level procedure has received both significant support and strong criticism. Naturally, the position so far taken by the FASB is clearly supportive. So too is the recent expression by Haskins and Sells (one of the Big Eight auditing firms) of an unqualified opinion on financial statements presented on the price-level basis of a Brazilian subsidiary of a United States parent corporation.

On the critical side is a powerful force, namely, the Securities and Exchange Commission. The SEC has leaned toward current value specific, rather than general, price adjustment methods. Other influential voices, such as another Big Eight firm—Touche Ross & Co.—have expressed either direct criticism of, or lack of enthusiasm for, general price-level adjustments.

If we were asked whether we would support general price-level adjustments if the only alternative was retaining historical cost, we probably would. We believe, however, that other superior alternatives exist; the remainder of this book is devoted to an exploration of those alternatives.

Appendix

Inflation Accounting

What will general price level
adjusted income statements show?*

Sidney Davidson and Roman L. Weil

Income Statement Effects of General Price Level Adjustments

Using the procedures described in the next section, we calculated what net income on an adjusted basis would be, both before and after recognizing "the general price-level gains and losses from holding monetary assets and liabilities" (hereafter described as monetary gains and losses), for 60 major corporations.[3] The procedures used conform generally with those recommended in APB Statement No. 3, although we diverged from those procedures in three areas where we felt that different procedures would make the statements more realistic and that these different procedures might be those required by the FASB if it issues a definitive pronouncement on this subject.[4]

For all companies, we measured both adjusted net income before monetary gain and adjusted net income as percentages of net income reported on a conventional basis. The results for the Dow 30 companies are shown in Table 1 and for the 30 other large companies in Table 2. The reader is warned that these percentages are in no way a criterion of the firm's inflation-adjusted performance, but instead merely relate adjusted income to income as conventionally reported. For a firm that reported high profits on a conventional basis, an adjustment percentage of 80 may still mean a better profit performance after adjustments than does an adjustment percentage of 115 for a firm that reported unsatisfactory profits on a conventional basis. Eighty percent of very good may still be good, while 115 percent of terrible may still be very bad.

Effects Differ Among Firms

The results demonstrate clearly the error of the frequently stated naive view that all firms are affected relatively equally by inflation, and that a single overall adjustment factor applied to the reported profits of all firms will yield satisfactory results.[5] Adjusted net income as a percentage of reported net income ranges from 18 to 153 percent for the Dow 30 and from 36 to 176 percent for the other 30. On the Dow list, AT&T and United Aircraft are outliers. If they are eliminated, the range is reduced to a spread from 62 to 112 percent of conven-

---

*This is an abbreviated version of the article published under the same title in the *Financial Analysts Journal* (January-February 1975). It is reproduced here by permission. Professors Davidson and Weil have refined some of their techniques further. These refinements are discussed in their article "Inflation Accounting: Some 1974 Income Measures," *Financial Analysts Journal* (September-October 1975). We have not incorporated these changes because they go into highly specialized aspects beyond the scope of this book.

tional income but, of course, this is still a wide spread. On the other 30 list, Trans Union and Loews are high with 176 percent and 159 percent, respectively, of reported income. The results for Trans Union and Loews, like the results for AT&T from the Dow list, indicate that when monetary gains are recognized, firms with large amounts of debt outstanding may do very much better in times of increasing prices than is shown on historical dollar accounting statements.

Table 1

DOW JONES COMPANIES ADJUSTED 1973 INCOME

AS A PERCENTAGE OF REPORTED INCOME

Company	Adjusted Net Income before Gain on Monetary Items, as a % of Reported Net Income*	Adjusted Net Income, including Gain on Monetary Items, as a % of Reported Net Income*
Allied Chemical	32%	62%
Alcoa	35	103
American Brands	51	92
American Can	32	83
AT&T	79	153
Anaconda	75	92
Bethlehem Steel	35	86
Chrysler	17	81
du Pont	72	72
Eastman Kodak.	86	90
Esmark	34	72
Exxon	82	97
General Electric	84	106
General Foods	71	102
General Motors	68	71
Goodyear	52	95
International Harvester	10	65
International Nickel	80	105
International Paper	70	85
Johns-Manville	84	98
Owens-Illinois	68	98
Procter & Gamble	87	96
Sears, Roebuck	76	82
Standard Oil of California	84	93
Texaco	83	100
Union Carbide	63	82
United Aircraft	29	18
U.S. Steel	29	68
Westinghouse Electric	76	112
Woolworth	31	95
Median	68 to 70	92

*See Table 5 for an example of what these columns show.

Table 2

THIRTY OTHER SELECTED COMPANIES ADJUSTED 1973 INCOME

AS A PERCENTAGE OF REPORTED INCOME

Company	Adjusted Net Income before Gain on Monetary Items as a % of Reported Net Income[a]	Adjusted Net Income, including Gain on Monetary Items, as a % of Reported Net Income[a]
Avon	93%	100%
Baxter Labs	71	100
Brunswick	60	75
Chemetron	10	60
Coca Cola	88	92
Dow Chemical	76	114
Genesco	−63[b]	36
Gould	57	92
Gulf and Western	47	134
Gulf Oil	71	99
Hilton Hotels	61	144
Holiday Inns	70	117
Inland Steel	61	100
IBM	89	93
IT&T	64	108
Koppers	40	61
Loews	70	159
MCA	75	108
Martin Marietta	34	97
Merck[c]	88	85
Pfizer	84	95
Phillip Morris	64	108
Pillsbury	45	100
Rockwell International	84	111
Shell Oil	58	80
Sunbeam	41	56
Trans Union	52	176
Walgreen	7	64
Weyerhaeuser	88	111
Zenith	78	85
Median	64	99 to 100

[a]See Table 5 for an example of what these columns show.

[b]A loss equal to 63 percent of reported income. See text for explanation of possible cause.

[c]Merck includes short-term securities with cash. We cannot tell how much they are or what portion of them are nonmonetary. All are included in monetary assets.

Income Before Monetary Gain Reduced for All Firms

The figures for adjusted income before monetary gains confirm the often-stated view that conventionally reported earnings have a substantial inflation component. In every case, this partially adjusted income figure was lower than the net income shown in the published financial statements. For the Dow companies the range is from 10 to 87 percent of conventional income with no conspicuous outliers, although the median of 68 to 70 percent indicates the distribution is skewed toward the higher percentages. The range of percentages for the other 30 was from −63 to +93 percent of reported net income, with a median of 64.

Genesco here is clearly an outlier, since Walgreens, the next lowest company in these percentages, stands at seven percent. (The −63 percent for Genesco means that its adjusted income before monetary gains showed a *loss* equal to 63 percent of conventionally reported net income.) The fiscal year for Genesco ended on July 31, 1974. Prices increased during the first half of 1974 at a rate almost twice as large as during the first half of 1973. Thus the results for Genesco may merely indicate that its adjusted income before monetary gain is penalized in our tables because the reporting period for Genesco is significantly different from that for the other companies. To test this, we processed the Genesco data assuming its fiscal year ended on December 31, 1973 (like most of the rest of the 60 companies), but used the same operating data actually reported in the financial statements for the year ending July 31, 1974. In this hypothetical case, Genesco showed a 125 percent—as opposed to a 163 percent—decline in income before monetary gain and a 51 percent—as opposed to a 74 percent—decline, in net income. Thus even if Genesco had experienced the lower rate of inflation, it would remain at the bottom of the lists. This analysis raises the point discussed at greater length in the last section of this article: What do we expect to see in the annual reports for the year 1974 when prices increased at a rate much faster than in 1973?

A closer look at the companies in the lower end of the range reveals one possible shortcoming of the method of presentation used here. Inflation adjustments of equal dollar amounts will have a greater percentage effect on the income of a low profit company than on the income of a high profit company. Nineteen seventy-three was not a good year for International Harvester or United Aircraft. The inflation adjustments for International Harvester and United Aircraft, although not especially large relative to other firms, reduced adjusted income before monetary gains to 10 percent and 18 percent, respectively, of the modest reported net incomes.

Adjusted Net Income Surprisingly High in Relation to Reported Net Income

When monetary gains from net debtor position are included, the resulting net income was a surprisingly high percentage of conventional income (surprising to us and to most other observers, we believe). For the Dow companies, adjusted net income for more than half the companies was 90 percent or more of reported net income and in seven cases exceeded the reported income. For the other 30, adjusted income in half the cases was equal to or greater than the reported net income. The significance of the monetary gains factor responsible for these results is discussed in the concluding section of this article.

The Estimating Procedure for General Price Level Adjusted Income

The procedure used in making the inflation adjustments reported in the previous section can also be used by analysts in estimating what the general price level adjusted income for any company will be. The procedure requires a copy of the financial statements, including the usual notes, as published in the annual report. An analyst who also has a copy of the Form 10-K filed with the SEC can refine the calculations somewhat, as will be made clear below.

Price Index and Computing Rates of Change in Prices Over Time

To compute general price level adjusted income one must have a set of GNP Deflators for each of the five quarters preceding the balance sheet date, plus quarterly or annual data for one or two earlier periods. The handiest source is a table of the GNP Deflator by quarters for the past 10 or 15 years. (An abbreviated list is supplied in a following section.)

Consider, for the purpose of exposition, the problem of analyzing a company whose reporting year ends on December 31, 1974. Assume the GNP Deflator for the fourth quarter of 1974 is reported to be 178 and the GNP Deflator for the fourth quarter of 1973 was reported to be 159.[6] Then the rate of price change for the year 1974 is computed as

$$\frac{178}{159} - 1 = 1.12 - 1 = 12 \text{ percent.} \tag{1}$$

In the instructions that follow there are statements such as "adjust (a given financial statement item) for one-half year (or some other fraction of a year)." For example, revenues for the year, which are to be adjusted for one-half year of price change, are adjusted six percent (equal to one-half of 12 percent).[7]

In general, if you are required to adjust prices for a fraction of a year, say 62 percent, then the proportionate price change for that fraction of a year is, in our example, 62 percent of 12 percent (= 7.44 percent).[8]

Adjusting Revenues and Other Income

Revenues and other income are, for the most part, spread fairly evenly throughout the year, and adjusting the historically reported amounts for one-half year of price change is usually satisfactory. If the annual report or other information indicates that revenue or other income occurred unevenly throughout the year, then one can adjust that portion of revenues separately.

Adjusting Cost of Goods Sold

The adjustment we use for cost of goods sold depends upon whether the company uses a first-in, first-out (FIFO), last-in, first-out (LIFO), or weighted-average cost flow assumption. Some companies use both FIFO and LIFO—one for a part of inventories and the other for the remainder. For those companies we use both the FIFO and LIFO techniques and compute the proper average of the two separate adjustments. (The example discussed later involves this complication.) Companies that merely report using "lower-of-cost-or-market inventory valuation" are assumed to use FIFO, unless the notes give contrary information.

The adjustment for cost of goods sold requires data from the income statement on cost of goods sold and data on beginning and ending inventories from the balance sheet. If the income statement does not disclose the cost of goods sold, then the notes to the financial statements as reported to the SEC must show it. (The annual report of the General Electric Company, for example, discloses cost of goods sold in the notes to the income statement.)

FIFO Adjustment: Under FIFO, we know that beginning inventory entered cost of goods sold and that the remainder of cost of goods sold consists of the earlier purchases during the year. We assume that the purchases occurred fairly evenly throughout the year. Then the average purchase which entered cost of goods was made

$$\left[\frac{\text{Cost of Goods Sold} - \text{Beginning Inventory}}{\text{Purchases}} \right] \times \tfrac{1}{2} \times 12$$

months after January 1. Purchases for the year can be computed from the relation

Purchases = Ending Inventory + Cost of Goods Sold − Beginning Inventory.

General price level adjusted cost of goods sold for FIFO companies is, then,

Beginning Inventory Adjusted for a Full Year plus

Cost of Goods Sold Minus Beginning Inventory
Adjusted for the Fraction of a Year Equal to

$$1 - \left[\frac{\text{Cost of Goods Sold} - \text{Beginning Inventory}}{\text{Purchases}} \right] \times \tfrac{1}{2} \ .$$

LIFO Adjustment (Inventory Increase—Normal Case): The adjustment for LIFO cost of goods sold in estimating general price level income depends upon whether inventory increased or decreased during the year. For most companies, most of the time, inventory amounts increase. The items that enter cost of goods sold under normal conditions are then the later purchases during the year. When inventories are not declining, the average dollar of cost of goods sold was acquired

$$\tfrac{1}{2} \times \frac{\text{Cost of Goods Sold}}{\text{Purchases}} \times 12$$

months before the end of the year. Thus LIFO cost of goods sold is adjusted for a fraction of the year equal to

$$\tfrac{1}{2} \times \left[\frac{\text{Cost of Goods Sold}}{\text{Cost of Goods Sold} + \text{Ending Inventory}} \right] - \text{Beginning Inventory}$$

LIFO Adjustment (Inventory Decrease): When inventory amounts decline during a year, part of cost of goods sold comes from beginning inventory. Under LIFO, the beginning inventory for a year reported on comparative balance sheets is at least two years old as of the current balance sheet date. In our procedures we adjust the "dip into old LIFO layers" for two years, but information in a given annual report may indicate that even more adjustment is necessary. The dip into old LIFO layers is equal to

$$\text{Beginning Inventory} - \text{Ending Inventory}$$

and this amount of cost of goods sold is adjusted for two years of price change, at a minimum. The rest of cost of goods sold (Cost of Goods Sold − Beginning Inventory + Closing Inventory) is adjusted for one-half year of price change.

Weighted-Average Adjustment: Under a weighted-average cost flow assumption, a firm assumes it uses equal portions of all goods available for sale. The total of goods available for sale is beginning inventory plus all purchases, which is also equal to cost of goods sold plus ending inventory. Purchases are assumed to be spread evenly throughout the year. Thus, total goods available for sale in end-of-year dollars is

$$\text{Beginning Inventory Adjusted for a Full Year}$$
$$\text{plus}$$
$$\text{Purchases Adjusted for One-half Year.}$$

The weighted-average cost of goods sold restated in December 31 dollars is

$$\frac{\text{Cost of Goods Sold}}{\text{Goods Available for Sale}} \times \frac{\text{Goods Available for Sale}}{\text{Stated in End-of-Year Dollars}}$$

and can be computed as

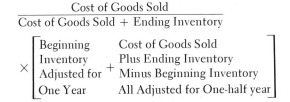

Adjusting Depreciation

To compute price level adjusted depreciation, ascertain the depreciation charges for the year and the accumulated depreciation as of the end of the year. Often, as for example in the annual reports of American Brands (1973) and Sears, Roebuck (1974), the amount of depreciation is not shown separately in the income statement, but is included in the cost of goods sold. In that case, the amount of depreciation charges can be read from the statement of changes in financial position. (If depreciation is included in cost of goods sold, then subtract the depreciation from cost of goods sold before adjusting cost of goods sold with the method described in the preceding section.) The amount of accumulated depreciation is shown either directly on the balance sheet or in notes.

If a company uses straight-line depreciation, then the average age of its depreciable assets in years is computed from[9]

$$
\begin{aligned}
\begin{matrix} \text{Average Age of} \\ \text{Depreciable} \\ \text{Assets in Years} \end{matrix} &= \begin{matrix} \text{Average Life of} \\ \text{Depreciable Assets} \end{matrix} \times \begin{matrix} \text{Fraction of Life} \\ \text{Which Has Expired} \end{matrix} \\[2ex]
&= \frac{\text{Total Cost of Depreciable Assets}}{\text{Depreciation Charges for Year}} \times \frac{\text{Accumulated Depreciation}}{\text{Total Cost of Depreciable Assets}} \\[2ex]
&= \frac{\text{Accumulated Depreciation}}{\text{Depreciation Charges for Year}}
\end{aligned}
\tag{2}
$$

If the company uses straight-line depreciation, then adjust the depreciation charges for the average age of the depreciable assets in years computed from (2).

If the company uses an accelerated depreciation method, then the computation of the average age of depreciable assets in (2) is an overestimate of the average age. How much of an overestimate it is depends upon the average age and the growth rate over time of depreciable assets for that company.

We have solved a series of linear difference equations to provide age-reducing factors to compute the average age of assets depreciated on the sum-of-the-years'-digits and double-declining-balance accelerated depreciation methods. These age-reducing factors are shown in Tables 3 and 4.

To use the tables to estimate the average age of assets depreciated on an accelerated basis requires an estimate of growth rate in depreciable assets. The information for estimating growth rates is typically found in the historical summary of the annual report. Ideally, we want to find the growth rate in depreciable assets. Many published historical summaries do not provide this information and some surrogate will be necessary. A good surrogate is the growth in the annual depreciation charge. Another substitute, but one not so good, is the growth in the total of noncurrent assets. (For General Motors, we had to use the growth in yearly expenditures for depreciable assets to compute the growth rate of total depreciable assets.) If the average age of depreciable assets is computed from equation (2) to be n, then the growth rate to use in entering the age-reducing tables is

$$
\sqrt[n]{\frac{\text{Depreciable Assets (or Surrogate) as of Balance Sheet Date}}{\text{Depreciable Assets (or Surrogate) as of } n \text{ Years Ago}}} - 1.
$$

Enter the appropriate table (Table 3 or Table 4) of age-reducing factors with the age found in equation (2) and the growth rate in depreciable assets. Typically, the age found and the implied growth rate will lead one to some point within a block of four numbers in the table. The simplest procedure is to "eyeball" an interpolation corresponding to the proper point within the block, but in our computer program we use an exact linear interpolation.

Once one has the age-reducing factor from the table, he multiplies the result of equation (2) by that factor and adjusts the reported depreciation charges for the resulting number of years.

Table 3

AGE-REDUCING FACTORS FOR DEPRECIABLE ASSETS
SUM-OF-THE-YEARS'-DIGITS (SYD) METHOD

Unadjusted Life in Years*	Annual Growth Rate of Depreciable Assets (or Surrogate)					
	0%	5%	10%	15%	20%	30%
3	.857143	.865991	.874202	.881823	.888898	.901575
4	.833333	.846666	.858928	.870188	.880513	.898633
5	.818182	.835965	.852168	.866872	.880169	.902953
6	.807692	.829889	.849913	.86785	.883822	.910458
7	.800000	.826571	.850291	.871241	.889576	.919252
8	.794118	.825025	.852309	.876041	.896423	.928347
9	.789474	.824677	.855390	.881666	.903779	.937203
10	.785714	.825173	.859175	.887756	.911283	.945519
11	.782609	.826282	.863428	.894070	.918707	.953141
12	.780000	.827845	.867988	.900449	.925903	.959998
13	.777778	.829752	.872742	.906780	.932775	.966081
14	.775862	.831921	.877607	.912985	.939262	.971411
15	.774194	.834294	.882520	.919008	.945330	.976036
20	.768293	.847901	.906506	.945383	.969205	.990728
25	.764706	.862605	.927800	.964872	.983715	.996701
30	.762295	.877202	.945545	.978234	.991789	.998891

*Accumulated Depreciation/Depreciation Charges for Year.

Adjusting All Other Expenses and Deductions

We have now discussed adjustment of all revenues and other income as well as cost of goods sold and depreciation. All other deductions from revenues to determine net income should be adjusted for one-half year.

Computing Gain or Loss on Monetary Items

To compute gain or loss on monetary items, first compute the average net monetary item positon for the year. We use the average of the beginning and ending balances of monetary items. Monetary assets include cash, accounts receivable, bonds and notes held, and any other item that will be eventually converted into a definite amount of cash that is known today. Monetary liabilities generally include all liabilities. The exceptions are the estimated liabilities for future expenditures under warranties and the liability shown when the company has received cash in advance of delivering goods or services. This latter liability is often called "Advances from Customers" or "Rental Payments Received in Advance" or "Prepaid Subscriptions" or "Deferred Income." (Such items are often so small in proportion to total liabilities that they can safely be ignored for many companies. We have not ignored these items in our calculations.) APB Statement No. 3 also indicated that deferred taxes, deferred investment tax credits, and debts denominated in foreign currencies should be excluded from monetary liabilities. This treatment is so much at odds with the theory underlying the construction of general price level adjusted statements that we think the FASB may include deferred taxes and investment tax credits as well as items denominated in foreign currencies among monetary items.[10]

The major difficulty in practice in considering monetary items is deciding whether or not the asset "Marketable Securities" is a monetary asset. If the marketable securities are bonds, commerical paper, or government notes, then they are monetary. If the marketable securities are equity securities, then they are not monetary. Unfortunately, most firms do not disclose exactly what their marketable securities are.

To compute the average net monetary liability position for the year, add together the monetary liabilities at the beginning of the year and at the end of the year; then subtract the sum of monetary assets at the beginning and the end of the year. Divide the result by two. If positive (as it usually is), the result shows the average net borrowing position of the company during the year; if negative, the average net lending position. The monetary gain for the year is the average net liability position multiplied by the rate of price change for the year. If the company was a net lender during a year of rising prices, it will have a loss on holdings of monetary items. (Only one of the Dow Jones companies, United Aircraft, and one of the 30 other companies, Merck, show losses on holding of monetary items. On the other hand, several of the banks we have examined show losses on holdings of monetary items, as did Company H shown in Table 6.)

If the company swapped nonmonetary items for monetary items, or vice versa, in large amounts at some time other than near mid-year, then you may want to adjust separately for the resulting monetary gain or loss. If, for example, a company sold a large plant near the end of the year, and the proceeds of the sale are still held in monetary assets, then our averaging process will overstate average monetary assets for the year and understate the gain (or overstate the loss) on holding monetary items.

Preparing the Adjusted Statements

The estimated adjustments are now complete. Revenues, other income, and all expenses except cost of goods sold and depreciation are adjusted for one-half year's price change. Gain or loss on monetary items is computed using the entire year's price change. The figures can be summarized as shown in Table 5.

Comments on the Procedure

Although the procedure is somewhat complicated to describe, our computer program carries out the estimating procedure for a single company in less than half a second. It takes us about 30 minutes to compute all the adjustments for a single company by hand.

If the FASB should decide that deferred taxes and items denominated in foreign currencies are not monetary after all, then the gains on monetary items we have reported in the previous section are nearly all overstated. If the FASB condones the ABP Statement No. 3 computation of one-half year's price change, as described in a later section, then our estimates of income are again overstated. Our estimating procedure tries, however, to mirror the logic of the general price level adjustment wherever we can make it do so.

Table 4

AGE-REDUCING FACTORS FOR DEPRECIABLE ASSETS
DOUBLE-DECLINING-BALANCE (DDB) METHOD

Unadjusted Life in Years*	Annual Growth Rate of Depreciable Assets (or Surrogate)					
	0%	5%	10%	15%	20%	30%
3	.764706	.779434	.793105	.805796	.817576	.838674
4	.765306	.783763	.800807	.816513	.830958	.856400
5	.764997	.787301	.807768	.826454	.843444	.872744
6	.764619	.790793	.814637	.836176	.855495	.888002
7	.764285	.794327	.821473	.845701	.867098	.902108
8	.764006	.797901	.828260	.854994	.878200	.915005
9	.763774	.801503	.834974	.864019	.888754	.926670
10	.763581	.805120	.841596	.872745	.898728	.937116
11	.763417	.808741	.848107	.881150	.908101	.946384
12	.763278	.812359	.854496	.889216	.916864	.954534
13	.763158	.815967	.860750	.896930	.925017	.961645
14	.763054	.819560	.866861	.904286	.932565	.967801
15	.762962	.823134	.872822	.911279	.939523	.973094
20	.762634	.840616	.900195	.940831	.966249	.989670
25	.762432	.857275	.923311	.962058	.982189	.996331
30	.762297	.872956	.942215	.976483	.991014	.998766

*Accumulated Depreciation/Depreciation Charges for Year.

Illustration of the Estimating Procedure

To make the estimating procedure clear and to provide a guide for analysts to follow in preparing their own estimates, we illustrate the estimating procedure in this section. The illustration is for the General Electric (GE) Company's operations for 1973, as reported in the financial statements of its annual report for that year.

Price Index and Rate of Price Change during 1973

The GNP Deflator has the following values for these dates important to the estimating procedure:

Quarter[a]	GNP Deflator (1958 = 100)
4th, 1973	158.93
3rd, 1973	155.67
2nd, 1973	152.61
1st, 1973	149.95
4th, 1972	147.96
4th, 1967[b]	118.9
3rd, 1967[b]	117.7
Annual Average	
1967[c]	117.59
1966[c]	113.94

[a]The GNP Deflator is an average for the quarter.

[b]These are required for the depreciation calculations.

[c]These are required for the alternative depreciation calculations.

The rate of price increase for the year 1973 is $158.93/147.96 - 1 = 1.0741 - 1 = 7.41$ percent. If prices are assumed to have increased uniformly throughout the year, price change during half a year is equal to:[11]

$$\text{Price Change for one-half 1973} = \sqrt{1.0741} - 1 = 3.64 \text{ percent.}$$

Adjustment of Revenues

GE's revenues for the year 1973 were $11,759 million (equals "Sales" + "Other income"). Revenues are to be adjusted for one-half year. GE's price level adjusted revenues are then

$$1.0364 \times \$11,759 \text{ million} = \$12,187 \text{ million.}$$

Adjustment of Cost of Goods Sold

GE uses LIFO for about 84 percent of its inventories and uses FIFO for about 16 percent.[12] Historical cost of goods sold was $8,515.2 million.[13]

LIFO Adjustment: Under a LIFO cost flow assumption for inventories the purchases that enter cost of goods sold are the last purchases of the year. Total purchases for the year are the cost of goods sold (COGS) plus the increase in inventories for the year.

Purchases = COGS + Increase in Inventories
Purchases = COGS + Closing Inventory (12/31) − Beginning Inventory (1/31)
Purchases = $8,515.2 + $1,986.2 − $1,759.0
            = $8,742.4 in millions.

Assuming LIFO, an amount of purchases equal to COGS/Purchases = $8,515.2/ $8,742.4 = 97.4 percent of all purchases during the year entered cost of goods sold. These purchases *on average* occurred $0.974/2 \times 12 = 5.844$ months before the end of the year. Thus the average dollar of cost of goods sold was dated about July 4, 1973. (December 31 less 5.844 months is about July 4.)

The rate of price change in the last 5.844 months of 1973 was 3.545 percent. Thus the entire cost of goods sold adjusted for a 3.545 percent increase in prices is

LIFO COGS = $8,515.2 × 1.03545 = $8,817. Adjusted in millions.

FIFO Adjustment: Under a FIFO cost flow assumption for inventories, the cost of goods sold consists of beginning inventory plus the purchases from the earlier part of the year.

The purchases that enter cost of goods sold for GE in 1973 are the beginning inventory (BI) of $1,759.0 million plus the first $6,756.2 (equals $8,515.2 − $1,759.0 equals COGS − BI) million of purchases for the year. Thus the average dollar of purchases that entered cost of goods sold for GE in 1973 occurred $\frac{1}{2}$ × $6,756.2/$8,742.4 × 12 months equals 4.64 months after January 1, 1973, or about May 20, 1973. The quantity cost of goods sold minus beginning inventory must be adjusted for 7.36 (equals 12 − 4.64) months—61.3 percent of a year. The beginning inventory must be adjusted for an entire year.

$$\begin{aligned} \text{FIFO COGS} = {} & \text{Beginning Inventory Adjusted in millions.} \\ & \times \text{Year's Price Change Adjusted in millions} \\ & + (\text{Cost of Goods Sold} - \text{Beginning Inventory}) \\ & \times \text{Price Change for 0.613 of One Year.} \\ = {} & \$1,759.0 \times 1.0741 + \$6,756.2 \times 1.0449 \\ = {} & \$8,948.9. \end{aligned}$$

Combining LIFO and FIFO Adjustments: The adjusted LIFO cost of goods sold was computed to be $8,817.0 and the adjusted FIFO cost of goods sold was computed to be $8,948.7. GE used LIFO for 84 percent of its inventory and FIFO for 16 percent. Thus GE's combined-average adjusted cost of goods sold is

$$\begin{aligned} \text{COGS Adjusted in Millions.} = {} & 0.84 \times \$8.817.0 + 0.16 \times \$8,948.9 \\ = {} & \$8,838.1. \end{aligned}$$

Depreciation: GE's depreciation charge for the year 1973 was $334.0 million. The accumulated depreciation at December 31, 1973, was $2,559.3 million. Thus, if straight-line depreciation were used, the average dollar's worth of depreciable assets would have been acquired

$$\frac{\$2,559.3}{\$334.0 \text{ per year}} = 7.663 \text{ years}$$

before December 31, 1973.

GE, however, uses sum-of-the-years'-digits (SYD) depreciation so that estimate must be reduced somewhat.

To use the SYD adjustment table requires an estimate of GE's annual growth rate in depreciable assets. GE presents the depreciation charges for several past years in its historical summary.[14] The growth rate in depreciation charges provides a surrogate for the growth rate in depreciable assets. Depreciation charges for 1965 (eight years—the closest one shown to 7.663 years—prior to balance sheet date) was $188.4 million. Thus, the depreciation charges increased, on average, at a rate of 7.42 percent (equals $\sqrt[8]{334.0/188.4} - 1$) per year between January 1, 1965, and December 31, 1974.

Entering the SYD adjustment table (Table 3) for age 7.663 years and growth rate 7.42 percent, and interpolating as necessary, yields an adjustment factor of 0.8124. Thus GE's depreciable assets, according to our formula are on average 0.8124 × 7.663 years equals 6.225 years old.

Therefore, depreciation charges must be adjusted for 6.225 years of price change. 6.225 years before December 31, 1973, occurred during the fourth quarter of 1967. Refer to the GNP Deflator for the last two quarters of 1967. We compute that prices increased by 34.9 percent during the 6.225 years before December 31, 1974.[15] The adjusted depreciation charge for GE in 1973 is then

$$1.349 \times \$334.0 \text{ million equals } \$450.54 \text{ million.}$$

All "Other" Deductions from Income

GE's total "other" deductions from income in 1973 were $2,324.7 million. These other deductions consist of interest charges, income taxes, income applicable to minority interests and all operating expenses except cost of goods sold and depreciation.

The other deductions are assumed to be spread evenly throughout the year and are adjusted for one-half year's price change.

$$\text{Adjusted Other Deductions in millions} = \$2,324.7 \times 1.0364$$
$$= \$2,409.3.$$

Computing Gain on Holding of Net Monetary Items

GE's monetary items for 1973 were reported as follows:[16]

	($ in Millions)	
	Dec. 31, 1973	Dec. 31, 1972
Monetary Liabilities		
All Liabilities	$4,901.7	$4,273.8
Monetary Assets		
Cash, Receivables, Customer Financing,		
Deferred Taxes, and Recoverable Costs.	2,980.8	2,642.1
Net Monetary Liabilities	$1,920.9	$1,631.7

The average net monetary liabilities for the year 1973 was $1,776.3 [equals 0.5 × ($1,920.9 + $1,631.7)] million. The price change for the year was 7.41 percent. Thus GE's gain from being a net debtor during 1973 when prices increased by 7.41 percent was about 0.0741 × $1,776.3 equals $131 million.

Preparing the General Price Level Adjusted Income Statement

The computations just described for the General Electric Company's income statement are summarized in Table 5.

Table 5

GENERAL ELECTRIC COMPANY

INCOME STATEMENT FOR 1973

	(Amounts Shown in Millions of Dollars)		
	Historical Dollars (Shown in Annual Report)	Constant Dollars Dated 12/31/73 As Estimated	Percentage Change
Revenue and Other Income	$11,759	$12,187	+3.64%
Expenses and Deductions:			
Cost of Goods Sold[a]	$ 8,515	$ 8,838	+3.79
Depreciation (SYD)[b]	334	451	+34.89
Other	2,325	2,409	+3.64
Total	$11,174	$11,698	+4.69
Net Income before Gain on Monetary Items	$ 585	$ 489	−16.40[c]
Gain on Monetary Items	——	131	——
Net Income	$ 585	$ 620	+6.11[d]

[a]Inventories are 84 percent LIFO; 16 percent FIFO.

[b]Average life of depreciable assets is 6.225 years; price index for 6.225 years before balance sheet date was 117.8.

[c]The numbers shown in the first columns of Tables 1, 2, and 7 are 100 plus this number.

[d]The numbers shown in the second columns of Tables 1, 2, and 7 are 100 plus this number.

How Accurate Is The Estimating Procedure?

The previous sections have presented procedures for estimating general price level adjustments to reported income and have shown the results of those procedures for 1973 operations of 60 major corporations. We have suggested that analysts can use these procedures for preparing general price level adjustments for companies of interest to them. How similar are the results using these procedures to the results that would be reported by major companies if general price level adjusted statements were required?[17] We attempt to answer that question, insofar as we can, in this section.

We have partial, reported ("actual") general price level adjusted accounting figures for three companies on a current basis—Gulf Oil Corporation, Shell Oil Company, and Indiana Telephone Corporation. A fourth company, called Company R, helped us assess the accuracy of our procedures on a confidential basis. In addition, the AICPA commissioned a study of general price level accounting in 1968–69.[18] The AICPA made available to us the financial statements for a dozen or so companies in that study. Those data contain three companies for which we can apply our estimating procedures. (The others cannot be tested because some vital information—such as the start of the year balance sheet— was not given to us.) These are real companies, but their names were withheld.

Next the AICPA published results for a fictitious XYZ Company in APB Statement No. 3 that explains the general price level restatement procedure. Finally, one standard accounting reference book contains a chapter on inflation accounting which shows a comprehensive example of general price level adjustments for another fictitious company, Demonstrator Corporation. Table 6 presents partial comparisons of our results and reported figures for these ten companies. The results are partial in the sense that some of the real companies made available (published) only parts of their general price level adjusted financial statements. We compare our numbers with the published excerpts.

You can judge for yourself the results shown in Table 6. Our estimated bottom line figures—net income—for Gulf and Company R are within six percent of the companies' numbers. For Shell we are off by 10 percent. Indiana Telephone does not report gains on monetary items as suggested in APB Statement No. 3, but our estimates of their net income before gain on monetary items is within five percent of the reported figure.

At first glance the following may appear puzzling. For some companies (such as Company P of the Rosenfield Study) the estimates of the income items are in error by substantially more than the components of income are in error. Recall however, that the denominator for each error calculation is the reported figure of that financial statement item and keep in mind that net incomes are typically less than five percent of revenues or cost of goods sold. Errors in estimates of the same absolute dollar amounts are, then, a much larger percentage of net income than they are of total revenues or of cost of goods sold.

For the fictitious AICPA example (XYZ Company) we do well for 1967, but poorly for 1968. The XYZ Company comparisons should not be given much weight because the GNP Deflator Series has been changed since the 1968 publication date of Statement No. 3. That is, the AICPA used numbers for the GNP Deflator Series different from the ones now considered official.

Furthermore, the assumed 1968 operations of XYZ Company resulted in a drastic decline in income from 1967. Whereas revenues for 1968 were about 10 percent less than in 1967, income was about 75 percent less. When computing the deviation of our estimate of net income from the reported result, we divide by reported net income, which is small for 1968. When the denominator is small, the resulting percentage can be large even when the absolute deviation is not, as suggested in our comment on International Harvester and United Aircraft in an earlier section.

The large difference between our estimate for gain on monetary items for XYZ in 1968 and the reported figure is caused by XYZ's selling a nonmonetary asset on December 31, 1968. The cash realized from that sale is larger than the total amount of net monetary liabilities. Our standard procedure assumes that all inflows of cash occur evenly throughout the year; that assumption substantially reduced both the estimated average net monetary liability and the gain on monetary items for the year from that reported by the XYZ Company. Since the nonmonetary asset sold was converted into the monetary asset cash on December 31, 1968, this transaction did not affect *reported* gain on monetary items at all. When we account separately for this one transaction, the error in reporting gain on monetary items for XYZ Company in 1968 is reduced from 45 percent to less than 20 percent.

Table 6

Percentages by Which the Davidson-Weil Estimates Deviate
from the Reported General Price Level Adjusted Items

[For each item, the number shown is the Davidson-Weil estimate divided by the general price level adjusted item as reported (by the Company or by the AICPA) minus one: Number shown = DW/Reported − 1. A positive number indicates an over-estimate by Davidson-Weil, a negative number, an underestimate.]

General Price Level Adjusted Financial Statement Item	Gulf Oil (1973)[a]	Shell Oil (1973)[b]	Company R (1973)[c]	Indiana Telephone (1973)[d]	AICPA—Rosenfield Study Co. H (1968)[e]	Co. J (1968)[e]	Co. P (1968)[e]	AICPA XYZ Company (1967)[f]	(1968)[f]	Demonstrator Company (1960)[g]
Revenues and Other Income	*	3.63%	0.68%	0.90%	0.72%	0.05%	0.25%	0.13%	1.38%	0.35%
Cost of Goods Sold	*	*	0.02	**	0.79	0.11	−1.78	0.07	0.75	0.18
Depreciation[h]	5.93%	*	18.74	0.65	6.33	2.99	3.45	2.62	−4.29	0.41
Other Expenses and Deductions	*	*	0.62	0.81	0.94	−0.29	0.31	−0.23	6.30	0.03
INCOME BEFORE GAIN OR LOSS ON MONETARY ITEMS	*	*	−9.97	1.76	10.77	−1.43	24.67	−3.41	60.76[i]	5.01
Gain or Loss on Monetary Items	*	*	5.80	***	11.17[j]	−6.08	−53.33	−1.00	−45.12[i]	−4.21
NET INCOME	5.23[k]	−10.13	−5.78	***	−3.03	−2.46	7.33	−3.38	30.53	4.62

*Not reported by the Company.

**Indiana Telephone Company has no cost of goods sold.

****Not computed by Indiana Telephone in accordance with APB Statement No. 3

Footnotes to Table 6

[a]Gulf Oil Corporation. *The Orange Disc.* July–August 1974. p. 31.

[b]Shell Oil Company. *Shell Shareholder News.* June 1974. p. 1.

[c]From the company itself on a confidential basis. The company reports that its depreciable assets are only about half as old as our computation (Accumulated Depreciation/Depreciation for the Year) indicates.

[d]Indiana Telephone Corporation. *Annual Report for 1973.*

[e]AICPA data compiled by Paul Rosenfield. See Paul Rosenfield. "Accounting for Inflation—A Field Test." *The Journal of Accountancy.* June 1969. pp. 45–50.

[f]American Institute of Certified Public Accountants. Accounting Principles Board Statement No. 3. "Financial Statements Restated for General-Price Changes." June 1969. Exhibit B-R-3 (12/31/68).

[g]Robert T. Sprouse. "Adjustments for Changing Prices." in S. Davidson (editor). *Handbook of Modern Accounting.* New York: McGraw-Hill Book. Co.. 1970. Chapter 30. page 26.

[h]Straight-line method is used by all companies.

[i]See text for explanation of these large deviations. The Davidson-Weil estimates are off by only $95,000 for income items and less than $40,000 on monetary items. Revenues for the year were $27 million.

[j]DW overstate the amount of the *loss* on monetary items.

[k]We include marketable securities in monetary items; it is not clear what Gulf does.

The estimates for the Demonstrator Corporation are gratifyingly accurate. The primary cause of the over adjustments for ordinary income items is the same as the cause of our other over adjustments, which is explained next.

The major cause of the difference between the results of our estimating procedure and the published company results, as far as we can tell, comes from the adjustment for revenues and other items spread evenly throughout the calendar year. APB Statement No. 3 suggests that the adjustment factor be:

$$\frac{\text{GNP Deflator (4th Quarter)}}{\text{GNP Deflator (Average for Year)}}.$$

But the GNP Deflator (4th Quarter) is the *average* for the fourth quarter (about November 15), not the price level as of December 31. Hence, the AICPA procedure adjusts items "spread fairly evenly throughout the year" on average from about June 30 to about November 15—four and one-half months. The adjustment is supposed to be for six months, a time period one-third longer.[19] We believe the AICPA procedure under adjusts for the items spread fairly evenly throughout the year. In our own procedures we use the factor

$$\sqrt{\frac{\text{GNP Deflator (4th Quarter This Year)}}{\text{GNP Deflator (4th Quarter Last Year)}}}$$

for items requiring, on average, one-half year's adjustment. We suggest that a reasonable approximation to this geometric mean is[20]

$$1 + 0.5 \times \left[\frac{\text{GNP Deflator (4th Quarter This Year)}}{\text{GNP Deflator (4th Quarter Last Year)}} - 1 \right]$$

At any rate, our adjustments for a half year are always larger than those found by following the AICPA procedures. We surmise, but cannot be sure, that the four real companies used in our comparisons with 1973 data have followed the AICPA method for adjusting for four and one-half months on average, rather than the six months we suggest. We know that Demonstrator Corporation's adjustments for items spread evenly throughout the year were made using the four and one-half month AICPA technique. In general, during times of increasing prices, the result of using only four and one-half rather than six months for adjusting items spread fairly evenly throughout the year is to underestimate general price level adjusted profits. The items spread evenly throughout the year are (1) nearly all revenues and (2) many expenses. Since the sum of "nearly all revenues" exceeds the sum of "many expenses" for almost all companies, the excess—a partial gross margin—is understated.

Once the FASB makes official its standards for general price level adjustments, those who want to estimate results will want to pay careful attention to the half-year adjustment suggested (or required) and to build an analogous computation into the estimating procedure. We think we have used the most logical procedure, but we can change it if, as has happened before, the FASB does not agree with us about what is logical.

All the companies for which we can assess the accuracy of our methods use straight-line depreciation. We cannot, however, test the accuracy of our methods for firms using accelerated depreciation until some such firms publish their general price level adjusted depreciation figures.

Footnotes

[3]This long title is used in the FASB discussion memorandum of February 15, 1974, on the subject. APB Statement No. 3 indicates a preference for the briefer "general price level gain or loss." The FASB uses that title in the illustration in the discussion memorandum, but it also uses the phrase "purchasing power gain or loss" that was recommended in Accounting Research Study No. 6. We have chosen to use the simpler, and in our opinion, more meaningful, phrase "monetary gain or loss."

[4]The three areas are: (1) the method of calculating the adjustment factor for revenues and other items spread fairly evenly throughout the year; (2) treating deferred taxes and deferred investment credit as monetary items, and (3) treating foreign debt as a monetary item. Each of the items is discussed in later sections.

[5]We are not the first to challenge the validity of the naïve view that a constant adjustment factor will suffice. See Russell J. Petersen, "Interindustry Estimation of General Price-Level Impact on Financial Information," *The Accounting Review*, 48, 1 (January 1973), pp. 34–43.

[6]These numbers only approximate the actual GNP Deflator for those two quarters.

[7]A more accurate computation is to use

$$\sqrt{1.12} - 1 = (1.12)^{1/2} - 1 = 1.0583 - 1 = 5.83 \text{ percent}$$

as the average of price change for a half-year when prices went up by 12 percent for the whole year. This more exact computation, and the analogous ones for other fractions of a year, can be done if you have a calculator or computer that raises numbers to fractional powers. We use the simpler, but less exact, procedure explained in the text for hand calculations but our computer program uses the more accurate method described in this footnote and the next.

The AICPA in APB Statement No. 3 actually recommends a different procedure, explained below. It is so clearly inferior to both the methods described here that we are hopeful the FASB will use one or the other of these two.

[8]The more accurate computation, analogous to the one described in footnote 7, is to use

$$(1.12)^{0.62} - 1 = 7.28 \text{ percent}$$

as the rate of change in prices for 62 percent of a year during which prices increased by 12 percent.

[9]To see how this computation works, consider an asset costing $10,000 on which accumulated depreciation is $3,000 at year-end and for which annual straight-line depreciation charges are $1,000. We know that the asset has a 10-year life ($10,000/$1,000 per year) and that the asset is 30 percent gone as of the end of the year ($3,000/$10,000). Thus the asset is 30 percent of 10 years, or three years old, at the end of the year.

[10]We have counted these items among monetary items except in some of our "calibrating" calculations where the company has reported a different treatment.

[11]A simpler computation of the price change during one-half year is $1/2 \times 7.41$ percent $= 3.705$ percent. $(1.03705)^2$ is, however, greater than 1.0741. Using one-half the year's price change (3.705 percent) rather than the price change for one-half a year (3.64 percent) will bias the computations by assuming, in effect, that prices increased more rapidly in the second half of the year than in the first half. Such a bias results in slight *over*-adjustments.

[12]This information is given on page 36 in the notes to GE's 1973 annual report. That annual report is reproduced and annotated in *Accounting: The Language of Business*, Sidney Davidson, James S. Schindler, and Roman L. Weil, Glen Ridge, New Jersey (07028): Thomas Horton & Daughters, Inc., 1974.

[13]Page 34 of GE's 1973 annual report.

[14]GE annual report, pp. 42–43.

[15]The exact computation of the rate of price increase is

$$\left(\frac{158.93}{118.9}\right) \times \left(\frac{118.9}{117.7}\right)^{0.225/0.25} - 1 = 34.9 \text{ percent.}$$

An adequate approximation, much easier to carry out by hand, is

$$158.93/[118.9 - {}^{0.225}/_{0.25}(118.9 - 117.7)] - 1.$$

This approximation results in the calculation of a 34.7 percent increase in prices in the 6.225 years preceding December 31, 1973.

A simpler approach would use year-average figures for the GNP Deflators of the earlier years since they may be more readily available. This, in effect, assumes a "half-year convention" for depreciation charges in the first year. This procedure would have for the denominator of the calculation, the following:

Denom. = −0.225 × (1967 average GNP Deflator − 1966 average GNP Deflator)
= 117.59 − 0.225(117.59 − 113.94)
= 116.77

The percentage increase in prices over the 6.225 years preceding December 31, 1973, using this method would then be equal to

$$\frac{158.93}{116.77} - 1 = 36.1 \text{ percent.}$$

This method will always yield slightly higher adjusted depreciation charges than the method illustrated in the body of the text.

[16]Annual report, pp. 32 and 39.

[17]Others have devised estimating procedures for the same purpose. See *Business Week,* September 14, 1974, page 96. The estimates shown there for the Dow Jones Companies differ substantially from ours. See also Russell J. Petersen, "An Examination of the Effects of Changes in the General Price Level on Published Financial Statements," Doctoral Dissertation, University of Washington, June 1971.

[18]Paul Rosenfield, "Accounting for Inflation—A Field Test," *The Journal of Accountancy,* June 1969, pp. 45–50.

[19]These comments assumed a relatively uniform change in prices during the year. Since the AICPA procedure uses year-average prices, it eliminates the need for such an assumption, but in most cases that factor is far less significant than the one-third shortening of the time period.

The U.S. Department of Commerce reports that the fourth quarter average is computed as of the middle of the second week of November. If the annual average is for June 30, then the AICPA procedure does not adjust for four and one half months, but for even less than that. Then the AICPA procedure is in error by 37 percent, not $33\frac{1}{3}$ percent.

[20]One might consider using

$$\frac{\text{GNP Deflator (4th Quarter This Year)}}{\text{GNP Deflator (2nd Quarter This Year)}}$$

for half-year adjustments, but he should not. This latter approximation has the weakness that the average price change for one half-year is much misstated if the prices did not increase at a fairly uniform rate throughout the year. Consider, for example, a year when prices were up by 10 percent in the first six months and were stable during the last six months. This procedure of dividing the fourth quarter index by the second quarter index would show average price change for six months to be zero, while in fact prices went up by about five percent for an average six-month period.

Accounting for Changes in Specific Prices

4

Financial statements adjusted for changes in the general price level (as presented in Chapters 2 and 3) represent one way of responding to the deterioration in purchasing power caused by inflation. Those procedures continue to rely on historical cost data. They merely restate the historical cost figures in common dollars, or dollars of equivalent purchasing power. In this process we correctly identify the gain or loss in purchasing power directly attributable to the monetary items held by the firm. Beyond that, however, the procedures in Chapter 2 succeed in translating the dollars used to measure past events into their current purchasing-power equivalents and nothing more. The restated financial statements do not reflect current economic values, although they may provide more reliable approximations of those values than do unadjusted historical cost statements.

As mentioned before, inflation does not affect all prices in the same way (see the price index data in Table 1.1 and the "swarm of bees" analogy). Intuition suggests that a more complete accounting for the effects of inflation must of necessity deal with movements in the *specific prices* of individual items, for concentrating solely on general price-level move- ✓ ments is not sufficient. In the present chapter, then, we develop a procedure to reflect the effects of changes in specific prices. It is important to recognize that this procedure involves a clear departure from historical costs: reflection of changes in specific prices means that new bases for valuation are required. Historical cost figures cannot be used except as the starting point for calculating the specific price *changes.*

Another problem with conventional historical cost accounting must be faced when prices are changing. This problem is created by the *realization criterion,* under which income is not recognized until realized, typically at the time of sale. Periodic income measurement will, however, be enhanced by recognizing the effects of changing prices *as they occur,* and not delaying until realization via completed market transactions.

There are several possible approaches to the recognition of specific price changes in the accounts. We prefer to use the *replacement cost* approach, where changes in replacement costs become the basis of accounting for specific price changes. This choice is defended in Chapter 5. Since it is convenient to introduce the subject of accounting for changing prices through the framework of *replacement cost accounting*, we therefore temporarily defer the discussion of alternative measures of specific prices, and our reasons for selecting *replacement cost*, until Chapter 5.

The Securities and Exchange Commission is currently moving toward requiring that certain replacement cost data be disclosed in the footnotes to financial statements. The SEC, on August 21, 1975, released "Notice of Proposed Amendments to Regulation S-X to Required Disclosure of Certain Replacement Cost Data in Notes to Financial Statements (S7–579)." The following quotation from this proposal summarizes the nature of and rationale for these new proposed disclosure rules.

> In the light of the current rate of inflation and price changes, therefore, the Commission has concluded that it is necessary to propose amendments to its Regulation S-X which would require registrants to disclose in the footnotes to financial statements the current cost at the end of the reporting period of replacing inventories and productive capacity as well as the cost of sales and depreciation, depletion, or amortization expense computed on the basis of replacement cost during the reporting period. The Commission believes that these data will make it possible for investors to obtain a better understanding of the current costs of operating the business which cannot be obtained from historical cost financial statements taken alone and that such an understanding is necessary in order to make informed investment decisions.

In addition, the SEC's belief that disclosure of replacement cost information has implications for the economy as a whole is reflected in the following statement from the proposal.

> While the Commission's objective in proposing these rules is to improve investment decision making, it believes the data will also be useful to managers for internal purposes and to macro-economic decision makers who have responsibility for determining economic policies which affect business activities.

The period for public commentary is to expire on January 31, 1976, while this book is in production. Developments during this period, especially vis-à-vis the SEC proposal and the FASB's "Price Level Accounting" proposal should be of interest to all who rely on financial statements.

Shortly after release of the SEC proposal, a "blue-ribbon" British commission issued its report recommending how British companies might reflect the effects of changing prices in their financial statements. Headed by Francis Sandilands, the commission came out in favor of replacement cost accounting, reversing an earlier position by Britain's accounting profession which favored a version of price-level accounting. The commission suggests that its recommendations be put into effect on Christmas Eve, 1977.

The Sandilands Commission also recommends that their version of current operating income be adopted for tax purposes. This would drastically affect the tax structure; a royal commission may be appointed to study the effects of these and other proposed changes in Britain's tax laws.

The determination of income based on replacement costs has two distinct advantages over conventional historical cost income measurement. First, the use of replacement costs enables us to match current costs and current revenues. Current costs are measured by the replacement cost of the resources used at the time revenue is realized. Second, in calculating replacement cost income we separately disclose two components of income which are intermingled in the conventional historical cost income measure: *operating income* and *holding gains*. Operating income measures the current profitability of normal production-sales operations. Holding gains are a direct result of changes in the specific prices of resources held over time.

Introduction to Replacement Cost Accounting

To illustrate these points and to contrast replacement cost income with conventional historical cost income, consider the following example.

The ABC Corporation sells tractors through a number of distributors. Early in 19x5, the firm buys a specially equipped tractor at a cost of $6,000. The tractor is not sold during 19x5, and its replacement cost rises to $7,500 by the end of 19x5 and remains at $7,500 until the tractor is sold. During 19x6, the tractor is finally sold for $10,000. Historical cost accounting would record no profit on the tractor in 19x5 and would record $4,000 profit in 19x6 [$10,000 minus the historical cost of $6,000]. Replacement cost accounting, however, recognizes the $4,000 total profit in two stages. First, replacement cost income in 19x5 will include $1,500 of the total profit of $4,000 as a holding gain. Second, additional profit of $2,500 will be recognized in 19x6. The $2,500 represents the difference between the current sale price of $10,000 and the outlay required at time of sale to replace the tractor, $7,500. Observe that only the *timing* of profit recognition differs between historical cost and replacement cost accounting; the total profit is the same.* The timing and amount of profit under the two methods are summarized below.

---

*This is an important concept. Over the life of a firm, *total* profit under replacement cost and historical cost accounting would be the same; the timing of profits would be different. General price-level accounting, however, bears no such relationship to historical cost accounting. Both the timing *and* amounts of total profit under general price-level accounting are likely to differ from their historical cost counterparts.

	Profit Recognized in		Total Profit
	19x5	19x6	
Historical Cost	—	$4,000	$4,000
		($10,000 − $6,000)	
Replacement Cost . .	$1,500	$2,500	$4,000
	($7,500 − $6,000)	($10,000 − $7,500)	

Advocates of replacement cost accounting believe that the historical cost treatment of this sequence of events is misleading. They argue that recognition of the entire $4,000 profit in 19x6 fails to disclose the fact that $1,500 of this profit is a *holding gain* or *cost saving*.* That is, the increase in the replacement cost of the asset while it was *held* generates a gain. The firm has *gained* by purchasing the tractor for less than it would have cost at the end of 19x5. The advocates of replacement cost accounting also maintain that the operating profit is but $2,500, not the $4,000 reported under conventional historical cost accounting. The reason is that sale of a tractor in the future (barring subsequent price changes) will generate only $2,500 in profit. Of the historical cost and replacement cost methods, only the latter reveals the separate holding and operating components of profit *and* records them in the time periods in which they actually occurred. General price-level accounting, of course, is not designed to differentiate between operating profits and holding gains.

Replacement cost accounting is not restricted to textbook examples. An actual case is provided by N. V. Philips Gloeilampenfabrieken, a large international corporation headquartered in Holland. In 1973, Philips had sales in excess of $8 billion; for purposes of comparison, General Electric's 1973 sales were $11.5 billion. Philips has used a replacement cost accounting system for many years. Exhibit 4.1 contrasts Philips' reported net income for 1974, 1973 and 1972 under both replacement cost accounting *and* conventional historical cost accounting (see further discussions in Chapter 10).

The following, more complex example introduces the treatment of inventories and depreciation under replacement cost accounting in contrast to conventional historical cost accounting. Exhibit 4.2 shows the historical cost statement of financial position at December 31, 19x5, and other data for the LL Corporation.

---

*As far as we know, the term *cost saving* was coined by Edwards and Bell on page 93 of *The Theory and Measurement of Business Income* (University of California Press, 1961). We are heavily indebted to Edwards and Bell, not only for the notion of cost saving, but for much of the theoretical and procedural subject matter discussed in the remainder of this book. *The Theory and Measurement of Business Income* is, in our opinion, a classic work; it should be read by all serious students of accounting.

Exhibit 4.1

N.V. PHILIPS' GLOEILAMPENFABRIEKEN

	Reported Net Income (in millions of guilders)		
	1974	1973	1972
Historical Cost Basis	857.3	918.3	832.3
Replacement Cost Basis	679.3	846.5	675.9
Excess of Historical Cost Income over Replacement Cost Income	178.0	71.8	156.4
Excess as a Percentage of Replacement Cost Income	26.2%	8.5%	23.1%

NOTE: These large differences between net income reported under the two methods are primarily due to the treatment of inventories and depreciation of fixed assets under replacement cost accounting.

Exhibit 4.2

LL CORPORATION
Statement of Financial Position
December 31, 19x5 (Historical Cost)

ASSETS		LIABILITIES AND STOCKHOLDERS' EQUITY	
Inventory.	$20,000	Liabilities.	$14,000
Delivery Equipment (1) . . .	8,000	Capital Stock	6,000
Land	10,000	Retained Earnings	18,000
Total Assets	$38,000	Total Liabilities and Stockholders' Equity .	$38,000

(1) Purchased new on December 28, 19x5; 4-year life; no salvage value; to be depreciated by the straight-line method—none allocated in 19x5.

INFORMATION RELATING TO 19x6 OPERATIONS:

Sales	$49,000
Cost of Inventory Purchased	$30,000
Inventory, December 31, 19x6	$28,000
Replacement Cost of Inventory, December 31, 19x6.	$40,000
Cost of Goods Sold (at replacement cost at date(s) of sale)	$35,000
Cost to Replace Delivery Equipment, Effective January 5, 19x6 . . .	$10,000
Cost to Replace the Land Rose to $12,000 in April 19x6	

From these data, we can prepare a conventional historical cost income statement for the LL Corporation at December 31, 19x6. This is shown in Exhibit 4.3.

The important point is that conventional historical cost accounting reflects only the results of completed market transactions. The effects of

Exhibit 4.3

LL CORPORATION

Statement of Income

for the Year Ended December 31, 19x6 (Historical Cost)

SALES	$49,000
Cost of Goods Sold:	
Inventory, January 1, 19x6	$20,000
Merchandise Purchases	$30,000
Cost of Goods Available for Sale	$50,000
Less: Inventory, December 31, 19x6	$28,000
	$22,000
Contribution Margin	$27,000
Less: Depreciation on Delivery Equipment ($8,000 / 4)	2,000
NET INCOME	$25,000

Exhibit 4.4

LL CORPORATION

Statement of Income

for the Year Ended December 31, 19x6 (Replacement Cost)

SALES	$49,000
Cost of Goods Sold (at replacement cost at date(s) of sale)	35,000
Contribution Margin	$14,000
Less: Depreciation on Delivery Equipment	
(based on replacement cost; $10,000 / 4)	2,500
CURRENT OPERATING INCOME	$11,500
REALIZABLE COST SAVINGS (HOLDING GAINS):	
Realized through sale or use during 19x6:	
Excess of replacement cost of goods sold ($35,000)	
over historical cost of goods sold ($22,000)	$13,000
Excess of replacement cost depreciation ($2,500)	
over historical cost depreciation ($2,000)	500
	$13,500
REALIZED INCOME	$25,000
Unrealized at December 31, 19x6:	
Excess of replacement cost ($40,000) over historical	
cost ($28,000) of ending inventory	$12,000
Excess of replacement cost book value ($7,500) over	
historical cost book value ($6,000) of delivery equipment	1,500
Excess of replacement cost ($12,000) over	
historical cost ($10,000) of land	2,000
	$15,500
REPLACEMENT COST INCOME	$40,500

changing prices are not recorded until realized by transactions with outside entities.

We now compare historical cost income with *replacement cost income*. A replacement cost income statement for the LL Corporation at December 31, 19x6, follows in Exhibit 4.4.

The replacement cost income statement provides three useful measures of income. *Current operating income* reflects the excess of current revenues over the current cost of assets used or sold during the period. *Realized income* represents the sum of current operating income plus those cost savings (holding gains) which were reali*zed* through use (depreciation) or sale (cost savings on inventory sold). Reali*zed* income is the same as conventional historical cost income. *Replacement cost income* includes, in addition, cost savings which became reali*zable* during the period, but which have not been reali*zed* through completed transactions and remain unreali*zed* at the end of the period. In other words,

Analysis of the Replacement Cost Income Statement

Replacement Cost Income = Current Operating Income
+ Reali*zable* Cost Savings

If the cost to replace an asset increases before the asset is disposed of, a holding gain or cost saving has occurred. By having the wisdom (or good fortune) to acquire assets at lower prices than those presently prevailing, the firm achieves a *cost saving*. This cost saving equals the *increase* in replacement cost. To put it another way, the *increase* in replacement cost has been *avoided* because the asset was purchased at a lower cost in the past.

A *realizable cost savings* account is established to keep track of all cost savings arising during the current year. For bookkeeping purposes, this account serves as a *suspense account*. At the end of the period, the reali*zable* cost savings account is *closed* and the balance transferred to accounts entitled *realized cost savings* and *unrealized cost savings* and eventually into replacement cost income.

It is important to understand that reali*zable* cost savings are *flows*. Even though they will normally arise in each period, only the *current period realizable cost savings* enter current period replacement cost income. In our example, reali*zable* cost savings arising during 19x6 totaled $29,000. This is shown below in Exhibit 4.5, using two alternative calculations.

Of this $29,000, $13,500 was *realized* during 19x6 through sale or use of the assets to which the cost savings related. The remaining $15,500

Realizable Cost Savings

Exhibit 4.5

Realizable Cost Savings—With Reference to Increases in Replacement Costs during 19x6

Increase in Replacement Cost of Inventory Available for Sale	$25,000
Increase in Replacement Cost of Delivery Equipment	2,000
Increase in Replacement Cost of Land	2,000
Total Realizable Cost Savings (increases in replacement costs)	$29,000

Realizable Cost Savings—With Reference to Cost Savings Realized during 19x6 and Cost Savings Unrealized at December 31, 19x6

Increase in Replacement Cost of Inventory Sold	$13,000
Depreciated Portion of Increase in Replacement Cost of Delivery Equipment	500
Realized Cost Savings	$13,500
Increase in Replacement Cost of Inventory on Hand	12,000
Undepreciated Portion of Increase in Replacement Cost of Delivery Equipment	1,500
Increase in Replacement Cost of Land	2,000
Unrealized Cost Savings	$15,500
Total Realizable Cost Savings (realized and unrealized)	$29,000

measures the increase in replacement cost of those assets still on hand at year end. This $15,500 in realiz*able* cost savings is *unrealized* at year end.

The journal entries which would have been made in the books of the LL Corporation to record the realiz*able* cost savings occurring during 19x6 are shown below.

> Dr. Inventory. 25,000   (1)
>   Cr. Realizable Cost Savings 25,000

To record the increase in the replacement cost of inventory sold at date(s) of sale, $13,000 and of inventory on hand at December 31, 19x6, $12,000.

> Dr. Delivery Equipment 2,000   (2)
>   Cr. Realizable Cost Savings 2,000

To record the increase in replacement cost of the delivery equipment.

> Dr. Land. 2,000   (3)
>   Cr. Realizable Cost Savings 2,000

To record the increase in replacement cost of the land.

Note that if we desired to retain the historical cost figures, the write-ups could easily be made to "asset valuation adjustment" accounts. For example, in the case of inventory, the entry would be:

Dr. Inventory Valuation Adjustment   25,000
    Cr. Realizable Cost Savings   25,000

To record the increase in the replacement cost of inventory available for sale as a separate valuation adjustment.

All cost savings are initially identified as realiz*able*, pending reclassification as realiz*ed* or *un*realiz*ed* at year end. Therefore,

> Realiz*able* Cost Savings = Realiz*ed* Cost Savings
>   + *Un*realiz*ed* Cost Savings

Like realiz*able* cost savings, realiz*ed* cost savings are also *flows*. Realiz*ed* cost savings arise as the assets to which realiz*able* cost savings relate are sold or used up. The journal entries to record cost savings realiz*ed* by the LL Corporation during 19x6 are shown below. Looking first at inventory, we begin with the replacement cost of goods sold.

Realized Cost Savings

Dr. Cost of Goods Sold   35,000   (4)
    Cr. Inventory   35,000

To record the cost of goods sold, measured by replacement cost as of the date(s) of sale.

As this merchandise has now been sold, the realiz*able* cost savings associated with it have now become realiz*ed*.

Dr. Realizable Cost Savings   13,000   (5)
    Cr. Realized Cost Savings   13,000

To recognize the realization of $13,000 of realizable cost savings on the inventory sold during 19x6. (These cost savings were initially recorded in entry (1) as realiz*able*.)

Next, we show the treatment of replacement cost depreciation. At this point, after entry (2), the carrying value (and depreciable amount) of the delivery equipment is equal to its current replacement cost of $10,000. The entry to record replacement cost depreciation is as follows.

Dr. Depreciation Expense   2,500   (6)
    Cr. Accumulated Depreciation   2,500

To record straight-line depreciation for 19x6, based on replacement cost of $10,000, a 4-year life and no salvage value.

As in the case of asset revaluations, historical cost may also be preserved in accumulated depreciation. This is achieved by recording the difference between replacement cost depreciation and historical cost depreciation in a separate account, as shown in the following entry.

Dr. Depreciation Expense	2,500	
Cr. Accumulated Depreciation		2,000
Cr. Accumulated Depreciation Valuation Adjustment . . .		500

To record replacement cost straight-line depreciation for 19x6, keeping the amount attributable to the increase in replacement cost separate as a valuation adjustment to accumulated depreciation.

Replacement cost depreciation exceeds historical cost depreciation by $500, one-fourth of the increase in replacement cost. Since one-fourth of the delivery equipment's service potential has been used, this $500 represents a cost saving that has been *realized through use*. The journal entry is:

Dr. Realizable Cost Savings	500		(7)
Cr. Realized Cost Savings		500	

To record the realization of the cost saving represented by the excess of replacement cost depreciation over historical cost depreciation. (These cost savings were initially recorded in entry (2) as realiz*able*.)

All that remains now is to reclassify the remaining realiz*able* cost savings which relate to those assets still on hand as *un*realiz*ed* at the end of 19x6.

Unrealized Cost Savings

Unlike realiz*able* and realiz*ed* cost savings, *un*realiz*ed* cost savings are *stocks,* not *flows*. They represent cost savings attributable to assets *still on hand* at the end of the period. The *un*realiz*ed* cost savings do not disappear at the end of the accounting period; they remain in the *unrealized cost savings* account until realiz*ed* in a subsequent period.

At December 31, 19x6, a total of $15,500 in cost savings which became realiz*able* during the year have not been realiz*ed* through sale or use. This includes $12,000 on the ending inventory, $1,500 on the undepreciated portion of the delivery equipment and $2,000 on the land. A single entry will reclassify these cost savings as *un*realiz*ed*, thus closing out the realiz*able* cost savings account.

Dr. Realizable Cost Savings	15,500		(8)
Cr. Unrealized Cost Savings		15,500	

To reflect the fact that $15,500 in cost savings which became realiz*able* during 19x6 on inventory, delivery equipment and land are unrealized at December 31, 19x6. (These cost savings were initially recorded in entries (1), (2) and (3) as realiz*able*.)

Exhibit 4.6—Flow of Revenues, Costs and Cost Savings in Replacement Cost Accounting

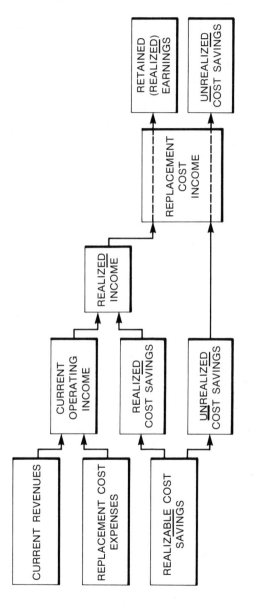

Note: Observe that replacement cost income consists of current operating income plus realizable cost savings. Replacement cost income, like historical cost income, is a temporary account and will be closed to stockholders' equity. Two equity accounts have been provided for this purpose. Since separate disclosure of unrealized cost savings is desirable, the realized and unrealized portions of replacement cost income are accumulated in separate stockholders' equity accounts.

Closing Entries. To place journal entries (1)–(8) in proper perspective, consider Exhibit 4.6, a representation of the flow of revenues, costs and cost savings in replacement cost accounting. The flow chart also suggests the form of the closing entries, which complete the replacement cost accounting cycle.

The replacement cost closing entries can now be shown.

Dr. Sales	49,000		(9)
Cr. Cost of Goods Sold		35,000	
Cr. Depreciation Expense		2,500	
Cr. Current Operating Income		11,500	

To close current revenues and replacement cost expenses to current operating income.

Dr. Current Operating Income	11,500		(10)
Dr. Realized Cost Savings	13,500		
Cr. Realized Income		25,000	

To close current operating income and realiz*ed* cost savings to realiz*ed* income.

Dr. Realized Income.	25,000		(11)*
Dr. Unrealized Cost Savings	15,500		
Cr. Replacement Cost Income		40,500	

To close realiz*ed* income and *un*realiz*ed* cost savings to replacement cost income.

Dr. Replacement Cost Income	40,500		(12)*
Cr. Retained (Realized) Earnings		25,000	
Cr. Unrealized Cost Savings		15,500	

To close replacement cost income to stockholders' equity, with appropriate identification of the realiz*ed* and *un*realiz*ed* portions.

These entries are posted to the appropriate general ledger "T" accounts, as shown in Exhibit 4.7.

---

*As an alternative, an account for replacement cost income need not be set up. Rather, realiz*ed* income could be closed directly to retained (realiz*ed*) earnings, leaving the balance in *un*realiz*ed* cost savings undisturbed.

Exhibit 4.7

Partial General Ledger of the LL Corporation, 19x6

Inventory			
Beg. Balance	50,000	(4)	35,000
(1)	25,000	To Balance	40,000
	75,000		75,000
Balance	40,000		

Delivery Equipment			
Beg. Balance	8,000	To Balance	10,000
(2)	2,000		
	10,000		10,000
Balance	10,000		

Land			
Beg. Balance	10,000	To Balance	12,000
(3)	2,000		
	12,000		12,000
Balance	12,000		

Cost of Goods Sold			
(4)	35,000	(9)	35,000

Accumulated Depreciation			
To Balance	2,500	(6)	2,500
		Balance	2,500

Realizable Cost Savings			
(5)	13,000	(1)	25,000
(7)	500	(2)	2,000
(8)	15,500	(3)	2,000
	29,000		29,000

Realized Cost Savings			
(10)	13,500	(5)	13,000
		(7)	500
	13,500		13,500

Unrealized Cost Savings			
(11)	15,500	(8)	15,500
To Balance	15,500	(12)	15,500
	31,000		31,000
		Balance	15,500

Sales			
(9)	49,000	Beg. Bal.	49,000

Depreciation Expense			
(6)	2,500	(9)	2,500

Current Operating Income			
(10)	11,500	(9)	11,500

Realized Income			
(11)	25,000	(10)	25,000

Replacement Cost Income			
(12)	40,500	(11)	40,500

Retained (Realized) Earnings			
To Balance	43,000	Beg. Balance	18,000
		(12)	25,000
	43,000		43,000
		Balance	43,000

It will be useful to elaborate on the treatment of the realiz*able* cost savings. First, the astute reader will observe that the realiz*ed* cost savings in 19x6 exactly offset the excess of replacement cost expenses over historical cost expenses [$13,500 = $37,500 − $24,000]. Indeed, the replacement cost income method merely *reclassifies* and *identifies* these cost savings. Thus, the results of operations as expressed by the current operating income figure are not distorted. As previously indicated, realiz*ed* income (current operating income plus realiz*ed* cost savings) is identical with historical cost net income. The difference lies in the *separate disclosure* of operating profits and holding gains (cost savings).

Second, the *un*realiz*ed* cost savings of $15,500 exactly equals the increase in the undepreciated values of the assets due to increases in replacement costs. We have elected to include them on the income statement. Of course, total profit is thus increased by $15,500, precisely the difference between replacement cost income ($40,500) and historical cost income ($25,000). This does *not* represent a mere reclassification between operating profit and holding gains. In fact, many accountants prefer to take the *un*realiz*ed* cost savings directly to stockholders' equity, bypassing the income statement. Disclosure of *un*realiz*ed* cost savings on the income statement, however, provides more useful information. If *un*realiz*ed* cost savings were carried straight to stockholders' equity, the bottom line of the replacement cost income statement would be *realized income* and, hence, would be equal to historical cost net income.

Other Financial Statements.   This example would not be complete without the statements of financial position and changes in financial position for the LL Corporation. Exhibits 4.8 and 4.9 show both statements prepared under historical cost and replacement cost accounting. We assume that all sales and purchases in 19x6 were made in cash.

A Brief Analysis and Evaluation of Replacement Cost Accounting

Replacement cost accounting has two major advantages in its presentation of significant financial information. The statement of financial position, under historical cost accounting, loses its economic significance when large price movements have rendered its historical valuations virtually meaningless. Indeed, many historical cost valuations have only limited significance in the sense that they represent past expenditures awaiting eventual write-off to the income statement. Replacement cost valuations, however, *do* reflect the effects of changing prices. Position statement valuations are stated at the *amounts* the firm would have to pay, at the financial statement date, to replace the assets included in the statement. Thus, replacement cost accounting generates currently meaninful position statements.

Second, replacement cost income statements disclose considerably more information than do conventional historical cost income statements.

Exhibit 4.8

LL CORPORATION
Statement of Financial Position
December 31, 19x6

ASSETS	Historical Cost	Replacement Cost	LIABILITIES AND STOCKHOLDERS' EQUITY	Historical Cost	Replacement Cost
Cash	$19,000	$19,000	Liabilities	$14,000	$14,000
Inventory	28,000	40,000	Stockholders' Equity:		
Total Current Assets	$47,000	$59,000	Capital Stock	6,000	6,000
Delivery Equipment	$ 8,000	$10,000	Retained (Realized)		
Less: Accumulated			Earnings	43,000	43,000
Depreciation	2,000	2,500	Unrealized Cost Savings		15,500
	$ 6,000	$ 7,500	Total Liabilities and		
Land	10,000	12,000	Stockholders' Equity	$63,000	$78,500
Total Assets	$63,000	$78,500			

NOTE: Under the replacement cost method, assets are stated at their replacement costs. The difference of $15,500 in total assets (equities) between the two methods is equal to the *unrealized* cost savings attributable to the assets on hand at December 31, 19x6.

Exhibit 4.9

LL CORPORATION
Statement of Changes in Financial Position
for the Year Ended December 31, 19x6

	Historical Cost	Replacement Cost
SOURCES OF WORKING CAPITAL		
Historical Cost Net Income	$25,000	
Replacement Cost Income		$40,500
Add Depreciation Expense		
Not Using Working Capital	2,000	2,500
		$43,000
Subtract Realizable Cost Savings		
Not Providing Working Capital:		
On Delivery Equipment		$ 2,000
On Land		$ 2,000
		$ 4,000
Working Capital Provided by Operations	$27,000	$39,000
TOTAL SOURCES OF WORKING CAPITAL	$27,000	$39,000
Increases in Working Capital Accounts		
Cash	$19,000	$19,000
Inventory	8,000	20,000
Increase in Working Capital	$27,000	$39,000

NOTE: This statement does not provide for applications or uses of working capital during 19x6, as there were none in our example. The differences attributed to the replacement cost method are three. (1) An additional $500 for depreciation was added back. This is the excess of replacement cost depreciation over historical cost depreciation. (2) *Realizable* cost savings on nonworking capital assets must be removed from the increases in working capital. Although included in replacement cost income, they do not affect working capital. (3) An additional $12,000 in working capital was provided by the increase in replacement cost of inventory on hand. This is included in replacement cost income (as *unrealized* cost savings) and accounts for the larger increase in working capital under replacement cost accounting.

Operating profits are clearly separated from holding gains; in this way, the efficiency of operations can be evaluated through reference to current operating income. Furthermore, the effects of price changes are clearly identified as realiz*able* cost savings which were either realiz*ed* during the year or remain *un*realiz*ed* at year end. Since realized income is the sum of current operating income and realiz*ed* cost savings, we are able to observe the significance of each component of historical cost income. //

Consider for a moment the implications of the *contribution margin* (revenues less variable expenses, excluding depreciation) under both methods. The replacement cost contribution margin reflects current costs and revenues. In the absence of further price changes, an amount equal to the replacement cost contribution margin of $14,000 could be paid out in dividends without impairing the *physical capacity* of operations, that is, management could continue operations at the same level in the future without additional external financing. On the other hand, if the historical cost contribution margin of $27,000 was all paid out in dividends, future operations would decline because insufficient funds would be retained within the firm to replace the inventory that was sold at prevailing prices. Furthermore, it is the replacement cost contribution margin of $14,000 that management can expect similar operations to yield in the future, again assuming no further changes in prices.

In the long run, sufficient revenues must be generated to cover all costs, including the depreciation on fixed assets. To assess long-run profitability, then, the current cost of all resource inputs must be measured. Current operating income provides this measure; historical cost income does not. Indeed, when prices are changing, historical cost income is of little value in predicting future profits and in assessing long-run profitability. In our example, the $11,500 current operating income is useful in assessing long-run profitability, for it measures all costs at their current replacement prices.

To complete this brief analysis, Exhibit 4.10 provides a reconciliation between historical cost income and replacement cost income.

Exhibit 4.10

LL CORPORATION

Reconciliation of Historical Cost Income and Replacement
Cost Income for the Year Ended December 31, 19x6

Replacement Cost Income	$40,500
Less: Realizable Cost Savings	29,000
Replacement Cost Current Operating Income	$11,500
Plus: Realized Cost Savings	13,500
Historical Cost Income (= Realized Income)	$25,000

Historical cost income, then, consists of both operating income (i.e., current operating income) *and* holding gains (i.e., realiz*ed* cost savings). The realiz*ed* cost savings are attributable wholly to changes in prices of assets sold or used up to the time of their sale or use. Failure to disclose this fact may be misleading. In our example, almost one-half of the historical cost income is due to price changes, *not* to operations. This problem is compounded by the fact that such gains are reflected (but not separately identified) in historical cost income *only* when they are realized. Although our example does not treat this problem specifically, if some of the realiz*ed* cost savings had in fact become realiz*able* in 19x5 (the previous year), historical cost net income would not disclose this. In fact, historical cost net income includes operating income and all cost savings realiz*ed* during the current period, regardless of when those cost savings first became realiz*able*.

A final comment on the reconciliation concerns the disclosure of the cost savings which became realiz*able* during 19x6. This $29,000 reflects the effects of price changes on the firm during 19x6. It serves as a measure of the overall effect of management's holding activities in 19x6. Historical cost net income, of course, fails to address this issue at all.

Attention should be given to the disposition of *un*realiz*ed* cost savings if they become realiz*ed* in subsequent periods. To do so, we must reconcile three apparently conflicting statements. (1) Realiz*able* cost savings refer to those cost savings arising in a given year. (2) Realiz*able* cost savings = realiz*ed* cost savings + *un*realiz*ed* cost savings. (3) Cost savings realiz*ed* in any given year will normally include cost savings which became realiz*able* in the current year *and* cost savings which were *un*realiz*ed* at the beginning of the year (i.e., they became realiz*able* in previous years).

Once we admit the likely possibility of statement (3), that current period realiz*ed* cost savings will include some cost savings which were *un*realiz*ed* at the beginning of the period, statements (1) and (2) become incompatible. If realiz*able* cost savings are those which arose in the current year, then they must exclude any prior period cost savings. And if realiz*ed* cost savings reflect both current and prior period realiz*able* cost savings, then the identity expressed in statement (2) cannot hold. The way out of this dilemma is to modify the identity in statement (2) in the following way.

Treatment of Cost Savings in Subsequent Periods

Realiz*able* Cost Savings = Realiz*ed* Cost Savings +
  Change in *Un*realiz*ed* Cost Savings

Prior period cost savings realized in the current period reduce unrealized cost savings and increase realized cost savings. On the other hand, whenever realizable cost savings remain unrealized at year end, unrealized cost savings increase. Thus, the *change* in unrealized cost savings is the net effect of decreases associated with realization of prior period cost savings and increases associated with unrealized realizable cost savings.

Exhibit 4.11 shows cost savings data for each of three years. Each year's realizable cost savings which remain unrealized are assumed to be realized in the next period. Exhibit 4.11 indicates that realizable cost savings, current period realized and unrealized cost savings, and total realized cost savings plus the change in unrealized cost savings are all equal.

Exhibit 4.11

Realiz*able*, Realiz*ed* and *Un*realiz*ed* Cost Savings

Year	Current Period Realizable Realizable =	Realized +	Unrealized =	Current and Prior Period Realizable Realized +	Change in Unrealized	Balance in Unrealized
1	10,000	8,000	2,000	8,000	2,000	2,000
2	15,000	10,000	5,000	12,000	3,000	5,000
3	18,000	8,000	10,000	13,000	5,000	10,000
Total	43,000	26,000	17,000	33,000	10,000	10,000

Therefore, when only current period realizable cost savings are involved, total realizable cost savings is the sum of the realized and unrealized portions. However, when prior period cost savings are realized in the current period, realizable cost savings is the sum of total realized cost savings and the *change* in the balance of unrealized cost savings.

Summary   In the overview of the main concepts of replacement cost accounting, we highlighted two important aspects of replacement cost accounting. First, the method values assets on the position statement at the cost currently required to replace them. Second, operating income is separated from holding gains and the overall impact of changing prices is disclosed. Now it is time to pursue the conceptual and technical aspects of replacement cost accounting in more detail. We turn to a discussion of the theoretical basis for replacement cost accounting in Chapter 5.

Questions and Problems

4.1. In a period of *changing* prices, net income determined in accordance with generally accepted accounting principles (GAAP) may not adequately measure a firm's performance. How? What performance *should* be measured?

4.2. "In a period of *stable* prices, net income determined in accordance with GAAP will generally be a useful measure of performance." Is this likely to be true? Why?

4.3. Briefly discuss the meaning and usefulness of a statement of financial position prepared in accordance with GAAP (a) when prices are changing and (b) when prices are stable.

4.4. Why is replacement cost accounting a topic worth studying?

4.5. A firm purchased 100 widules for $4.00 each on July 1, year 1. On December 20, year 1, 50 widules were sold for $5.00 each; the cost to replace the sold widules was $4.50 each. On March 31, year 2, the remaining widules were sold for $5.50 each; their replacement cost had risen to $5.10.

Required: Contrast the treatment of the above transactions under historical cost accounting and replacement cost accounting.

4.6. What is a holding gain (loss)? As a user of financial statements, would you be interested in the magnitude of holding gains (losses)? Why or why not?

4.7. What is meant by realizable holding gains? Explain the relationship between realizable holding gains, realized holding gains and unrealized holding gains.

4.8. In a replacement cost accounting system, we choose to refer to holding gains as *cost savings*. What is a cost saving and why is it usually more descriptive of a price-change event than holding gain?

4.9. The newly formed Jamestown Company is considering the adoption of replacement cost accounting after its second year of operation. Its statement of financial position at the end of year 1 and year 2 data appear below.

Jamestown Company
Statement of Financial Position
December 31, Year 1

ASSETS
Cash	$ 2,000
Inventory	5,000
Fixed Asset	18,000
Total Assets	$25,000

LIABILITIES AND STOCKHOLDERS' EQUITY

Accounts Payable.	$ 4,000
Capital Stock.	15,000
Retained Earnings	6,000
Total Liabilities and Stockholders' Equity	$25,000

YEAR 2 DATA

The fixed asset was purchased at the end of year 1; it has a 10-year life and no salvage value. Straight-line depreciation is to be used (none allocated in year 1). Early in year 2, the asset's replacement cost rose to $20,000.

Cash sales = $40,000.
Inventory purchases = $18,000, paid in cash.
Ending inventory = $3,000 (replacement cost = $4,000).
Replacement cost of goods sold (at dates of sale) = $21,700.
During the year, $2,000 was spent on land; its replacement cost at year end was $2,300.

Required:

a. Prepare journal entries to record all transactions during the year, including the year-end replacement cost adjustments (use "valuation adjustment" accounts).

b. Prepare a complete set of financial statements for the Jamestown Company in year 2 (including a statement of changes in financial position) under both historical cost and replacement cost accounting.

c. Prepare a reconciliation between current operating income, historical cost net income and replacement cost income.

The Theory behind   5
Replacement Cost Accounting

Replacement cost accounting relies heavily on the notion that income can arise in more than one way. Disclosure of the various ways in which income arises is therefore important. We now consider the definition of income, as well as the nature and disclosure of its components, more carefully.

For accounting purposes, net income or loss has been traditionally defined as the difference between revenues earned and expenses incurred during a period of time. We argued in Chapter 4 that the traditional historical cost income calculation falls short of reflecting all income-related events occurring during a period. We believe that a more complete and conceptually superior net income calculation should be based on the so-called Hicksian or economic definition of income, after the well-known British economist, Sir John Hicks. According to this definition, income is "the maximum amount which he [a man] can consume during a week, and still expect to be as well off at the end of the week as he was at the beginning."*

Net Income: Operating Income and Realizable Income

In those terms, net income carries with it the connotation of relative degrees of *well-offness* and implies that the total change in net worth (adjusted for capital changes), including increases and decreases in asset and liability values, is a useful measurement of income. In our opinion, accounting income should be augmented to more nearly reflect economic income, especially during periods in which prices and values are changing significantly.

It must be recognized that income has two basic components. *Operating income* of a firm results from producing and selling goods and services. *Realizable income* accrues to the firm over time as the prices of its assets and liabilities change; it does not relate to sales at all. Reali*zable* income refers to holding gains and cost savings that are generated by changes in the specific prices of assets and liabilities.

---

*J. R. Hicks, *Value and Capital* (Oxford: Clarendon Press, 1946), p. 172.

Operating income is usually a guide to long-run profitability, whereas realiz*able* income (holding gains and cost savings) is often irregular, and hence may not be of a recurring nature. Therefore, to maintain the predictive power of the operating income figure, operating income should be shown separately and not be distorted by combining it with income not generated by operations. Conventional historical cost accounting statements, of course, do not separate operating income from realiz*able* income.

Realized Income vs.
Realizable Income

Realiz*ed* income refers to the gains associated with the sale of the firm's products or other assets. These gains may be in the form of realiz*ed* operating income or realiz*ed* holding gains. Realiz*able* income refers to the gains which *could* be realiz*ed* if the product (at any stage in the production process) or other asset were to be sold at current market prices. In the context of replacement costs, realiz*able* income arises whenever the current replacement cost of assets held exceeds their acquisition cost. Realiz*able* income, then, refers to realiz*able* cost savings and realiz*able* holding gains. Furthermore, the realiz*able* income concept suggests that income is being earned continually as products move through the stages of production toward their eventual sale and as the prices of other assets and liabilities change.

Income or loss, therefore, could be recognized when the value of assets at any point in time differs from the value of all inputs used in their production up to that point or from their acquisition cost. For example, suppose a firm could sell a semifinished product for $100 on June 1 and the same product for $105 on June 30. If the cost of raw materials used to produce the semifinished product was $50 and the cost of labor and overhead was $25 (assume no storage cost), the realiz*able* income is $25 on June 1 and $30 on June 30.

Theoretically, income could be recorded continually as it becomes realiz*able*. In the real world, of course, this would be highly impractical. So we choose intervals for recording realiz*able* income (normally 12-month intervals). At the end of each interval we propose establishing the values of assets and liabilities on hand so that the realiz*able* income can be determined. These values reflect the changes in the specific prices of those assets.

One widely accepted approach to the calculation of realiz*able* income involves *replacement costs*.* The *replacement cost income* method uses replacement costs as measures of the effects of *changes* in specific prices. When replacement costs are used, realiz*able* income is designated *realizable cost savings*.

---

*Other bases for valuation and for use in determining realiz*able* income are discussed later in the chapter.

For temporary investments such as marketable securities, however, we prefer to designate realiz*able* income as realiz*able* holding gains rather than cost savings. Although *holding gains* and *cost savings* have the same fundamental meaning, we believe that holding gains are more descriptive of the price changes accruing to temporary investments. Until the product or asset is actually sold, increases in prices result in realiz*able* cost savings, as the replacement costs of the input resources exceed their historical costs. Realiz*able* income in the context of replacement cost accounting refers to those gains which accrue to the firm because it purchased input resources or other assets at prices *lower* than those currently prevailing. The following example relates the realiz*ed* and realiz*able* income concepts to operating income, holding gains and cost savings.

Consider a retail firm, in its first year of operation, which has the following historical cost account balances at the end of the year.

Merchandise Sales	$100,000
Merchandise Purchases	80,000
Ending Merchandise Inventory	10,000
Cost of Goods Sold	70,000
Purchases of Marketable Securities	20,000
Proceeds from Sales of One-Fourth of the Marketable Securities	16,000
Marketable Securities on Hand at Year End (three-fourths)	15,000

The relevant replacement cost information follows.

Cost of Goods Sold (at replacement cost at date(s) of sale)	$ 75,000
Ending Merchandise Inventory	14,000
Replacement Cost of Marketable Securities When Sold	8,000
Marketable Securities on Hand at Year End	18,000

Using these data, we prepare statements of income under historical cost accounting (Exhibit 5.1) and replacement cost accounting (Exhibit 5.2).

Exhibit 5.1

Statement of Income (Historical Cost)

SALES	$100,000
Cost of Goods Sold	70,000
Operating Income	$ 30,000
Gain on Sale of Securities	1,000
NET INCOME	$ 31,000

Exhibit 5.2

Statement of Income (Replacement Cost)

SALES	$100,000
Cost of Goods Sold	75,000
CURRENT OPERATING INCOME	$ 25,000
Realized Cost Savings—Excess of Replacement Cost of Goods Sold over Historical Cost of Goods Sold	5,000
Realized Holding Gain on Sale of Securities	$ 1,000
REALIZED INCOME	$ 31,000
Unrealized Cost Savings at Year End: Excess of Replacement Cost over Historical Cost of Ending Inventory	$ 4,000
Unrealized Holding Gains at Year End: Excess of Replacement Cost over Historical Cost of Marketable Securities on Hand	3,000
	$ 7,000
REPLACEMENT COST INCOME	$ 38,000

NOTE: Realiz*able* income consists of all realiz*able* cost savings and holding gains, both realiz*ed* and *un*realized. In this example, realiz*able* income is $13,000.

In Exhibits 5.1 and 5.2, historical cost net income ($31,000) includes both current operating income ($25,000) and realiz*ed* cost savings and holding gains ($6,000) and is equal to realiz*ed* income. Therefore, realiz*ed* income actually splits historical cost income into two parts: current operating income and realiz*ed* cost savings and holding gains. Separate disclosure of each of these parts is important, even though they do add up to the historical cost net income.

Furthermore, historical cost net income does not recognize the *un*realiz*ed* effects of price changes, so *un*realized cost savings and holding gains are excluded. When price changes have been significant, these items can be material and should be disclosed. Realiz*able* income, of course, includes and separately discloses these *un*realized effects of specific price changes.

We believe, therefore, that periodic income measurement reflecting *both* operating income and realiz*able* income comes close to meeting the Hicksian definition of income.

The essence of accounting for changes in specific prices is to recognize these price changes in asset valuation when the financial statements are prepared. Replacement cost is only one of several possible bases of valuation.

At least three dimensions to the valuation of an asset should be considered: (1) *form*, whether initial (raw material), present (work in process), or ultimate (finished product); (2) *valuation date*, past, present, or future; and (3) the *market* in which the firm could *buy* the asset in the specified form or in which the firm could *sell* the asset in its specified form.

The prices obtained in markets in which the asset is bought are referred to as *entry prices* because they are the prices at which assets enter or could enter the firm. The prices obtained in markets in which the asset is sold are referred to as *exit prices* because they are the prices at which assets are or could be disposed of by the firm.

**Alternative Bases
for Valuation and
Income Measurement**

In the valuation of an asset, *entry prices* can be measured in at least four ways. (1) *Historical cost*, the actual past amount paid to acquire the inputs which the firm used to produce or acquire the asset in its present form. (2) *Present cost*, the amount currently required to acquire (not produce) the asset in its present form. (3) *Replacement cost*, the amount currently required to acquire and convert the inputs to produce, using current technology, the service potentials represented by the asset in its present form. (4) *Reproduction cost*, the amount currently required to reproduce the asset in its present form without regard to changes in technology which may affect the service potentials inherent in the asset.

Entry Prices

And in the valuation of an asset, *exit prices* can be measured in at least three ways. (1) *Expected value*, the amount the firm feels that it can receive in the future for a specified asset when sold in the ultimate form contemplated in the firm's planned course of action. (2) *Current value*, the amount actually realized during the current period for a specified asset which was sold. (3) *Opportunity value*, the amount which could currently be realized if the asset (whether a finished or semifinished good or a raw material) were to be sold in its present form. The amount would be the best price immediately obtainable outside the firm. (Also known as opportunity cost.)

Exit Prices

We now examine the uses of these valuation concepts in calculating income based on alternative valuation assumptions. In order to compare income determination using entry and exit prices as measures of specific prices, we need to select both an entry price and an exit price from the alternatives presented above. We regard *replacement cost* as the "best" entry price and *opportunity value* as the "best" exit price for purposes of income determination.

Entry price. Of the four possible entry prices (historical cost, present cost, replacement cost and reproduction cost), historical cost may be quickly deleted from further consideration. Historical costs must be preserved for income tax purposes and because they provide the starting point in measuring price changes. For financial reporting, however, we believe that inflation has destroyed the usefulness of historical cost data.

Consider the choice between replacement cost and reproduction cost. If a building or manufacturing facility was acquired or constructed several years ago, its reproduction cost would be the current cost to reproduce that asset *as it was originally constructed*, without regard to changes in technology. On the other hand, its replacement cost would be the current cost to replace the *service potentials* of the asset, given current technology. We believe that replacement cost is more relevant. Of what use is it to know how much it would cost today to produce the same electric power-generating facility originally constructed many years ago? If the facilities are to be replaced, a "new" old plant would not be built. Rather, current technology would be used to construct a plant which replaces (or even expands) the generating capacity of the old plant. Therefore, reproduction cost often becomes irrelevant. Of course, in the case of currently manufactured inventories or other assets, reproduction cost may be the same as replacement cost. In general, however, replacement rather than reproduction cost is most useful.

Looking now to the choice between *replacement cost* and *present cost*, we need to recall the definition of each. Replacement cost refers to the current cost of the *input resources* used to produce the asset in its present form; present cost, however, refers to the current cost of *acquiring the asset* in its present form. Why will replacement cost normally be different from (indeed *less than*) present cost?* *Present cost* will include not only the current cost of resource inputs but *also* any *value added* in production. This *value added* refers to the transformation of input resources, by some production process, into semifinished or finished goods. For a firm which manufactures television sets, one would normally expect that it could produce those television sets for less than it would have to pay to acquire completed television sets of equal quality on the market. Hence, the difference between the current cost of *producing* a given product internally and the current cost of *acquiring* a given product externally is the difference between replacement cost and present cost. We assume that the time lag associated with production is not significantly different from that associated with acquiring the item externally.

---

*This will be true for manufacturing firms. For retail firms, which deal only in finished products, replacement cost and present cost must be the same. In addition, firms that *purchase* rather than *construct* their plant and equipment will normally find that replacement cost is the same as present cost.

Now, a prominent feature of replacement cost accounting is that it measures and discloses current operating income (the value added in production) and realizable cost savings. If present costs were used in lieu of replacement costs, current operating income would not adequately measure value added because the costs charged against income would include the value added by another producer. This point is illustrated in the following example.

A firm manufactures and sells television sets. We are given the following data for a recent accounting period.

	Replacement Cost	Present Cost
Sales	$1,000,000	$1,000,000
Cost of Goods Manufactured and Sold	800,000	950,000
Other Operating Expenses	100,000	100,000

We assume no beginning or ending inventories and prepare income statements using these two cost concepts.

	Replacement Cost	Present Cost
SALES	$1,000,000	$1,000,000
Cost of Goods Manufactured and Sold	800,000	950,000*
Other Operating Expenses	100,000	100,000
CURRENT OPERATING INCOME	100,000	(50,000)
Realized Cost Savings: Excess of Current Cost of Goods Manufactured and Sold over Historical Cost of Goods Manufactured and Sold ($600,000)	200,000	350,000
REALIZED INCOME	$ 300,000	$ 300,000

*Based on wholesale price quotations from other producers.

Which of the two methods best reports the results of the firm's operations? Realiz*ed* income based on present cost is not adequate because current operating income based on present cost fails to measure the profitability of the firm's production-sales activities. Why? Because the cost of goods sold measured in present costs does not represent the current production costs of *this firm*. Instead, it represents the production costs and profit margins (or value added) of *another firm* or *firms*. Only current operating income based on replacement costs provides a proper measure of *our* firm's profitability.

Replacement cost, then, is the best entry price because it is the best measure of current cost and it has none of the disadvantages of the other entry price possibilities. In addition, it contains whatever advantages the other entry prices possess, with the possible exception of the objectivity inherent in historical costs. As prices change, however, the objectivity of historical cost becomes less and less relevant.

Exit Price. The three alternative exit prices we are considering are expected value, current value and opportunity value. Expected value is what the firm *expects to realize* from the future sale of a specified asset in the *ultimate* form planned by the firm. Current value is the amount *actually realized* for an asset sold during the current period. Opportunity value is the amount which *could be realized* if the asset in its *present* form were to be sold. In other words, if the asset were kept rather than sold, the firm forgoes the best selling price obtainable outside the firm, its opportunity value. Opportunity value is usually measured by *net realizable value* (selling price less cost of sale or disposal).

Of the three possible exit prices, current value is appropriate for assets actually sold, normally in their final form. But for semifinished products and for assets unsold at year end, current value is not a defined exit price. Expected value is not suitable either, for it depends on expectations about the uncertain future and is not very objective. Furthermore, it is based on the assumption that the asset will be sold in the ultimate form contemplated by the firm. Therefore, it is not suitable for valuing semifinished products. Since opportunity value represents an objective current price for the asset or product in its present form (finished or semifinished), we believe that it is the most appropriate of the possible *exit* prices.

The example given below compares income determination under historical costs, replacement costs and opportunity values. The data have been compiled for a manufacturing firm just completing its first year of operations. We assume that the opportunity values of the resource inputs when they were acquired equaled their historical costs and that the opportunity value of the delivery equipment at year end is represented by its net realizable value.

	Historical Cost	Opportunity Value	Replacement Cost
Sales (10,000 units)	$100,000	$100,000	$100,000
Cost of Goods Sold (10,000 units)	60,000	60,000	70,000
Ending Inventory (4,000 units)	24,000	40,000	31,000
Delivery Equipment (5-year life, no salvage value, straight-line depreciation)	10,000	5,000	12,000

Comparative statements of income under these alternative valuation methods are presented in Exhibit 5.3.

Exhibit 5.3

Statement of Income

	Historical Cost	Opportunity Value	Replacement Cost
SALES	$100,000	$100,000	$100,000
Cost of Goods Sold	60,000	60,000	70,000
Depreciation	2,000	5,000	2,400
CURRENT OPERATING INCOME		$ 35,000	$ 27,600
Realized Cost Savings—Goods Sold			10,000
Realized Cost Savings—Depreciation			400
Historical Cost Net Income (= realized income)	$ 38,000		$ 38,000
Increase in Opportunity Value of Inventory		16,000	
OPPORTUNITY VALUE NET INCOME		$ 51,000	
Unrealized Cost Savings—Inventory			7,000
Unrealized Cost Savings—Delivery Equipment			1,600*
REPLACEMENT COST INCOME			$ 46,600

*$1,600 = [($12,000 − $10,000) − ($2,400 − $2,000)]

Exhibit 5.4 presents a reconciliation of the three income measures.

Exhibit 5.4

Reconciliation of Historical Cost Net Income, Opportunity Value Net Income and Replacement Cost Income

CURRENT OPERATING INCOME	$27,600
Realized Cost Savings	10,400
REALIZED INCOME (HISTORICAL COST NET INCOME)	38,000
Unrealized Cost Savings	8,600
REPLACEMENT COST INCOME	46,600
Delivery Equipment: Difference between Opportunity Value and Replacement Cost Depreciation (5,000 − 2,400)	(2,600)
Delivery Equipment: Realizable Cost Savings	
Realized Cost Savings	(400)
Unrealized Cost Savings	(1,600)
Ending Inventory: Difference between Opportunity Value and Replacement Cost Unrealized Increase (16,000 − 7,000)	9,000
OPPORTUNITY VALUE NET INCOME	$51,000

As mentioned previously, historical cost net income ($38,000) includes both current operating income ($27,600) and realized cost savings ($10,400). However, only replacement cost accounting separates the respective amounts of these two components. Income computed using opportunity values *augments* replacement cost income. The extent to which the net change in the opportunity values of assets still on hand exceeds the net change in their replacement cost book values is included in opportunity value net income. In our example, this amount is $4,400 [= $9,000 − $4,600].

The opportunity value of inventory on hand rose by $16,000, while the replacement cost rose by only $7,000. This difference of $9,000 represents value added by production and is recognized in the current year. On the other hand, the opportunity value of the delivery equipment, which is now *used* rather than *new*, fell by $5,000. This is $4,600 more than the decline of $400 in the replacement cost book value of the equipment ($2,400 depreciation less cost savings totaling $2,000).

This example illustrates the fundamental distinction between net income based on opportunity values and replacement cost income. Replacement cost income, of course, includes realiz*able* income based on replacement costs. We believe that replacement costs are preferred over opportunity values for purposes of income determination. We base our preference on the following reasons.

Bases for Preferring a Replacement Cost Entry Price over an Opportunity Value Exit Price

Opportunity value is not necessarily *unique*. The net realizable value of an asset may depend on how quickly it must be sold or whether it is to be sold singly or in conjunction with other assets. Many people who have sold homes will agree that a quick sale usually results in a lower selling price than might be obtainable if time were not a factor. In addition, an entire plant would probably bring a different price than the total of the separate prices of the building and individual pieces of equipment. Similarly, the sale of an entire division or line of business would be expected to generate more revenue than the sum of the individual sales of portions of the division or line of business. Consequently, many opportunity values might be chosen; it is not clear which would be appropriate.*

Opportunity value is not as *objective* as replacement cost. Opportunity value is based on hypothetical sales, while replacement costs are usually, but not always, derived from market transactions. Replacement costs

*One could argue that replacement cost may also lack uniqueness. However, replacement cost of facilities, equipment or other assets would be based on the scale with which they are being used by the firm. Net realizable values, however, are based on the state of the secondhand sales market in which disposal could be arranged in a variety of ways, some of which would surely involve piecemeal sales.

should be more easily audited, especially where replacement costs are calculated using price indexes specific to particular types of assets.

Some assets have value in *use*, but little or no value in *exchange*. For example, one's eyeglasses or contact lenses have significant value in use but virtually no value in exchange. Many firms own assets which are similarly valuable only when used by the firm. Indeed, the decision of a firm to keep an asset, rather than sell it, is *prima facie* evidence that management believes its value in use is at least as great as its net realizable value. In such circumstances, net realizable value is a poor measure of the asset's current value to the firm. The opportunity values of assets having characteristics unique to a particular production process or line of business would significantly understate their value to the firm.

Like historical cost, opportunity value fails to clearly identify the results of *holding* activities. Realiz*able* cost savings in replacement cost accounting reflect the effects of pure price changes. Since our aim *is* accounting for changing prices, we attach great importance to this.

Opportunity values do not provide us with *current operating income*, which has *predictive* usefulness. Current operating income is a repetitive measure and excludes past prices and their effects on this period. By matching current costs with current revenues, it is a good indicator of *current profitability*. If there are no further price changes, it provides a good forecast of the *future profitability* of the same level of operations.

Replacement cost, not opportunity value, preserves the *cost* basis of accounting, which has merit because it provides information regarding the *current* cost and profitability of operations. For example, such information may be used as a guide to whether to leave an industry, whether competitors may be expected to enter the industry, or whether to expand or contract our investment in that industry.

The use of an exit price such as opportunity value obtained in a market in which the firm is usually a *buyer* (such as markets for buildings and equipment) would report *unusual* values suitable for *unusual* situations.* This might be suitable in a liquidation situation but seems inappropriate for a going concern.

The use of opportunity values obtained from markets in which the firm is usually a *seller* (such as the goods markets) cannot be objected to as being unusual. However, such a practice would tend to lead to the recognition of operating income (or value added) in advance of its realization. This would weaken the usefulness of current operating income.

We recognize that there are problems in obtaining the current replacement costs of assets which are unique in nature, or which are not regularly traded in competitive markets. While formidable, this is not an insoluble

---

*This discussion is based on arguments presented in E. O. Edwards, "The State of Current Value Accounting," *The Accounting Review* (April 1975): especially pp. 239–42.

problem. It will be eased if the concepts discussed here become accepted and widely used, because the demand for more accurate replacement cost data will rise and more effort will be made to supply these data. We will return to this problem in our detailed discussion of the treatment of fixed assets in a replacement cost accounting system, in Chapter 7 and again in Chapter 10.

Summary of the Components of Replacement Cost Income

Replacement cost income consists of two main components. *Current operating income* is the current value of the output sold less the replacement cost of related resource inputs, measured at the date(s) the output was sold. *Realizable income* as measured by realiz*able* cost savings and holding gains represents the difference between the replacement cost of assets held during the period (which were either sold or remain on hand at the end of the period) and their replacement cost at the beginning of the period (or acquisition cost if they were acquired during the period). Any realiz*able* cost savings attributable to assets *sold* or *used* during the period are deemed realiz*ed*. The remaining realiz*able* cost savings relate to assets still on hand and are *un*realiz*ed*.

Income determined by conventional historical cost accounting procedures would differ from replacement cost income by the amount of the *un*realiz*ed* cost savings during the period. Furthermore, historical cost operating income (current value of outputs sold less historical cost of inputs) would include, but not separately disclose, the realiz*ed* cost savings.

We now proceed to discuss in detail the actual functioning of a replacement cost accounting system. Specifically, we will provide examples of how to apply the replacement cost measure of new specific prices to the accounts which would typically be affected. Recall that monetary assets represent fixed quantities of dollars, regardless of changes in prices. Since their value is fixed at these stated dollar amounts, this is the same whether we use replacement cost, historical cost or any other valuation approach. Hence, no adjustments are required for monetary assets. Consequently, we begin in the next chapter with a discussion of replacement cost accounting as applied to inventories.

Questions and Problems

5.1. Compare net income measured according to generally accepted accounting principles (GAAP) with the Hicksian or economic definition of income. Indicate both similarities and differences in the two income concepts.

5.2. Critically evaluate "well-offness" as it relates to income measurement. What, in your opinion, are its strengths and weaknesses?

5.3. Briefly discuss the meanings of operating income and realizable income and clearly state the difference between the two concepts.

5.4. What do you see as similarities between the Hicksian concept of income and replacement cost income? What differences do you perceive?

5.5. In your own words, define entry price and exit price. Give an example which clearly indicates the difference between the two concepts.

5.6. We have stated a preference for the use of replacement cost entry price data in measuring realizable income. All accountants do not agree with this preference. Briefly argue for the "exit price" position.

5.7. Define "value added." Why is this concept important in discussing various ways of measuring income?

5.8. Unless significant evidence exists to the contrary, economic entities are accounted for as "going concerns." What does the entry/exit price controversy imply about the "going concern" assumption?

5.9. Consider the following data for the Mycroft Corporation. The firm has just completed its first year of operations. The plant, equipment and patents were acquired early in the year.

	Historical Cost	Opportunity Value	Replacement Cost
Sales	$75,000	$ 75,000	$ 75,000
Cost of Goods Sold	50,000	50,000	60,000
Inventory.	20,000	32,000	25,000
Patents (5-year life)	1,000	100,000	?
Cost of Plant and Equipment	40,000	15,000	80,000
(10 percent straight-line depreciation)			

Required:

a. Briefly discuss how the replacement cost of the patents might be determined.

b. Assume that the year-end replacement cost of the patents is $79,000, and that replacement cost depreciation and amortization is based on the average replacement cost for the year. Prepare comparative income statements using the historical cost, opportunity value and replacement cost data.

c. For the assets given, show their presentation on the statement of financial position, after any depreciation and amortization, using the historical cost, opportunity value and replacement cost data. Comment on the usefulness of the three presentations.

Replacement Cost Treatment of Inventories

In conventional historical cost accounting, inventories are generally valued at acquisition cost. Application of the "lower of cost or market" rule leads to occasional write-downs below acquisition cost. However, it is not always possible to determine the acquisition cost of inventory on hand with a high degree of precision. When costs are changing and products are similar, it is difficult to know which costs apply to units that have been sold and which costs apply to units remaining in inventory. There are several cost flow assumptions commonly used to resolve this problem. The cost flow assumption selected in a given situation depends upon financial accounting theory and income tax considerations.

Our approach in this chapter will be to review three widely used cost flow assumptions in accounting for inventories under historical cost accounting. We will then develop a replacement cost approach to inventory accounting and show how it would be applied when each of these historical inventory cost flow assumptions is being used.

When periodic inventory accounting is used, the following simple equation can be used to determine the cost of goods sold.

Cost of Goods Sold = Beginning Inventory + Purchases
− Ending Inventory

We will employ the periodic method of accounting for inventories but will discuss perpetual inventory accounting in a later section. The following data will be used throughout most of the chapter.

	Units	Price/Unit	Total
Beginning Inventory, 1/1	200	$14.00	$2,800.00
Purchases:			
3/1	80	14.75	$1,180.00
5/15	150	15.20	2,280.00
8/29	90	15.80	1,422.00
12/1	120	16.10	1,932.00
Total Purchases			$6,814.00

Ending Inventory, 12/31   220

   Purchase Price at December 31 of the previous period = $14.45
   Purchase Price at December 31 of the current period = $16.25

Review of Historical Cost Inventory Accounting

FIFO (first-in, first-out).   Under the FIFO cost flow assumption, the first units purchased were the first units sold. The ending inventory will therefore consist of the most recent purchases and be valued at the most recent purchase prices.* If we apply this cost flow assumption to the data, ending inventory (220 units) would be valued as follows:

Units	Price/Unit	Total
120.	$16.10	$1,932.00
90.	15.80	1,422.00
10.	15.20	152.00
Ending Inventory (FIFO)		$3,506.00

The cost of goods sold is $6,108.00, as shown below.

Beginning Inventory.	$2,800.00
Plus Purchases	6,814.00
Cost of Goods Available for Sale.	$9,614.00
Less Ending Inventory	3,506.00
Cost of Goods Sold	$6,108.00

LIFO (last-in, first-out).   Under the LIFO cost flow assumption, the last units purchased were the first ones sold. The ending inventory will consist of the oldest purchases and be valued at the oldest purchase prices.** In this case, the 220 units on hand at the end of the period will be valued as follows:

Units	Price/Unit	Total
200	$14.00	$2,800.00
20	14.75	295.00
Ending Inventory (LIFO)		$3,095.00

---

*When FIFO is being used, it is often convenient to think of LISH (last-in, still-here) in connection with the ending inventory. That is, think of *first-in, first-out* in computing the cost of goods sold and *last-in, still-here* in computing the ending inventory value. These notions of LISH and FISH (to be discussed in connection with LIFO) were developed by George H. Sorter.

**When LIFO is being used, think of FISH (first-in, still-here) in connection with the ending inventory. That is, think of *last-in, first-out* in computing the cost of goods sold and *first-in, still-here* in computing the ending inventory value.

The cost of goods sold is $6,519.00, as shown below.

Beginning Inventory.	$2,800.00
Plus Purchases	6,814.00
Cost of Goods Available for Sale	$9,614.00
Less Ending Inventory	3,095.00
Cost of Goods Sold	$6,519.00

The LIFO cost flow assumption has little to recommend it in terms of flow of goods. Indeed, it represents an *ad hoc* attempt to react to inflation by charging against current revenue the most recent costs of the units sold.

Weighted Average.   This cost flow assumption presumes that the ending inventory consists of units from the beginning inventory, as well as units from the purchases made during the year. Therefore, the cost per unit of the ending inventory is equal to the cost of goods available for sale divided by the total number of units available for sale.

Cost of Goods Available for Sale	$9,614.00
Total Units Available for Sale	640.00
Average Unit Cost ($9,614/640).	$ 15.02
Ending Inventory (220 units × $15.02/unit)	$3,304.40
Cost of Goods Available for Sale	$9,614.00
Less Ending Inventory	3,304.00
Cost of Goods Sold	$6,309.60

These three historical inventory cost flow assumptions are compared in Exhibit 6.1.

Exhibit 6.1

A Comparison of the Closing Entries and T-Accounts Under Each of the Three Historical Inventory Cost Flow Assumptions

	FIFO		LIFO		Weighted Average	
Inventory, 12/31	3,506.00		3,095.00		3,304.40	
Cost of Goods Sold	6,108.00		6,519.00		6,309.60	
Inventory 1/1		2,800.00		2,800.00		2,800.00
Purchases		6,814.00		6,814.00		6,814.00

To close the inventory and purchases accounts to cost of goods sold and record the ending inventory valuation.

Exhibit 6.1 (continued)

Income Summary	6,108.00		6,519.00		6,309.60	
Cost of Goods Sold		6,108.00		6,519.00		6,309.60

To close the cost of goods sold to the income summary account.

NOTE: If sales = $12,000.00 and cost of goods sold is the only expense, net income under the three historical inventory cost flow assumptions is as follows.

	Sales	−	Cost of Goods Sold	=	Net Income
FIFO	$12,000.00	−	$6,108.00	=	$5,892.00
LIFO	12,000.00	−	6,519.00	=	5,481.00
Weighted Average	12,000.00	−	6,309.60	=	5,690.40

FIFO

Inventory

(A)	2,800.00	
(B)	3,506.00	2,800.00
	6,306.00	2,800.00
(C)	3,506.00	

Purchases

(A)	6,814.00	
(B)		6,814.00
	6,814.00	6,814.00

Cost of Goods Sold

(B)	6,108.00	
(B)		6,108.00
	6,108.00	6,108.00

Income Summary

(B)	6,108.00	
	6,108.00	
(C)	6,108.00	

LIFO

Inventory

(A)	2,800.00	
(B)	3,095.00	2,800.00
	5,895.00	2,800.00
(C)	3,095.00	

Purchases

(A)	6,814.00	
(B)		6,814.00
	6,814.00	6,814.00

Cost of Goods Sold

(B)	6,519.00	
(B)		6,519.00
	6,519.00	6,519.00

Income Summary

(B)	6,519.00	
	6,519.00	
(C)	6,519.00	

Weighted Average

Inventory

(A)	2,800.00	
(B)	3,304.40	2,800.00
	6,104.40	2,800.00
(C)	3,304.40	

Purchases

(A)	6,814.00	
(B)		6,814.00
	6,814.00	6,814.00

Cost of Goods Sold

(B)	6,309.60	
(B)		6,309.60
	6,309.60	6,309.60

Income Summary

(B)	6,309.60	
	6,309.60	
(C)	6,309.60	

(A) Balances Just Prior to Year-End Closing Entries

(B) Closing Entries

(C) Ending Account Balances

In the determination of current operating income, gains which result from operations should be separated from gains (or cost savings) resulting from holding activities. This is accomplished by matching current replacement costs with current revenues. Theoretically, every time a unit is sold, its replacement cost at that time should be obtained and used as the cost of goods sold.* This, however, would be highly impractical.

Just as historical cost accounting makes assumptions about the flow of inventory costs (FIFO, LIFO, etc.), replacement cost accounting makes assumptions as to when units were sold. Replacement cost information may not be known for *all* dates during the period, but clearly replacement costs are known on *inventory purchase* dates. It is therefore convenient to assume that sales occurred on inventory purchase dates. If a firm can arrive at a more accurate assumption for sales dates and current costs for those dates, the more accurate assumption should be used. For example, an automobile dealer may know the sales date and replacement cost on that date for every automobile sold. It may be practical for him to use *actual* sale dates. Each firm should make an analysis of sale date assumptions which are the most accurate and practical in its situation. We now return to our example.

Since 420 units were sold out of 640 units available for sale, assume that 65.6 percent [=420/640] of purchases were sold on each inventory purchase date. Therefore, sales would be assumed to occur as follows.

Purchase Date	Proportion Sold		Units Sold		Unit Replacement Cost at Time of Sale		Total
3/1	65.6% × 280	=	184	×	$14.75	=	$2,714.00
5/15	65.6% × 150	=	98	×	15.20	=	1,489.60
8/29	65.6% × 90	=	59	×	15.80	=	932.20
12/1	65.6% × 120	=	79	×	16.10	=	1,271.90
			420				

Replacement Cost of Goods Sold $6,407.70

NOTE: The amount on 3/1 includes 200 units from beginning inventory and 80 units purchased on 3/1.

The replacement cost of the ending inventory is easily determined: multiply the number of units on hand by the unit replacement cost at December 31.

Ending Inventory = 220 × $16.25 = $3,575.00
(Replacement Cost)

---

*Although this is the conventional way of computing replacement cost of goods sold, we will return to this point later in the chapter. In effect, we will then argue that the use of replacement cost on inventory purchase dates (or dates of *replacement*) may enhance the usefulness of current operating income as a measure of distributable income.

Computation of
Realized Cost Savings

Cost savings realized on goods sold are simply the excess of replacement cost over historical cost of goods sold. The calculations are as follows.

$$\text{FIFO} \quad \text{Realized Cost Savings} = \frac{\text{Replacement Cost}}{\text{of Goods Sold}} - \frac{\text{Historical Cost}}{\text{of Goods Sold}}$$
$$(\text{FIFO})$$
$$\$299.70 \quad\quad = \quad\quad \$6,407.70 \quad - \quad \$6,108.00$$

$$\text{LIFO} \quad \text{Realized Cost Savings} = \frac{\text{Replacement Cost}}{\text{of Goods Sold}} - \frac{\text{Historical Cost}}{\text{of Goods Sold}}$$
$$(\text{LIFO})$$
$$(\$111.30) \quad\quad = \quad\quad \$6,407.70 \quad - \quad \$6,519.00$$

$$\text{WEIGHTED AVERAGE} \quad \frac{\text{Realized}}{\text{Cost Savings}} = \frac{\text{Replacement}}{\text{Cost of}} - \frac{\text{Historical Cost}}{\text{of Goods Sold}}$$
$$\text{Goods Sold} \quad (\text{Weighted Average})$$
$$\$98.10 \quad = \quad \$6,407.70 \quad - \quad \$6,309.60$$

Computation of
Realizable Cost Savings

We can now compute the realizable cost savings associated with the current year's inventory transactions. First, we must recognize that there are *unrecorded* *unrealized* cost savings in the beginning inventory. This amount is $90.00, as shown below.

$$\frac{\textit{Unrealized} \text{ Cost Savings}}{\text{in Beginning Inventory}} = \frac{\text{Replacement Cost}}{\text{of Beginning}} - \frac{\text{Historical Cost}}{\text{of Beginning}}$$
$$\text{Inventory} \quad\quad \text{Inventory}$$
$$\$90.00 \quad\quad = \quad\quad \$2,890.00 \quad - \quad \$2,800$$
$$[= 200 \times \$14.45] \quad [= 200 \times \$14.00]$$

Since there are *unrealized* cost savings in the beginning inventory, our computation of the *realizable* cost savings is based on the identity introduced in Chapter 4.

$$\frac{\text{Realizable}}{\text{Cost Savings}} = \frac{\text{Realized}}{\text{Cost Savings}} + \frac{\textit{Change} \text{ in } \textit{Unrealized}}{\text{Cost Savings}}$$

Recall that we must consider the *change* in *unrealized* cost savings to account for the interaction between the flow of *realized* cost savings and the stock of *unrealized* cost savings. The total *realizable* cost savings on current year inventory transactions is $278.70. The use of different historical inventory cost flow assumptions, however, makes it necessary to show separately the computation of the realiz*able* cost savings for each of those assumptions.

Realizable Cost Savings: FIFO. In this case, the ending inventory is assumed to consist of goods acquired in the most recent purchases (i.e., LISH). The cost savings in the ending inventory are *unrealized* at the end of the current year. They reflect the increases in inventory purchase prices which occurred between the purchase dates and the end of the current year and are calculated as follows. The total quantity on hand is 220 units.

Units	Replacement Cost at December 31	Historical Purchase Price	Increase per Unit since Purchase	Total Increase since Purchase
120	$16.25	$16.10	$ .15	$18.00
90	16.25	15.80	.45	40.50
10	16.25	15.20	1.05	10.50
Unrealized cost savings in ending inventory				$69.00

NOTE: This $69.00 is, of course, equal to the difference between replacement cost ending inventory ($3,575.00) and FIFO ending inventory ($3,506.00).

Realiz*ed* cost savings (excess of replacement cost of goods sold over historical cost of goods sold) *include* the $90.00 of *unrealized* cost savings attributable to the beginning inventory. Since FIFO assumes that the oldest units are sold first, these cost savings were realiz*ed* during the current year. Therefore, they already are included in the realiz*ed* cost savings on cost of goods sold calculated previously. The calculation of realiz*able* cost savings under FIFO is shown below.

$$\text{Realizable Cost Savings} = \frac{\text{Realized Cost}}{\text{Savings}} + \frac{\text{Change in Unrealized}}{\text{Cost Savings}}$$
$$\$278.70 \quad = \quad \$299.70 \quad + \quad (\$21.00)$$
$$[= \$69.00 - \$90.00]$$

Realizable Cost Savings: LIFO. With LIFO, the ending inventory is assumed to consist of the oldest goods (i.e., FISH). The 220 units on hand have increased in price to $16.25 since they were purchased; the related cost savings are *unrealized* at year end. Recall that since the number of units on hand increased during the year, the LIFO method assumes that the goods in the beginning inventory are still on hand at the end of the year. Therefore, the *unrealized* cost savings on the ending inventory are calculated as follows.

Units	Replacement Cost at December 31	Historical Purchase Price	Increase per Unit since Purchase	Total Increase since Purchase
200	$16.25	$14.00	$2.25	$450.00
20	16.25	14.75	1.50	30.00
Unrealized cost savings on ending inventory				$480.00

NOTE: This $480.00 is the same as the difference between the replacement cost ending inventory ($3,575.00) and the LIFO ending inventory ($3,095.00). Since the beginning inventory is assumed to be still on hand, the $480.00 includes the *unrealized* cost savings of $90.00 in the beginning inventory.

The realiz*able* cost savings under LIFO are

$$\text{Realiz}able\text{ Cost Savings} = \frac{\text{Realiz}ed\text{ Cost}}{\text{Savings}} + \frac{\text{Change in Un}realized}{\text{Cost Savings}}$$
$$\$278.70 \quad = \quad (\$111.30) \quad + \quad \$390.00$$
$$[= \$480.00 - \$90.00]$$

Realizable Cost Savings: Weighted Average. When weighted average is used, inventory is valued at an average cost. Hence, the ending inventory represents not the oldest or the newest units, but average units purchased at the average cost of all units available for sale. The 220 units in ending inventory were valued at an average historical unit cost of $15.02. The unit replacement cost is $16.25 at year end; hence the *unrealized* cost savings in the ending inventory are $270.60 [= 220 × ($16.25 − $15.02)]. This amount is the same as the difference between replacement cost ending inventory ($3,575.00) and the weighted average ending inventory ($3,304.40).

With the help of the identity and the $98.10 of realiz*ed* cost savings previously calculated, realiz*able* cost savings can be easily computed.

$$\text{Realiz}able\text{ Cost Savings} = \frac{\text{Realiz}ed\text{ Cost}}{\text{Savings}} + \frac{\text{Change in Un}realized}{\text{Cost Savings}}$$
$$\$278.70 \quad = \quad \$98.10 \quad + \quad \$180.60$$
$$[= \$270.60 - \$90.00]$$

Realiz*able* cost savings refer to those cost savings arising in a given year due to changes in replacement cost *in that year*. For a given set of inventory transactions, realiz*able* cost savings will be the same, regardless of the historical cost flow assumption employed. The replacement cost of goods sold and inventory valuation is the same in all cases. The historical cost flow assumption used merely affects the division of the realiz*able* cost savings between realiz*ed* and *un*realiz*ed*.

We can now analyze this division of the realiz*able* cost savings under the three historical cost flow assumptions.

| | Current Year Realizable Cost Savings | | |
	Total	Realiz*ed* During the Year	Unrealiz*ed* at Year End
FIFO	$278.70	$209.70	$ 69.00
LIFO	278.70	(111.30)	390.00
Weighted Average	278.70	39.06	239.64

Regarding *FIFO*, the entire beginning inventory was assumed sold. Thus the $90.00 of *un*realiz*ed* cost savings in the beginning inventory were all realiz*ed*. This leaves $209.70 [= $299.70 − $90.00] of the realiz*ed* cost savings which became realiz*able* this year. The *un*realiz*ed* cost savings of $69.00 in the ending inventory all became realiz*able* this year.

With *LIFO*, the situation is reversed. The entire beginning inventory is assumed to be on hand at year end. Hence the $90.00 of *un*realiz*ed* cost savings in the beginning inventory remain *un*realiz*ed* at year end. This leaves $390.00 [= $480.00 − $90.00] of the *un*realiz*ed* cost savings that became realiz*able* this year. Since LIFO cost of goods sold exceeded replacement cost of goods sold, the difference ($111.30) represented negative realiz*ed* cost savings. These are all realiz*able*, since none of the beginning inventory was sold.

The use of Weighted Average, however, results in the assumption that some portion of the beginning inventory was sold and some portion remains at year end. Recall that of the 640 units available for sale, 420 were sold. Therefore, 65.6 percent [= 420/640] of all units available for sale were sold. Since units available for sale include the beginning inventory, the presumption is that 65.6 percent of the beginning inventory was sold and 34.4 percent remains on hand.

Consequently, $59.04 [= 65.6% × $90.00] of the *un*realiz*ed* cost savings in the beginning inventory were realiz*ed*, while $30.96 [= 34.4% × $90.00] remain *un*realiz*ed*. This means, of course, that of the $98.10 of realiz*ed* cost savings, only $39.06 [= $98.10 − $59.04] became realiz*able* this year. Similarly, of the $270.60 of *un*realiz*ed* cost savings in the ending inventory, only $239.64 [= $270.60 − $30.96] became realiz*able* this year.

It will be useful to show replacement cost income statements under the three historical cost flow assumptions. We assume that sales for the period amounted to $12,000 and that cost of goods sold is the only expense item. Comparative income statements are shown in Exhibit 6.2.

Exhibit 6.2

Comparative Replacement Cost Income Statements
Under Three Historical Inventory Cost Flow Assumptions

	FIFO	LIFO	Weighted Average
SALES	$12,000.00	$12,000.00	$12,000.00
Less Replacement Cost of Goods Sold	6,407.70	6,407.70	6,407.70
CURRENT OPERATING INCOME.	$ 5,592.30	$ 5,592.30	$ 5,592.30
Realized Cost Savings.	299.70	(111.30)	98.10
REALIZED INCOME	$ 5,892.00	$ 5,481.00	$ 5,690.40
Less Realized Cost Savings of Prior Period (1)	90.00	—	59.04
	$ 5,802.00	$ 5,481.00	$ 5,631.36
Unrealized Cost Savings	69.00	390.00	239.64
REPLACEMENT COST INCOME	$ 5,871.00	$ 5,871.00	$ 5,871.00

(1) Since replacement cost income equals current operating income plus realiz*able* cost savings, any prior period cost savings realiz*ed* in this period must be deducted after realiz*ed* income is computed. This deduction, combined with the *unrealized* cost savings arising in this period, gives us the *change* in *unrealized* cost savings which fits the now familiar identity,

Realiz*able* Cost Savings = Realiz*ed* Cost Savings + *Change* in *Unrealized* Cost Savings

The comparison in Exhibit 6.2 clearly shows that both current operating income ($5,592.30) and replacement cost income ($5,871.00) are insensitive to the historical inventory cost flow assumption employed. This is true, of course, because sales ($12,000), replacement cost of goods sold ($6,407.70) and realiz*able* cost savings ($278.70) are the same in all three cases.

On the other hand, as we have seen, realiz*ed* income is affected by the historical inventory cost flow assumption, which determines the amount of realiz*ed* (and *unrealized*) cost savings. In addition, realiz*ed* income under each cost flow assumption is identical to its historical cost net income counterpart.

Introducing Replacement Costs into the Accounts

The replacement cost data we have calculated can easily be incorporated into the historical cost records. To avoid destroying the historical data, we use "valuation adjustment" accounts when replacement costs are recorded. Pertinent journal entries for each of the historical cost valuation cases are shown in Exhibit 6.3. In Exhibit 6.4, the entries are posted to general ledger accounts. We assume sales for the period amounted to $12,000.

Exhibit 6.3

Comparative Journal Entries

	FIFO DR	FIFO CR	LIFO DR	LIFO CR	Weighted Average DR	Weighted Average CR
(1) Inventory Valuation Adjustment	90.00		90.00		90.00	
Unrealized Cost Savings		90.00		90.00		90.00
To record the unrealized cost savings in the beginning inventory.						
(2) Inventory Valuation Adjustment	21.00		390.00		180.60	
Realizable Cost Savings		21.00		390.00		180.60
To adjust the ending inventory to its replacement cost and record the related realizable cost savings.						
(3) Cost of Goods Sold Valuation Adjustment	299.70		111.30		98.10	
Realizable Cost Savings		299.70		111.30		98.10
To adjust the cost of goods sold to its replacement cost at date(s) of sale and record the related realizable cost savings						
(4) *Realizable* Cost Savings	278.70		278.70		278.70	
Realized Cost Savings		299.70	111.30			98.10
Unrealized Cost Savings	21.00			390.00		180.60
To reclassify the current year's realizable cost savings on inventory as realized through sale or unrealized at year end.						
(5) Sales	12,000.00		12,000.00		12,000.00	
Cost of Goods Sold		6,108.00		6,519.00		6,309.60
Cost of Goods Sold Valuation Adjustment		299.70	111.30			98.10
Current Operating Income		5,592.30		5,592.30		5,592.30
To close sales and replacement cost of goods sold to current operating income.						
(6) Current Operating Income	5,592.30		5,592.30		5,592.30	
Realized Cost Savings	299.70			111.30	98.10	
Realized Income		5,892.00		5,481.00		5,690.40
To close current operating income and realized cost savings to realized income.						
(7) *Realized* Income	5,892.00		5,481.00		5,690.40	
Retained (*Realized*) Earnings		5,892.00		5,481.00		5,690.40
To close realized income to retained (realized) earnings.						

Exhibit 6.4

Comparative General Ledger Posting

FIFO

Inventory			
(A)	3,506.00	To Balance	3,506.00
Balance	3,506.00		

Cost of Goods Sold			
(A)	6,108.00	(5)	6,108.00

Sales			
(5)	12,000.00	(A)	12,000.00

Inventory Valuation Adjustment			
(1)	90.00	(2)	21.00
		To Balance	69.00
	90.00		90.00
Balance	69.00		

Cost of Goods Sold Valuation Adjustment			
(3)	299.70	(5)	299.70

Realizable Cost Savings			
(2)	21.00	(3)	299.70
(4)	278.70		
	299.70		299.70

Realized Cost Savings			
(6)	299.70	(4)	299.70

Unrealized Cost Savings			
(4)	21.00	(1)	90.00
To Balance	69.00		
	90.00		90.00
		Balance	69.00

Realized Income			
(7)	5,892.00	(6)	5,892.00

Current Operating Income			
(6)	5,592.30	(5)	5,592.30

Retained (Realized) Earnings			
To Balance	5,892.00	(7)	5,892.00
		Balance	5,892.00

(A) Historical Cost End-of-Year Balance

Exhibit 6.4 (continued)

LIFO

Inventory		
(A)	3,095.00	To Balance 3,095.00
Balance	3,095.00	

Cost of Goods Sold		
(A)	6,519.00	(5) 6,519.00

Sales		
(5)	12,000.00	(A) 12,000.00

Inventory Valuation Adjustment		
(1)	90.00	
(2)	390.00	
	480.00	To Balance 480.00
Balance	480.00	

Cost of Goods Sold Valuation Adjustment		
(5)	111.30	(3) 111.30

Realizable Cost Savings		
(3)	111.30	(2) 390.00
(4)	278.70	
	390.00	390.00

Realized Cost Savings		
(4)	111.30	(6) 111.30

Unrealized Cost Savings		
To Balance	480.00	(1) 90.00
	480.00	(4) 390.00
		480.00
	Balance	480.00

Current Operating Income		
(6)	5,592.30	(5) 5,592.30

Realized Income		
(7)	5,481.00	(6) 5,481.00

Retained (Realized) Earnings		
To Balance 5,481.00	(7)	5,481.00
	Balance	5,481.00

(A) Historical Cost End-of-Year Balance

Exhibit 6.4 (continued)

Weighted Average

Inventory		
(A)	3,304.40	To Balance 3,304.40
Balance	3,304.40	

Cost of Goods Sold		
(A)	6,309.60	(5) 6,309.60

Sales		
(5)	12,000.00	(A) 12,000.00

Inventory Valuation Adjustment		
(1)	90.00	
(2)	180.60	To Balance 270.60
	270.60	270.60
Balance	270.60	

Cost of Goods Sold Valuation Adjustment		
(3)	98.10	(5) 98.10

Realizable Cost Savings		
(4)	278.70	(2) 180.60
		(3) 98.10
	278.70	278.70

Realized Cost Savings		
(6)	98.10	(4) 98.10

Unrealized Cost Savings		
To Balance	270.60	(1) 90.00
	270.60	(2) 180.60
		270.60

Current Operating Income		
(6)	5,592.30	(5) 5,592.30

Realized Income		
(7)	5,690.40	(6) 5,690.40

Retained (Realized) Earnings		
To Balance 5,690.40	(7) 5,690.40
	Balance 5,690.40

(A) Historical Cost End-of-Year Balance

Note that entry (1) has been used to record the $90.00 of *unrealized* cost savings in the beginning inventory. In this example, we have assumed that these *unrealized* cost savings amount to $90.00 for each of the historical inventory cost flow assumptions. A real situation, however, would normally disclose a *different* beginning balance in *unrealized* cost savings because, as we have seen, the historical inventory cost flow assumption used will affect the amounts of realiz*able* cost savings that are realiz*ed* and *unrealized*.

We can now make the following observations about the example.

1. Current operating income ($5,592.30) is the same, regardless of which of the three historical cost inventory methods is used, because replacement cost of goods sold is the same with each method. The different cost of goods sold valuation adjustments were necessary to revise the historical cost of goods sold to $6,407.70 (the replacement cost of goods sold).

2. Care must be exercised in treating the end of year *un*realized cost savings. If they are included in *replacement cost income*, they must not be included in replacement cost income again subsequently when realiz*ed*. This is to avoid double counting of these cost savings. To ensure that realiz*ed* income will equal historical cost net income, we include all realiz*ed* cost savings. Then, in the calculation of current period replacement cost income, any realiz*ed* cost savings which became realiz*able* in a prior period must be subtracted, as was shown in Exhibit 6.2 (see also Chapter 9).

3. Realiz*ed* income under each of the three historical inventory cost flow assumptions is the same as its historical cost net income counterpart.

	FIFO	LIFO	Weighted Average
Realized income, per Exhibit 6.2	$5,892.00	$5,481.00	$5,690.40
Historical cost net income, per Exhibit 6.1	$5,892.00	$5,481.00	$5,690.40

4. Realiz*ed* income is not the same under the three historical cost inventory valuation methods because realiz*ed* (and *unrealized*) cost savings differ as a result of the alternative historical cost flow-of-goods assumptions. The difference lies in the treatment of both the *un*realized cost savings attributed to the beginning inventory ($90.00) and the current period realiz*able* cost savings ($278.70). Of this total of $368.70 [$90 + $278.70], all but $69 is realiz*ed* under FIFO. With LIFO, none of this is realiz*ed*; indeed, an additional $111.30 (the excess of LIFO cost of goods sold over replacement cost of goods sold) is *unrealized*. Under LIFO, then, a total of $480.00 in cost savings is

*un*realized at year end. In the case of weighted average, only part of the *un*realized cost savings attributed to the beginning inventory ($90.00) and current year realiz*able* cost savings ($278.70) has been realiz*ed*. This amounts to $98.10 [$59.04 + $39.06]. A reconciliation of these three realiz*ed* income measures is shown in Exhibit 6.5.

Exhibit 6.5

Reconciliation of Realized Income Computed under
Three Alternative Historical Cost Flow-of-Goods Assumptions

Realiz*ed* Income (FIFO).	$5,892.00
Excess of Realiz*ed* Cost Savings (FIFO) over Realiz*ed* Cost Savings (LIFO) [$299.70 − ($111.30)]	(411.00)
Realiz*ed* Income (LIFO).	$5,481.00
Excess of Realiz*ed* Cost Savings (LIFO) over Realiz*ed* Cost Savings (Weighted Average) [($111.30) − $98.10]. . . .	209.40
Realiz*ed* Income (Weighted Average)	$5,690.40

Effects When Inventories Are Decreasing

The preceding example involved a situation in which inventory increased (from 200 to 220 units) during the year. Suppose that the inventory decreased during the year. Does this create any special accounting problems for us? The answer is that it does not. To illustrate the procedure, we return to the basic data in our example. We assume that 480 units were sold during the period (instead of 420); the ending inventory would then stand at 160 units, down from 200 units at the beginning of the year. Using the LIFO cost flow assumption, we work through the adjustments to arrive at replacement cost of goods sold and ending inventory.

To calculate the replacement cost of goods sold, we again assume that sales took place on inventory purchase dates because we have objective replacement cost data on those dates. Since 480 units were sold out of 640 units available for sale, assume that 75 percent [=480/640] of purchases were sold on each purchase date. Therefore, sales would be assumed to occur as follows and replacement cost of goods sold on a given date would equal the number of units assumed sold on each purchase date times the replacement cost prevailing at that date.

Purchase Date	Proportion Sold		Units Sold		Unit Replacement Cost at Time of Sale		Total
3/1	75% × 280	=	210	×	$14.75	=	$3,097.50
5/15	75% × 150	=	113	×	15.20	=	1,717.60
8/29	75% × 90	=	67	×	15.80	=	1,058.60
12/1	75% × 120	=	90	×	16.10	=	1,449.00
			480				
Replacement Cost of Goods Sold							$7,322.70

The historical cost of goods sold under LIFO will be as shown below.

Beginning Inventory.	$2,800.00
Purchases	6,814.00
Cost of Goods Available for Sale.	$9,614.00
Ending Inventory (160 × $14.00)	(2,240.00)
Cost of Goods Sold (LIFO).	$7,374.00

Realiz*ed* cost savings are equal to the difference between replacement cost of goods sold ($7,322.70) and historical cost of goods sold ($7,374.00), or −$51.30. *Un*realiz*ed* cost savings on the ending inventory are $360.00 [=160 × $2.25]. Under LIFO, the ending inventory of 160 units consists entirely of units on hand at the beginning of the year; the replacement cost of these units rose to $16.25 from $14.00, a change of $2.25. The cost savings realiz*ed* through sales, however, did not all become realiz*able* in this year. Specifically, 40 units from the *beginning inventory* were sold. The cost savings attributable to the increase in replacement cost of these units to $14.45 from $14.00 on last December 31 became realiz*able* last year and were *un*realiz*ed* at the beginning of this year. This amount, $18.00 [=40 × $.45], is included in realiz*ed* cost savings. Now total realiz*able* cost savings for the year can be computed under the LIFO method using the identity:

$$\text{Realiz\textit{able} Cost Savings} = \frac{\text{Realiz\textit{ed} Cost}}{\text{Savings}} + \frac{\text{\textit{Change in Un}realiz\textit{ed}}}{\text{Cost Savings}}$$
$$\$218.70 \quad = \quad (\$51.30) \quad + \quad \$270.00$$
$$[= \$360 - \$90.00]$$

NOTE: Realiz*able* cost savings in the ending inventory are $288.00 [=160 × ($16.25 − $14.45)] and realiz*ed* cost savings which arose this year are ($69.30) [=($51.30) − $18.00]. Therefore, realiz*able* cost savings are $218.70 [=$288.00 + ($69.30)].

This differs from the realizable cost savings calculated previously by $60 [=$278.70 − $218.70]. In the earlier example, the ending inventory consisted of the 200 units from the beginning inventory and 20 units purchased on 3/1. The present example reflects the sale of the 20 units purchased on 3/1 and 40 units from the beginning inventory, assumed sold at the average replacement cost for the year of $15.25 [=$7,322.70/ 480], thereby generating the following cost savings.

Units	×	($15.25 − Purchase Price)	=	Cost Savings
20	×	($15.25 − $14.75)	=	$10.00
40	×	($15.25 − $14.00)	=	50.00
				$60.00

If the units had been held throughout the year, as in the earlier example, the cost savings would be based on the end of year purchase price of $16.25. In this case, the cost savings would be calculated as follows.

Units	×	($16.25 − Purchase Price)	=	Cost Savings
20	×	($16.25 − $14.75)	=	$ 30.00
40	×	($16.25 − $14.00)	=	90.00
				$120.00

The $60 difference [= $278.70 − $218.70], of course, is the difference between $120 and $60 and represents cost savings foregone by selling the units instead of holding them in inventory until the end of the year.

A Note on Perpetual Inventories

The use of a *perpetual* rather than a *periodic* inventory system will often result in different historical cost of goods sold and inventory valuations. Under LIFO perpetual, for example, the timing of purchases and sales is important. If purchases are heavy and sales are light near the end of the year, the ending perpetual inventory will include some of these recent purchases. This will lead to a lower cost of goods sold with LIFO perpetual than with LIFO periodic.

The use of a perpetual inventory method should create no special problems in a replacement cost accounting system. It will, of course, affect the respective amounts of realiz*ed* and *un*realiz*ed* cost savings, as did the various periodic cost flow assumptions.

Lower of Cost or Market and Replacement Cost Accounting

In Chapter 2 we mentioned that conventional accounting practice applies the "lower of cost or market" rule when valuing certain assets (such as inventories and marketable securities) and nonmonetary liabilities (such as estimated warranty obligations). What is the relevance of lower of cost or market in a replacement cost accounting system?

First, to anticipate a later chapter, the replacement cost of marketable securities is their market value; the replacement cost of liabilities is also their market value. As a result, replacement cost accounting would be consistent with lower of cost or market in terms of marketable securities and nonmonetary liabilities for downward movements only. With respect to inventories, we believe that lower of cost or market should also be applied in replacement cost accounting. Unless inventories have value in use which exceeds their net realizable value (selling price less normal cost of selling), the effects of specific price changes are best reflected by net realizable value. Such changes in specific prices would, of course, be automatically reflected in the replacement cost inventory valuation of a retailing firm. In a manufacturing firm, however, the replacement cost of production may exceed the net realizable value of the production. In this case, inventories should be valued at the lower of net realizable value (or "market") or replacement cost of production. When write-downs are required, the amount of write-down would be treated as a holding loss or negative cost saving.

Such a holding loss would be *unrealized* in replacement cost accounting. However, when inventory is written down from cost to market in a historical cost system, the loss is taken as *realized*. Hence the identity shown, up to now, between historical cost net income and replacement cost realized income is not maintained in this special circumstance. To our knowledge, this is the only exception to that identity.

One of the inflation-related problems which concerns many firms today is the matter of "inventory profits." Briefly, the argument is that the determination of income under historical cost accounting results in the recognition of profit which is fictitious because of the rising replacement cost of inventories. To the extent that the cost of replacing inventory which was sold exceeds the historical cost of goods sold, historical operating profits are said to be overstated. The portion of reported net income under historical costs referred to as fictitious "inventory profits" is the difference between cost of goods sold stated at replacement and historical costs.* This amount is, of course, the cost savings realized when inventory is sold. In other words, the inventory profits are the realized cost savings on goods sold which, when added to current operating income and other realized cost savings, give us realized income, the same as historical cost net income.

Replacement Costs, Inventory Profits, Operating Income and Distributable Profits

We sympathize with this concern because if any of these fictitious inventory profits are paid out in taxes or dividends, the physical capacity of the firm will be impaired. Without additional external financing, the firm will be unable to fully replace the inventory that was sold.

A major advantage of replacement cost accounting is that it separates current operating income from realized cost savings and hence from inventory profits as defined by the SEC. Current operating income serves as a guide to future profitability. It also indicates the maximum amount of profit (after taxes) which could be paid out in dividends without impairing the physical capacity of the firm. However, some modification of this meaning of current operating income may be required, depending on movements in inventory prices and inventory replacement policies.

Recall that the calculation of replacement cost of goods sold reflects the replacement cost at date(s) of sale. This can be approximated by using

---

*This is the meaning of *inventory profits* according to the SEC. In our opinion, however, a more useful and complete definition of inventory profits would also include the *un-realized* cost savings in ending inventories.

replacement costs on inventory purchase dates, as in our example. The usefulness of the current operating income figure will depend on first, whether the inventory which was sold has in fact been replaced; and second, whether the replacement cost *at time of replacement* differs from replacement cost *at time of sale*. Our conclusion is that current operating income is most useful as a measure of distributable income when replacement cost of goods sold reflects replacement cost at time of replacement. If physical inventory has declined during the year, all units sold have not been replaced. These units should be costed on a NIFO (next-in, first-out) basis. Any other cost figure will misstate current operating income as a measure of distributable income.

A firm begins the year with cash of $40 and three units of inventory valued at $10 each. During the year, one unit is sold for $25. Replacement cost at date of sale is $17. Replacement cost at year end is $22. The beginning statement of financial position appears below.

Statement of Financial Position
January 1

ASSETS		EQUITIES	
Cash	$40	Capital Stock.	$50
Inventory	30	Retained Earnings	20
Total Assets	$70	Total Equities	$70

In case *a*; the unit sold is not replaced.

Statement of Income

Sales	$25
Replacement Cost of Goods Sold	17
Current Operating Income	$ 8
Realized Cost Savings	7
Realized Income	$15
Unrealized Cost Savings (2 × $12)	24
Replacement Cost Income	$39

Statement of Financial Position
December 31

ASSETS		EQUITIES	
Cash	$ 65	Capital Stock.	$ 50
Inventory	44	Retained Earnings	35
		Unrealized Cost Savings	24
Total Assets	$ 109	Total Equities	$ 109

NOTE: If the $8 of current operating income is paid out as a dividend, the net increase in cash (i.e., ending cash of $65, less the dividend of $8, less beginning cash of $40) is $17. This will not be sufficient to replace the inventory of $22.

In case *b*, the unit sold is replaced at a cost of $20.

Statement of Income

Sales	$25
Replacement Cost of Goods Sold	17
Current Operating Income	$ 8
Realized Cost Savings	7
Realized Income	$15
Unrealized Cost Savings [(2 × $12) + (1 × $2)]	26
Replacement Cost Income	$41

Statement of Financial Position
December 31

ASSETS		EQUITIES	
Cash	$ 45	Capital Stock	$ 50
Inventory	66	Retained Earnings	35
		Unrealized Cost Savings	26
Total Assets	$111	Total Equities	$111

NOTE: If the $8 of current operating income is paid out as a dividend, the net increase in cash of $17 would not have covered the replacement cost of $20.

In both cases, current operating income overstates the amount which may be distributed as a dividend without impairing the physical capacity of the firm. Cost of goods sold is measured by replacement cost at *date of sale*, rather than at *date of replacement*. In case *a*, the inventory had not been replaced at year end. Hence, the appropriate replacement cost of goods sold would either be the $22 price at December 31, an actual replacement cost incurred early in the subsequent period (before the financial statements are finalized) or some other "best estimate." Otherwise, current operating income will not adequately reflect profitability in the sense of maintaining physical capacity.

In case *b*, the inventory was replaced at a cost of $20 prior to year end. Hence, the $20 is the appropriate replacement cost of goods sold. Current operating income would now reflect the cost of replacement and could be paid out while leaving the firm no worse off in terms of physical capacity. In case *b*, then, the firm would gain by replacing at $20 instead of $22, an adequate representation of the facts. To illustrate this concretely, statements of income and financial position are prepared below for cases *a* and *b*, with cost of goods sold measured at date of replacement. The $22 replacement cost is assumed for case *a*.

Statement of Income

	Case a	Case b
Sales	$25	$25
Replacement Cost of Goods Sold	22	20
Current Operating Income	$ 3	$ 5
Realized Cost Savings.	12	10
Realized Income	$15	$15
Unrealized Cost Savings	24	26
Replacement Cost Income.	$39	$41

The firm is better off in case *b* because it replaced at a lower cost than will be required in case *a*.

Statement of Financial Position
December 31

ASSETS	Case a	Case b	EQUITIES	Case a	Case b
Cash	$ 65	$ 45	Capital Stock	$ 50	$ 50
Inventory	44	66	Retained Earnings	35	35
			Unrealized Cost Savings	24	26
Total Assets	$109	$111	Total Equities	$109	$111

For case *a*, $3 could be paid out, while leaving an increase in cash of $22 sufficient to replace the inventory. In case *b*, $5 could be paid without changing the cash and physical inventory positions. Of course, if selling prices are expected to remain constant, use of the $22 replacement cost in case *a* generates a current operating income figure which is a better *predictor* of future profitability.*

Manufactured Inventories

The discussion so far has implicitly dealt with a merchandising firm, that is, the inventories have been *purchased* rather than *manufactured*. Although the principles discussed here are also appropriate for manufactured inventories, the process of determining replacement cost may be complex when manufactured inventories are involved. Specifically, the

---

*Roman L. Weil has suggested that measurement of replacement cost of goods sold at date of replacement may mix *operating* and *speculative* gains. That is, the decision *when* to replace the inventory may be a speculative rather than an operating decision. Weil argues that the amount of speculative gain or loss is equal to the difference between replacement cost at date of sale and replacement cost at date of replacement. Although Weil's argument has merit, we believe that it is often quite difficult to differentiate between operating and speculative gains (or losses); and that the determination of current operating income based on replacement cost of goods sold at date of replacement is a more satisfactory measure of distributable income.

firm will need to ascertain the current cost of the direct labor, direct materials, variable overhead and fixed overhead used in the manufacturing process. Firms using a standard cost system based on *currently attainable standard costs* will have an advantage here. Currently attainable standard costs are the costs that should be incurred under current operating conditions and normal efficiency. With this system, standard costs are revised periodically to reflect current conditions. Hence the standard costs associated with direct labor, direct materials and variable overhead should be reasonably representative of the replacement costs of these items. The fixed manufacturing overhead, however, is a different matter.

Fixed manufacturing overhead includes rent, taxes, other current costs of an unvarying nature and *depreciation on manufacturing plant and equipment*. Let us assume that replacement cost depreciation exceeds historical cost depreciation. Now even currently attainable standard costs will not reflect replacement cost depreciation. Consequently, manufacturing firms will have to revise their fixed overhead rates to reflect depreciation and amortization based on the current replacement cost of manufacturing facilities. Realiz*able* cost savings on manufactured inventories, then, would consist primarily of a *pro rata* share of the excess of replacement cost depreciation and amortization over historical cost depreciation and amortization.

A short example will clarify these points. Suppose a firm allocates fixed manufacturing overhead to production on a historical cost basis of $1.00 per completed unit produced. If that overhead rate increases to $1.20 per completed unit after inclusion of current replacement costs, realiz*able* cost savings will be equal to $.20 for each completed unit produced. The increased overhead would be taken first through a "fixed manufacturing overhead control valuation adjustment" account and then allocated to valuation adjustment accounts for work in process, finished goods inventories and cost of goods sold. The allocation would be made according to the proportions of historical cost fixed manufacturing overhead charged to those accounts. In this way, realiz*able* cost savings on partially completed as well as fully completed production could be recognized.

LIFO Inventory Accounting and Inflation

Historical cost of goods sold under LIFO approximates or even exceeds replacement cost of goods sold in a period of rising prices. Indeed, the use of LIFO tends to eliminate "inventory profits." But when inventory prices are rising, the use of LIFO places a low value on ending historical cost inventories because the inventories are assumed to consist of the *oldest* goods, acquired when prices were *lower*. Thus, when prices are rising, the use of LIFO generates more realistic income measurement but at the cost of less realistic asset measurement.

Many firms are currently switching (or have recently switched) to LIFO inventory accounting.* Exhibit 6.6 illustrates the effect of the switch to LIFO on 1974 earnings and the change from 1973 earnings.

Exhibit 6.6*

Effect of the Switch to LIFO on the Earnings of Selected Firms

Company	1974 Earnings Per Share	LIFO Net Earnings Decrease From LIFO Total (millions)	Per Share	1973–74 Earnings Change With LIFO	Without LIFO
American Can	$5.48	$ 27.6	$1.56	53%	96%
American Cyanamid	3.24	26.0	0.54	36	59
American Standard	2.40	15.6	0.90	11	53
AMF	1.19	15.5	0.83	−62	−35
Cities Service	7.58	13.3	0.49	50	59
Clark Equipment	3.19	26.6	1.96	−21	27
Continental Can	4.07	40.1	1.37	25	67
Crown Zellerbach	5.06	6.8	0.28	18	25
Dow Chemical	6.35	141.5	1.53	116	168
E I du Pont	8.20	145.0	3.02	−32	−7
Ethyl	7.41	6.5	0.68	48	61
General Tire & Rubber	3.60	22.8	1.06	1	30
Hercules	2.21	19.1	0.45	1	22
Ingersoll-Rand	5.62	8.1	0.45	15	24
Kennecott Copper	5.08	19.9	0.61	6	18
Kimberly-Clark	4.10	11.0	0.47	24	38
Martin Marietta	3.58	14.0	0.62	40	65
Owens-Illinois	5.74	18.6	1.34	22	51
Pfizer	1.93	9.9	0.14	11	19
PPG Industries	4.51	17.9	0.86	1	20
Pullman	5.69	1.7	0.24	12	17
RCA	1.45	16.5	0.22	−39	−30
Reynolds Metals	6.23	16.4	0.95	159	198
Rohm & Haas	5.83	13.2	1.04	13	33
St. Regis Paper	4.76	3.0	0.14	65	70
Scott Paper	2.00	16.3	0.47	23	52
Standard Oil (Calif.)	5.71	250.0	1.47	15	44
Texaco	5.84	196.7	0.72	23	38
TRW	3.05	13.0	0.47	3	19
Union Carbide	8.69	14.3	0.23	82	87

*Reproduced with permission from *Forbes* (March 1, 1975).

---

*The *Wall Street Journal* (October 7, 1974) reported a study by Gary S. Shieneman of Arthur Young & Co. disclosing that about 10 percent of the 2,600 NYSE and AMEX companies were using LIFO at the end of 1973. Twenty percent of those had switched during 1973 alone.

For the thirty firms surveyed, the switch to LIFO tends to significantly depress earnings computed without LIFO. In addition, the *change* in earnings from 1973 to 1974 was generally quite different when LIFO was employed.

It should be understood that the quest for more realistic income measurement is not the only motivating force behind the many switches to LIFO. Tax effects also play an important role. The method of inventory accounting employed in the books must also be used for income tax purposes. Firms switching to LIFO, then, may often realize large tax savings. Each additional dollar in tax deductions (i.e., reductions in taxable income) will reduce federal income taxes by about $.48. As Exhibit 6.6 shows, firms such as du Pont and Standard Oil of California had large increases in cash flow from the tax savings associated with the bookkeeping switch to LIFO.

LIFO, however, can be a two-edged sword. The problem with LIFO arises during periods of declining inventories. As long as physical inventories are constant or increasing, the use of LIFO will generate a reasonably current cost of goods sold. When inventories decline, however, LIFO cost of goods sold will consist, in part, of very old inventory costs. Thus, in a period of rising prices, a draw-down of inventory will throw some old, and perhaps very low, inventory costs into cost of goods sold, thus distorting income measurement and generating additional income taxes. This situation must be understood when management considers adopting LIFO.

In sum, LIFO is of some help in measuring income when prices are changing and inventories are not declining, but it does not deal with the entire problem of realistic income measurement, only the "cost of goods sold" portion. On the other hand, LIFO leads to outdated inventory valuations on the statement of financial position. Its use is not an adequate substitute for replacement cost treatment of inventories.

Much of the application of replacement costs to inventories is mechanical and will not be repeated here. However, the informed replacement cost accountant needs to clearly understand the following points.

First, current year realiz*able* cost savings for a given set of inventory transactions will be identical under any historical cost flow-of-goods assumption. The use of LIFO, FIFO or another historical inventory method will affect only the division between realiz*ed* and *un*realiz*ed* cost savings. Hence, current operating income will be the same, although realiz*ed* income will differ depending on the historical inventory method employed.

Second, if *un*realiz*ed* cost savings on inventory are included in current replacement cost income, they must not be included a second time when realiz*ed* in the future. Consequently, if they are shown as part of replacement cost income currently, they must be deducted from realiz*ed* income for the period in which they are realiz*ed*. Thus, we can be sure that they will be counted in replacement cost income only once.

Third, the most useful measure of distributable income is given by current operating income when cost of goods sold is based on replacement cost at date of replacement. Indeed, looking to inventory purchase dates for measures of replacement costs generates a useful current operating income figure. Inventory which has not been replaced in the current year, however, should be costed at its year-end replacement cost, unless a future replacement cost is more appropriate.

Questions and Problems

6.1. The Argonaut Corporation had the following inventory transactions during the current year.

	Units	Price/Unit
Inventory, January 1	500	$10.00
Purchases:		
3/31	350	12.00
6/20	270	13.50
9/5	100	14.00
11/25	220	15.00
Inventory, December 31	750	

Replacement cost at December 31 is $15.50.

Required:

a. Compute the historical cost of goods sold for FIFO, LIFO and weighted average cost flow assumptions.

b. For purposes of computing the replacement cost of goods sold, it is assumed that sales took place on inventory purchase dates. Compute the number of units assumed to have been sold on each purchase date.

c. Compute the replacement cost of goods sold.

d. Compute realizable cost savings, realized cost savings and unrealized cost savings under the FIFO, LIFO and weighted average inventory methods.

6.2. You are given the following information for Moxie, Inc.

	Beginning Inventory		Cost of Goods Sold		Ending Inventory	
	Hist. Cost	Rep. Cost	Hist. Cost	Rep. Cost	Hist. Cost	Rep. Cost
FIFO	$25,000	$30,000	$145,000	$175,000	$32,000	$40,000
LIFO	15,000	30,000	149,000	175,000	18,000	40,000
Weighted Average*	20,000	30,000	147,000	175,000	25,000	40,000

*Assume that 90% of all goods available for sale were sold.

Required:

a. For the current year, compute realizable, realized and unrealized cost savings under each of the three inventory methods.

b. Prepare journal entries to record all cost savings arising during the current and previous years under each of the three inventory methods.

6.3. Briefly discuss the meaning and implications of "inventory profits."

6.4. Replacement cost of goods sold based on costs prevailing at inventory *replacement* dates rather than inventory *sale* dates may lead to a more useful measurement of operating profitability. Do you agree? Explain.

6.5. It was stated in the text that application of the "lower of cost or market" rule to historical cost financial statements will cause a divergence between realized income and historical cost net income. Explain.

6.6. Historical cost of goods sold under LIFO may be almost as good a measure as replacement cost of goods sold. However, the use of LIFO in a period of changing prices is still inadequate for financial statement purposes. Why?

Replacement Cost Treatment of Fixed Assets   **7**

The accounting for fixed assets under a replacement cost system is based on the principles used in the preceding chapter, although the technique is somewhat different than the inventory accounting procedures previously discussed. Aside from the accounting techniques, however, one major difficulty lies in arriving at the replacement cost of fixed assets.

The replacement cost of a fixed asset which was purchased new may easily be determined if the asset is marketed continuously and is not subject to significant technical or styling changes. In the case of a fixed asset which was purchased used, the replacement cost may be estimated by depreciating the replacement cost of a similar new asset or by determining the replacement cost of a similar used asset. But assets built to individual specifications, assets subject to rapid technological change and assets which are no longer manufactured will require an alternative method of estimating replacement cost.

There are basically two alternative methods available: (1) appraisal; and (2) the use of specific price index numbers for similar fixed assets to adjust the original cost base to the amount which would currently have to be paid for such an asset. Numerous price indexes are compiled by U.S. government agencies and by other organizations: wholesale price indexes, for example, are published by the Bureau of Labor Statistics. Some of the available indexes are suitable for determining the replacement cost of many kinds of assets (see Chapter 10).

To illustrate the treatment of fixed assets by means of a specific price index in a replacement cost system, assume that a firm has a group of assets which has a 10-year life and is depreciated on a straight-line basis. To simplify the computation, assume that no assets are bought or sold during the period and that it is not possible to obtain a replacement cost figure directly from the market. There are, however, specific price index figures available on comparable assets. The following information is obtained.

Replacement Cost Accounting and Fixed Assets

Equipment cost $10,000
Date of purchase   1/1/71
Expected life   10 years
Depreciation basis—Straight-line, no salvage value
Historical cost depreciation each year = $1,000

Specific price index values:

1967–1969 100
Beginning of 1971 125
End of 1975 175
End of 1976 210

The first step is to compute the replacement cost depreciation on the equipment during 1976. We assume that replacement cost depreciation for the year is based on the average of the beginning-of-year and end-of-year equipment replacement cost, although other "averaging" methods are available. The replacement cost at any point in time may be found by multiplying the historical cost by the ratio of the current specific price index over the specific price index at the time the asset was originally procured. Therefore, annual replacement cost depreciation is 1/10 times the average replacement cost of equipment for the year.

Replacement cost at the beginning of 1976:
($10,000 × 175/125) = $14,000

Replacement cost at the end of 1976:
($10,000 × 210/125) = $16,800

Average replacement cost in 1976:
($14,000 + $16,800)/2 = $15,400

Replacement cost depreciation for 1976:
1/10 × ($15,400) = $1,540

This $1,540 is the depreciation figure to be used in determining current operating income.

Realiz*able* cost savings result when the current replacement cost of an asset exceeds the historical cost book value of the asset. These realiz*able* cost savings, however, are *not* simply the difference between the beginning and end-of-period replacement costs: the change in replacement cost during the period must be *weighted* by the proportion of the asset's services *which still remains* to be used.

Consider an asset with four years of its ten-year estimated life remaining. The asset was originally purchased for $5,000; the first change in its replacement cost occurred early this year. To replace the asset today with a similar new asset would require an outlay of $8,000. What are the realiz*able* cost savings this year? At first glance, one might respond with "$3,000." If this were true, the asset would be written up to $8,000 and the $3,000 valuation adjustment would be depreciated over the remaining four years of life at an annual amount of $750. But the $3,000 relates to an asset with a life of *ten years*. Therefore, the increased depreciation charge, on a straight-line basis, should be only $300. To achieve this result, we weight the $3,000 change in replacement cost by 4/10, the proportion of the asset's services remaining. We thereby generate realiz*able* cost savings of $1,200, of which $300 will be realized during the current year through depreciation.

Keeping this point in mind, we now continue our previous illustration.

Computation of Realizable Cost Savings.   At the beginning of 1976, five years of the assets' life had expired, that is, 5/10 of the original assets remained. Furthermore, 4/10 would be available for use at the end of 1976. We assume that the 5/10 available at the beginning of 1976 was held while replacement cost rose from $14,000 to the average of $15,400 in 1976. Similarly, we assume that the 4/10 remaining at the end of 1976 was held while replacement cost rose from the average of $15,400 to $16,800 at the end of 1976.

$$\begin{aligned} \text{Realiz\emph{able} cost savings} \\ \text{during 1976} \end{aligned} \quad \begin{aligned} &= 5/10 \ (\$15,\!400 - \$14,\!000) \\ &\quad + 4/10 \ (\$16,\!800 - \$15,\!400) \\ &= \$700 + \$560 \\ &= \$1,\!260 \end{aligned}$$

Realized Cost Savings.   Cost savings realiz*ed* on the equipment during 1976 amounted to $540, the difference between replacement cost depreciation ($1,540) and historical cost depreciation ($1,000). Note that only a portion of the realiz*ed* cost savings became realiz*able* in 1976. This amount is $140, the difference between replacement cost depreciation of $1,540 for 1976 and hypothetical depreciation of $1,400 [= $14,000 × 1/10] based on the replacement cost at the beginning of 1976. The balance of $400 [= $540 − $140] represents realization during 1976 of cost savings which became realiz*able* prior to 1976, as the equipment increased in price to $14,000. The $400, then, was *unrealized* at the beginning of 1976.

Unrealized Cost Savings.   At the beginning of the year, there were $2,000 of unrealized cost savings in the equipment. The $2,000 is equal to the increase in replacement cost at the beginning of the year ($4,000) times the proportion of the assets' services remaining at the beginning of the year (5/10). During the year, realiz*able* cost savings of $1,260 arose, of which $140 were realiz*ed* through replacement cost depreciation. In addition, $400 of the beginning *un*realiz*ed* cost savings were realiz*ed* through replacement cost depreciation. Therefore, the ending balance in *un*realiz*ed* cost savings is $2,720 [= $2,000 + $1,260 − $540]. Of this amount, $1,120 [= $1,260 − $140] became realiz*able* this year and will be included in replacement cost income as *un*realized cost savings.

Replacement Cost Book Value. The replacement cost book value at the end of a period is equal to the replacement cost book value at the beginning of the period plus realiz*able* cost savings for the period (i.e., the amount by which the asset is written up to reflect its increased replacement cost) minus replacement cost depreciation for the period. We can compute the replacement cost book value at the beginning of 1976 by taking the historical cost book value and adding the *un*realized cost savings at the beginning of 1976. As previously mentioned, since we assume that replacement cost rose to $14,000 at the end of 1975, the *un*realized portion of the $4,000 [$14,000 − $10,000] in realiz*able* cost savings would be $2,000 [= 5/10 × $4,000] at the beginning of 1976. In Exhibit 7.1, we compute the replacement cost book value at the end of 1976, using both replacement cost and historical cost figures.

Exhibit 7.1

Computation of Replacement Cost Book Value
of Equipment, December 31, 1976

Historical cost	$10,000
Accumulated historical cost depreciation (5 years @ $1,000)	5,000
Historical cost book value, January 1, 1976	$ 5,000
Unrealized cost savings, January 1, 1976 (= $4,000 × 5/10)	2,000
Replacement cost book value, January 1, 1976	$ 7,000
Realizable cost savings in 1976	1,260
Replacement cost depreciation in 1976	(1,540)
Replacement cost book value, December 31, 1976	$ 6,720

Proof: Historical cost book value, December 31, 1976	$ 4,000
Unrealized cost savings, December 31, 1976:	
Unrealized cost savings, January 1	$ 2,000
Add Realizable cost savings in 1976	1,260
Less Realized cost savings in 1976	(540)
	$ 2,720
Replacement cost book value, December 31, 1976	$ 6,720

NOTE: We can now show the computation of realiz*able* cost savings using the identity,

Realiz*able* Cost Savings = Realiz*ed* Cost Savings + *Change* in *Un*realized Cost Savings

$1,260 = $540 + $720 (= $2,720 − $2,000)

The preceding calculation of replacement cost book value, although technically correct, is generally inadequate for financial reporting. Contemporary financial reports normally disclose more information about fixed assets than their book values. The statement of financial position will usually report the following information on fixed assets.

Property, Plant and Equipment, at cost. . . . . $xxxx
    Less Accumulated Depreciation xx
    (Book Value) . . . . $xxxx

The "Property, Plant and Equipment" line states the total cost of fixed assets, including, of course, the cost of assets acquired *new* in the past which are now *used*. A replacement cost statement of financial position should report the same information, but in terms of current replacement costs. In other words, assets acquired new in the past should be stated at the cost to replace them with new assets today. Similarly, replacement cost accumulated depreciation should be based on the replacement cost "new," to generate the net book value calculated above. This requirement gives rise to the so-called *revalorization problem*, which involves adjusting both the asset and its accumulated depreciation to a replacement cost "new" basis.

At December 31, 1976, the cost of replacing our equipment with similar new equipment is $16,800, based on the change since acquisition in the specific price index. Assume that the entries to record the previous years' increase in replacement cost, the current year realiz*able* cost savings and replacement cost depreciation have been made (these are shown later). The equipment account has a balance of $15,260 [=$10,000 + $4,000 + $1,260] and the accumulated depreciation account has a balance of $8,540 [= $5,000 + $2,000 + $1,540]. The difference is $6,720, the replacement cost book value. We need to write up the equipment account by $1,540 so it will show the December 31 replacement cost of $16,800. We also need to increase accumulated depreciation by $1,540 to reflect six years of depreciation based on a $16,800 depreciable base. This six years of depreciation amounts to $10,080 [= $8,540 + $1,540, or 6 × $1,680]. Once the entry to adjust the equipment and accumulated depreciation accounts has been made, the revalorization problem is solved. The journal entries required to record the replacement cost data in 1976 follow, as do the postings to the appropriate ledger accounts. To preserve the historical cost data, we record the replacement cost increments in *valuation adjustment* accounts.

The first journal entry records the increase in replacement cost to $14,000 at the beginning of the year, the related increase in accumulated depreciation ($2,000) and the *unrealized* cost savings ($2,000) at the beginning of the year.

Dr. Equipment Valuation Adjustment. 4,000   (1)
   Cr. Accumulated Depreciation
       Valuation Adjustment 2,000
   Cr. Unrealized Cost Savings. 2,000

To record the increase in replacement cost, accumulated depreciation and *unrealized* cost savings at the beginning of the year.

Dr. Depreciation Expense. 1,000   (2)
Dr. Depreciation Expense Valuation
    Adjustment   540
   Cr. Accumulated Depreciation. 1,000
   Cr. Accumulated Depreciation
       Valuation Adjustment   540

To record replacement cost straight-line depreciation for 1976, keeping the amount attributable to the increase in replacement cost separate as a valuation adjustment to accumulated depreciation.

Dr. Equipment Valuation Adjustment. 1,260   (3)
   Cr. Realizable Cost Savings 1,260

To record the cost savings which became realiz*able* on the equipment during 1976.

Dr. Realizable Cost Savings.   140   (4)
Dr. Unrealized Cost Savings   400
   Cr. Realized Cost Savings   540

To record the realization of the cost savings represented by the excess of replacement cost depreciation over historical cost depreciation, charging current year realiz*able* cost savings and (prior-year) *unrealized* cost savings for their respective amounts.

Dr. Realizable Cost Savings. 1,120   (5)
   Cr. Unrealized Cost Savings. 1,120

To reflect the fact that $1,120 in cost savings which became realiz*able* during 1976 on equipment are *unrealized* at December 31, 1976.

Dr. Equipment Valuation Adjustment. 1,540   (6)
   Cr. Accumulated Depreciation
       Valuation Adjustment 1,540

To restate the equipment and accumulated depreciation accounts on a replacement cost "new" basis; $1,540 = $16,800 − $15,260. (This is the *revalorization* entry.)

Equipment		
Beg. Balance 10,000	To Balance	10,000
Balance 10,000		

Equipment Valuation Adjustment		
(1) 4,000	To Balance	6,800
(6) 1,540		
6,800		6,800
Balance 6,800		

Accumulated Depreciation		
To Balance 6,000	Beg. Balance	5,000
	(2)	1,000
6,000		6,000
	Balance	6,000

Accumulated Depreciation Valuation Adjustment		
(3) 1,260		
To Balance 4,080	(1)	2,000
	(2)	540
	(6)	1,540
4,080		4,080
	Balance	4,080

Unrealized Cost Savings		
(4) 400	(1)	2,000
To Balance 2,720	(6)	1,120
3,120		3,120
	Balance	2,720

Depreciation Expense		
(2) 1,000	(A)	1,000

Depreciation Expense Valuation Adjustment		
(2) 540	(A)	540

Realizable Cost Savings		
(4) 140	(3)	1,260
(5) 1,120		
1,260		1,260

Realized Cost Savings		
(B) 540	(4)	540

(A) To Current Operating Income
(B) To Realized Income

In each of the remaining four years of the equipment's life, one-fourth ($680) of the *unrealized* cost savings will be *realized*. If replacement cost remains at $16,800, this amount ($680) will exactly equal the difference between replacement cost depreciation ($1,680) and historical cost depreciation ($1,000).

The presentation of the equipment account in the replacement cost statement of financial position is shown below.

Equipment (Replacement Cost New)	$16,800
Less Accumulated Depreciation	10,080
(Replacement Cost Book Value)	$ 6,720

Other Issues in the Replacement Cost Treatment of Fixed Assets

Accelerated Depreciation: Sum-of-the-Years'-Digits

The examples in this chapter so far have incorporated two simplifying assumptions—straight-line depreciation and zero salvage value. We now examine the effects of relaxing these assumptions.

First we consider accelerated depreciation methods in the context of replacement cost accounting. One such method is *sum-of-the-years'-digits*. For an asset with a useful life of four years, the annual depreciation rate is shown below.

Years' Digits	Rate
1	4/10 = 40%
2	3/10 = 30%
3	2/10 = 20%
4	1/10 = 10%
10	

With this method, the appropriate rate would be applied to the average replacement cost of the asset during each year. No additional problems would be introduced. Each year, a revalorization entry would be required to state the asset and its accumulated depreciation at the amounts which would have resulted if sum-of-the-years'-digits depreciation had been applied to current replacement cost *since date of acquisition*.

Consider an asset which cost $10,000, has no salvage value and has a four-year life. Sum-of-the-years'-digits depreciation is to be used. There is no change in replacement cost during year 1 and during most of year 2. Replacement cost rises to $15,000 at the *end* of year 2, giving an average replacement cost of $12,500 during year 2. At the end of year 1, the historical cost accounts show the following balances.

Asset.	.$10,000
Accumulated Depreciation	4,000
Book Value	.$ 6,000

The journal entries to record the developments in year 2 are:

Dr. Depreciation Expense.	3,000	
Dr. Depreciation Expense Valuation		
Adjustment	750	
Cr. Accumulated Depreciation.		3,000
Cr. Accumulated Depreciation Valuation		
Adjustment.		750

To record replacement cost sum-of-the-years'-digits depreciation in year 2, applying the 30% rate to the average replacement cost for the year ($12,500).

Dr. Asset Valuation Adjustment 2,250
    Cr. Realizable Cost Savings 2,250

To record realiz*able* cost savings where 6/10 of the asset was held while replacement cost rose from $10,000 to $12,500 and 3/10 of the asset was held while replacement cost rose from $12,500 to $15,000. [$2,250 = 6/10 ($12,500 − $10,000) + 3/10 ($15,000 − $12,500).]

Dr. Realizable Cost Savings. 2,250
    Cr. Realized Cost Savings 750
    Cr. Unrealized Cost Savings. 1,500

To record realization of the cost savings represented by the excess of replacement cost depreciation over historical cost depreciation and to reclassify the remaining realiz*able* cost savings as *unrealized* at year end.

Dr. Asset Valuation Adjustment 2,750
    Cr. Accumulated Depreciation Valuation
        Adjustment. 2,750

To restate the asset and accumulated depreciation accounts on a replacement cost "new" basis; [$2,750 = $15,000 − ($10,000 + $2,250)]. (This is the *revalorization* entry.)

After the entries are posted to the ledger accounts, the books show the following replacement cost balances at the end of year 2.

Asset. $15,000
Accumulated Depreciation   10,500
Book Value . . . . $ 4,500

The replacement cost book value can be verified as follows. Recall that ending replacement cost book value equals beginning replacement cost book value ($6,000), plus current year realiz*able* cost savings ($2,250), less replacement cost depreciation ($3,750). The *unrealized* cost savings of $1,500 will be realiz*ed* according to the schedule shown below.

Year	Replacement Cost Depr.	Historical Cost Depr.	Realized Cost Savings
3	20%(15,000) = 3,000	20%(10,000) = 2,000	1,000
4	10%(15,000) = 1,500	10%(10,000) = 1,000	500
			1,500

Double-declining balance is another common accelerated depreciation method. Each year's depreciation is twice the straight-line rate times the undepreciated basis of the asset. For an asset having a four-year life, the rate would be 50 percent [= 2 × 25%] per year. Firms using double-

Accelerated Depreciation: Double-Declining Balance

declining balance often switch to straight-line during the year in which the accelerated depreciation charge drops to or below the straight-line depreciation charge on the remaining depreciable balance. Using the data from the example on sum-of-the-years'-digits depreciation, we work through double-declining balance depreciation in a replacement cost accounting system.

Recall that the asset cost $10,000, has no salvage value and has a four-year life. Double-declining balance depreciation is to be used. Replacement cost rose to $15,000 at the end of year 2, giving an average replacement cost of $12,500 during year 2. At the end of year 1, the historical cost accounts show the following balances.

$$\begin{array}{ll} \text{Asset} & \text{\$10,000} \\ \text{Accumulated Depreciation} & \underline{5,000} \\ \text{Book Value} & \underline{\$\ 5,000} \end{array}$$

The following journal entries record the developments in year 2.

Dr. Depreciation Expense 2,500
Dr. Depreciation Expense Valuation
    Adjustment   625
    Cr. Accumulated Depreciation 2,500
    Cr. Accumulated Depreciation Valuation
        Adjustment   625

To record replacement cost double-declining balance depreciation in year 2, applying the 50% rate to the average *undepreciated* replacement cost balance for the year of $6,250 [= ($5,000 + $7,500)/2].*

Dr. Asset Valuation Adjustment 1,875
    Cr. Realizable Cost Savings 1,875

To record realiz*able* cost savings where 50% of the asset was held while replacement cost rose from $10,000 to $12,500 and 25% (50% × 50%) was held while replacement cost rose from $12,500 to $15,000. [$1,875 = 50%($12,500 − $10,000) + 25%($15,000 − $12,500).]

Dr. Realizable Cost Savings 1,875
    Cr. Realized Cost Savings   625
    Cr. Unrealized Cost Savings 1,250

To record the realization of the cost savings represented by the excess of replacement cost depreciation over historical cost depreciation and to reclassify the remaining realiz*able* cost savings as *un*realiz*ed* at year end.

---

*Since 50 percent of the asset was depreciated at the beginning of year two, its beginning undepreciated balance was $5,000. After replacement cost rose to $15,000 at the end of year 2, its (50 percent) undepreciated balance rose to $7,500.

Dr. Asset Valuation Adjustment   3,125
   Cr. Accumulated Depreciation Valuation
      Adjustment. 3,125

To restate the asset and accumulated depreciation accounts on a replacement cost "new" basis; $3,125 = [\$15,000 - \$10,000 - \$1,875]$. (This is the *revalorization* entry.)

After the entries are posted to the ledger accounts, the books show the following replacement cost balances at the end of year 2.

Asset. \$15,000
Accumulated Depreciation . . . . <u> 11,250</u>
Book Value . . . . <u>\$ 3,750</u>

The replacement cost book value can be verified by adding beginning replacement cost book value ($5,000) to current year realiz*able* cost savings ($1,875) and subtracting replacement cost depreciation ($3,125). The un*realized* cost savings of $1,250 will be realiz*ed* according to the schedule shown below, assuming a switch to straight-line depreciation in year 3.

	Straight-Line Depreciation		
Year	Replacement Cost	Historical Cost	Realized Cost Savings
3	3,750/2 = 1,875	2,500/2 = 1,250	625
4	3,750/2 = 1,875	2,500/2 = 1,250	<u>625</u>
			<u><u>1,250</u></u>

NOTE: At the end of year 2, historical cost book value is $2,500. This is equal to the historical cost book value ($5,000) at the end of year 1 less year-2 historical cost depreciation [$2,500 = 50% × $5,000].

The use of accelerated depreciation based on historical costs does *not* adequately reflect the effects of inflation. Even though it involves depreciating an asset *faster* than the straight-line method, the total amount depreciated will not exceed historical cost. (Indeed, this is usually done for tax purposes—i.e., to increase the present value of the tax savings associated with the depreciation deduction.) We have shown that replacement cost depreciation combined with an accelerated depreciation method has a significant impact in excess of historical cost accelerated depreciation. Finally, historical cost accelerated depreciation ignores the increase in replacement cost of the undepreciated balance. In fact, in a period of rising prices, historical cost accelerated depreciation understates asset values even more than straight-line depreciation.

Accounting for fixed assets requires that any *salvage value* be excluded from the depreciable basis. If an asset costing $10,000 is projected to have

Replacement Cost
Salvage Value

a salvage or scrap value of $1,000 at the end of its useful life, then only $9,000 will be depreciated. Hence, in a period of rising replacement costs, care must be taken to properly apportion these increases between the depreciable basis and the salvage value.

If the replacement cost rises from $10,000 to $15,000, a decision must be made regarding the replacement cost salvage value. If management's historical experience suggests that salvage value is typically 10 percent of cost, then the salvage value rises to $1,500 and the depreciable basis rises to $13,500. Replacement cost depreciation would be calculated on the depreciable basis of $13,500. Realiz*able* cost savings would be $5,000 for the year in which the replacement cost rose to $15,000. Of this $5,000, $4,500 would be realiz*ed* during the life of the asset through replacement cost depreciation. The remaining $500, attributed to the salvage value, would be *un*realiz*ed* until the asset is finally retired and disposed of.

It is important, then, (1) to make certain that the salvage value is measured in replacement cost terms and (2) not to depreciate any realiz*able* cost savings which pertain to the salvage value. Increases in depreciable basis will, of course, be handled consistently with the previous examples in this chapter.

Sometimes, when double-declining balance depreciation is used, the undepreciated balance at the end of the asset's life is viewed as its salvage value. In this case, a change in the replacement cost of the asset would result in a change in this remaining undepreciated balance and would represent *un*realiz*ed* cost savings until the asset is retired.

It is useful at this time to review the notion of revalorization. When replacement cost increases after an asset has been placed in service, current period realiz*able* cost savings accrue only to the unused portion of the asset. The unused portion is assumed to be represented by 100 percent minus the percentage that has been depreciated. Hence, the entry which records realiz*able* cost savings writes up only the unused portion of the asset. Proper financial statement disclosure normally requires that asset costs at acquisition and depreciation allocated since acquisition be reported. A revalorization entry is necessary, to adjust the entire asset balance and the accumulated depreciation to reflect the current replacement cost "new." After revalorization, both the asset balance and the accumulated depreciation appear as if the current replacement cost had been paid at acquisition. The replacement cost book value is unchanged by revalorization, but the gross asset and accumulated depreciation balances will be increased.

Replacement Cost Depreciation in Fixed Manufacturing Overhead Rates

When a firm *manufactures*, rather than *purchases*, its inventory, depreciation of manufacturing plant and equipment becomes a part of the fixed overhead allocated to production. As mentioned in the chapter on inventories, such overhead rates must be revised to reflect current costs.

Therefore, replacement cost depreciation of manufacturing plant and equipment must be charged to *factory overhead* rather than *depreciation expense*. The problem remains, of course, how to allocate the new current cost overhead. An example will illustrate how this might be accomplished in practice.

A firm manufactures widgets. Fixed manufacturing overhead is applied to production according to a predetermined rate, allocated on the basis of direct labor hours worked. We assume that the period's historical cost fixed manufacturing overhead was $10,000. Increased replacement costs result in replacement cost manufacturing overhead of $12,000 for the period. The total increase in replacement cost of fixed manufacturing facilities is $20,000. The historical cost overhead rate of $1.00 per direct labor hour is based on normal activity of 10,000 hours. The replacement cost overhead rate therefore becomes $1.20 per direct labor hour. During the period, 6,000 direct labor hours were worked on widgets that were completed (of which one-half were sold) and 4,000 direct labor hours on widgets that remained in work in process. The following journal entries record the overhead incurrence and application during the year.

Dr. Fixed Manufacturing Overhead 10,000
    Cr. Accumulated Depreciation — Factory Equipment 8,000
    Cr. Prepaid Expenses 2,000

To record the actual historical fixed manufacturing overhead for the year.

Dr. Finished Goods Inventory 3,000
Dr. Cost of Goods Sold 3,000
Dr. Work in Process Inventory 4,000
    Cr. Fixed Manufacturing Overhead 10,000

To allocate historical fixed manufacturing overhead to the period's production and sales.

Dr. Manufacturing Facilities Valuation
    Adjustment 20,000
    Cr. Realizable Cost Savings 20,000

To record the cost savings which became realiz*able* during the year on the manufacturing facilities.

Dr. Fixed Manufacturing Overhead Valuation
    Adjustment 2,000
    Cr. Accumulated Depreciation Valuation
        Adjustment — Manufacturing Facilities 2,000

To record the increase in fixed manufacturing overhead due to re-placement cost depreciation on manufacturing facilities.

Dr. Cost of Goods Sold Valuation Adjustment 600
Dr. Finished Goods Inventory Valuation
    Adjustment 600
Dr. Work in Process Inventory Valuation
    Adjustment 800
  Cr. Fixed Manufacturing Overhead Valuation
    Adjustment. 2,000

To record the increase in replacement cost of production and sales due to the excess of replacement cost fixed manufacturing overhead over historical cost fixed manufacturing overhead.

Dr. Realizable Cost Savings. 20,000
  Cr. Realized Cost Savings   600
  Cr. Unrealized Cost Savings. 19,400

To reclassify realiz*able* cost savings as either realiz*ed* or *un*realiz*ed*. Under *full* or *absorption* costing, fixed manufacturing overhead is considered a *product cost* rather than a *period expense*. Therefore, only the portion of the realiz*able* cost savings in cost of goods sold [$600 = 3,000/10,000 × $2,000] is deemed to have been realiz*ed*. The remaining $1,400 of realiz*able* cost savings associated with the $2,000 increase in depreciation of manufacturing facilities has, in effect, increased the replacement cost of the work in process and finished goods inventories. Hence, the $1,400 in inventory will remain *un*realiz*ed* until the inventory is sold. In addition, the other $18,000 of realiz*able* cost savings relates to the undepreciated manufacturing facilities and is also *un*realiz*ed*.

As a practical matter, factory overhead would typically not be allocated in this way. It would flow through work in process to finished goods and then to cost of goods sold rather than being charged directly to the inventory and cost of goods sold accounts, as we have treated it for the sake of simplicity. The net result, of course, would be the same.

Questions and Problems

7.1. Briefly discuss and evaluate the ways in which the replacement cost of fixed assets can be estimated.

7.2. "Fixed asset replacement costs are every bit as objective as inventory replacement costs." Do you agree? Why or why not?

7.3. On January 1, 19x5, the Cyclops Corporation purchased a computerized drill press. The press cost $100,000, has an expected life of five years and no salvage value. Cyclops uses straight-line depreciation to allocate the cost of its fixed assets over their useful lives. At the end of 19x9, we observe that the replacement cost of the drill press rose in each year subsequent to 19x5 according to the following schedule.

Date	Replacement Cost
12/31/x6	$115,000
12/31/x7	125,000
12/31/x8	140,000
12/31/x9	160,000

Required:

a. Compute the annual historical cost depreciation charge.

b. Compute the replacement cost depreciation for each year (assume that the increases in replacement cost occurred more or less evenly over each year).

c. Compute realizable cost savings for each year.

d. Prepare a schedule of changes in replacement cost book value and the amount of the revalorization adjustment required in each of the five years, 19x5–19x9.

e. Prepare a schedule showing realizable cost savings, realized cost savings and unrealized cost savings over the life of the drill press.

7.4. A machine is purchased on January 1, 19x0, for $5,000. The machine is to be depreciated by the straight-line method over a ten-year useful life and has no salvage value. Specific price index values for similar machinery appear below.

Date	Specific Price Index—Machinery
1/1/x0	110
12/31/x3	132
12/31/x4	165

The firm is switching to replacement cost accounting in 19x4.

Required:

a. Compute replacement cost depreciation for 19x4 and give the journal entry to record it.

b. Compute realizable, realized and unrealized cost savings for 19x4.

c. Give the journal entries necessary to record the machine at its 12/31/x4 replacement cost, including the revalorization adjustment and all entries required to record the realizable, realized and unrealized cost savings.

7.5. Refer to the data in problem 7.3. In each of the following two situations, compute replacement cost depreciation, realizable cost savings and give the journal entries related to the drill press for the years 19x6 and 19x7.

a. The firm uses sum-of-the-years'-digits depreciation.

b. The firm uses double-declining balance depreciation.

Suppose that at the end of 19x6 it was determined that the drill press had a salvage value of $5,000. In each of the following two situations, compute replacement cost depreciation and realizable cost savings in 19x6 and 19x7. Also give the revalorization entries at 12/31/x6 and 12/31/x7.

c. The firm uses straight-line depreciation.

d. The firm uses sum-of-the-years'-digits depreciation.

Replacement Cost Treatment of Other Accounts

Short-term monetary assets and liabilities such as cash and accounts receivable and payable are already stated in current dollars which, by definition, will equal their current values. Therefore, no replacement cost adjustments are necessary for these accounts.

This category includes investments in common stocks. Returns on common stocks consist of uncertain dividends and capital gains. Capital gain returns, of course, are classic examples of holding gains. As the market value of such investments fluctuates, the firm experiences pure realiz*able* holding gains (or losses). Historical cost accounting does not adequately deal with these investments for two reasons. First, such investments are recorded and carried at cost, or lower of cost or market, with no upward adjustments until they are sold. Second, holding gains which accrue over time are not recognized until realized, although holding losses would be recognized under the "lower of cost or market" rule. Then when realized, holding gains are attributed in their entirety to the period of sale. Consequently, evaluation of management's holding activities in this area is difficult if not impossible. In addition, the historical cost statement of financial position carries these investments at amounts which, if holding gains have occurred, are not representative of their current market values. Under replacement cost accounting, both of these defects are rectified. Realiz*able* holding gains are recorded *as they occur* and position statements will reflect current values. A numerical example follows, to illustrate the replacement cost treatment of investments in securities with no fixed return.

A firm has investments in the following common stocks.

Investments in Securities with No Fixed Return

Issues	Historical Cost, Last Year	Market Value Beg. of Year	Market Value September 30	End of Year Market Value of Securities on Hand
Amalgamated Industries Ltd.	$300	$400	$440	$350
Integrated Conglomerates, Inc.	350	340	320	286
Total	$650	$740	$760	$636

On September 30, 10 percent of the firm's holdings in each of the two securities is sold. We now prepare journal entries to record the current year's developments and post them to the appropriate ledger accounts. In the case of marketable securities, we think the term *holding gains* is more descriptive than *cost savings*. The first entry is necessary to record the unrealized holding gains at the beginning of the year.

Dr. Marketable Securities Valuation Adjustment. . 90   (1)
    Cr. Unrealized Holding Gains 90

To record holding gains *unrealized* at the beginning of the year [$90 = $740 − $650].

Dr. Marketable Securities Valuation Adjustment. . . . 2   (2)
    Cr. Realizable Holding Gains. 2

To record the current year's realiz*able* holding gains pertaining to the securities which were sold [$2 = 10% ($760 − $740)].

Dr. Cash 76   (3)
    Cr. Marketable Securities 65
    Cr. Marketable Securities Valuation Adjustment 11

To record the sale of 10 percent of the marketable securities for $76.

Dr. Realizable Holding Gains 30   (4)
    Cr. Marketable Securities Valuation Adjustment 30

To record the decrease in replacement cost of marketable securities on hand at year end [$30 = 90% × $740 − $636].

Dr. Unrealized Holding Gains 39   (5)
    Cr. Realized Holding Gains 11
    Cr. Realizable Holding Gains. 28

To reclassify the realiz*able* holding gains (losses) as realiz*ed* ($2 gain) and *un*realized ($30 loss) and to record the realization of the prior period *un*realized holding gain ($9). (Thus the debit to *un*realized holding gains consists of the $9 which was realiz*ed* and the $30 loss which is *un*realized.)

Marketable Securities			
Beg. Balance	650	(3)	65
		To Balance	585
	650		650
Balance	585		

Marketable Securities Valuation Adjustment			
(1)	90	(3)	11
(2)	2	(4)	30
		To Balance	51
	92		92
Balance	51		

Cash			
(3)	76	To Balance	76
Balance	76		

Unrealized Holding Gains			
(5)	39	(1)	90
To Balance	51		
	90	Balance	90
			51

Realizable Holding Gains			
(4)	30	(2)	2
		(5)	28
	30		30

Realized Holding Gains			
(A)	11	(5)	11

(A) To Realized Income

It is clear that investments in securities with variable returns create no additional problems under replacement cost accounting, even when holding losses occur.

Bonds and other fixed income securities are like stocks in the sense that their prices may fluctuate; the coupon (interest) payments, however, are fixed in the bond contract. Replacement costs are important in two respects here: (1) to reflect changes in the market value of the securities; (2) to restate the coupon interest to bring it into line with current market rates of interest. The replacement cost treatment of bonds payable is, in principle, identical with the treatment of investments in bonds, except for the reversal of debits and credits and the different account titles (e.g., *credit* bonds *payable* on issue versus *debit* investment in bonds on acquisition). The following example illustrates only the treatment of bonds payable.

Securities with Fixed Return

Several years ago, the firm issued $1,000 of 6 percent bonds at par. Interest is paid semiannually and the bonds are due to be retired at the end of next year. During the current year, rising interest rates caused the price of the bonds to gradually fall, and the yield to maturity to gradually rise. At year end, the market value of the bonds stood at $981 and the yield to maturity at 8 percent. During the year, the only bond-related transactions entered in the books were the two semiannual interest payments of $30 each. We now show the adjustments required at year end to bring the bonds into a replacement cost accounting system. We then show the posting of the adjustments to the appropriate ledger accounts.

Dr. Bonds Payable Valuation Adjustment.   19   (1)
   Cr. Realizable Cost Savings   19
To record the decrease in the market value of bonds payable and to recognize the related reali*zable* cost savings [$19 = $1,000 − $981].

Dr. Interest Expense Valuation Adjustment   10   (2)
    Cr. Realizable Cost Savings   10
To adjust interest expense to reflect the current (replacement) cost of borrowed capital and to recognize realiz*able* cost savings. Average current interest rate during the year is 7 percent [= (6% + 8%)/2]; [$10 = (7% − 6%) × $1,000].*

Dr. Realizable Cost Savings.   29   (3)
    Cr. Realized Cost Savings   10
    Cr. Unrealized Cost Savings.   19

To reclassify as realiz*ed* cost savings the excess of replacement cost interest expense over historical cost interest expense and to show the cost savings attributable to the decline in value of the bond liability as *un*realized at year end.

Before posting to the ledger accounts, we should make a few comments on the realiz*able* cost savings generated above. The $19 adjustment to bonds payable and the related realiz*able* cost savings can be explained in two ways. First, given current money market conditions, only $981 could be borrowed today under the terms of the bond contract. Hence, the firm has *gained* $19 because it issued the bonds when interest rates were lower and $1,000 was borrowed under the terms of the bond contract. Second, the firm has gained because it could liquidate a $1,000 liability today for $981 by simply purchasing the bonds in the market. Both interpretations clarify the credit of $19 to realiz*able* cost savings.

The $10 adjustment which increases current interest expense also represents a cost saving to the firm. The firm originally issued its bonds when the interest rate was 6 percent, thereby requiring annual interest payments of $60. If the firm had issued the same quantity of bonds at the current year's average interest rate of 7 percent, annual interest payments of $70 would be required. As a consequence, $10 in cost savings for the current year has been realiz*ed* because the replacement cost interest expense exceeded the historical cost (contractual) interest expense by $10. The firm has saved on annual interest expense because it borrowed when the interest rate was lower than that presently prevailing. The ledger accounts are shown below.

---

*Another approach is to multiply the average interest rate (7 percent) by the average liability [$990.50 = ($1,000 + $981)/2] and subtract the historical cost interest expense of $60. If this were done, the interest expense adjustment would be $9.34 [= $69.34 − $60.00].

	Bonds Payable		
To Balance	1,000	Beg. Balance	1,000
		Balance	1,000

	Bonds Payable Valuation Adjustment		
(1)	19	To Balance	19
Balance	19		

	Interest Expense		
Beg. Balance	60	(A)	60

	Interest Expense Valuation Adjustment		
(2)	10	(A)	10

	Realizable Cost Savings		
(3)	29	(1)	19
		(2)	10
	29		29

	Realized Cost Savings		
(B)	10	(3)	10

	Unrealized Cost Savings		
To Balance	19	(3)	19
		Balance	19

(A) To Current Operating Income
(B) To Realized Income

Note that in the subsequent year, when the bonds are retired at face value, the *un*realiz*ed* cost savings of $19 will vanish, as realiz*able* cost savings will be *debited* for this amount. If the market interest rate of 8 percent stays the same, however, an additional $20 in cost savings will be realiz*ed* on the interest expense [(8% − 6%) × $1,000]. Therefore, the net realiz*able* cost savings in the year of retirement will be $1, the difference between the interest "savings" of $20 in the year of retirement and $19, the *present value* of those interest "savings" (discounted at 8 percent) at the end of the current year. In other words, realiz*able* cost savings occurred because of the drop in the market value of the bonds at the end of the current year; the contractual interest payments of $60 are exactly $20 less than the current interest rate requires. Discounting this $20 (two semiannual payments of $10 each) to its present value at the current interest rate of 8 percent gives us the $19.

Questions and Problems

8.1. How are current monetary assets and liabilities treated under replacement cost accounting? Draw an analogy with the treatment of these items under the price-level restatements discussed in Chapter 2.

8.2. The treatment of noncurrent monetary assets and liabilities under replacement cost accounting differs from that prescribed in Chapter 2. What is the nature of the difference(s) and which treatment seems more logical?

8.3. The Atlanta Corporation is beginning a program of short-term investments in marketable securities. Despite mounting evidence to the contrary, Atlanta's financial vice-president feels that the market can be "beaten" by astute trading. The following information for the portfolio is given.

	Stock A	Stock B	Stock C
1/1 Purchase	100 @ $100	1,000 @ $300	
3/1 Sale	50 @ $120	100 @ $380	
6/1 Purchase			500 @ $500
9/1 Sale		100 @ $440	
12/31 Closing Price	$175	$500	$600

Required:

a. Compute the replacement cost of securities on hand at December 31.

b. Compute realizable, realized and unrealized gains for the year.

c. Give the journal entries to record all historical cost and replacement cost related transactions during the year. Valuation adjustments are made at year end only.

d. Using the data for Stock B only, compute realizable, realized and unrealized gains under the following assumptions: (1) the stock had been purchased for $400 per share, rather than $300; (2) the closing price on December 31 was $275 rather than $500.

8.4. A firm issued $2,000,000 of ten-year 8 percent semiannual bonds at par on 1/1/x6. By 12/31/x6, the market value of the bonds had fallen to $1,860,939 as the market rate of interest gradually increased to 10 percent during 19x6.

Required:

a. From the point of view of the issuing firm, give all entries relative to the sale of the bonds, the two semiannual interest payments during the year and the replacement cost adjustments at year end.

b. Assume that a single firm purchased the entire bond issue on 1/1/x6. From the point of view of the purchasing firm, give all entries relative to the purchase of the bonds, the two semiannual interest payments during the year and the replacement cost adjustments at year end.

c. Suppose the bonds had been sold at a discount of $100,000 (i.e., for $1,900,000) and, alternatively, at a premium of $100,000 (i.e., for $2,100,000). How would each of these situations affect (1) the issuing firm and (2) the purchasing firm with respect to interest expense (income) and realizable, realized and unrealized cost savings. Assume that the bond discount or premium is to be amortized by the straight-line method. Journal entries are not required.

9 Illustration of Comprehensive Replacement Cost Financial Statements

To present a complete set of financial statements, our examples on inventories, fixed assets, marketable securities and bonds payable have been incorporated into the following data for the CVA Corporation for 19x6. Exhibit 9.1 shows historical and replacement cost statements of financial position at December 31, 19x5. The replacement cost statement of financial position reflects the replacement cost of marketable securities, inventories and equipment and the related *un*realize*d* cost savings at the end of 19x5.

Exhibit 9.1

CVA CORPORATION
Statement of Financial Position
December 31, 19x5

	Historical Cost	Replacement Cost
ASSETS		
Cash and Receivables	$ 1,800	$ 1,800
Marketable Securities	650	740
Inventories	2,800	2,890
Total Current Assets	$ 5,250	$ 5,430
Equipment, at Cost	$10,000	$14,000
Less: Accumulated Depreciation	5,000	7,000
Total Fixed Assets	$ 5,000	$ 7,000
Total Assets	$10,250	$12,430
LIABILITIES		
Accounts Payable	$ 2,500	$ 2,500
Bonds Payable	1,000	1,000
Total Liabilities	$ 3,500	$ 3,500

196

Exhibit 9.1 (continued)

STOCKHOLDERS' EQUITY

Capital Stock	$ 2,000	$ 2,000
Retained (Realized) Earnings	4,750	4,750
Unrealized Cost Savings/Holding Gains		2,180
Total Stockholders' Equity	$ 6,750	$ 8,930
Total Liabilities and Stockholders' Equity.	$10,250	$12,430

We assume that the firm accounts for its inventories on a FIFO (first-in, first-out) basis, and that the equipment is being depreciated on a straight-line basis over ten years with no salvage value. We also assume that all sales were made for cash and all merchandise purchases and expenses were paid for in cash. The journal entries summarizing all transactions made during the year will provide enough information for the preparation of historical cost and replacement cost financial statements. They have also been posted and summarized in the appropriate general ledger accounts.

Comprehensive Replacement Cost Financial Statements

Dr. Cash 12,000   (1)
    Cr. Sales 12,000

A summary entry to record sales for the year.

Dr. Operating Expenses 3,600   (2)
    Cr. Cash 3,600

A summary entry to record operating expenses for the year.

Dr. Merchandise Purchases 6,814   (3)
    Cr. Cash 6,814

A summary entry to record merchandise purchases for the year.

Dr. Inventory 706   (4)
Dr. Cost of Goods Sold 6,108
    Cr. Purchases 6,814

To record cost of goods sold (FIFO) for the year and adjust inventory to the amount on hand at year end.

Dr. Cost of Goods Sold Valuation
    Adjustment 299.70   (5)
    Cr. Realizable Cost Savings 278.70
    Cr. Inventory Valuation Adjustment 21.00

To adjust ending inventory and cost of goods sold to replacement cost and record the related realiz*able* cost savings.

Dr. Depreciation Expense 1,000   (6)
Dr. Depreciation Expense Valuation
    Adjustment 540
    Cr. Accumulated Depreciation 1,000
    Cr. Accumulated Depreciation Valuation
       Adjustment 540

To record historical cost and replacement cost depreciation for the year.

Dr. Equipment Valuation Adjustment. 1,260   (7)
   Cr. Realizable Cost Savings 1,260

To record the cost which became realiz*able* on the equipment during the year.

Dr. Equipment Valuation Adjustment. 1,540   (8)
   Cr. Accumulated Depreciation Valuation
      Adjustment. 1,540

To restate the equipment and accumulated depreciation accounts on the basis of replacement cost "new." (This is the *revalorization* entry.)

Dr. Marketable Securities Valuation Adjustment. . . . 2   (9)
   Cr. Realizable Holding Gains. 2

To record the current year's realiz*able* holding gains pertaining to the securities which were sold.

Dr. Cash 76   (10)
   Cr. Marketable Securities 65
   Cr. Marketable Securities Valuation Adjustment 11

To record the sale of 10 percent of the marketable securities for $76.

Dr. Realizable Holding Gains 30   (11)
   Cr. Marketable Securities Valuation Adjustment 30

To record the decrease in replacement cost of marketable securities on hand at year end.

Dr. Interest Expense. 60   (12)
   Cr. Cash 60

To record payment of interest on $1,000 of 6 percent bonds payable.

Dr. Bonds Payable Valuation Adjustment. 19   (13)
Dr. Interest Expense Valuation Adjustment 10

   Cr. Realizable Cost Savings 29

To record the realiz*able* cost savings associated with the decline in market value of the bonds payable and the increase in replacement cost interest expense.

Dr. Realizable Cost Savings. 1,567.70   (14)
   Cr. Realized Cost Savings 849.70
   Cr. Realized Holding Gains 11.00
   Cr. Realizable Holding Gains. 28.00
   Cr. Unrealized Cost Savings/Holding Gains. 679.00

To reclassify realiz*able* cost savings and holding gains during the period as either realiz*ed* or *un*realiz*ed*.

Dr. Sales 12,000.00   (15)
     Cr. Operating Expenses 3,600.00
     Cr. Cost of Goods Sold 6,108.00
     Cr. Cost of Goods Sold Valuation Adjustment . . .   299.70
     Cr. Depreciation Expense 1,000.00
     Cr. Depreciation Expense Valuation Adjustment .   540.00
     Cr. Interest Expense 60.00
     Cr. Interest Expense Valuation Adjustment 10.00
     Cr. Current Operating Income 382.30

To close all revenue and expense accounts (reflecting replacement costs) to current operating income.

Dr. Current Operating Income 382.30   (16)
Dr. Realized Cost Savings 849.70
Dr. Realized Holding Gains 11.00
     Cr. Realized Income 1,243.00

To close current operating income and realiz*ed* cost savings and holding gains to realiz*ed* income.

Dr. Realized Income 1,243   (17)
     Cr. Retained (Realized) Earnings 1,243

To close realiz*ed* income to retained (realized) earnings.

Cash and Receivables			
(A)	1,800	(2)	3,600
(1)	12,000	(3)	6,814
(10)	76	(12)	60
		To Balance	3,402
	13,876		13,876
Balance	3,402		

Marketable Securities			
(A)	650	(10)	65
		To Balance	585
	650		650
Balance	585		

Marketable Securities Valuation Adjustment			
(A)	90	(10)	11
(9)	2	(11)	30
		To Balance	51
	92		92
Balance	51		

Inventory			
(A)	2,800	To Balance	3,506
(4)	706		
	3,506		3,506
Balance	3,506		

Inventory Valuation Adjustment			
(A)	90	(5)	21
		To Balance	69
	90		90
Balance	69		

Equipment			
(A)	10,000	To Balance	10,000
Balance	10,000		

(A) Balance, January 1, 19x6

Equipment Valuation Adjustment			
(A)	4,000		
(7)	1,260		
(8)	1,540	To Balance	6,800
	6,800		6,800
Balance	6,800		

Accumulated Depreciation			
To Balance	6,000	(A)	5,000
		(6)	1,000
	6,000		6,000
		Balance	6,000

Accumulated Depreciation Valuation Adjustment			
To Balance	4,080	(A)	2,000
		(6)	540
		(8)	1,540
	4,080		4,080
		Balance	4,080

Accounts Payable			
To Balance	2,500	(A)	2,500
		Balance	2,500

Bonds Payable			
To Balance	1,000	(A)	1,000
		Balance	1,000

Bonds Payable Valuation Adjustment			
(13)	19	To Balance	19
Balance	19		

Capital Stock			
To Balance	2,000	(A)	2,000
		Balance	2,000

Retained (Realized) Earnings			
To Balance	5,993	(A)	4,750
		(17)	1,243
	5,993		5,993
		Balance	5,993

Unrealized Cost Savings / Holding Gains			
To Balance	2,859	(A)	2,180
		(14)	679
	2,859		2,859
		Balance	2,859

Operating Expenses			
(2)	3,600	(15)	3,600

Sales			
(15)	12,000	(1)	12,000

Merchandise Purchases			
(3)	6,814	(4)	6,814

(A) Balance, January 1, 19x6

Cost of Goods Sold		
(4)	6,108	(15) 6,108

Cost of Goods Sold Valuation Adjustment		
(5)	299.70	(15) 299.70

Depreciation Expense		
(6)	1,000	(15) 1,000

Depreciation Expense Valuation Adjustment		
(6)	540	(15) 540

Interest Expense		
(12)	60	(15) 60

Interest Expense Valuation Adjustment		
(13)	10	(15) 10

Realizable Cost Savings		
(14)	1,567.70	(5) 278.70
		(7) 1,260.00
		(13) 29.00
	1,567.70	1,567.70

Realized Cost Savings		
(16)	849.70	(14) 849.70

Realizable Holding Gains		
(11)	30	(9) 2
		(14) 28
	30	30

Realized Holding Gains		
(16)	11	(14) 11

Current Operating Income		
(16)	382.30	(15) 382.30

Realized Income		
(17)	1,243	(16) 1,243

(A) Balance, January 1, 19x6

After all transactions have been posted and the income and expense accounts have been closed out, we are able to prepare a complete set of financial statements for the CVA Corporation on both the historical cost and replacement cost bases. Statements of income appear in Exhibit 9.2, statements of financial position in Exhibit 9.3 and statements of changes in financial position in Exhibit 9.4.

Exhibit 9.2

CVA CORPORATION

Statement of Income

for the Year Ended December 31, 19x6

	Historical Cost	Replacement Cost
SALES	$12,000.00	$12,000.00
Less: Cost of Goods Sold	6,108.00	6,407.70
Operating Expenses	3,600.00	3,600.00
Depreciation Expense	1,000.00	1,540.00
Interest Expense	60.00	70.00
	$10,768.00	$11,617.70
OPERATING INCOME	$ 1,232.00	
CURRENT OPERATING INCOME		$ 382.30
Prior Periods Cost Savings/Holding Gains Realized during 19x6:		
Through Sale of Inventory		90.00
Through Equipment Depreciation		400.00
Through Sale of Securities		9.00
		$ 499.00
Current Period Realizable Cost Savings/Holding Gains Realized during 19x6:		
Through Sale of Inventory		$ 209.70
Through Equipment Depreciation		140.00
Through Sale of Securities		2.00
Through Interest Expense		10.00
		$ 361.70
Gain on Sale of Securities	11.00	
NET INCOME = REALIZED INCOME	$ 1,243.00	$ 1,243.00
Less: Prior Periods Cost Savings/ Holding Gains Realized in 19x6		499.00
		$ 744.00
Current Period Realizable Cost Savings/ Holding Gains Unrealized at December 31, 19x6:		
On Ending Inventory		$ 69.00
On Equipment		1,120.00
On Securities		(30.00)
On Bonds Payable		19.00
		$ 1,178.00
REPLACEMENT COST INCOME		$ 1,922.00

Exhibit 9.3

CVA CORPORATION
Statement of Financial Position
December 31, 19x6

	Historical Cost	Replacement Cost
ASSETS		
Cash and Receivables.	$ 3,402	$ 3,402
Marketable Securities.	585	636
Inventories.	3,506	3,575
Total Current Assets.	$ 7,493	$ 7,613
Equipment, at Cost	$10,000	$16,800
Less: Accumulated Depreciation	6,000	10,080
Total Fixed Assets	$ 4,000	$ 6,720
Total Assets	$11,493	$14,333
LIABILITIES		
Accounts Payable	$ 2,500	$ 2,500
Bonds Payable	1,000	981
Total Liabilities	$ 3,500	$ 3,481
STOCKHOLDERS' EQUITY		
Capital Stock	$ 2,000	$ 2,000
Retained (Realized) Earnings	5,993	5,993
Unrealized Cost Savings/Holding Gains		2,859
Total Stockholders' Equity.	$ 7,993	$10,852
Total Liabilities and Stockholders' Equity	$11,493	$14,333

Exhibit 9.4

CVA CORPORATION
Statement of Changes in Financial Position
for the Year Ended December 31, 19x6

	Historical Cost	Replacement Cost
SOURCES OF WORKING CAPITAL		
Historical Cost Net Income	$1,243	
Replacement Cost Income		$1,922
Add Depreciation Expense		
Not Using Working Capital	1,000	1,540
	$2,243	$3,462
Subtract Realizable Cost Savings		
Not Providing Working Capital:		
On Equipment		$1,260
On Bonds Payable		19
		$1,279
TOTAL SOURCES OF WORKING CAPITAL	$2,243	$2,183

Increase (Decrease) in Working Capital Accounts

Cash and Receivables.	$1,602	$1,602
Marketable Securities.	(65)	(104)
Inventories.	706	685
Increase in Working Capital	$2,243	$2,183

Deferred Income Taxes on Unrealized Cost Savings/ Holding Gains

We stated in Chapter 3 that it is customary to report income tax expense based on the appropriate relationship between net income per books and the existing income tax structure. When net income per books differs from taxable income on the tax return because of *timing differences*, the reported income tax expense will differ from the income tax assessed on the tax return. Therefore, when income is recognized on the books earlier (or deductions recognized later) than on the tax return, the reported income tax expense exceeds the income tax liability.

As an example, consider a firm with net income per books of $10,000. The firm reports income for *tax* purposes on the installment sale method, which is not acceptable for *financial reporting* purposes. Assume that current period collections on installment sale contracts generate net taxable income of only $8,000. With a tax rate of 40 percent, the following journal entry would be made to record the income tax expense.

Dr. Income Tax Expense 4,000
    Cr. Income Tax Payable 3,200
    Cr. Deferred Income Taxes 800

To record the current period income tax expense based on book net income of $10,000, the current income tax liability based on taxable income of $8,000 and deferred income taxes of $800.

In subsequent periods, as the balance of the installment sale income is collected, the income tax payable on those collections will be charged to deferred taxes rather than income tax expense.

Recall that in Chapter 3 we argued that deferral of income taxes on income differences which arise because of general price-level adjustments is inappropriate. We took this position because, under current income tax regulations, general price-level adjustments are not relevant. They represent *permanent differences* rather than *timing differences,* and never enter into the computation of taxable income. Under replacement cost accounting, however, what should be our position regarding deferred income taxes on *unrealized* cost savings/holding gains, currently not relevant in the computation of taxable income?

We believe that one of the major advantages of replacement cost accounting is its treatment of the *timing* of gains and losses, which are recognized *as they occur;* realization is *not* necessary. Since such gains and losses are based on actual current costs, the recognition of *unrealized* cost savings/holding gains *prior to* their realization for either book or tax purposes represents a timing difference. However, only those *unrealized* gains which will eventually find their way to the tax return through realization by *sale* represent timing differences on which deferred tax treatment is appropriate. Hence, following the deferred income tax treatment required in APB Opinion No. 11, taxes should be recorded and deferred on the appreciation in ending inventory and fixed asset salvage values, but generally not on appreciation of the fixed asset depreciable base itself.

When the replacement cost of a fixed asset rises, there will be a future effect on *taxable income* if the salvage value also rises. When the asset is eventually retired and sold, presumably for an amount close to its replacement cost salvage value, there will be a taxable gain on the sale, equal to the difference between the replacement cost and historical cost salvage values.

One could argue that *unrealized* cost savings in fixed manufacturing facilities should also be accorded deferred tax treatment. The replacement cost of *future* manufactured inventories would rise, as the replacement cost depreciation is charged to product. Hence, deferred tax treatment of these *unrealized* cost savings in fixed manufacturing facilities *in advance* of their inclusion in future product costs might be justified. *Unrealized* holding gains on temporary investments (e.g., marketable securities) should qualify for deferred tax treatment but *unrealized* cost savings associated with changes in the market value of bond liabilities generally should not. In other words, *unrealized* gains accruing to assets which are to be *sold* in the normal course of operations are timing differences. *Unrealized* gains which accrue to assets which are to be *used* in the normal course of operations are not timing differences. The same principles will apply when the firm experiences *unrealized* holding losses.

To illustrate the suggested deferred tax treatment of *unrealized* holding gains/cost savings, we use the data from the comprehensive financial statements (Exhibits 9.2, 9.3, 9.4). In any given year, only those *unrealized* gains which became *realizable* during that year would require deferred tax treatment. This is necessary to avoid deferred tax treatment on *unrealized* gains in more than one year. Historical cost net income (*realized* income) is $1,243 on the statement of income. We assume that no conventional permanent or timing differences exist and that taxable income is also $1,243. Of the *unrealized* gains (losses) which became *realizable* during the year, only $39 is eligible for deferred income tax treatment, according to the principles discussed above. This amount is the net of $69 of *unrealized* cost savings on ending inventory and $30 of *unrealized* holding losses on marketable securities. For these data, we make the following journal entry to record federal income taxes for the year. The tax rate is 40 percent.

Dr. Income Tax Expense. 512.80
   Cr. Income Tax Payable 497.20
   Cr. Latent Income Taxes. 15.60

To record the current period income tax expense based on historical cost net income of $1,243 plus *unrealized* holding gains/cost savings of $39, the current income tax liability based on taxable income of $1,243 and latent income taxes of $15.60 attributed to the *unrealized* cost savings/holding gains of $39.

The account entitled *latent income taxes* is based on similar terminology used by N. V. Philips Gloeilampenfabrieken in disclosing its "latent income tax obligation" on revaluations recognized in its replacement cost accounting system. We believe that this terminology is both descriptive and appropriate for two reasons. First, the timing differences giving rise to the deferred tax treatment in replacement cost accounting are not conventional. Since the current income tax regulations say nothing about such differences, appropriate terminology is required to distinguish them from conventional timing differences. Second, we feel that separate disclosure of the *magnitude* of this contingent income tax liability is important. There is more uncertainty regarding the future realization of these "revaluation" timing differences than there is for conventional timing differences. Hence, the use of *latent income taxes* will adequately describe and disclose the nature and amount of the deferred taxes on *unrealized* cost savings/holding gains.

It will be useful to pursue this into the following period. Let us assume that there is no further change in the value of the marketable securities and that none are purchased or sold. In addition, assume that the *un*realized cost savings associated with this period's ending inventory are all realized next period, but that there is an additional $40 of (realiz*able*) *un*realized cost savings in next period's ending inventory. If our firm has taxable income (=historical cost net income) of $1,000, the following journal entry records the period's income taxes. The tax rate is 40 percent.

Dr. Income Tax Expense.	388.40
Dr. Latent Income Taxes	11.60
Cr. Income Tax Payable	400.00

To record the current period income tax expense based on historical cost net income of $1,000 less prior period *un*realized gains of $69 which were realiz*ed* this period, plus current period *un*realized gains of $40, and the income tax liability. [$11.60 = 40% ($69 − $40)].

The net change in "taxable" *un*realized gains is − $29[= $40 − $69], leaving a year-end balance of $10, the difference between the *un*realized holding loss of $30 on the marketable securities and the *un*realized gain of $40 on the ending inventory. The above entry adjusts latent income taxes to $4, the latent income tax on the net *un*realized gains of $10. It also reflects the fact that the income tax expense on the prior period gains was recorded previously and is not an expense of the current period.

We believe that deferred income tax treatment is appropriate for certain current year realiz*able* cost savings/holding gains which remain *un*realized at year end. Latent income taxes should be disclosed in connection with *un*realized holding gains/cost savings in the equity section of the statement of financial position as well as in the liability section with conventional deferred income taxes. The specific procedures involved will depend on the treatment of these *un*realized gains. There are two possibilities.

Disclosure on the Statement of Financial Position

In case *a*, the *un*realized gains arising in the current period are included in replacement cost income. The previous example illustrates this treatment and the income tax expense reflects the latent taxes attributed to the *un*realized gains. The amount of *un*realized gains carried to the equity section would therefore be *net* of the applicable latent taxes, and would lead to the following disclosure in the equity section of the position statement.

Unrealized Cost Savings/Holding Gains, Net
  of Latent Income Taxes of $xx. . . . . $xxxx

In case *b*, the *un*realized gains arising in the current period are carried directly to the equity section of the statement of financial position and are *not* included in replacement cost income. Income tax expense would presumably be based on realiz*ed* income, rather than replacement cost income, and therefore would not reflect the latent taxes. In this case, a special journal entry is required each year to enter (or adjust) the latent income taxes in the books. We suggest charging the *un*realiz*ed* gains for the amount of latent taxes as shown below.

Dr. Unrealized Cost Savings/Holding Gains xx
    Cr. Latent Income Taxes. xx

To record the latent income tax liability on unrealized cost savings/holding gains.

This would also lead to the following disclosure in the equity section of the position statement.

Unrealized Cost Savings/Holding Gains, Net of
    Latent Income Taxes of $xx. . . . . $xxxx

Now, in case *b*, one additional bookkeeping complication arises. When the *un*realiz*ed* gains are carried directly to the position statement (i.e., not via replacement cost income), *income tax expense* is not recorded but *latent taxes* are. When these gains are realiz*ed* (and included in income), the latent taxes must be eliminated. In order to do this and show the correct income tax expense for the period in which realization occurs, the previous journal entry charging *un*realiz*ed* gains and crediting latent taxes must be *reversed*. In this way, the amount of tax attributable to those gains would be properly charged to income tax expense, and *not* against latent income taxes. To illustrate this, consider the following data. The income tax rate is 40 percent.

	Period 1	Period 2
Realized Income (= taxable income)	$1,000	$1,000
Unrealized Cost Savings/Holding Gains. . . .	100	—

At the end of period 1, the following journal entries would be made.

Dr. Income Tax Expense 400
    Cr. Income Tax Payable 400

To record current period income tax expense and the related liability.

Dr. Unrealized Cost Savings/Holding Gains 40
    Cr. Latent Income Taxes. 40

To record the latent income tax liability on *unrealiz*ed* cost savings/holding gains.

At the end of period 2, now that period 1's *un*realiz*ed* gains have been realiz*ed,* two journal entries are required.

Dr. Latent Income Taxes 40
    Cr. Unrealized Cost Savings/Holding Gains. 40

To eliminate latent income taxes on *unrealized* gains which were realiz*ed* this period.

Dr. Income Tax Expense 400
    Cr. Income Tax Payable 400

To record current period income tax expense and the related liability.

These entries permit us to (1) take the gross amount of the gains into realiz*ed* income and (2) record the proper income tax expense on those gains. If the first entry at the end of period 2 had not been made, $40 of income tax expense would have been charged against latent income taxes and would never be properly reflected in the books.

Summary

The chapters on replacement cost accounting were designed to provide an overview of the subject as well as careful, detailed analyses of the major areas of application in the accounts. Specifically, the treatments of inventories and fixed assets explored not only the general procedures but also the technicalities essential to the actual implementation of a replacement cost accounting system. It should be clear that replacement cost accounting can be implemented, since both the principles and the techniques for its use presently exist. Furthermore, large companies, such as Philips, have used replacement cost accounting for a number of years. The main advantage of replacement cost accounting, in our view, is that it restores the usefulness of accounting information by restating position statement accounts at their current values and by providing an income statement that clearly identifies current profitability in the current operating income figure and the effects of price changes in the disclosure of cost savings and holding gains. In addition, the accounting records may be easily modified so that historical cost and replacement cost data are both readily available.

On the other hand, determining the replacement cost of many assets may well be a subjective process to some extent and therefore more difficult to audit. Of course, adoption of these procedures will create a demand for such information which in turn will probably evoke increased supplies of replacement cost information. In the final analysis, however, it may be that the effects of changing prices are so serious as to require us to be *approximately right* rather than *precisely wrong*.

Questions and Problems

9.1. Why is preparation of the statement of changes in financial position more important under replacement cost accounting than under historical cost accounting?

9.2. Consider the following data for the RC Corporation.

RC CORPORATION
Statement of Financial Position, December 31, 19x5

	Historical Cost	Replacement Cost
ASSETS		
Cash	$ 1,000	$ 1,000
Accounts Receivable	1,500	1,500
Marketable Securities	2,000	1,900
Inventories	3,200	3,400
Total Current Assets	$ 7,700	$ 7,800
Plant and Equipment	$12,000	$15,000
Less: Accumulated Depreciation	3,000	3,750
	$ 9,000	$11,250
Land	4,000	9,000
Total Fixed Assets	$13,000	$20,250
Total Assets	$20,700	$28,050
LIABILITIES		
Accounts Payable	$ 4,000	$ 4,000
Long-Term Debt	3,000	3,000
Total Liabilities	$ 7,000	$ 7,000
STOCKHOLDERS' EQUITY		
Capital Stock	$10,000	$10,000
Retained (Realized) Earnings	3,700	3,700
Unrealized Cost Savings/Holding Gains	—	7,350
Total Stockholders' Equity	$13,700	$21,050
Total Liabilities and Stockholders' Equity	$20,700	$28,050

19x6 Transaction Data:

Cash Sales	$40,000
Merchandise Purchases, Cash	28,000
Ending Inventory, Historical Cost	3,800
Interest Expense, Cash	270
Replacement Cost of Goods Sold	29,700
Cash Operating Expenses, Excluding Depreciation	5,200
Ending Inventory, Replacement Cost	4,650

Other 19x6 Data:

(1) On June 1, 19x6, one-fifth of the land was sold for $2,000. The remaining land has a replacement cost of $7,500 at year end.

(2) On June 30, 19x6, a patent was purchased for $8,000 cash. The patent has an eight-year life; its cost is to be amortized on the straight-line basis. At year end, the patent was estimated to be worth $8,800. One-half year of amortization is to be taken in 19x6.

(3) Plant and equipment is being depreciated over twenty years on the straight-line basis, no salvage value. It was acquired on 1/5/x1. Its replacement cost new at 12/31/x6 is $18,000.

(4) The long-term debt carries a coupon rate of 9 percent and matures on 12/31/x9. During 19x6, interest rates gradually declined to 7 percent. Interest is paid annually at year end.

(5) Cost to replace the marketable securities was $2,100 at 12/31/x6.

(6) Inventories are accounted for under the FIFO cost flow assumption.

Required:

a. Prepare historical cost and replacement cost statements of income for 19x6.

b. Prepare historical cost and replacement cost statements of financial position at 12/31/x6.

c. Prepare historical and replacement cost statements of changes in financial position for 19x6, including an analysis of changes in working capital accounts.

9.3. Given the following data and assuming an income tax rate of 40 percent, compute the latent income tax liability.

	Historical Cost	Replacement Cost
Inventory	$ 8,000	$ 8,400
Temporary Investments	2,500	2,000
Delivery Equipment (salvage value = 0)	2,000	2,700
Land	10,000	12,000

10 The Practical Determination
of Replacement Costs

The main criticism of replacement cost accounting probably concerns the practical difficulty of making the necessary measurements. This can be a real problem, though not so great a difficulty as has been suggested in some quarters. Clearly, replacement costs can be—and have been—measured in a practical manner by companies such as Philips and others that have been doing so for many years. The degree of subjective estimating involved may be no more severe than the many subjective estimates which provide the basis for conventional financial statements—such as the useful life of assets, or "percentage of completion" approximations. We may forget how subjective some of those estimates are, simply because long usage and custom have made us feel safe or comfortable with them. Current value estimates may be no more subjective, just less familiar and thus somewhat intimidating.*

Determination of Replacement Costs

For *purchased* inventories of raw materials and merchandise, replacement cost is relatively easy to ascertain. However, for *manufactured* inventories of work in process and finished goods, the undertaking is more complex. It becomes necessary to identify the various components of manufacturing costs that are embodied in the inventories, such as raw materials, direct labor and factory overhead—which in turn consists of elements such as indirect labor, depreciation, maintenance, and so on.

For each of these components of cost, it is necessary to determine a measure of current replacement costs. Because overhead items are indirect, determining their current replacement cost will require a review and possible reestimation of standard costs. This of course will cost money. The question is not whether the job can be done, but rather how much it will cost.

---

*Because of auditors' understandable concern with respect to potential lawsuits against them, current values may appear somewhat unconservative and litigious to the cautious auditor, who feels protected by precedent in regard to historical cost.

The current replacement costs of fixed assets have to be determined as well. With respect to standardized items, such as automobiles, trucks and office equipment, the current replacement costs can be obtained from dealers in the second-hand markets for these types of assets. The determination of replacement cost of many other fixed assets, however, is more difficult and less precise.

Manufacturing and trade associations, professional appraisers and some government agencies prepare specific indexes of current cost for certain types of plant and equipment. These can be used, provided that care is taken to ascertain that the index in question is suitable for the intended purpose. For other fixed assets, current replacement cost information is less readily available. It then becomes necessary to resort to professional valuations and appraisals. Some of this information may already be in existence for insurance purposes or other reasons. Otherwise it needs to be obtained on a regular basis. The question, again, is not whether it can be done, but rather what will it cost?

We cannot give precise figures for the extra accounting expense that would be incurred by a current replacement cost system. There are, however, some broad indications we can consider. First, companies which use the current replacement cost method must be convinced that its benefits outweigh its costs, since these firms have used it for many years. Second, Dr. Wessel Van Bruinessen, the president of Nederlands Instituut Van Registeraccountants (the Netherlands Institute of Registered Accountants),* recently stated** that the technical problems of current replacement costs accounting appear to be greatly overestimated.

Perhaps this question is best dealt with in the following comment in a Philips publication.

> Although it is not possible to calculate the additional costs connected with the application of replacement value in our accounting systems, modern accounting methods and computer equipment reduce these costs to a minimum. Of far greater importance is the conviction that a more appropriate basis for policy decisions is thereby created, and that is of tremendous value. Any extra cost is certainly negligible as compared with this benefit.

Generally, the question whether replacement cost accounting is feasible is no longer the major issue. Rather, the question is what kind of disclosure may be required. An insight into this aspect is provided by the following comment by John C. Burton, Chief Accountant of the U.S. Securities and Exchange Commission.***

---

*Our translation.

**Presentation to the U.S. Financial Accounting Standards Board, April 23–24, 1974.

***"Accounting that Allows for Inflation," *Business Week* (November 30, 1974), p. 14. reflect those of the SEC. The proposal referred to in the quotation was subsequently issued on August 21, 1975, and is discussed in Chapter 4 of this book.

At the present time, the most significant inflation-related deficiencies in financial statements exist in the areas of inventories and productive facilities. Supplemental disclosures in these areas, including disclosure of income effects, would be a productive first step. The Securities and Exchange Commission has already proposed such disclosure in the area of inventory and cost of goods sold, and it has urged disclosure of "inventory profits," which can arise in an inflationary environment. The next step may be a proposal for requiring expanded supplemental replacement cost data.

In order to move from the level of broad generalization toward a discussion of specific problems, we now consider some real-world applications of replacement cost accounting, and how the firms in question resolved the (replacement cost) valuation problem. First, we present an example of inventory valuation.

Valuation of Tobacco Leaf Inventory

The example that follows is drawn from John R. Hanna, *Accounting Income Models: An Application and Evaluation* (Hamilton, Ontario: The Society of Industrial Accountants of Canada, 1974). Hanna describes inventory valuation procedure of Imasco Limited (formerly Imperial Tobacco Company of Canada Limited).

Tobacco leaf is aged for approximately three years before being used in production. Aged leaf is more valuable than freshly harvested leaf because of the maturation process. The slowness of the aging process made inventory values quite susceptible to inflation. While use of LIFO would help to approximate replacement cost more closely so far as the income statement was concerned, there remained the problem of inventory valuation for position statement purposes. There was, in Canada, no replacement for aged tobacco leaf; hence, no replacement cost prices actually existed. Aged tobacco could be purchased in the United States, but import duties would be high. In addition, United States leaf types and grades differed somewhat from Canadian green (i.e., unmatured) tobacco.

One alternative considered was to approximate current replacement cost by adding the costs of handling and storage required to age tobacco to the current crop price for green Canadian tobacco. Replacement of all leaf inventories with green Canadian leaf, however, would be a hypothetical exercise because Imperial's inventories were very large relative to the size of the Canadian crop in any one year. In addition, the inventory value so arrived at would represent the cost of aged leaf several years in the future, rather than the current replacement cost at the present time. While these considerations suggest that it is worth exploring other alternatives, they do not rule out use of the above approach.

Another approach contemplated was to forecast the long-term trend of tobacco leaf prices and use this price for valuing leaf inventories for the year-end position statement. Although Imperial recognized that actual leaf prices would fluctuate above and below the long-term trend, the belief was that the price trend over the long run would give a fair measure of inventory replacement costs. After some study, however, Imperial decided that sufficiently accurate and dependable forecasts of long-run prices could not be developed. Therefore, this approach was not pursued.

After careful consideration, it was decided that current entry price approximations were in fact the best valuation method. Although aged tobacco leaf was not actually available in the Canadian market, it was possible to estimate current entry prices for green leaf which could then be adjusted to allow for storage and handling costs. The estimated entry prices were taken from published Canadian government agricultural statistics showing the average price per pound for green tobacco. These green leaf prices were translated into current raw material cost per pound of stripped leaf by the use of conversion factors based on past manufacturing experience. The resulting valuation represents replacement at the present cost of green leaf, plus current costs of stripping, handling and storing.

This method is consistent with the theoretical basis of replacement cost accounting, presented in Chapter 5. By using it, we avoid inclusion of value added by other firms in counting the current cost of replacing our own services in converting raw materials to finished goods.

Using the above method, and appropriate replacement cost estimation procedures for all assets applied to extensive data made available by the company, Hanna constructed comprehensive current value financial statements for Imperial Tobacco for the years 1962–1967. These provide a convincing demonstration of the practicality of the current cost method. For the interest of the readers, we reproduce below the Imperial Tobacco income statements and balance sheets for 1962–1967 as prepared by Hanna on a current value basis.

Buildings, Plant and Equipment

In the United States, generally accepted accounting principles require plant and equipment to be stated at historical cost. Accounting Principles Board Opinion No. 6 states that property, plant and equipment should not be written up by an entity to reflect appraisal, market or current values which are above cost (i.e., historical cost) to the entity. Examples of U.S. replacement cost valuation are therefore difficult to find.* However, illustrations from other countries have been known for a number of years. For example, the 1963 Accounting Research Study No. 6 of the AICPA, entitled *Reporting the Financial Effects of Price-Level Changes*, cites

---

*Nevertheless, although sparse, U.S. examples do exist. As one case of supplementary information on replacement cost valuation, consider the following, from the 1974 Annual Report of Koppers Company, Inc.

Replacement Costs Calculated

. . . we have calculated the cost of replacing Koppers plant, equipment and property at today's prices, using appropriate, generally accepted construction cost indices for various types of Koppers facilities.

The original cost of the property, plants, and equipment now owned by Koppers was $441 million. It would require approximately $800 million, nearly double the original cost, to replace these same assets today.

Exhibit 10.1

Imperial Tobacco Company of Canada Limited
Current Value Consolidated Balance Sheets
at December 31, 1962–1967* (000s)

Year	1962	1963	1964	1965	1966	1967
Current Assets						
Cash and term deposits	$ 13,037	$ 13,662	$ 13,165	$ 11,263	$ 11,559	$ 10,182
Marketable securities	13,417	11,578	13,112	11,146	11,907	13,349
Accounts receivable less allowance for doubtful accounts	10,763	11,156	14,889	16,849	16,509	17,044
Leaf tobacco, manufacturing materials. supplies, and merchandise	83,204	83,305	89,691	92,343	86,087	83,821
Total Current Assets	$120,421	$119,701	$130,857	$131,601	$126,062	$124,396
Current Liabilities						
Accounts payable and accrued liabilities	$ 6,272	$ 6,265	$ 6,924	$ 8,331	$ 9,961	$ 9,521
Income, excise, and other taxes	21,505	19,838	21,087	21,079	17,727	22,896
Provision for dividends	1,571	1,317	1,313	1,793	1,065	1,057
Debt maturing within one year	700	700	700	1,789		
Total Current Liabilities	$ 30,048	$ 28,120	$ 30,024	$ 32,992	$ 28,753	$ 33,474
Net Working Capital	$ 90,373	$ 91,581	$100,833	$ 98,609	$ 97,309	$ 90,922
Other Assets						
Loans and advances to nonconsolidated subsidiaries	$	$	$	$ 786	$ 1,251	$ 2,503
Investment in nonconsolidated subsidiaries				12,412	12,333	12,665
Other investments	2,028	3,417	7,323	1,834	1,715	1,793
Special refundable tax					540	359
Prepaid expenses and deferred charges	754	770	1,365	1,331	1,288	1,410
Fixed assets	42,039	44,279	43,630	44,057	48,561	47,993
Goodwill, trade marks, and patents	1	1	1	1	234	1
	$135,195	$140,048	$153,152	$159,030	$163,231	$157,646
Other Liabilities						
Debentures	$ 8,974	$ 7,797	$ 6,503	$ 2,036	$ 2,024	$ 2,058
Deferred income taxes	1,220	2,504	7,550	10,248	10,738	6,182
	$ 10,194	$ 10,301	$ 14,053	$ 12,284	$ 12,762	$ 8,240
Excess of Assets over Liabilities	$125,001	$129,747	$139,099	$146,746	$150,469	$149,406
Provided by:						
Share capital:						
Common	$ 48,353	$ 48,353	$ 48,353	$ 48,353	$ 48,353	$ 48,353
Preferred	8,030	7,215	6,973	6,766	6,518	5,973
Capital surplus		815	1,057	1,264	1,512	2,057
Retained earnings	68,618	73,364	82,716	90,363	94,086	93,023
	$125,001	$129,747	$139,099	$146,746	$150,469	$149,406

*John R. Hanna, *Accounting Income Models: An Application and Evaluation* (Hamilton, Ontario: The Society of Industrial Accountants of Canada, 1974), p. 69. Reproduced with kind permission.

Exhibit 10.2

Imperial Tobacco Company of Canada Limited Current Value
Consolidated Income and Retained Earnings Statement, 1962–1967* (000s)

Year	1962	1963	1964	1965	1966	1967
Net Sales	$373,392	$355,065	$351,456	$366,262	$373,069	$393,315
Cost of Sales						
Federal sales and excise taxes, and excise duty	$223,836	$210,764	$204,798	$209,495	$212,434	$216,845
Manufacturing costs excluding depreciation	119,775	114,603	123,497	133,917	141,176	155,122
Depreciation	3,757	4,050	4,243	4,539	4,864	5,034
	$347,368	$329,417	$332,538	$347,951	$358,474	$377,001
Earnings from Operations	$ 26,024	$ 25,648	$ 18,918	$ 18,311	$ 14,595	$ 16,314
Income from investments in nonconsolidated subsidiaries	$	$	$	$ 222	$ 374	$ 337
Income from other investments	893	1,056	1,198	1,648	1,670	1,448
Interest on funded debt	(371)	(511)	(508)	(502)	(72)	(102)
Increase in value of nonmonetary assets:						
Inventories	(3,048)	(2,475)	11,435	9,869	6,424	(2,654)
Fixed assets	2,008	1,918	2,634	2,185	657	128
Other	(19)	19	24	65	40	24
Earnings before Income Taxes and Nonrecurring Items	$ 25,487	$ 25,655	$ 33,701	$ 31,798	$ 23,688	$ 15,495
Gain or loss on disposal of fixed assets	(92)	(395)	(686)	(148)	(300)	(439)
Write off of goodwill				(322)	(80)	(233)
Cost of purchase of 6% preferred shares for cancellation		(269)	(79)	(74)	(68)	(138)
Earnings before Income Taxes	$ 25,395	$ 24,991	$ 32,936	$ 31,254	$ 23,240	$ 14,685
Income taxes	12,139	11,971	15,908	15,251	11,100	7,101
Net Earnings	$ 13,256	$ 13,020	$ 17,028	$ 16,003	$ 12,140	$ 7,584
Retained earnings, January 1	62,855	68,618	73,364	82,716	90,324[a]	94,086
Dividends	(7,493)	(7,459)	(7,434)	(8,149)	(8,130)	(8,102)
Transfer to capital surplus		(815)	(242)	(207)	(248)	(545)
Retained earnings, December 31	$ 68,618	$ 73,364	$ 82,716	$ 90,363	$ 94,086	$ 93,023

[a]Opening balance adjusted to reflect $39,000 loss to January 1, 1966 on operation of Beau Chatel Wines first consolidated in 1966.

*John R. Hanna, *Accounting Income Models: An Application and Evaluation* (Hamilton, Ontario: The Society of Industrial Accountants of Canada, 1974), p. 72. Reproduced with kind permission.

the following companies which at that time were already users of replacement cost for the valuation of fixed assets:

>Creole Petroleum Corporation (Venezuela)
>
>Compania Minera Aguilar, S.A. (an Argentinian subsidiary of St. Joseph head company)
>
>Bowater Paper Corporation Limited (England)
>
>Electric and Musical Industries Limited (England)
>
>Selfridges Limited (England)
>
>Broken Hill Proprietary Company Limited (Australia)

As an illustration, let us briefly look at the last corporation. The Broken Hill group of companies engages in mining, steelmaking, oil and natural gas drilling and production. In 1972, the Broken Hill financial statements, which reflected a profit in excess of $148 million, contained the following note.

>The charge for fixed asset utilization represents a proportion of the current replacement cost of plant and machinery used in producing income. The proportion is determined by the expected total useful life of each asset, this being periodically reviewed and reassessed in the light of technical and economic developments. The book values of fixed assets have been reduced by that part of the fixed asset utilization charge designated depreciation, this being calculated by applying the percentage rate appropriate to the assessed asset life to the book value of the asset. The remainder of the charge for fixed asset utilization has been included in reserves as fixed asset value adjustment.

The 1972 fixed asset utilization charge of approximately $125 million includes depreciation of $87 million and a fixed asset value adjustment of $38 million. The financial statements note that the methods used for fixed asset accounting "follow on close consultation with our auditors, and have their support." The auditors' report contains the usual opinion that the statements "give a true and fair view of the state of affairs of the company and the result of its operations for the year."

In addition to the list of illustrative companies given above, several large corporations in the Netherlands (in addition to Philips) make use of replacement cost for fixed asset valuation.* Examples are Koninklijke

---

*Other large Netherlands corporations, however, do not use replacement cost accounting. For a recent survey, see Morton Backer, *Current Value Accounting* (New York: Financial Executives Research Foundation, 1973). An article by A. W. Knol, "Accounting in Holland," in the British periodical *Accountancy* (January 1973), reported on the accounting practices applied in 1967 to property and depreciation by 259 of the 289 commercial and industrial Dutch companies listed on the Amsterdam Stock Exchange. Approximately 50 percent of the companies surveyed give some recognition to current values in their financial statements, and 39 companies have stated property at, and based depreciation on, current value.

Nederlandsche Hoogovens en Staalfabrieken NV, one of Europe's largest steel companies, and Heineken's Bierbrouwerij Maatschappij NV, the international brewery whose products are probably familiar to those Americans who enjoy beer.

Morton Backer comments on the Heineken's replacement cost system:*

Replacement costs for buildings and machinery are determined by means of independent, and admittedly costly, appraisals. The company operates four large breweries in the Netherlands. Each year the plant and equipment of a different brewery is appraised and the resultant percentage increase in replacement cost is used as the basis for adjusting the company's aggregate fixed asset accounts. Although the appraiser calculates changes in replacement costs for different categories of assets, this is combined into a single index for machinery and equipment and applied to all such property owned by the company in Holland. Replacement cost increases are charged to asset accounts and credited to the Revaluation Surplus Account. Depreciation is then charged to income on the basis of replacement cost. Heineken does not give effect to technological improvements in its determination of replacement costs. The company's management is aware of this deficiency but finds it very difficult to estimate the extent of increased productivity in future replacements.

Land values are adjusted on the basis of the value of comparable properties on the outside of town. For example, assume that the company actually paid 50 guilders per square meter for land located in the center of a city which is now worth 1,000 guilders. Suppose, however, that industrial land on the periphery of the city is now available for 100 guilders. Since the present land can not be sold as long as the brewery is on it, the replacement cost is adjusted to 100 rather than 1,000 guilders per square meter.

Raw materials are repriced at replacement cost at the end of each year. The adjustment is based on current rather than expected prices. Work in process and finished goods are not revised because of rapid turnover.

The benefits perceived by Heineken's management from its replacement cost system are indicated in the following conversation with Mr. J. F. Stap, the Controller:

Q. What are the principal benefits obtained by Heineken from this system?

A. In the first place, our insurance contract requires that new asset evaluations be made every three years. This is quite common in Holland, although some of the larger companies, unlike Heineken, use a self insurance plan. Were it not for this requirement, we would still use a replacement cost system but probably not reappraise our assets as frequently.

Q. Do you use return on capital as a basis for evaluating performance of internal sectors?

---

*Morton Backer, *Current Value Accounting* (New York: Financial Executives Research Foundation, 1973). Reproduced by permission.

A. Yes. We do not make this calculation for each brewery but for different product lines. It is one of the goals we plan at the beginning of the year for beer, soft drinks, real estate business and foreign investments. We believe this is the only meaningful measurement of performance.

Q. Are your return on investment goals related to your cost of capital?

A. Yes, but this is a complicated subject. We give effect to the cost of equity and debt capital but attach a risk premium according to the type of investment.

Q. What about the use of replacement costs in product pricing?

A. This is very important in export sales. Although we may make exceptions at times for desired penetration of a particular foreign market, we try to avoid export business that will not produce a full replacement cost recovery plus interest on capital. The situation within Holland is different since we have governmental price control which prevents general price increases.

Q. Has your dividend policy been affected by the use of replacement costs?

A. Of course dividend policy is influenced greatly by the financial market. There also are legal requirements in Holland as to minimum dividend payouts (as percentage of profits). It is difficult to say categorically whether our dividend policy might have been different in the absence of replacement costs. Certainly this system provides a better guide since profits are reported more realistically.

Q. Do you think your stock is being quoted at a lower price because of replacement costs or that you have been disadvantaged in take-overs?

A. Yes, it might be. I think where financial analysts make comparisons of our company with other beer companies they often ignore the fact that our profits are based on replacement costs. This might hurt in raising capital. However, when it comes to take-overs, our auditors evaluate these companies at replacement cost.

The question of technological change brought up in the Heineken material above is an important one. We discuss it in more detail below.

Replacement versus Reproduction Cost

It is necessary to distinguish very clearly between replacement cost and reproduction cost. These are key terms not only for accountants but also for engineers and appraisers in the estimation of current value. It is most important to ensure that the terms are used consistently but not interchangeably.

Reproduction cost is the current cost of replicating assets *in their identical form*. Replacement cost is the current cost of duplicating the *services* or *output* of present assets by whatever facilities can do so most economically at this time.

When assets are replaced in kind, and there have been no changes in technology, reproduction cost and replacement cost should be identical.

However, when technological change has taken place, reproduction of the past form of assets may become irrelevant. Replacement cost, which takes into account technological change, becomes a more accurate representation of current value. Consider, for example, the older tube-type television receivers and electromechanical desk calculators. Replacement of the former would most probably be by solid state (transistorized) TV receivers, and of the latter by electronic calculators using the current chip technology. In both cases, technological change has made reproduction economically undesirable and thus replacement cost is the relevant measure.

Accountants who support the replacement cost concept have not done much exploration of the technological change question. Clearly this is an important issue that requires careful attention, since it is plausible that there are many situations where reproduction cost, replacement cost and historical cost are all significantly different from one another.

One of the authors* studied electric utility plant costs for the 20-year period 1945–1964. Using a well-known published reproduction cost index (the Handy-Whitman Index of Public Utility Construction Costs), he found that the *reproduction cost* of actual operating facilities approximately doubled over the 20-year period. However, a replacement cost index (measuring the cost of productive *capacity* rather than productive *facilities*) specially computed for this purpose showed virtually no change for the 20 years. In other words, the greatly increased costs of reproduction of given facilities had been totally offset by technological progress and economies of scale due to larger plant sizes. This striking example highlights the potentially material error involved in using *reproduction cost* estimates instead of *replacement cost* estimates.

Basically, there are three main approaches to ascertaining replacement cost when market prices are not readily available.

(1) Appraisal, including a detailed physical inventory in order to reprice all items on a current basis. This method, usually the most costly and the most reliable, takes a reproduction cost approach, insofar as technologically complex equipment is concerned. For buildings and other simpler items, the equivalent modern replacement would be considered where obsolescence is a factor. Therefore, where there has been little technological change, or only simpler assets are affected, or the appraisers are appropriately expert, this method is suitable. However, under other conditions, it does run the risk of giving reproduction rather than replacement costs.

Replacement Cost Estimation: Summary and Final Examples

---

*J. Leslie Livingstone, "Electric Utility Plant Replacement Costs," *The Accounting Review* (April 1967): 233–40.

(2) An engineering study, not entailing a fully detailed inventory. The accuracy of this method is normally reliably high, and its expense is likely to be less than detailed appraisal. An engineering study is most desirable when technological change in complex plant and equipment has occurred. In that case, the new plant and equipment requirements must first be designed, to obtain equivalent output. Only then can their current cost be approximated.

(3) Simplest and least costly is the application of a suitable specific cost index to each major class of fixed asset involved. Where an appropriate index can be obtained or developed, this method is excellent. There are available a large number of indexes, published by government and by private agencies. For example, firms such as the American Appraisal Company and Marshall and Stevens prepare and publish many indexes for construction and building costs, and for machinery and equipment.

The purchasing department of a company may be able to provide good estimates of certain replacement costs. In the case of Philips Lamp, for example, the purchasing department maintains a large number of replacement cost indexes for this purpose. In the case of Barber-Ellis of Canada, Limited (see below), prices of equipment suppliers were used to determine the current replacement cost of machinery and equipment.

In order to provide a recent example of the use of current replacement costs in actual practice, Illustrative Example 10.1 presents the 1974 financial statements of Barber-Ellis of Canada, Limited. This company published, as supplementary information, a set of current replacement cost financial statements for the first time in 1974. Included is the report of their independent auditors on the current value statements. In this connection, we thank Mr. Michael Alexander, a partner in the international auditing firm of Touche Ross & Co., who made these statements available to us.

Illustrative Example 10.1

Barber-Ellis of Canada, Limited

BARBER-ELLIS OF CANADA, LIMITED

Current Replacement Cost Financial Statements

Inflation, and rapid price changes, have raised questions about the usefulness of traditional accounting reports. Therefore, the Board of Directors of Barber-Ellis, in addition to the historical accounts, is presenting a Balance Sheet and Statement of Earnings on a current replacement cost basis. This presentation brings all costs and asset values to a common point in time (in this case, December 31, 1974) rather than mixing asset values of various dates, in some cases many years ago, with those of recent months.

The current replacement cost statements relate the current costs of Barber-Ellis' production and distribution capability with the current revenues from those capacities. They also isolate price-change 'profits' from the manufacturing and trading 'profits'. The 'profits' which result from price-changes are included with and taxed on historical accounting statements; in fact, these 'profits' are needed to maintain the company's current operating capacity by replenishing product inventories at higher prices and replacing plant and machinery as it wears out, at higher current prices. The taxes the company pays on these price-change 'profits' are in effect taxes on the shareholders' invested capital.

It is generally conceded that inflation is producing considerable distortion; replacement cost statements identify this distortion.

It is significant that in the process one can see that in the case of Barber-Ellis:

1. 21% of the company's 1974 pretax earnings on an historical cost basis relate to price-change 'profits', which are related to inflation and are illusory by nature.

2. The company is being taxed very heavily. The effective income tax rate is 60% of corporate earnings after price-change 'profits' are eliminated.

3. The company's performance, even after eliminating price-change 'profits', is improving.

4. The company's dividend rate, while apparently 30% of historical earnings, is, in fact, 49% of the restated earnings.

If our economy is to function effectively, it is essential that management, investors and governments clearly understand the changed financial conditions that inflation creates. For managers and investors, it is to understand and avoid decisions based on the illusory profits created by historical costs; for governments it is to stop taxation at levels which now impair the capital of business and discourage investment in Canadian enterprise.

It is hoped that these current replacement cost statements will assist the management, the shareholders, investors and others in Canada, in a greater understanding of the effects of inflation on the capital invested in a business and the income it earns.

BARBER-ELLIS OF CANADA, LIMITED

Report on Supplementary Financial Statements

To the Shareholders,
Barber-Ellis of Canada, Limited.

In conjunction with our examination of and report on the financial statements of Barber-Ellis of Canada, Limited for 1974 we have also examined the accompanying supplementary financial statements which have been prepared on a current replacement cost basis.

Uniform criteria for the preparation and presentation of such supplementary financial information have not yet been established and accordingly, acceptable alternatives are available as to their nature and content. In our opinion, however, the accounting basis described in the notes to the supplementary financial statements has been applied as stated and is appropriate in these circumstances.

Touche Ross & Co., Chartered Accountants.   Toronto, Ontario, February 21, 1975

BARBER-ELLIS OF CANADA, LIMITED

Current Replacement Cost Balance Sheet
As of December 31, 1974

(with comparative historical cost figures)

ASSETS

	Current Replacement Cost (Note 1)	Historical Cost (Note 3)
CURRENT		
Cash	$ 29,783	$ 29,783
Accounts receivable	12,074,945	12,074,945
Inventories	10,366,804	10,117,804
Prepaid expenses	249,545	249,545
	$22,721,077	$22,472,077
Property, plant and equipment	$15,164,198	$11,261,927
Accumulated depreciation	(8,074,486)	(5,817,772)
Unamortized excess of purchase price of subsidiaries over fair value of net assets required	—	816,067
	$29,810,789	$28,732,299

LIABILITIES

CURRENT		
Bank indebtedness	$ 7,573,983	$ 7,573,983
Accounts payable and accrued liabilities	4,109,189	4,109,189
Income taxes	1,296,693	1,296,693
Dividends—preference shares	700	700
Current portion of long-term debt	486,650	486,650
	$13,467,215	$13,467,215
Deferred income taxes	$ 278,362	$ 278,362
Long-term debt (Note 1)	4,133,650	4,133,650
	$17,879,227	$17,879,227

SHAREHOLDERS' EQUITY

CAPITAL STOCK	$ 565,705	$ 565,705
Contributed surplus	45,000	45,000
Retained Earnings	7,001,653	10,242,367
Revaluation surplus	4,319,204	—
	$29,810,789	$28,732,299

BARBER-ELLIS OF CANADA, LIMITED

Current Replacement Cost Statement of Earnings and Retained Earnings
For the year ended December 31, 1974

(with comparative historical cost figures)

	Current Replacement Cost (Note 2)	Historical Cost (Note 3)
NET SALES	$69,058,300	$69,058,300
COSTS AND EXPENSES		
Cost of products sold	$51,373,580	$50,389,580
Selling, general and administration	10,705,281	10,705,281
Depreciation and amortization	1,095,567	786,969
Interest — long-term debt.	381,884	381,884
Interest—current	590,284	590,284
	$64,146,596	$62,853,998
Earnings before income taxes.	$ 4,911,704	$ 6,204,302
Provision for income taxes.	2,927,442	2,927,442
NET EARNINGS	$ 1,984,262	$ 3,276,860
Retained earnings, beginning of year	7,939,344	7,939,344
	$ 9,923,606	$11,216,204
Adjustment of prior years' depreciation on current replacement cost of plant and equipment	$1,948,116	—
Dividends	973,837	$ 973,837
RETAINED EARNINGS, END OF YEAR	$ 7,001,653	$10,242,367
EARNINGS PER SHARE		
Basic	$ 4.30	$ 7.09
Fully diluted	4.22	6.96

BARBER-ELLIS OF CANADA, LIMITED

Statement of Revaluation Surplus
For the year ended December 31, 1974

Revaluation of physical assets to reflect current replacement cost as at December 31, 1974	
Inventories.	$ 249,000
Property, plant and equipment	3,902,271
Excess of purchase price over fair value of assets acquired	(816,067)
Revaluation of cost of products sold during the year ended December 31, 1974	
Portion of 1974 earnings determined on historical cost basis which are required to replace inventory sold at the current cost in effect at the date of sale	984,000
Revaluation surplus December 31, 1974	$4,319,204

BARBER-ELLIS OF CANADA, LIMITED

Notes to Current Replacement Cost Financial Statements
December 31, 1974

1. Current replacement cost accounting

The essence of current replacement cost accounting is that it gives recognition to maintaining the invested capital of the business and to the current costs of earning a satisfactory return. Since the company is viewed as a 'going concern', income is not considered to have been earned without first providing for the replenishment of capital consumed in the operations. The company maintains its productive capability by being able to replace its plant and equipment as it is used and its inventories as they are sold. The current replacement costs of inventories and of property, plant and equipment are shown on the balance sheet and earnings are determined by matching current costs with current revenues. Adjustments of the historical cost of physical assets to their current replacement cost are considered as restatements of shareholders' equity and are shown on the balance sheet under revaluation surplus.

Since 1974 is the first year the company has prepared current replacement cost financial statements, comparative figures for 1973 are not available.

The current replacement cost financial statements do not represent the current value of the company as a whole because the human resources and the intangible assets such as the excess of purchase price of subsidiaries over fair value of net assets acquired and the goodwill have not been included. The current replacement cost of assets is not necessarily their net realizable value should they be sold.

The principles of valuation are:

(a) Property, plant and equipment

During 1973 and 1974 land and buildings have been independently appraised by quantity surveyors of The Canadian Institute of Quantity Surveyors or by accredited appraisers of The Appraisal Institute of Canada. The basis of valuation is the current replacement cost of facilities with similar productive capacities. Where appraisals for buildings were completed at dates other than at December 31, 1974, the appraised values were adjusted by the non-residential construction price index developed by Statistics Canada.

Machinery and equipment are valued at their current replacement costs which are determined from recent suppliers' prices and estimates made by an equipment supplier. The machinery and equipment are of a specialized nature and their current replacement costs do not necessarily represent the amounts for which the assets could be sold.

(b) Accumulated depreciation

The accumulated depreciation for plant and equipment has been adjusted by $1,948,116 to reflect that portion of the current replacement cost of the assets which would have been charged to earnings in prior years.

(c) Cash, accounts receivable and prepaid expenses

These assets are shown at historical cost which is also their current value to the company.

(d) Inventories

Inventories are valued at the lower of current replacement cost and net realizable value. Replacement costs for inventories are based on current prices and labour costs.

(e) Current and long-term liabilities

These liabilities are shown at their historical amounts. The difference between current and stated interest rates on long-term debt would have only a minimal effect on earnings.

2. Principles of calculating earnings

Net sales represent the net proceeds from products sold to customers. Cost of products sold is calculated on the basis of the current replacement cost of the item sold on the date of sale. Depreciation of buildings and equipment is computed on the diminishing balance method on current replacement costs at the following rates:

Buildings	5%
Plant and equipment	20%

3. Historical cost financial statements

The column of historical costs should be read in conjunction with the notes to the historical cost financial statements.

We offer the following comments on the Barber-Ellis replacement cost statements. First, recall that we have defined three separate income concepts with respect to replacement cost accounting: current operating income, realized income and replacement cost income. Let us consider the figure of $1,984,262 reported as net earnings by Barber-Ellis. Which of the above income concepts, if any, does this represent?

In the Barber-Ellis statements, the earnings statement reflects expenses on a replacement cost basis, but does not reflect any holding gains or cost savings, realiz*ed* or *unrealized*. The holding gains are separately shown in the statement of revaluation surplus and are therefore carried directly to the balance sheet. The income concept that excludes all holding gains (both realiz*ed* and *unrealized*) is current operating income, which is reported by Barber-Ellis under the descriptions of net earnings. In the company's introductory comments to the replacement cost statements, a description is given of the meaning of the reported income figure. Note that this description corresponds closely indeed to the notion of current operating income.

Next, let us compute the realiz*ed* cost savings. These will relate to cost of goods sold and to property, plant and equipment.

	Cost of Goods Sold	Depreciation on Property, Plant and Equipment
At Current Replacement Cost	$51,373,580	$1,095,567
Deduct Historical Cost	50,389,580	786,969
Realiz*ed* Cost Savings	$ 984,000	$ 308,598

The cost of goods sold is much larger than depreciation—about 50 times as large, in fact. Yet the realiz*ed* cost savings on depreciation are almost one-third of those on cost of goods sold. Why? Because the historical and replacement costs of inventories are much closer to one another than the historical and replacement cost amounts for depreciation. The reason, not surprisingly, is that inventory costs (even on a historical basis) are more current than those of the longer-lived plant assets.

Now that we know the realiz*ed* cost savings (which total $1,292,598), we can make the following calculation:

Current Operating Income	$1,984,262
Add Realiz*ed* Cost Savings	1,292,598
Equals Realiz*ed* Income	$3,276,860

We check this result by noting that realiz*ed* income must equal historical cost income; since historical cost net income is $3,276,860, the equality is satisfied.

The treatment given *un*realiz*ed* cost savings is best seen in the statement of revaluation surplus. The statement seems to show *un*realiz*ed* cost savings, which we can figure out as follows.

December 31, 1974	Inventories	Property Plant and Equipment (Gross)
Replacement Cost	$10,366,804	$15,164,198
Less Historical Cost	10,117,804	11,261,927
*Un*realiz*ed* Cost Savings	$ 249,000	$ 3,902,271

The above amounts agree with those in the statement of revaluation surplus. However, the cost savings on property, plant and equipment are partially realiz*ed* and partially *un*realiz*ed*; these two components must therefore be separated.

Property, Plant and Equipment

	Gross	Less Accumulated Depreciation	Net
Replacement Cost	$15,164,198	$8,074,486	$7,089,712
Historical Cost	11,261,927	5,817,772	5,444,155
Cost Savings	$ 3,902,271	$2,256,714	$1,645,557

Thus the cost savings realiz*ed* through depreciation are $2,256,714, which leaves *un*realiz*ed* cost savings of $1,645,557.

Given the above information and using the concepts presented in this book, we believe that a different presentation should be made. This presentation would consist of the determination of realiz*ed* income, its subsequent inclusion in retained (realiz*ed*) earnings and the determination of the ending balance in *un*realiz*ed* cost savings/holding gains. Unfortunately, the omission of information about the beginning balance in *un*realiz*ed* cost savings/holding gains prohibits the calculation of realiz*able* cost savings for 1974 and replacement cost income for 1974. Further, the adjustment for prior years' depreciation of $1,948,116 should not be charged against retained earnings but rather should be netted out in computing the *un*realiz*ed* cost savings in property, plant and equipment shown in the statement of revaluation surplus. For Barber-Ellis, these items are summarized in Exhibit 10.3.

We have omitted discussing the item of $816,067 entitled "Excess of Purchase Price over Fair Value of Assets Acquired." There is not sufficient information given to determine the precise nature of this item. It could be goodwill, in which case it should appear on the replacement cost balance sheet as an asset—which it does not. The treatment given to it by Barber-Ellis implies that it has a replacement cost of zero. If this is in fact the case, then it would be treated as an *un*realiz*ed* holding loss. We have shown it as a reduction to *un*realiz*ed* cost savings/holding gains in Exhibit 10.3.

We now consider how the revalorization problem has been approached. In the statement of retained earnings, the amount of $1,948,116 has been charged against retained earnings as "Adjustment of Prior Years' Depreciation on Current Replacement Cost of Plant and Equipment." Under our method, this would be the revalorization amount, to be debited to the fixed asset valuation adjustment account and credited to the accumulated depreciation valuation adjustment account.

This treatment would be more consistent than the one used by Barber-Ellis. Their approach has the prior years' excess of replacement cost over historical cost for depreciation charged against retained earnings, but does not do the same with respect to cost of goods sold. In effect,

Exhibit 10.3

Analysis and Presentation of Barber-Ellis Cost Savings Data

| | Cost Savings | | | | | |
	Realized in Prior Years	Unrealized at 12/31/73	Realized in 1974	Unrealized at 12/31/74	Realizable in 1974	Total Realizable All Years
Inventories	?	?	$ 984,000	$ 249,000	?	?
Property, Plant and Equipment	$1,948,116	?	$ 308,598	$1,645,557	?	$3,902,271
Total	$1,948,116	?	$1,292,598	$1,894,557	?	$3,902,271

NOTE: Recall that Realizable Cost Savings = Realized Cost Savings + Change in Unrealized Cost Savings. Since unrealized cost savings at 12/31/73 are not available, the change in unrealized cost savings cannot be determined; hence, realizable cost savings and replacement cost income cannot be determined.

Realized Income

Current Operating Income		$1,984,262
Cost Savings Realized in 1974:		
On Inventory Sold	$984,000	
Through Depreciation	308,598	1,292,598
Realized Income		$3,276,860

Balance in Retained (Realized) Earnings:
$10,242,367 (= $7,001,653 + $1,948,116 + $1,292,598)

Balance in Unrealized Cost Savings/Holding Gains (Revaluation Surplus):
$1,078,490 (= $249,000 + $1,645,557 − $816,067)

the realiz*ed* cost savings for fixed assets are excluded from retained earnings, but the realiz*ed* cost savings for inventory have been included in retained earnings. If the revalorization entry had been made, realiz*ed* cost savings for depreciation would not have been excluded from retained earnings and would thus be treated consistently with realiz*ed* cost savings from cost of goods sold.

With the information above, we can go a step farther in analyzing the realiz*ed* cost savings on property, plant and equipment.

```
Realized Cost Savings as of 12/31/74 . . . . . . . . . . . . . . . $2,256,714
Less Prior Year's Portion . . . . . . . . . . . . . . . . . . . . . . . .   1,948,116
Realized in 1974   . . . . . . . . . . . . . . . . . . . . . . . . . . . . $   308,598
```

The $308,598 is the excess in 1974 of replacement cost depreciation ($1,095,567) over historical cost depreciation ($786,969). This verifies our calculation.

Finally, Barber-Ellis has not taken into account the question of future income taxes on the *un*realiz*ed* cost savings relating to inventories, what we have called the latent tax adjustment. It should be taken into account in order to reflect *un*realiz*ed* cost savings on an after-tax basis.

We should make it emphatically clear that our purpose is not to find fault with or display superior knowledge to Barber-Ellis or their auditors. Clearly both are to be commended for taking a leadership role in striving for superior statement presentation. They have gone beyond mere lip service and have made a practical contribution. It is easier for us to suggest improvements than it was for them to take the first major step. We recognize both the value of a pioneer effort and its vulnerability to criticism.

The purposes of our comments are to illuminate and compare our methods with a real-world example and to show how our framework provides useful techniques for analyzing and, where necessary, augmenting and improving replacement cost financial statements. According to the auditors' report, "Uniform criteria for the preparation and presentation of [current replacement cost] financial information have not yet been established and accordingly, acceptable alternatives are available as to their nature and content." However, we feel that we have shown that the various alternatives are not *equally* acceptable; some *are* better than others. In this area, theory is clearly ahead of practice. Therefore our purpose is also to compare our methods with others and to determine and demonstrate where the advantages lie.

Our discussion did not cover all aspects of the Barber-Ellis statements. In order to allow the reader an opportunity to both review and to venture out alone, there is a set of problems on the Barber-Ellis statements at the end of the chapter. Some of these problems deal with aspects we have not

discussed in specific relation to Barber-Ellis; the topics in question have
been covered elsewhere in this book. We challenge you to challenge your-
selves!

In addition, the appendices to this chapter show portions of recent
annual reports for two corporations which use current replacement cost.
Appendix A deals with the well-known example of Philips Lamp. Appendix B shows portions of a current value annual report for Sea Pines
Corporation, a large real estate developer. Since this is not a published
annual report, we have removed all dollar amounts from the pages here
reproduced. However, the remaining material is still informative. Since
real estate presents one of the most difficult areas of current value estimation, we include a discussion of some of the practical problems of using
appraisal information in accounting reports. The Sea Pines materials deal
mainly with appraisal values, consisting of supporting schedules detailing
property values, plus related notes to the financial statements. Each appendix contains a short commentary on its contents, and the end-of-
chapter problems include some dealing with the materials in the appendices. If these appendices do nothing else, at least they show that the
valuation problems—difficult as they may be—can be successfully overcome.

Summary   Some critics of the current value approach emphasize that this method
entails practical difficulties and added effort and expense in order to arrive at replacement costs. In comparison with historical cost accounting,
this is true. But the usefulness of the current value information is much
greater than that provided by historical cost accounting. Comparing the
greater expense with the greater usefulness, we feel that the extra effort
is well worthwhile. In this chapter we have discussed the major problems
in the development of replacement cost estimates and available methods
of dealing with them. We have focused on the practical issues, and have
presented several illustrations from the real world. The fact that a number
of major corporations have already produced current replacement cost
financial statements is to us the best indicator that the practical difficulties
are not insurmountable.

Appendix A

Philips Lamp

Auditors' Report

We have examined the Accounts for the year 1973 of N.V. Philips' Gloeilampenfabrieken and of N. V. Gemeenschappelijk Bezit van Aandeelen Philips' Gloeilampenfabrieken. With respect to certain subsidiaries and associated companies, mainly
outside Europe, we have also made use of the reports of other auditors.

In our opinion, the accompanying Accounts of N. V. Philips' Gloeilampenfabrieken
and of N.V. Gemeenschappelijk Bezit van Aandeelen Philips' Gloeilampenfabrieken
give a true and fair view of these companies' state of affairs as at 31 December
1973 and of their results for the year 1973.

We have also examined the Combined Statements of Financial Position and of
Results, which combine the consolidated accounts for the year 1973 of N.V.
Philips' Gloeilampenfabrieken and of the United States Philips Trust. In conducting
our examination we have also made use of the other auditors' reports referred to
above.

As regards the consolidated accounts of the United States Philips Trust we have
relied on the report, dated 21 February 1974, of Messrs. Hurdman and Cranstoun,
Certified Public Accountants, New York.

In our opinion, based on our examination and on the aforementioned report
of Messrs. Hurdman and Cranstoun, the accompanying Combined Statements
give a true and fair view of the combined state of affairs as at 31 December 1973
and of the combined results for the year 1973.

Eindhoven, 12 March 1974   KLYNVELD KRAAYENHOF & CO.

Combined Statement of Results

(in millions of guilders)

	1973		1972	
SALES		22,562.8		19,924.5
Cost and expenses:				
Cost of sales	−15,484.8		−13,752.2	
Selling and general expenses	−4,481.2	−19,966.0	−4,197.4	−17,949.6
TRADING PROFIT		2,596.8		1,974.9
Other income and charges:				
Interest paid	−520.7		−537.6	
Interest received	120.7		99.3	
	−400.0		−438.3	
Extraordinary income	88.1		99.9	
Extraordinary charges.	−356.0	−667.9	−172.6	−511.0
PROFIT BEFORE TAX		1,928.9		1,463.9
Tax on profit		−962.9		−719.3
PROFIT AFTER TAX		966.0		744.6
Share in net profit of non-consolidated companies		61.4		62.7
GROUP PROFIT		1,027.4		807.3
Minority interests		−128.3		−90.1
NET PROFIT		899.1		717.2

Combined Statement of Financial Position

(in millions of guilders)

	1973		1972	
PROPERTY, PLANT AND EQUIPMENT				
Replacement value	15,758.6		14,105.8	
Depreciation	−7,401.1	8,357.5	−6,518.5	7,587.3
INTANGIBLE ASSETS		—		—
INVESTMENTS IN NON-CONSOLIDATED				
SUBSIDIARIES AND ASSOCIATED COMPANIES		608.8		578.2
SUNDRY NON-CURRENT ASSETS		690.5		622.4
STOCKS				
Factory stocks	3,591.7		2,905.8	
Advance payments by customers	−403.9		−421.3	
	3,187.8		2,484.5	
Commercial stocks	3,242.5	6,430.3	2,938.7	5,423.2

ACCOUNTS RECEIVABLE

Trade debtors	6,415.7		5,737.8	
Discounted bills	−403.8		−392.6	
	6,011.9		5,345.2	
Other accounts receivable	490.8		445.0	
Prepaid expenses	349.2	6,851.9	316.2	6,106.4

LIQUID ASSETS

Marketable securities	223.1		195.2	
Cash at bank and in hand	1,024.0	1,247.1	1,618.4	1,813.6
		24,187.1		22,131.1

	1973		1972	
SHAREHOLDERS' EQUITY INTEREST				
Ordinary share capital	1,636.3		1,274.1	
Share premium account	280.1		619.3	
Retained profit	4,520.2		3,821.0	
Revaluation surplus	2,013.9	8,450.5	1,715.8	7,430.2
MINORITY INTERESTS		1,022.6		907.0
SUNDRY PROVISIONS				
Long-term provisions	2,554.7		2,092.7	
Short-term provisions	899.1	3,453.8	744.3	2,837.0
LONG-TERM LIABILITIES				
Convertible debenture loans	742.4		773.1	
Other debenture loans	548.1		611.7	
Other long-term liabilities	2,460.9	3,751.4	2,722.1	4,106.9
CURRENT LIABILITIES				
Banks	1,886.8		2,256.5	
Accounts payable	3,250.8		2,716.9	
Tax on profit	994.8		638.8	
Accrued expenses	1,127.4	7,259.8	1,043.6	6,655.8
PROFIT AVAILABLE FOR DISTRIBUTION	347.2		270.6	
Interim dividend made payable in December	−98.2	249.0	−76.4	194.2
		24,187.1		22,131.1

Explanatory Notes to the Combined Statements*

Principles of valuation

Property, plant and equipment
These assets and their depreciation are valued on the basis of replacement value.
Changes in the replacement value are credited or charged to Revaluation Surplus.

*These statements combine the consolidated data of N.V. Philips' Gloeilampenfabrieken and those of the United States Philips Trust.

Intangible assets
Intangible assets are shown in the balance sheet at no value.

Investments in non-consolidated subsidiaries and associated companies
Non-consolidated investments are valued at their net tangible asset value, determined in accordance with the principles adopted in these annual accounts.

Sundry non-current assets
These assets are valued at purchase price or at estimated realizable value, whichever is the lower.

Stocks
Stocks are valued at replacement value or at estimated realizable value, whichever is the lower. Changes in replacement value are credited or charged to Revaluation Surplus. The provision for the risk of obsolescence is deducted from the total figure for stocks. Profits arising from transactions within the Philips organization are eliminated.

Accounts receivable
Accounts receivable are shown at nominal value, less the provision for the risk of bad debts.

Liquid assets
Securities are valued at purchase price or at their listed stock exchange price at the end of the financial year, whichever is the lower. Shares in N.V. Gemeenschappelijk Bezit van Aandeelen Philips' Gloeilampenfabrieken and debentures of N.V. Philips' Gloeilampenfabrieken and of their associated companies are included at par.

Minority interests
Minority interests in consolidated subsidiaries are valued on the basis of net tangible asset value, determined in accordance with the principles adopted in these annual accounts.

Sundry provisions
These provisions do not relate to specific assets; they are formed to meet commitments and risks connected with the course of business. Pension provisions are included under this heading at present value.

Long-term and current liabilities
These liabilities are taken up at nominal value.

Replacement value
The replacement value is determined on the basis of the price trends of the various assets, making use inter alia of indices. Transfers to Revaluation Surplus pursuant to changes in the replacement value are made after deduction of latent tax liabilities.

Foreign currencies
In the Combined Statement of Financial Position amounts in foreign currency are converted into guilders at the official exchange rates applicable on the balance sheet date, unless circumstances, as, for instance, the trend of the purchasing power of the currency concerned, call for the adoption of a lower rate.

Exchange differences due to the conversion into guilders of property, plant and equipment and stocks are offset against Revaluation Surplus in the relevant country.

Exchange differences due to the conversion in guilders of nominal assets and liabilities are credited or charged to Profit and Loss Account.

In the Combined Statement of Results, sales and income in foreign currencies are converted at the rates applicable in the relevant periods.

The balance of the relevant profit and loss account is converted at the end of the year at the rates applied in the Combined Statement of Financial Position. The resultant difference is credited or charged to Profit and Loss Account.

Property, plant and equipment	replacement value	depreciation	book value
Land and buildings	6,327.7	2,071.3	4,256.4
Machinery and equipment	6,799.0	4,188.0	2,611.0
Equipment leased out	455.7	173.9	281.8
Dwellings and land	325.5	85.3	240.2
Vacant land	197.9	—	197.9
Balance at 31 December 1972	14,105.8	6,518.5	7,587.3

Investments in:

Land and buildings	216.7	
Machinery and equipment	799.5	
Equipment leased out	170.4	
Dwellings and land	24.1	
Vacant land	11.8	
Decrease due to assets sold and withdrawn from use	−217.9	
Net acquisitions		1,004.6

Depreciation on:

Land and buildings	−183.9	
Machinery and equipment	−659.1	
Equipment leased out	−81.0	
Dwellings and land	−6.6	−930.6
Revaluation		293.8
Net changes due to new and discontinued consolidations		402.4
Total changes in 1973		770.2

	replacement value	depreciation	book value
Land and buildings	7,181.3	2,479.0	4,702.3
Machinery and equipment	7,515.8	4,613.4	2,902.4
Equipment leased out	546.2	219.4	326.8
Dwellings and land	301.1	89.3	211.8
Vacant land	214.2	—	214.2
Balance at 31 December 1973	15,758.6	7,401.1	8,357.5

Investments in non-consolidated subsidiaries and associated companies

This item includes loans to these companies totalling f 29.8 m (f 39.0 m last year); the interest received on this amount is comprised in the Combined Statement of Results under "Other income and charges." Other amounts due from these companies are included under "Trade debtors."

Balance at 31 December 1972 . . . .   578.2

Changes:
    Included in the consolidation as at 1 January 1973 . . . . .   −57.4
    Investments 64.2
    Changes in loans . . . .   −4.8
    Share in the net profit of 1973 . . . .   61.4
    Dividends received . . . .   −27.9
    Revaluation. . . . .   −2.3
    Others . . . .   −1.6

Balance at 31 December 1973 . . . .   609.8

Sundry non-current assets	1973	1972
Loans secured by mortgage	213.3	234.3
Other loans and sundry non-current receivables	244.2	181.1
Securities not officially quoted	28.3	28.7
Sundry assets not immediately realizable.	204.7	178.3
	690.5	622.4

The securities not officially quoted include securities with a value of f 15.0 m (f 17.7 m last year) which are not freely disposable.

Stocks

Stocks were increased in 1973 by f 123.0 m to the credit of Revaluation Surplus (f 32.9 m last year).

Accounts receivable

•Trade debtors
This item includes amounts owing under instalment sales contracts totalling f 684.1 m (f 658.5 m last year) and amounts due from non-consolidated subsidiaries and associated companies totalling f 237.2 m (f 208.6 m last year).

Liquid assets

•Marketable securities
This item includes f 5.3 m (f 4.0 m last year) in ordinary shares of N.V. Gemeenschappelijk Bezit van Aandeelen Philips' Gloeilampenfabrieken. The total holding includes securities with a value of f 27.2 m (f 39.3 m last year) which are not freely disposable.
The market value of the total holding of securities is f 232.4 m (f 223.8 m last year).
•Cash at bank and in hand
This item includes an amount of f 77.8 m (f 194.1 m last year) repayable at not less than three months' notice.

Shareholders' equity interest

Balance at 31 December 1972
Ordinary share capital (issued and fully paid up) 1,274.1
Share premium account 619.3

Retained profit N.V. Philips	3,202.5	
Beneficiaries' interest in U.S. Philips Trust	618.5	
Retained profit		3,821.0
Revaluation surplus		1,715.8
Shareholders' equity interest at 31 December 1972		7,430.2

Changes:
Share premium conversion into ordinary share capital:

Ordinary shares issued	326.8	
Decrease of Share premium account	−326.8	——

Conversion of convertible debentures:

Ordinary shares issued	4.7	
Added to Share premium account	18.3	23.0

Distribution in connection with final dividend 1972,
charged to Share premium account:

Ordinary shares issued	30.7	
Decrease of Share premium account	−30.7	
Added to Retained profit	147.2	147.2

Transfer to Retained profit from net profit 1973

of N.V. Philips	557.6	
Decrease in net asset value of U.S. Philips Trust	−5.6	552.0

Increase in Revaluation surplus after deduction

of latent tax liability totalling f 280.1 m		298.1
Balance at 31 December 1973		8,450.5
Ordinary share capital (issued and fully paid up)		1,636.3
Share premium account		280.1*
Retained profit N.V. Philips	3,907.3**	
Beneficiaries' interest in U.S. Philips Trust	612.9	
Retained profit		4,520.2
Revaluation surplus		2,013.9

Total shareholders' equity interest

at 31 December 1973		8,450.5

	1973	1972
Long-term provisions		
Provisions for latent tax liabilities	937.2	713.7
Provisions for pensions	917.1	752.0
Provisions for statutory payments		
to laid-off personnel	159.7	150.4
Others	540.7	476.6
	2,554.7	2,092.7

*Share premium account includes an amount of f 101.0 m, free from Netherlands tax (f 440.1 m last year).

**This includes an amount of f 3,528.7 m pursuant to article 42, para 4, of the Articles of Association (last year f 2,971.1 m) and f 378.6 m in respect of final dividends not taken up in cash (last year f 231.4 m).

Long-term liabilities

•Convertible debenture loans	conversion price	amount outstanding	conversion period
4³⁄₄% U.S. dollar debenture loan . . . . N.V. Philips' Gloeilampenfabrieken	f 44.30	338.2*	from 1 Jan. 1969 to 30 June 1983
6½% Debenture loan . . . . N.V. Philips' Gloeilampenfabrieken	f 53.20	172.9	from 1 Jan. 1971 to 31 Dec. 1974
5% Personnel debentures N.V. Philips' Gloeilampenfabrieken			
issued in 1968	f 45.20	2.5	from 1 Jan. 1969 to 31 Dec. 1978
issued in 1969	f 49.30	2.8	from 1 Jan. 1970 to 31 Dec. 1979
6% Personnel debentures N.V. Philips' Gloeilampenfabrieken			
issued in 1970	f 48.—	2.8	from 1 Jan. 1971 to 31 Dec. 1980
issued in 1971	f 26.—	4.6	from 1 Jan. 1972 to 31 Dec. 1981
issued in 1972	f 43.60	5.5	from 1 Jan. 1973 to 31 Dec. 1982
issued in 1973	f 39.—	8.8	from 1 Jan. 1974 to 31 Dec. 1983
5³⁄₄% Sterling debenture loan . . . . Philips Finance Ltd., England	per £ 50.— 7,566 shares	104.0	from 1 Jan. 1974 to 31 Dec. 1994
6% DM personnel debentures Allgemeine Deutsche Philips Industrie GmbH, Gemany			
issued in 1970	f 48.—	11.9	from 1 Jan. 1971 to 31 Dec. 1980
issued in 1971	f 26.—	10.5	from 1 Jan. 1972 to 31 Dec. 1981
issued in 1972	f 43.60	10.5	from 1 Jan. 1973 to 31 Dec. 1982
issued in 1973	f 39.—	10.3	from 1 Jan. 1974 to 31 Dec. 1983
4% Debenture loan North American Philips Corporation (N.A.P.C.)	$58.—	57.1	to 1 June 1982
Total convertible debenture loans		742.4	
Total last year		773.1	

The above debentures—except for those of N.A.P.C.—are convertible into ordinary shares of N.V. Gemeenschappilijk Bezit van Aandeelen Philips' Gloeilampenfabrieken and redeemable on or before the date the conversion period ends. The 4% convertible debentures of N.A.P.C. are convertible into ordinary shares of N.A.P.C. up to 1 June 1982 and redeemable on or before 1 June 1992.

If all outstanding convertible debentures were converted into ordinary shares of N.V. Gemeenschappelijk Bezit van Aandeelen Philips' Gloeilampenfabrieken, the result would be an increase of the ordinary share capital by 15,162,059 shares of f 10.

---

*This convertible U.S. dollar debenture loan has been valued at the conversion price of f3.60 per U.S. dollar, fixed at the time of issue.

	amount outstanding	falling due within one year from balance sheet date	falling due one or more years from balance sheet date	average remaining period
· Other debenture loans				
Rate of interest:				
4-10% (average 6.4%)	579.6	31.5	548.1	7 years
Last year	645.8	34.1	611.7	
· Other long-term liabilities				
—Private loans from banks				
Rate of interest:				
3.5-13% (average 8.4%)	512.0	79.3	432.7	4 years
—Other private loans				
Rate of interest:				
3.5-10% (average 6.6%)	1,726.0	262.6	1,463.4	5 years
—Participating personnel debentures				
Rate of interest:				
7% + 0.2% for every percent of dividend above 6%	251.5	—	251.5	
—Mortgages				
Rate of interest:				
4—9.5% (average 7.1%)	249.5	21.7	227.8	8 years
—Other debts				
Rate of interest:				
4.3—12% (average 8.4%)	100.8	15.3	85.5	5 years
Total other long-term liabilities	2,839.8	378.9	2,460.9	
Total last year	3,651.9	929.8	2,722.1	

Under "Long-term liabilities" an amount of f 1,911.8 m will become payable in the next five years. The part of these liabilities which becomes payable in 1974 is included under "Current liabilities". The personnel debentures, though redeemable on demand, are in fact in the nature of long-term loans.

The following liabilities are secured by collateral in the form of assets:

	1973	1972
Other debenture loans	6.5	7.5
Other long-term liabilities		
Private loans from banks	15.0	8.5
Other loans	62.1	78.7
Mortgages	227.8	172.5
Miscellaneous loans	32.9	54.5

The following liabilities involve commitments not to create a charge on certain assets:

Private loans from banks	7.6	10.0
Other loans	36.5	50.2

Current liabilities
· Banks
This item includes the part of long-term bank loans falling due in 1974.

·Accounts payable	1973	1972
Trade creditors	1,494.0	1,184.2
Short-term loans	498.7	493.5
Amounts payable in respect of pensions	2.6	1.9
Amounts payable to non-consolidated companies	23.8	43.4
Taxes payable (excl. tax on profit)	380.9	325.0
Other current liabilities	850.8	668.9
	3,250.8	2,716.9

The following current liabilities are secured by collateral in the form of assets:

Banks	188.6	87.8
Other current liabilities	80.9	68.5

The following liabilities involve commitments not to create a charge on certain assets:

Banks	23.2	105.4
Other current liabilities	8.1	33.7

Guarantees and other contingent liabilities
·Guarantees
The guarantees on behalf of non-consolidated companies and third parties amount to f 610.3 m (f 764.4 m last year).
·Other contingent liabilities
The other contingent liabilities, including long-term lease commitments, amount to f 1,491.6 m (last year f 1,821.5 m). Instalments falling due in the coming year with respect to commitments under leasing contracts amount to f 91.2 m (f 108.4 m last year). Collateral security has been given up to an amount of f 19.0 m (f 24.3 m last year).

Wages, salaries and other related costs
Wages, salaries and other related costs paid in 1973 totalled f 8,580.2 m (f 7,433.0 m last year).

Depreciation of property, plant and equipment
An amount of f 930.6 m (f 895.0 m last year) in respect of depreciation on property, plant and equipment was charged to Profit and Loss Account.

Tax on profit
In 1973 a provision for tax on profit was created, totalling f 962.9 m charged to Profit and Loss Account (last year t 719.3 m). Insofar as the cost of sales differs from historical cost, as a consequence of using the replacement value, the tax payable on that difference, amounting to f 124.4 m, is charged to the provision for latent taxes (f 72.8 m last year).

Supervisory Directors' fees
The remuneration paid to the 11 members of the Supervisory Board totalled f 640,000 (f 640,000 last year to 11 members). This amount consists of f 200,000 in fixed emoluments (last year f 200,000) and of f 440,000 (last year

f 440,000) in fees, which is included under the item "Supervisory Board, Management and Officers" in the Profit Appropriation on page 45.

Combined Statement of Changes in Financial Position

(in millions of guilders)

The statement below summarizes the changes in financial position in the years 1973 and 1972. "Internal funds" consist principally of:

> profit after tax;
> depreciation;
> the difference between the replacement value and the historical cost of goods sold;
> the changes in provisions.

	1973		1972	
Source of funds				
Internal funds	2,433.5		2,100.6	
Shareholders' equity interest	170.2		127.1	
Long-term liabilities	−355.5		−557.1	
Current liabilities	604.0		143.5	
Miscellaneous	−17.3		−26.8	
Total		2,834.9		1,787.3
Use of funds				
Investments in property, plant and equipment	1,407.0		946.7	
Investments in other fixed assets	72.4		−135.9	
Total fixed assets		1,479.4		810.8
Stocks at historical cost	884.1		−129.8	
Accounts receivable	745.5		306.0	
Liquid assets	−566.5		565.9	
Total current assets		1,063.1		742.1
Total assets		2,542.5		1,552.9
Profit distribution		292.4		234.4
Total		2,834.9		1,787.3

Calculation of Net Profit based on American Accounting Principles

The accounting principles applied by N.V. Philips' Gloeilampenfabrieken in calculating profit differ in some respects from those generally accepted in the United States of America. The main differences are:

•Depreciation on property, plant and equipment is based on the replacement value of the assets concerned.
•Stocks are in general valued at replacement value. This value is used for determining the cost of sales.
•In so far as the cost of sales differs from historical cost owing to the use of the replacement value, the tax payable on that difference is charged to the provision made for latent taxes at the time of revaluation.

•Net amounts paid in excess of the net tangible asset value for the acquisition of participations in any year are charged in that year to Profit and Loss Account.
•The share of profit due to the Supervisory Board, Management and Officers and to employees, in accordance with the Articles of Association, is not charged to Profit and Loss Account.

An attempt is made below to estimate what adjustment to net profit would be required if the principles generally accepted in the United States were applied, based on the first-in first-out method for the consumption of goods and using a write-off period of five years for net payments in respect of goodwill.

	in millions of guilders	in millions of U.S. dollars*
Net profit 1973 shown in the Combined Statement of Results.	899.1	321.1
Deduct: Profit-sharing with Supervisory Board Management and Officers and with employees	−52.6	−18.8
Adjustment of net profit on the basis of accounting principles generally accepted in the United States	71.8	25.6
Adjusted net profit.	918.3	327.9
Number of ordinary shares of f 10 of N.V. Philips' Gloeilampenfabrieken outstanding at 31 December 1973	163,628,632	
Per ordinary share of f 10 of N.V. Philips' Gloeilampenfabrieken:		
Adjusted net profit.	f 5.61	$2.00
Dividend	f 1.80	$0.64

Assuming conversion of all outstanding convertible debentures, the adjusted net profit per ordinary share would be f 5.23 ($1.87).

If the method of historical cost had been applied in the past, it is estimated that the item Revaluation Surplus as shown in the Combined Statement of Financial Position as at 31 December 1973, would have appeared as follows:

	in millions of guilders	in millions of U.S. dollars*
Addition to retained profit	1,199.3	428.3
Deduction from property, plant and equipment and stocks	814.6	290.9
	2,013.9	719.2

*Converted at the rate of f 2.80 per U.S. dollar.

Note that the Philips replacement cost statements are not supplementaries; they are the only statements presented. A brief amount of supplementary historical cost information is given in order to restate income on a historical cost basis.

Some European terminology may not be familiar to U.S. readers. Here is a short glossary:

European	U.S.
N.V. (prefix)	Inc. (suffix)
Accounts	Financial statements
Statement of Results	Income Statement
Trading Profit	Income before interest payable and receivable, extraordinary items and income taxes
Net profit	Net income
Stocks	Inventories
Sundry	Various
Debtors	Receivables
Ordinary shares	Common stock
Retained profit	Retained earnings

Philips, like Barber-Ellis, reports current operating income, which it calls profit, and excludes all cost savings/holding gains from the income statement. Cost savings/holding gains, both realiz*ed* and *un*realiz*ed* are taken directly to the position statement under the heading "Revaluation Surplus."

The Philips basis of replacement cost accounting is similar to that of Barber-Ellis. However, Philips gives very little historical cost information. Therefore we cannot make a detailed computation of cost savings/holding gains relative to individual classes of assets.

Appendix B

Sea Pines Company*

Exhibit I

Summary of Appraisal Valuation
For Land in Process of Development
December 31, 19x8 and 19x7

Community	Location	Type of Community	Estimated Sellout Date	Total Community Acreage (1)	Remaining Saleable Acreage (2)	19x8		19x7	
						Total Estimated Current Value (Exhibit II)	Cost (5)	Total Estimated Current Value	Cost (5)

								19x8	19x7

Notes:

(1) Total community acreage represents all acreage including acres that are unsaleable or used for business purposes.

(2) Remaining unsold acreage includes only acres available for future sale in the normal course of business.

Historical cost amounts are reduced by the liability for future development costs related to prior years' sales (as the estimated Current Value has also been reduced by this amount) as follows:

Cost, as reflected in Historical Cost Statements
Liability for future development related to prior years' sales
Other reclassifications and adjustments, net
Cost, net of liability for future development

*This material is reproduced here by kind permission of the Sea Pines Company.

The accompanying notes are an integral part of this exhibit.

Exhibit II

Summary of Appraisal Data by Project

Following is a summary of the appraisal data from the appraisals made by XYZ real estate appraisers, as of December 31, 19x8, to arrive at the estimated current wholesale value of each project. The wholesale value is the approximate market value of the project if sold in its present state to a purchaser who would continue the development in accordance with the present project master plan.

As more fully explained below by category, the appraisal techniques used are the "development approach" and the "comparable sales value approach." The development approach requires that estimates be made of the project's retail value, the effect of amenities and utilities, the amount of remaining development costs, selling, general and administrative expenses, and developer's profit. The net effect of these estimates is then discounted to its present value to arrive at a project's wholesale value. The comparable sales value approach arrives at the market value by the review of sales prices of comparable property and is used when significant development has not begun, and for which no dependable development master plan is available.

Current wholesale values are subject to significant changes based on numerous unpredictable factors such as interest rates, availability of credit to purchasers, inflation, buyer demand, income tax treatment of real estate purchases, ability to achieve satisfactory financing, governmental regulations, the "energy crisis," etc. There can be no assurance that estimates of current values reflected below could not decrease as a result of the above or other factors.

Development Appraisal Approach

Community	Estimated Gross Retail Value (1)	Net Effect of Operating Properties Including Utilities (2)	Development Costs (3)	Deduct Selling General and Administrative (4)	Estimated Allowance for Developer's Profit (5) Amount	Estimated Allowance for Developer's Profit (5) Percent	Investment Discount (6)	Estimated Wholesale Value	Comparable Sales Value Appraisal Approach Wholesale Value	Estimated Current Wholesale Value (7)

Notes:

(1) Gross retail value of the project is determined by estimating the current selling prices (potential future selling price changes are not considered) of all land in a fully developed state based on the use set forth in that project's master plan. See Exhibit II for a detail breakdown of the total estimated retail value of the project by homesite and parcel categories.

(2) The net effect of operating properties including utilities represents the estimated portion of the cost incurred for development of these properties that will not be recovered through their sale or profitable operation.

(3) The project's total development cost represents all such costs including provisions for contingencies (except for operating properties including utilities—see (2)) estimated to complete the project and in accordance with the project master plan. Since no provision is made for potential changes in future selling prices as explained in (1) above, no provision is made for potential changes in future development costs resulting from general price level changes.

(4) An allowance is made in the appraisal for estimated selling, general and administrative expenses that are necessary for a buyer to incur over the life of the project to market and administer the project. The amount of this allowance for all projects ranges from 10% to 20% of total retail value depending on the location of the project, type of property sold and other influencing factors.

(5) An allowance for developer's profit is made in the appraisal to arrive at a wholesale value of the project. The amount of the allowance is computed based on a percent of each year's estimated retail value. The percent is determined by evaluating the relative risk of each particular project and is shown in the percent column above.

(6) The investment discount represents an allowance in the appraisal, in addition to developer's profit, for an investment return on the wholesale value of the property. The total amount is computed by discounting each year's cash flow to its present value using 10% for the current rate of return in the above 19x8 appraisals.

(7) The total wholesale value of a project is a combination of the appraised value of all property whether appraised on a development approach or a comparable sales value approach.

The accompanying notes are an integral part of this exhibit.

Exhibit III

Summary of Estimated Retail Values by Project
December 31, 19x8

| | Homesites | | Parcels | Retail Values |
	Number Remaining	Average Selling Price (1)	Acres Remaining	Average Selling Price Per Acre (1)	Total (2) (Exhibit II)

NOTES:

(1) To arrive at total retail values, the appraiser values each homesite and parcel on an individual basis based on current selling prices. No provisions for potential future changes in selling prices are made. Further, no provisions for potential future changes in costs are made in the appraisal (see Note (3), Exhibit II).

Average selling price per homesite is computed by dividing the total estimated retail value of homesites per the appraisal by the estimated number of homesites to be available for sale per the appraisal. Refer to Exhibit IV for a comparison of the last three years average sales prices of homesites sold by the Company to current appraisal estimated selling prices for purposes of this exhibit.

Average selling price per acre for parcel property is computed by dividing the total estimated retail value of land designated as condominium acreage, apartment acreage and commercial acreage by the total acres estimated to be so allocated per the appraisal. Refer to Exhibit V for a comparison of selling prices of parcel sales in 19x8 with their appraisal value as of the previous year-end.

(2) Refer to Exhibit II where the appraisal information is summarized to arrive at a net wholesale appraised value by project. This Exhibit does not include property appraised under the comparable sales value appraisal approach, as explained in Exhibit II.

The accompanying notes are an integral part of this exhibit.

Exhibit IV

Comparison of Actual Selling Prices for Homesites
To Appraised Value of Homesites

| | 19x5 | | 19x6 | | | 19x7 | | | At December 31, 19x8 | |
	Number of Homesite Sales	Average Selling Price (5)	Percent Change from 19x4	Number of Homesite Sales	Average Selling Price (5)	Percent Change from 19x5	Number of Homesite Sales	Average Selling Price (5)	Percent Change from 19x6	Number of Homesites Remaining to Be Sold	Average Homesite Retail Value Per Appraisal
Community											

The accompanying notes are an integral part of this exhibit.

NOTE:

A greater proportion of either high or low value homesite sales in any one year
can distort comparability between years of average sales prices.

Exhibit V

Comparison of 19x8 Selling Prices of Developed
and Undeveloped Parcels to Appraised Values (1)

| | Actual Selling Price During Year Ended December 31, 19x8 | | Retail Values Per Appraisal as of December 31, 19x7 | |
Community and Number of Acres of Specific Parcels Sold	Total	Per Acre	Total	Per Acre

The accompanying notes are an integral part of this Exhibit.

NOTES:

(1) As prices for developed and undeveloped parcels vary significantly according to location and zoning, actual selling prices of developed and undeveloped parcels are compared on an individual parcel basis with their respective appraised values as opposed to using an average price per acre or parcel.

(2) Actual selling prices vary significantly in certain instances from the most recent appraised value due to changes in the density of the property in the Company's development master plan subsequent to the date of the appraisal.

Notes to Condensed Consolidated Financial Statements Reflecting Certain Estimated Current Value Adjustments

(Not in Conformity with Generally Accepted Accounting Principles)

December 31, 19x8

Current values, particularly related to real estate, are estimates and are subject to significant changes based on numerous unpredictable factors such as interest rates, availability of credit to purchasers, inflation, buyer demand, income tax treatment of real estate purchases, ability to achieve satisfactory financing, governmental regulations, the "energy crisis", etc. Many of the preceding factors are not within the control of the Company. Since these developments could significantly change the estimated value, there can be no assurance that estimates of current values reflected in the accompanying financial statements would not change as a result of the above or other factors.

Summary of Balance Sheet Accounts

Assets

In general, current value criteria give recognition in the balance sheet only to those assets capable of securing or satisfying the claims held by creditors or the equity of stockholders.

A summary and description of the method of stating asset accounts is as follows:

Balance Sheet Caption	Description
Properties	There is a significant difference between historical cost and estimated current value for certain of the properties included in this balance sheet caption. As shown on a project by project basis in Exhibit I elsewhere herein, land in process of development has been reflected at estimated current values based on appraisals by XYZ Appraisers.
	Land held for future development (that land for which no significant development activity has been initiated) has been recently acquired and has not been appraised and has therefore been stated at its cost for current value presentation.
	The land being developed as home and villa projects is included in the homes and villas under construction category and is valued at appraised value for estimated current

Balance Sheet Caption	Description

value presentation purposes. Homes and villas under construction are stated at cost for both the generally accepted accounting principles and current value presentation. This method allows recognition of construction profit, if any, under both methods on the sale of villas on a percentage of completion basis. To value the construction costs of homes and villas in excess of cost would result in recording economic resources before they are complete and exchangeable. Estimated current value is created only as the homes and villas are constructed for purchasers. Accordingly, no adjustment from cost value is made until services are rendered or projected losses require a downward adjustment to net realizable value.

Receivables

Generally accepted accounting principles require that receivables be discounted to reflect a market interest rate at the date of sale but require no subsequent adjustment to reflect changes in the interest rate. The current value procedures require that receivables be stated at their current realizable value considering present market interest rates. Accordingly, the current value presentation reflects homesite notes receivable discounted at an interest rate of 2% above the prime rate as of December 31, 19x8, which results in an effective yield of W%.

No additional discount was required as of December 31, 19x7, for changes in the market interest rate because, in management's opinion, notes receivable of the Company were marketable at that time at face value to banks without discount and without recourse at that date (during fiscal 19x7 and shortly thereafter, $X000 of land notes receivable were sold at face value without recourse).

Other Assets

Prepayments are presented at cost for current value presentation purposes are there is no significant difference between historical cost and current value.

Deferred charges do not represent economic resources capable of securing or satisfying the claims held by creditors so they are eliminated for the current value presentation. The stockholders' investment section is adjusted accordingly to reflect the reduction in the equity in the economic resources of the Company. Further, the current year amortization of deferred charges is eliminated from the current value Statement of Changes in Economic Resources.

Balance Sheet Caption	Description
	Merchandise inventory is presented at cost for the current value presentation because 19x8 shows no significant divergence between historical cost and current value.
Operating Properties	Current appraisals are not made on operating properties (inns, restaurants, golf courses, marinas, utility systems, etc.); accordingly, they are stated at historical costs in the accompanying financial statements.
	Operating properties are usually constructed during the initial phases of development projects. As such properties are completed, estimates are made by management to determine the portion of the cost that is not recoverable and therefore that should be transferred to the land in process of development category. These transfers represent the estimate of the initial cost of operating properties considered unrecoverable through successful future operations of the properties and attributable to land development activities. The estimates are based on the properties' achieving certain future levels of activity and profitability. In the opinion of management these levels of estimated activity and profitability will be attained.
Ownership in Joint Ventures	Appraisals or other estimates of current value were not made for the joint ventures and less than 50%-owned companies that the Company has invested in; accordingly, the ownerships are stated at the underlying equity in net assets of the investments.
Deferred Income Taxes	Deferred income taxes do not represent claims against existing resources but are valuations of certain asset accounts. Such valuation adjustments reflect the reduction in value attributable to using up the tax basis of these assets; accordingly, deferred tax amounts are offset against the related asset account for current value presentation purposes.

This section summarizes the appraisal considerations applicable to current value financial statement presentations. The summary focuses on some of the technical problems of using appraised values in current value financial statements, such as those which would be encountered in the Sea Pines presentation.

Appraisal Considerations for Current Value Reporting

Does the responsibility for the appraisal information included in financial statements belong to the appraiser or to the independent certified public accountant? The latter is not an expert in appraisal techniques, and so would have to limit any opinion expressed on current value financial statements that included appraisal information to the procedures utilized in accumulating this information in the financial statements.

Who Assumes Responsibility for the Appraised Values?

Sooner or later, accountants will probably assume the responsibility of expressing an opinion that the current value information based on appraisals is properly accumulated, in accordance with certain prescribed guidelines which would be disclosed in notes to the financial statements. However, independent certified public accountants would probably not be willing to accept the responsibility for the appraised values and for the appraisal assumptions and techniques utilized in connection with arriving at those values. The appraisal information must be the ultimate responsibility of the appraiser.

The independent certified public accountant should review the appraisals for reasonableness. The objective of this work would be to help the appraiser document the validity of the information and procedures used and to test the accumulation of the information in the financial statements. This review would include relating any factors in the appraisals to audit information available in the audit working papers. A review should also be made of these appraisals for consistent application. A critical step in this review process is to determine that the appraised values relate to the historical cost financial information presented. By this, we mean that in some cases it may be difficult to relate what is appraised to the actual cost elements the appraisal is supposed to relate to. This relationship is necessary, of course, to determine the holding gains or cost savings. If the wrong historical costs are related to the appraised values, an incorrect holding gain or cost saving will result.

Should the CPA Review Appraisal Information?

The discussion above refers to the problems inherent in comparing the costs in financial statements and records of the company to the appraised values of specific pieces of properties. Some of these problems are inherent in a fairly complex long-range real estate development process under percentage-of-completion accounting or installment sales accounting. As an example, under percentage-of-completion accounting, revenues relating to the incomplete portion of the project are deferred (as prescribed in the AICPA industry accounting guide). These deferred revenues are recognized as income as costs are incurred in connection with the development. The appraiser does not take into consideration the fact that certain of the sales revenues have been deferred. His approach is to determine what acres are available for sale and to make his calculations accordingly. This requires a reconciliation, to relate an appropriate book cost amount to the appraisal amount.

This is just one example of the intricacies that can become a problem in developing current value financial statements when you are attempting to isolate the current value increment or cost saving. There are other similar situations that result from the way utility costs and amenities are accounted for. But these problems are fairly technical in nature and relate more specifically to the subject company's accounting procedures. The point is that such situations may well create problems when one is involved in a fairly complicated accounting system.

Appraisal Standards?   For companies that report their financial information to the public and whose stock is traded in a public market, the appraiser must be aware that any financial information so reported which would mislead an investor could create a liability under the 1933 Act of the Securities and Exchange Commission. This is a whole new area of involvement for an appraiser, and a new concept in terms of appraiser responsibility. The appraisal profession has come a long way in terms of establishing guidelines and objectives to arrive at appraised values. There is, however, a great deal of flexibility allowed in terms of assumptions and approaches that can be used. Although accountants have a certain amount of flexibility, it is in a much more restrained form. Thus, this flexibility in appraisal will require greater standardization to provide reliable information to outside investors.

The question of independence is also raised if appraisers are to be associated with financial statements provided to investors. The Securities and Exchange Commission has prescribed guidelines for independence which, we believe, are stricter than the independence guidelines established by the appraisal professional associations.

Appraisers would have to accept legal responsibility similar to that of accountants and also allow for similar professional restraints in terms of generally accepted standards and procedures, independence and limitations with respect to acceptable alternative approaches and assumptions.

Can Accountants and   There are presently many appraisal firms with wide differences in abilities
Appraisers Work   and qualifications (probably not too different from the various accounting
Together?   firms). Presumably, large firms with the greatest degree of expertise would

be those involved in reporting appraisal values used in connection with financial statement presentation. The appraisers will have to be somewhat knowledgeable in the area of accounting, and be aware of how the appraisal information fits into financial statements. There will have to be a working relationship between the accountant and the appraiser, each understanding what the other is doing, to achieve a final product that will make sense. Working together in the preparation of current value financial statements will be difficult, until guidelines for responsibilities, procedures and objectives are established.

The time factor will also be significant if current value reporting is ever utilized to any great degree. The timing requirement for audits in connection with SEC filings leaves little room for flexibility. The involvement of appraisers in this process complicates the procedure and requires additional time for the company to prepare information for the appraisers. It may be extremely difficult to accumulate information and to make the appropriate reviews in order to provide current value information within the existing reporting deadline requirements of the Securities and Exchange Commission. Of course, this would not be a problem for nonpublic companies. The deadlines could be met by companies with excellent conventional accounting procedures that had tested the current value approach in the past.

Form of Appraisal Opinion

If the appraiser is to give an opinion regarding the appraised value of certain properties that will be shown in the financial statements, there should be some standard form of document for an appraiser to use that can be attached to the financial statements and that will establish responsibility in a specific manner.

The normal appraisal opinion is worded in such a manner that some of the "subject to" limitations could affect the ultimate worth of the appraisal. In many situations, the appraiser will indicate that the appraised value is subject to information provided by the client or based on certain assumptions that were made. We believe that it will be necessary for an appraiser to make an unequivocal statement of opinion on the appraised values and to extend his procedures to the extent necessary to make such an opinion. As previously mentioned, the guidelines for what can be done and the standards to use in an appraisal are fairly flexible and should probably be restricted somewhat to make appraised value a more reliable measurement.

Any Special Disclosure?

If all of the above matters are successfully resolved and if current value statements become an acceptable approach to providing financial information to investors, the actual information that should be used will require much study and consideration. We have concluded that current value financial statements will require additional disclosure over conventional financial statements. The aim of this current value project was to provide detailed information on appraised value, so that prior appraisal information could be evaluated by comparison with current actual experience. We feel that where appraisal information is utilized, it is important that the appraiser be held accountable and that there be some disclosure comparing actual results to prior appraisal information accompanied by explanations of variations. This would be a significant part of the current value financial statements, and was illustrated by some of the exhibits that were utilized in connection with the current value statements prepared in this project.

There are a number of factors which are beyond the appraiser's control but which can revise appraisal values. The primary factor that resulted in changed appraised values in this project was a number of changes in master plans. The "development approach" appraisal method used on most of the developments requires a projection of revenues and expenses of the development from a current date to the completion of the project. The results are then discounted back to present value in order to arrive at a current value for the project. The projection of sales required here is based on the existing master plan for the development project, which should not change significantly once the development starts. But there are instances where changes do occur. If there is a change in the density or utilization of any property, the value changes accordingly. This could have significant effects on the appraised value previously recorded.

Is There a "Best" Appraisal Method?

The development approach appraisal method is only one of a number of methods that can be used to appraise real estate, although many appraisers believe that the different methods should all result in approximately the same final appraised value. In addition, appraisers often utilize a number of methods and compare the results to determine if their end result makes sense. The development approach is the most sophisticated and refined approach for a development project in process with a set master plan. If there is no master plan available, a "comparable sales value" approach must be used. This assumes that there are comparable sales with which to make comparisons. However, for uncommon or unique developments, comparable sales value information can be almost nonexistent, thereby limiting this form of appraisal approach.

In sum, the information developed in this current value project is clearly useful to investors and others who are interested in the financial operations of an enterprise. The difficulties of working up this information on a complicated company (such as a real estate developer) are challenging. The time and cost of preparing such statements may be large, at least in the first instance that the current value method is applied. The problems that have been mentioned are not insurmountable, but would require more study and efforts at practical application in order to make current value reporting with appraisals a routine procedure.

Questions and Problems

Items 10.1 through 10.9 relate to the current replacement cost financial statements of Barber-Ellis of Canada, Limited, which appear in the chapter.

10.1. Consider the current replacement cost statement of earnings. Is the $1,984,262 net earnings:

  (a) current operating income?

  (b) realized income?

  (c) replacement cost income?

  (d) none of the above?

10.2. What is the amount of 1974 realized cost savings on (a) property, plant and equipment, and (b) inventories?

10.3. As of 12/31/74, what are the unrealized cost savings on (a) property, plant and equipment, and (b) inventories?

10.4. What is the amount of:

  (a) realized income?

  (b) replacement cost income?

  (c) realizable cost savings arising in 1974 on inventory, assuming that there were no unrealized cost savings in the beginning inventory?

10.5. Does the revaluation surplus include:

  (a) All cost savings/holding gains?

  (b) Anything besides cost savings/holding gains?

10.6. Consider the item "Unamortized Excess of Purchase Price of Subsidiaries Over Fair Value of Net Assets Acquired." Why does it not appear on the current replacement cost balance sheet? Comment on the treatment of this item.

10.7. Should provision be made for deferred income taxes associated with unrealized holding gains? Has the company made such provision?

10.8. How has Barber-Ellis handled the revalorization problem?

10.9. Are there any assets which Barber-Ellis has not restated at replacement cost? What about liabilities? Explain, and say what effects any additional adjustments would have on income and financial position.

10.10. For Philips Lamp, does the income statement reflect (a) current operating income; (b) realized income; (c) replacement cost income; (d) other?

10.11. How much are the Philips realiz*ed* cost savings/holding gains for 1973?

10.12. How much are the Philips cumulative cost savings/holding gains?

10.13. Realiz*ed* cost savings on inventory are a (a) source of funds; (b) a use of funds; (c) neither?

10.14. Realiz*ed* cost savings on fixed assets (via depreciation) are (a) a source of funds; (b) a use of funds; (c) neither?

Integration of General Price-Level and Specific Price-Change Adjustments

11

The preceding chapters presented two methods of adjusting financial statements to reflect the effects of inflation. Both methods were aimed at measuring monetary values and profits. The first, general price-level accounting (described in Chapters 2 and 3), converted all historical dollar balances into units of standardized purchasing power, by restated historical balances in end-of-period dollars through reference to changes in an appropriate general price index. The second, replacement cost accounting (described in Chapters 4–10), substituted the current replacement costs for historical costs of specific items. This method does not report entirely in units of standardized purchasing power but rather in the actual dollar values existing in the goods and capital markets during the period under review.

Importance of Measurement and Valuation Problems

The first method resolves a *measurement* problem. Since the value of money lies in its ability to command goods and services (i.e., in its *purchasing power*), dollars of different purchasing power are not equivalent; a measuring technique which combines them must be deficient. Restatement of dollars having *different* amounts of purchasing power in dollars having *common* amounts of purchasing power removes the deficiency in the unit of measurement. Therefore, *the restated amounts are the amounts to which the "old" dollars must increase in order to maintain equivalent purchasing power in the face of a changing general price level.* Monetary assets and liabilities, of course, are not restated. The amount of *potential restatement* of these items makes up the purchasing-power gain or loss.

The second method resolves a *valuation* problem, as opposed to a *measurement* problem. It employs *current values* (based on the current replacement costs of specific assets and liabilities) to reflect current conditions in the goods and capital markets. It does not standardize the measuring unit through restatement in dollars of common purchasing power; rather, it replaces historical valuations with current valuations. In determining periodic income, replacement cost accounting breaks the traditional historical cost net income figure into two important components. The first, current operating income, matches current costs against current revenues to show current profitability. The second, realiz*ed* cost savings/holding gains, shows the gains which result from the difference between the current cost of assets used and sold and their historical dollar amounts. In addition, replacement cost accounting supplements historical cost net income by also showing the *un*realiz*ed* cost savings/holding gains which arose during the year on assets and liabilities still retained by the firm.

In view of the above, we believe that general price-level accounting and replacement cost accounting should *not* be considered alternative solutions to the same problem. The two methods really address two distinct dimensions of a more fundamental problem. It seems to us that sound financial reporting should reflect *both* a constant unit of measurement and valuations based on current conditions in the goods and capital markets. In other words, the effects of inflation and deterioration in general purchasing power ought to be measured and disclosed within the framework of a current value replacement cost accounting system. Income statements should measure gains or losses in terms of purchasing power rather than in terms of money. Recall the "well-offness" notion implied in the Hicksian or economic concept of income. When general purchasing power is changing, well-offness becomes meaningful only when those changes are taken into account. In a period of inflation, when the effects of the deterioration in purchasing power are *removed* from income measured in terms of money, the amount remaining is referred to as *real* income (or loss). Hence, income statements should be designed to measure *real* income, money income deflated for changes in general purchasing power. The statement of changes in financial position would also be more useful when measured in real terms.

With respect to the replacement cost statement of financial position, assets and liabilities are already stated in current dollars (and hence in current units of purchasing power). The components of stockholders' equity, however, will have to be adjusted to reflect changes in the purchasing power of the dollar. This will involve determining *real* retained (realiz*ed*) earnings, *real un*realiz*ed* cost savings/holding gains and the current purchasing-power equivalent of capital stock.

This is an important distinction. General price-level accounting restates *historical* values, not *current* values, in units of equivalent general purchasing power. Thus, the general price-level restatement procedure falls short of measuring, in units of equivalent purchasing power, *current* financial position and the results of *current* operations. It works with equivalent units of purchasing power but not with current values. Furthermore, it measures purchasing-power gains and losses only in connection with monetary items. Replacement cost accounting, on the other hand, works with current values but not entirely with equivalent units of purchasing power. For example, in the replacement cost income statement, total revenue is measured in dollars which approximately represent the *average* purchasing power for the year. Similarly, the use of average replacement costs implies costs measured in dollars which approximately reflect the average purchasing power for the year. Cost savings and holding gains, however, are stated in dollars of varying purchasing power.

The task of this chapter, then, is threefold. Our first objective is to measure real income, net of changes in general purchasing power; second, to adjust the components of stockholders' equity to values in real terms; third, to prepare financial statements measured in dollars of equivalent purchasing power.

Perhaps another reference to the "swarm of bees" analogy which we used in Chapter 1 will help clarify these points. The swarm, of course, is the composite effect of a great many individual bees, all moving in different directions and at different speeds. We may be interested in knowing the current location of the swarm compared to its location yesterday. We may also be interested in knowing the current location of certain bees in the swarm. Put another way, we may be interested in both the movements of the swarm as a whole and the movements of specific bees in the swarm.

Now information about the swarm as a whole is not sufficient to pin down the location of individual bees. Similarly, information about certain individual bees will not enable us to pin down the exact location of the swarm. On the other hand, if we know the location of the individual bees relative to the swarm as a whole, *and* the location of the swarm, the location of both could be identified. Replacement cost accounting tells us about movements of prices of specific assets (individual bees), while general price-level accounting tells us about movements of a composite of specific asset prices (the swarm). Given both specific price information as well as general price-level information, we can measure movements in specific prices relative to movements in the general price level.

This important concept can be illustrated in yet another way. Say that we own stock in a mutual fund with a well-diversified portfolio (i.e., its *beta coefficient* is close to 1). The price of our stock has increased by 2 percent over the past year. How well has our fund performed? It depends on how the stock market as a whole has fared. If the market is down 25 percent, our fund has performed splendidly. However, if the market is up 25 percent, our fund's performance is disappointing.

Good performance, then, can be associated with an increase in the prices of what we own greater than the increase of prices in general. During inflation we gain if we hold goods that increase in price faster than the general price level. But we lose if the goods we hold do not increase in price as fast as the general price level. Therefore, to measure *real profit* we must take into account both changes in the *specific prices* of our goods and services and changes in the *general purchasing power* of the dollar. (In other words, using the swarm of bees analogy, how well are *our* bees doing, compared to the swarm as a whole?)

Introduction to Real Profit

Our objective is to remove the effects of inflation from the appropriate replacement cost accounts and, when necessary, restate the *real* balances in end-of-period dollars. The replacement cost position statement asset and liability accounts, of course, are already shown in end-of-period dollars, as is the total stockholders' equity. The replacement cost income statement and statement of changes in financial position, however, reflect average-of-period dollars. Cost savings and holding gains, reported in mixed dollars of various periods, must be broken down into two parts because we wish to identify the extent to which the recorded cost savings were sufficient to offset the effects of general inflation. Put another way, we wish to measure the effects of specific price changes which differ from changes in the general price level (in order to see how *our* bees are doing relative to the swarm as a whole.)

The gains represented by cost savings, measured in mixed dollars, consist of two separate components—*real* gains and *fictional* gains. A *real gain* is an increase in purchasing power. A *fictional gain* is the amount of gain required to maintain existing purchasing power in the face of inflation. Real gains will be equal to money gains (cost savings measured in dollar terms) less fictional gains. Therefore, if the specific price of an asset increases *faster* than the general price level, the increment in *purchasing power* (or real gain) will be measured by the amount of the specific price change *over and above* the change in the general price level. By analogy, this is how much better *our* bees have done compared with the swarm as a whole.

This relationship between money gains, fictional gains and real gains is summarized in the identity below.

Money Gains = Fictional Gains + Real Gains

or

Real Gains = Money Gains − Fictional Gains

Real replacement cost income, then, will be defined as current operating income plus real realiz*able* cost savings/holding gains.

Suppose an asset was purchased for $30,000. Its replacement cost subsequently rises by 50 percent to $45,000 while the general price level rises by 30 percent. The total cost saving is $15,000. The fictional cost saving is $9,000 [=30% × $30,000], the amount by which the specific price should increase merely to keep pace with the general price level. The fictional gain, then, does not represent an increase in purchasing power; it is the amount necessary to *preserve existing purchasing power*. The real gain is $6,000 [$15,000 − $9,000], because the asset's price increased by $6,000 *more* than was necessary to maintain existing purchasing power. In terms of the identity,

$$\text{Real Gains} = \text{Money Gains} - \text{Fictional Gains}$$
$$\$6,000 \quad = \quad \$15,000 \quad - \quad \$9,000$$

Much of our work in this chapter will be in measuring the real and fictional components in cost savings. In this way, we will be able to report *real* replacement cost income, income which measures the increment in purchasing power accruing to the firm during the accounting period. The effects of this differentiation between real and fictional income will then be reflected in the equity section of the statement of financial position.

To prepare these price-level adjusted replacement cost financial statements, we need to know how the price level has changed during the year. We assume the following general price-level values for the year.

General Procedure for the Preparation of Financial Statements Reporting Price-Level Adjusted Replacement Cost Data

19x6	General Price Index
Beginning of the year.	95
Average for the year.	100
End of the year.	105

We begin with the financial statements prepared in Chapter 9 under replacement cost accounting. The income statement reflects average current costs for the period, the position statement reflects end-of-period replacement costs. We will convert the average current cost replacement cost income statement measured in money terms to a statement of real income measured in average dollars for the period. We will also generate a statement of real income in end-of-period dollars which will articulate with the beginning and ending statements of financial position stated in end-of-period dollars. The 12/31/x6 position statement is already stated in end-of-19x6 dollars. To restate in end-of-period dollars the beginning statement of financial position at 12/31/x5, multiply each replacement cost balance by 105/95 to reflect the change in the general price level during the year.

The result of this work is to show beginning and ending statements of financial position and a statement of real income, all measured in dollars of the same vintage, namely, end-of-19x6 dollars. A real statement of changes in financial position measured in end-of-19x6 dollars can then be prepared. The general procedure for developing the complete set of financial statements is outlined in the following steps.*

(1) Compute fictional realiz*able* gains (Exhibit 11.1).

(2) Compute fictional realiz*ed* gains (Exhibit 11.2).

(3) Compute real gains, both realiz*able* and realiz*ed*, employing the "money gains = fictional gains + real gains" relationship (Exhibit 11.3).

(4) Compute the change in real *un*realiz*ed* gains (Exhibit 11.4).

(5) Prepare the statement of real income reflecting real gains (Exhibit 11.6).

(6) Prepare the replacement cost position statement at 12/31/x6 adjusted for changes in the general price level after adjusting the equity section in the beginning position statement to reflect the cumulative impact of price changes since inception (Exhibit 11.8).

(7) Prepare the replacement cost statement of changes in financial position adjusted for changes in the general price level (Exhibit 11.9).

Calculation of
Fictional Realizable
Gains

The first step, calculating *fictional realizable cost savings/holding gains* during the year, allows us to measure the extent to which asset and liability values *should have changed* to keep pace with the change in general purchasing power. We start with the beginning replacement cost balances and multiply them by 10/95, the change in the general price level over the year. Increases or decreases in the various accounts are assumed to have taken place at the *average price level* during the year. These increases and decreases are multiplied by 5/100, the change in the price level from its average value during the year to its year-end value. Replacement cost rather than *historical cost* balances are used because current year realiz*able* gains have meaning only in the context of *changing replacement costs*. The entire procedure for calculating fictional realiz*able* gains is illustrated for our asset and liability accounts in Exhibit 11.1.

---

*The subject matter of this chapter follows the principles developed by Edwards and Bell, *The Theory and Measurement of Business Income,* Chapter 8. We have, however, taken pains to clarify, elaborate and illustrate the difficult concepts involved and to present them in a more practical manner.

Exhibit 11.1

Computation of Fictional Realizable Gains
(Based on Replacement Cost Dollar Balances)

ACCOUNT				12/31/x6 Dollars × 100/105 =	Average 19x6 Dollars
CASH AND RECEIVABLES					
Balance, 12/31/x5	10/95 ×	1,800.00 =	189.00		
Increase during 19x6	5/100 ×	1,602.00 =	80.10	269.10	256.29
MARKETABLE SECURITIES					
Balance, 12/31/x5	10/95 ×	740.00 =	77.70		
Decrease during 19x6	5/100 ×	(104.00) =	(5.20)	72.50	69.05
INVENTORIES					
Balance, 12/31/x5	10/95 ×	2,890.00 =	303.45		
Increase during 19x6	5/100 ×	685.00 =	34.25	337.70	321.62
FIXED ASSETS					
Balance, 12/31/x5	10/95 ×	7,000.00 =	735.00		
Decrease during 19x6	5/100 ×	(280.00) =	(14.00)	721.00	686.67
ACCOUNTS PAYABLE					
Balance, 12/31/x5	10/95 ×	(2,500.00) =		(262.50)	(250.00)
BONDS PAYABLE					
Balance, 12/31/x5	10/95 ×	(1,000.00) =	(105.00)		
Decrease during 19x6	5/100 ×	19.00 =	.95	(104.05)	(99.10)
		10,852.00			
Total Fictional Realizable Gains.				1,033.75	984.53

The second step is the calculation of fictional realiz*ed* cost savings/holding gains during the year. Realiz*ed* gains include not only those which became realiz*able* during the current period but also the realization of any prior period realiz*able* gains. Hence, we start with the *historical cost* (rather than the replacement cost) balances and measure the extent to which the historical cost realiz*ed* gains or losses should have changed just to keep up with the change in general purchasing power. This is shown in Exhibit 11.2.

Calculation of Fictional Realized Gains

Exhibit 11.2

Computation of Fictional Realized Gains
(Based on Historical Cost Dollar Balances)

ACCOUNT	Average 19x6 Dollars	× 105/100 =	12/31/x6 Dollars
CASH AND RECEIVABLES (EXHIBIT 11.1)	256.29		269.10

MARKETABLE SECURITIES

Assume that the price index stood at 90 when the securities
sold were purchased.

Historical cost of securities sold (10/90 × 65)	7.22		7.58
	263.51		276.68

INVENTORIES (COST OF GOODS SOLD)

Assume that the price index stood at 90 when the beginning
inventory was purchased and at 103 when the ending
inventory was purchased.

Beginning Inventory (100/90 × 2,800)	3,110.80		
Purchases (100/100 × 6,814)	6,814.00		
Ending Inventory (100/103 × 3,506)	−3,403.88		
FIFO Cost of Goods Sold, Average 19x6 Dollars	6,520.92		
FIFO Cost of Goods Sold, Historical Dollars	−6,108.00		
Fictional Realized Cost Savings on Cost of Goods Sold	412.92		433.57

FIXED ASSETS (DEPRECIATION)

Assume that the price index stood at 75 when the fixed assets
were purchased.

Historical Cost Depreciation (25/75 × 1,000)	333.33		350.00
ACCOUNTS PAYABLE (EXHIBIT 11.1)	(250.00)		(262.50)
Total Fictional Realized Gains	759.76		797.75

Cash, receivables and payables are assumed to have "turned over" during
the year, so there are no *unrealized* gains in these accounts. Hence, the
total fictional realiz*able* gains (losses) computed in Exhibit 11.1 have
been realiz*ed*. Furthermore, the fictional gains (losses) will be exactly
offset by real losses (gains). These calculations are, in principle, similar to
the determination of the purchasing-power gain or loss on short-term
monetary items developed in Chapters 2 and 3 as part of the general
price-level restatement procedure.

In the following explanations, we use cash and receivables as our example. On 12/31/x5, cash and receivables amounted to $1,800. On
12/31/x6 the amount was $3,402, an increase of $1,602 which we assume

took place evenly over the year. These amounts have declined in purchasing power due to inflation. Specifically, the decline is:

$$
\begin{aligned}
\$1,800 \times 10/95 &\ldots\ldots\ldots\$189.00 \\
1,602 \times 5/100 &\ldots\ldots\ldots\underline{80.10} \\
&\underline{\$269.10} \text{ in } 12/31/\text{x6 dollars}
\end{aligned}
$$

When deflated to average 19x6 dollars, the decline is $256.29

This decline is a *real* loss, and it is realized. However, cash and receivables are "monetary items," and are thus already stated at their current value in 12/31/x6 dollars. Since it is unnecessary to write down their current value ($3,402), we have no *money* gain or loss. Thus the real gain (loss) is ($269.10); we use the following identity to calculate the fictional gain.

$$
\begin{aligned}
\text{Real Gains} &= \text{Money Gains} - \text{Fictional Gains} \\
(\$269.10) &= 0 - \text{Fictional Gains} \\
\text{Fictional Gains} &= 0 - (\$269.10) \\
\text{Fictional Gains} &= \$269.10
\end{aligned}
$$

Thus, the fictional gain of $269.10 is exactly offset by a real loss of $269.10, as the money gain is zero. Since money gains are always zero on monetary items, by definition, the fictional gains (losses) are always offset by equal real losses (gains) for monetary items.

The historical cost of the securities sold was $65. We assume that the general price index was 90 when the securities were originally purchased and 100 (i.e., average 19x6 dollars) when they were sold. The $65 is multiplied by 10/90, the price-level change since the securities were purchased, to determine the fictional realiz*ed* gain or gain which should have been realized at the time of sale, to keep pace with the increase in general purchasing power.

Realiz*ed* gains related to inventories are, of course, embodied in the cost of goods sold. Realiz*ed money* cost savings represent the difference between replacement cost of goods sold and historical cost of goods sold. Realiz*ed fictional* cost savings, on the other hand, represent the difference between historical cost of goods sold *restated for general price-level changes* and historical cost of goods sold measured in *historical dollars.* To prepare the restatements, it is necessary to know the level of the price index when the beginning and ending inventories were purchased. These values are assumed to be 90 and 103, respectively. We also assume that current period purchases were made at the average price level for the year (i.e., 100).

In our example, the only realiz*ed* gain attributable to fixed assets pertains to the depreciation expense. We assume that the price index stood at 75 when the equipment was purchased. By multiplying historical cost depreciation expense by 30/75, the change in the price index since date of purchase, we measure the extent to which depreciation expense *should* *have* increased to maintain constant purchasing power in the depreciation expense.

Another approach to calculating the fictional realiz*ed* gain on fixed assets involves restating the entire asset balance, taking 10 percent depreciation on the restated balance and subtracting historical cost depreciation of $1,000. The restated asset balance is $13,333 [=$10,000 × 100/75]. Ten percent depreciation is $1,333; the fictional realiz*ed* gain is $333 [=$1,333 − $1,000].

Calculation of Real Gains

Proceeding to the third step, we now have data on fictional realiz*able* and fictional realiz*ed* gains, the amounts developed in Exhibits 11.1 and 11.2. We also have data on money realiz*able* and money realiz*ed* gains, the amounts in the replacement cost financial statements in Chapter 9. Real realiz*able* gains and real realiz*ed* gains are derived in the now familiar relationship:

$$\text{Real Gains} = \text{Money Gains} - \text{Fictional Gains}$$

The computation of real gains, both in average and end-of-period dollars, is shown in Exhibit 11.3.

Exhibit 11.3

Computation of Real Gains

	Money Gains		Fictional Gains		Real Gains	
	Realizable	Realized	Realizable	Realized	Realizable	Realized
AVERAGE 19x6 DOLLARS						
Cash and Receivables.	—	—	256.29	256.29	(256.29)	(256.29)
Marketable Securities	(28.00)	11.00	69.05	7.22	(97.05)	3.78
Inventories.	278.70	299.70	321.62	412.92	(42.92)	(113.22)
Fixed Assets.	1,260.00	540.00	686.67	333.33	573.33	206.67
Accounts Payable	—	—	(250.00)	(250.00)	250.00	250.00
Bonds Payable and Interest .	29.00	10.00	(99.10)	—	128.10	10.00
Total	1,539.70	860.70	984.53	759.76	555.17	100.94
12/31/x6 DOLLARS						
Cash and Receivables.	—	—	269.10	269.10	(269.10)	(269.10)
Marketable Securities	(29.40)	11.55	72.50	7.58	(101.90)	3.96*
Inventories.	292.64	314.69	337.70	433.57	(45.06)	(118.88)
Fixed Assets.	1,323.00	567.00	721.00	350.00	602.00	217.00
Accounts Payable	—	—	(262.50)	(262.50)	262.50	262.50
Bonds Payable and Interest .	30.45	10.50	(104.05)	—	134.50	10.50
Total	1,616.69	903.74	1,033.75	797.75	582.94	105.98

*Includes ($.01) rounding error.

The change in real *un*realized gains in average and end-of-period dollars, step four, is easily computed from the data on real reali*zable* and real reali*zed* gains developed in Exhibit 11.3. The computation is based on the identity,

Calculation of the
Change in Real
Unrealized Gains

Reali*zable* Gains = Reali*zed* Gains + *Change in Un*realized Gains

or

Change in *Un*realized Gains = Reali*zable* Gains — Reali*zed* Gains

---

These amounts are shown in both average and end-of-period dollars in Exhibit 11.4.

Exhibit 11.4

Computation of Change in Real Unrealized Gains

	Change in Real Unrealized Gains	=	Real Realizable Gains	—	Real Realized Gains
AVERAGE 19x6 DOLLARS					
Cash and Receivables	—		(256.29)		(256.29)
Inventories	70.30		(42.92)		(113.22)
Fixed Assets	366.66		573.33		206.67
Marketable Securities	(100.83)		(97.05)		3.78
Accounts Payable	—		250.00		250.00
Bonds Payable and Interest	118.10		128.10		10.00
Total	454.23		555.17		100.94
12/31/x6 DOLLARS					
Cash and Receivables	—		(269.10)		(269.10)
Inventories	73.82		(45.06)		(118.88)
Fixed Assets	385.00		602.00		217.00
Marketable Securities	(105.87)		(101.90)		3.96*
Accounts Payable	—		262.50		262.50
Bonds Payable and Interest	124.00		134.50		10.50
Total	476.95		582.94		105.98

*Includes ($.01) rounding error.

The data in Exhibits 11.1, 11.2, 11.3 and 11.4 are summarized, by account, in Exhibit 11.5.

Exhibit 11.5

Summary of Computations of Fictional and Real Gains, by Account

	Money Gains (Losses)			Fictional Gains (Losses)			Real Gains (Losses)		
	Realizable	Realized	Change in Unrealized	Realizable	Realized	Change in Unrealized	Realizable	Realized	Change in Unrealized
AVERAGE 19x6 DOLLARS									
Cash and Receivables			—	256.29	256.29	—	(256.29)	(256.29)	—
Marketable Securities	(28.00)	11.00	(39.00)	69.05	7.22	61.83	(97.05)	3.78	(100.83)
Inventories	278.70	299.70	(21.00)	321.62	412.92	(91.30)	(42.92)	(113.22)	70.30
Fixed Assets	1,260.00	540.00	720.00	686.67	333.33	353.34	573.33	206.67	366.66
Accounts Payable				(250.00)	(250.00)		250.00	250.00	
Bonds Payable and Interest	29.00	10.00	19.00	(99.10)		(99.10)	128.10	10.00	118.10
Total	1,539.70	860.70	679.00	984.53	759.76	224.77	555.17	100.94	454.23
12/31/x6 DOLLARS									
Cash and Receivables			—	269.10	269.10	—	(269.10)	(269.10)	—
Marketable Securities	(29.40)	11.55	(40.95)	72.50	7.58	64.92	(101.90)	3.96	(105.87)
Inventories	292.64	314.69	(22.05)	337.70	433.57	(95.87)	(45.06)	(118.88)	73.82
Fixed Assets	1,323.00	567.00	756.00	721.00	350.00	371.00	602.00	217.00	385.00
Accounts Payable				(262.50)	(262.50)		262.50	262.50	
Bonds Payable and Interest	30.45	10.50	19.95	(104.05)		(104.05)	134.50	10.50	124.00
Total	1,616.69	903.74	712.95	1,033.75	797.75	236.00	582.94	105.98	476.95

For each type of gain, *money*, *fictional* or *real*, we can verify that

Realizable Gains = Realized Gains + *Change in* Unrealized Gains

Similarly, for *realizable*, *realized* and *change in unrealized* gains, we can verify that

Money Gains = Fictional Gains + Real Gains

We are now in a position to prepare the statement of real income (step five). Recall that our replacement cost income statement reflected average current costs and, hence, average dollars for the period. Starting with these data, we prepare the statement of real income measured in average dollars and then restate it, multiplying each item by 105/100, to measure it in end-of-period dollars. When measured in end-of-period dollars, the statement will articulate with the beginning and ending statements of financial position, both measured in end-of-period dollars. Let us now look at the various sections of the statement of real income as presented in Exhibit 11.6.

Statement of Real Income

Exhibit 11.6

CVA CORPORATION

Statement of Real Income for the Year Ended December 31, 19x6

	Average 19x6 Dollars	12/31/x6 Dollars
SALES	12,000.00	12,600.00
Less: Cost of Goods Sold	6,407.70	6,728.08
Operating Expenses	3,600.00	3,780.00
Depreciation Expense	1,540.00	1,617.00
Interest Expense	70.00	73.50
CURRENT OPERATING INCOME	382.30	401.42
Real Cost Savings/Holding Gains Realized during 19x6:		
Through Sale of Inventory	(113.22)	(118.88)
Through Equipment Depreciation	206.67	217.00
Through Sale of Securities	3.78	3.96
Through Interest Expense	10.00	10.50
Through Holding Cash, Receivables and Accounts Payable	(6.29)	(6.60)
Total Real Realized Gains (Losses)	100.94	105.98
REAL REALIZED INCOME	483.24	507.40
Change in Real Unrealized Cost Savings/Holding Gains:		
On Ending Inventory	70.30	73.82
On Equipment	366.66	385.00
On Securities	(100.83)	(105.87)
On Bonds Payable	118.10	124.00
Total Change in Real Unrealized Gains	454.23	476.95
REAL REPLACEMENT COST INCOME	937.47	984.35

Current operating income is taken directly from the replacement cost statement of income prepared in Chapter 9. Since it is already stated in average dollars for the period, it need not be restated for purposes of the average-dollar statement of real income. However, each element in current operating income is multiplied by 105/100 to restate it in end-of-period dollars.

Real realized cost savings/holding gains in average and end-of-period dollars were computed in Exhibit 11.3. The appropriate amounts are transferred directly from Exhibit 11.3 to the statement of real income.

Real unrealized cost savings/holding gains in average and end-of-period dollars were computed in Exhibit 11.4. The appropriate amounts have been transferred directly from Exhibit 11.4 to the statement of real income.

The statement of real income has a clear economic interpretation. When measured in average dollars, real replacement cost income represents the actual improvement in the firm's position, in terms of purchasing power, during the period. This improvement consists of current profitability (current costs matched against current revenues) plus the *real* portion of realiz*able* cost savings (i.e., money realiz*able* cost savings *deflated* by the change in the general price level). The shareholders are now in a better position to evaluate management's performance in terms of the *preservation* and *enhancement* of the purchasing power inherent in their equity in the firm. Notice the difference between money replacement cost income and real replacement cost income. Replacement cost income measured in money terms amounted to $1,922. Of this amount, however, only $937.47 was *real*; $984.53 was *fictional*. This, in itself, is a significant revelation.

The treatment of the real gains on bonds payable differs from the treatment of the purchasing-power gain on long-term debt discussed in the chapters dealing with general price-level restatements. In Chapter 3 we argued that such purchasing-power gains are realiz*ed* and should be included in restated net income. In the present chapter, these gains *are* included in real replacement cost income but *not* as being realized. This treatment is, we believe, more consistent with the general classification of cost savings (as realiz*ed* or *un*realiz*ed*) in replacement cost accounting.

The astute reader will have observed a slight difference in format from the replacement cost income statement in Chapter 9. In that statement, we showed realiz*able* cost savings, both realiz*ed* and *un*realiz*ed*, separately. We added those prior period cost savings which were realiz*ed* in this period to compute realized income and then deducted them in order to avoid double counting in replacement cost income. This refinement is not necessary, as the same amount of realiz*able* cost savings may be determined by summing total realiz*ed* cost savings and the change in *un*realiz*ed* cost savings. We have adopted the latter approach for the statement of real income. In that statement, real realiz*able* cost savings are shown to consist of two components: real realiz*ed* cost savings plus the *change* in real *un*realiz*ed* cost savings.

Exhibit 11.7

Adjustment of 12/31/x5 Stockholders' Equity

Item	Replacement Cost Balance 12/31/x5	Less Fictional Element	Real Balance	Plus Price Level Adjustment	Real Balance Restated in 12/31/x5 Dollars
(1) Capital Stock	2,000.00	—	2,000.00	440.00	2,440.00
	2,000.00		2,000.00	440.00	2,440.00
(2) Realized Income, 19x1	200.00	6.60	193.40	43.71	237.11
(2) Realized Income, 19x2	600.00	18.60	581.40	88.37	669.77
(2) Realized Income, 19x3	600.00	—	600.00	70.80	670.80
(2) Realized Income, 19x4	1,600.00	46.40	1,553.60	133.61	1,687.21
(2) Realized Income, 19x5	1,750.00	49.00	1,701.00	45.93	1,746.93
	4,750.00	120.60	4,629.40	382.42	5,011.82
(3) Unrealized Holding Gains— Marketable Securities	90.00	36.11	53.89	—*	53.89
(4) Unrealized Cost Savings— Inventories	90.00	155.56	(65.56)	—*	(65.56)
(5) Unrealized Cost Savings— Fixed Assets	2,000.00	666.67	1,333.33	156.86 (.34)**	1,490.19 (.34)**
	2,180.00	858.34	1,321.66	156.52	1,478.18
Total	8,930.00	978.94	7,951.06	978.94	8,930.00

*No price-level adjustment required here because these items are already stated in 12/31/x5 dollars.

**Rounding error.

NOTES:

(1) We assume that the firm began operations when the price level was 75 (the price level when the fixed assets were purchased). At that time, $1,600 of capital stock was issued. Subsequently, an additional $400 of capital stock was issued when the price level stood at 93.1 (near the end of 19x5). The total effect of price level changes on the historical capital stock balances, then, is

$$20/75 \ (1,600) + 1.9/93.1 \ (400) = .27 \ (1,600) + .02 \ (400) = 432 + 8 = 440$$

The average price level adjustment was $1,600/2,000 \ (.27) + 400/2,000 \ (.02) = .8(.27) + .2(.02) = .216 + .004 = .22.$

(2) We assume the following price levels over the five-year history of the CVA Corporation ending 12/31/x5. Realized income was earned in the increments as shown for each year, 19x1—19x5.

End of Year	Price Level	(a) Average Price Change during Year	(b) Price Change to 12/31/x5 from Average during Year
19x0	75	—	—
19x1	80	.033	.226
19x2	85	.031	.152
19x3	85	.000	.118
19x4	90	.029	.086
19x5	95	.028	.027

(a) These amounts were computed using the following formula.

$$[(P_t - P_{t-1})/2]/[(P_t + P_{t-1})/2]$$

They were multiplied by the realized income in each of the respective years to determine the fictional element.

(b) These amounts were computed using the following formula.

$$[95 - (P_t + P_{t-1})/2]/[(P_t + P_{t-1})/2]$$

They were multiplied by the "real balances" (i.e., the replacement cost money balances less the fictional elements) to restate these real increments in 12/31/x5 dollars.

(3) Marketable securities of $650 assumed purchased during 19x5 when price level stood at 90. Fictional gain = $[(95-90)/90] \times 650 = 36.11$.

(4) Inventories of $2,800 assumed purchased during 19x5 when price level stood at 90. Fictional gain = $[(95-90)/90] \times 2,800 = 155.56$.

(5) Replacement cost of fixed assets (originally purchased for $10,000 at end of 19x0) assumed to have risen to $14,000 at end of year 3 when price level stood at 85. Fictional gain as of 12/31/x3 on book value (50 percent of the asset has been depreciated) remaining at 12/31/x5 = $[(85-75)/75] \times 5,000 = 666.67$. Price-level adjustment = $[(95-85)/85] \times 1,333.33 = 156.86$.

Replacement Cost Statement of Financial Position Adjusted for Changes in the General Price Level

The major difference between the replacement cost position statement adjusted for changes in the general price level and the replacement cost position statement in money terms prepared in Chapter 9 lies in the equity section. Assets and liabilities are already measured in end-of-period dollars. Although the equity section total is also measured in 12/31/x6 dollars, it fails to disclose the *real* components of stockholders' equity. To develop these figures, we need to make some assumptions about the cumulative effect of price changes on the owners' equity in the firm *since inception*. This will be necessary only for the year in which the accounting techniques discussed in this chapter are to be implemented for the first time. In other words, the equity section should reflect the cumulative effect of operations and price changes over time *as if statements of real income had been prepared for each accounting period since the firm commenced operations*. It would be virtually impossible to go back and convert historical cost income statements to replacement cost income statements and then to statements of real income. Hence, we make some reasonable assumptions about the cumulative effects of price changes since inception and adjust the equity section accordingly. We adjust the beginning (i.e., 12/31/x5) equity section and then restate the entire 12/31/x5 position statement in 12/31/x6 dollars. The restated 12/31/x5 position statement, the 19x6 statement of real income and the 12/31/x6 position statement, all measured in 12/31/x6 dollars, will thus articulate with each other. The schedule in Exhibit 11.7 reflects the assumptions we have made about the cumulative effects of price changes since inception on the 12/31/x5 equity section.

Statements of financial position at December 31, 19x6, and December 31, 19x5, in 19x6 and 19x5 dollars, are presented in Exhibit 11.8 (step six).

Exhibit 11.8

CVA CORPORATION

Comparative Statements of Financial Position, December 31, 19x6 and 19x5
Replacement Costs Adjusted for Changes in the General Price Level

| | December 31, 19x6 | December 31, 19x5 | |
	($x6)	($x6)	($x5)
ASSETS			
Cash and Receivables.	3,402.00	1,989.00	1,800.00
Marketable Securities.	636.00	817.70	740.00
Inventories, at Lower of Cost or Market	3,575.00	3,193.45	2,890.00
Total Current Assets	7,613.00	6,000.15	5,430.00
Equipment, at Cost	16,800.00	15,470.00	14,000.00
Less: Accumulated Depreciation	10,080.00	7,735.00	7,000.00
Total Fixed Assets	6,720.00	7,735.00	7,000.00
Total Assets	14,333.00	13,735.15	12,430.00
LIABILITIES			
Accounts Payable	2,500.00	2,762.50	2,500.00
Bonds Payable	981.00	1,105.00	1,000.00
Total Liabilities	3,481.00	3,867.50	3,500.00
STOCKHOLDERS' EQUITY			
Capital Stock	2,696.20	2,696.20	2,440.00
Real Retained (Realized) Earnings	6,045.46	5,538.06	5,011.82
Real Unrealized Holding Gains/Cost Savings	2,110.34	1,633.39	1,478.18
Total Stockholders' Equity	10,852.00	9,867.65	8,930.00
Total Liabilities and Stockholders' Equity.	14,333.00	13,735.15	12,430.00

Using the data from the 12/31/x6 and restated 12/31/x5 equity sections and the statement of real income in 12/31/x6 dollars, we can now reconcile the change in the equity section during 19x6.

Reconciliation of Changes in Equity Accounts
during 19x6

	Capital Stock	Real Retained (Realized) Earnings	Real Unrealized Holding Gains/Cost Savings
Balance, 12/31/x5 ($x6)	2,696.20	5,538.06	1,633.39
Real Realized Income	——	507.40	——
Real Unrealized Cost Savings/Holding Gains	——	——	476.95
Balance, 12/31/x6 ($x6)	2,696.20	6,045.46	2,110.34

Replacement Cost
Statement of Changes
in Financial Position
Adjusted for Changes
in the General
Price Level

We now have all the information required to prepare the replacement cost statement of changes in financial position adjusted for changed in the general price level in 12/31/x6 dollars (step seven). This statement is presented in Exhibit 11.9.

Exhibit 11.9

CVA CORPORATION

Statement of Changes in Financial Position for the Year Ended December 31, 19x6
Replacement Costs Adjusted for Changes in the General Price Level

SOURCES OF WORKING CAPITAL	($x6)
Real Replacement Cost Income	984.35
Add Depreciation Expense Not Using Working Capital	1,617.00
	2,501.35
Subtract Real Realizable Cost Savings Not Providing Working Capital	
On Equipment	602.00
On Bonds Payable	124.00
	726.00
TOTAL SOURCES OF WORKING CAPITAL	1,875.35

Increase (Decrease) in Working Capital Accounts

	12/31/x6 ($x6)	12/31/x5 ($x6)	Increase	Decrease
Cash and Receivables	3,402.00	1,989.00	1,413.00	
Marketable Securities	636.00	817.70		181.70
Inventories	3,575.00	3,193.45	381.55	
Accounts Payable	2,500.00	2,762.50	262.50	
			2,057.05	
			(181.70)	181.70
Increase in Working Capital			1,875.35	

No new problems are created in the preparation of this statement. In our example, the only items affecting working capital are income statement items. Hence, the format is identical to the replacement cost statement of changes in financial position presented in Chapter 9.

Real data can easily be accumulated in a set of accounts which could constitute a self-balancing subsidiary ledger. Each period, after the end-of-period adjustments, these subsidiary accounts would provide the information necessary for the preparation of the financial statements illustrated in this chapter. The only accounts affected by the "real" adjustments are the owners' equity and cost savings accounts. The balances in these accounts would initially be those developed in the replacement cost accounting system summarized in Chapter 9. These and other necessary accounts have been duplicated in Exhibit 11.10, which will be our subsidiary ledger.

To illustrate the accounting procedures required to develop journal entries for these supplementary transactions and establish the subsidiary ledger, we use the data from our comprehensive example. The journal entries appear below and the T-account postings appear in Exhibit 11.10. The first entry is used to enter the net assets and stockholders' equity components from the 12/31/x5 replacement cost statement of financial position. The second entry records the cumulative effects of price changes from inception to 12/31/x5. The remaining entries show the current year developments. The journal entries which provide the basis for entries in our subsidiary ledger should be kept in a separate general journal.

Dr. Net Assets 8,930.00   (1)
   Cr. Capital Stock 2,000.00
   Cr. Real Retained (Realized) Earnings 4,750.00
   Cr. Real Unrealized Gains 2,180.00

To pick up the equity accounts and net assets in money terms from the 12/31/x5 replacement cost statement of financial position.

Dr. Real Unrealized Gains 701.82   (2)
   Cr. Capital Stock 440.00
   Cr. Real Retained (Realized) Earnings 261.82

To adjust the equity accounts at 12/31/x5 to eliminate the fictional realiz*ed* and *un*realiz*ed* gains and restate to 12/31/x5 dollars. The data are from Exhibit 11.7.

(701.82) = (858.34) fictional unrealized gains + 156.52
             price-level adjustment
  261.82 = (120.60) fictional realized gains + 382.42
             price-level adjustment

Dr. Net Assets 1,922.00   (3)
   Cr. Current Operating Income 382.30
   Cr. Real Realizable Gains 1,539.70

To pick up the increase in net assets and the components of replacement cost income during 19x6 from the replacement cost income statement.

Dr. Real Realizable Gains. 984.53   (4)
    Cr. Fictional Realizable Gains 984.53

To adjust money realiz*able* gains to real terms. Fictional realiz*able* gains were computed in Exhibit 11.1.

Dr. Real Realizable Gains. 100.94   (5)
    Cr. Real Realized Gains. 100.94

To transfer real realiz*ed* gains from real realiz*able* gains. See Exhibit 11.3 for the computation.

Dr. Current Operating Income 382.30   (6)
Dr. Real Realized Gains 100.94
    Cr. Real Realized Income 483.24

To close current operating income and real realiz*ed* gains (losses) to real realized income.

Dr. Real Realized Income. 483.24   (7)
Dr. Real Realizable Gains. 454.23
    Cr. Real Replacement Cost Income 937.47

To close real realized income and the change in real *un*realiz*ed* gains (the balance in real realiz*able* gains) to real replacement cost income.

Dr. Real Replacement Cost Income. 937.47   (8)
    Cr. Real Retained (Realized) Earnings 483.24
    Cr. Real Unrealized Gains. 454.23

To close real replacement cost income to real retained (realized) earnings and real *un*realiz*ed* gains.

Dr. Fictional Realizable Gains. 984.53   (9)
    Cr. Capital Stock 256.20
    Cr. Real Retained (Realized) Earnings 550.40
    Cr. Real Unrealized Gains. 177.93

To distribute fictional realiz*able* gains to the equity accounts. This reflects the total effect of general price-level movements during the year. The result is to restate the beginning equity account balances and the increment (i.e., real replacement cost income measured in average dollars) in end-of-period dollars.

Exhibit 11.10

Subsidiary Ledger for Real Data

Capital Stock				Real Retained (Realized) Earnings			
		(1)	2,000.00			(1)	4,750.00
		(2)	440.00			(2)	261.82
To Balance	2,696.20	(9)	256.20			(8)	483.24
	2,696.20		2,696.20	To Balance	6,045.46	(9)	550.40
					6,045.46		6,045.46
		Balance	2,696.20				
						Balance	6,045.46

Real Unrealized Gains				Current Operating Income			
(2)	701.82	(1)	2,180.00	(6)	382.30	(3)	382.30
		(8)	454.23				
To Balance	2,110.34	(9)	177.93				
	2,110.34		2,110.34				
		Balance	2,110.34				

Real Realizable Gains				Fictional Realizable Gains			
(4)	984.53	(3)	1,539.70	(9)	984.53	(4)	984.53
(5)	100.94						
(7)	454.23						
	1,539.70		1,539.70				

Real Realized Gains				Real Realized Income			
(6)	100.94	(5)	100.94	(7)	483.24	(6)	483.24

Real Replacement Cost Income				Net Assets			
(8)	937.47	(7)	937.47	(1)	8,930.00		
				(3)	1,922.00	To Balance	10,852.00
					10,852.00		10,852.00
				Balance	10,852.00		

Exhibit 11.11 presents an independent computation of the amounts distributed to the equity accounts.

Exhibit 11.11

Effect of General Price-Level Changes during 19x6 on the Equity Accounts and the Resulting Distribution of Fictional Realizable Gains

	Balance 12/31/x5 after Adjustments	×	Restatement Factor (10/95)	=	(1)	Increment from Real Replacement Cost Income in Average Dollars	×	Restatement Factor (5/100)	=	(2)	Total Effect of Price Level Changes = Fictional Realizable Gains (1) + (2)
Capital Stock	2,440.00		.105		256.20	—		—		—	256.20
Real Retained (Realized) Earnings	5,011.82		.105		526.24	483.24		.05		24.16	550.40
Real Unrealized Gains	1,478.18		.105		155.21	454.23		.05		22.72	177.93
Total	8,930.00				937.65	937.47				46.88*	984.53

*This is precisely the difference between real replacement cost income measured in end-of-period dollars (984.35) and average dollars (937.47) as calculated in Exhibit 11.6.

We believe that replacement cost accounting is, in general, superior to both historical cost and price-level adjusted historical cost accounting in providing useful information. This belief is based primarily on two characteristics of replacement cost accounting. First, all gains, both operating and holding, are recognized in the time period in which they arise. Second, realized income (= historical cost net income) is broken into two components—current operating income (which measures current operating profitability) and realized cost savings (which measures the realization of gains attributable only to specific price changes). In all likelihood, the cost of implementing a replacement cost accounting system will exceed the cost of general price-level accounting for most firms. We expect, however, that the benefits associated with replacement cost accounting will exceed its cost of implementation.

Once replacement cost data are available, the cost of making the price-level adjustments proposed here should be relatively insignificant. There are a few basic principles, such as the computation of fictional gains and the breakdown of money gains into real and fictional components, which, once understood, should be easy to implement. The subsidiary journal and ledger to keep track of the adjusted data represent rather small record-keeping requirements. Of course, all adjustments must be carefully documented through the use of working papers similar to those illustrated in this chapter. The major costs, which would arise when these procedures are first implemented, will relate to education and to development of the adjusted equity accounts at the beginning of the accounting period. Once begun, the additional costs required to maintain the system should be minimal. Consequently, objections to the proposed system should not rely heavily on anticipated system-related costs.

The immediate benefits are derived from the ability to measure *real income*. Real income refers to the increment (or decrement) in purchasing power in the firm's owners equity during each accounting period. Cries that "inflation is eating up (historical cost) profits" could be objectively evaluated. Indeed, the time may come when historical cost data no longer provide the basis for financial statements. Inflation, then, will have an effect on purchasing power, as it always does, and not on profit measurement.

The periodic measurement of real income will have a significant impact on the meaning of reported stockholders' equity. The real retained (realiz*ed*) earnings and real *un*realiz*ed* gains accounts will reflect the real changes in stockholders' equity over time. Of course, these real increments will be recorded in dollars of varying vintage and then restated in current end-of-period dollars. Even though *total* stockholders' equity would be the same as under replacement cost accounting without the price-level adjustments, its component items would have more meaning. Furthermore, calculation of a *real rate of return on equity* (RROR) would be possible. The use of current operating income, real realized income or real replacement cost income in the numerator of the RROR would enable information users to evaluate the productivity of stockholders' equity both in terms of real operating profits and total real gains, both operating and holding.

Another benefit of this procedure would probably come over the longer run, as the availability of real accounting data begins to shape tax policy. The determination of *real* rather than *money* tax burdens would probably reveal inequities and absurdities in the current tax structure which would require modification.

Finally, if this procedure were adopted universally, think of the improvement in economic and financial statistics of all kinds! Such statistics would almost certainly lead to more efficiency in private markets and governmental policies.

Questions and Problems

11.1. Briefly review the reasons why either general price-level accounting or replacement cost accounting alone is not fully adequate for financial reporting purposes.

11.2. Develop an analogy, other than the swarm of bees or mutual fund examples mentioned in the chapter, to illustrate the need for integration of adjustments for general and specific price changes.

11.3. Under general price-level restatement procedures, the historical cost of a fixed asset, such as land, is restated to reflect the change in the general price level since the asset was acquired. In the context of the current chapter, does the amount of such restatement represent a money gain, a real gain or a fictional gain? Explain.

11.4. How does the concept of purchasing-power gain or loss on monetary items (introduced in Chapter 2) relate to the treatment of such items in the present chapter?

11.5. A tract of land was purchased for $77,000 when the GNP Deflator stood at 128. It was sold more than a year later for $85,000, when the GNP Deflator had a value of 140.

a. Compute the money gain, fictional gain and real gain applicable to the land in end-of-period dollars.

b. Suppose that the land remained unsold at a financial statement date when its replacement cost was $83,000 and the GNP Deflator was 135. Compute realizable money gains, fictional gains and real gains at the financial statement date and when the land is subsequently sold (as in part a) in end-of-period (i.e., financial statement date and sale date) dollars. Indicate whether the gains are realized or unrealized.

11.6. The Marco Corporation purchased 500 shares of Flying Tiger Lines common stock at $6.75 per share on July 1 as a temporary investment. On December 31, the price per share was $7.40 and the price level had increased by 8 percent during the last half of the year.

a. Compute the money gain, real gain and fictional gain on this stock in end-of-period dollars. Identify the realizable, realized and unrealized components.

b. Compute the same requirements, assuming the year-end stock price was $6.30 and the change in the price index was 5 percent.

11.7. You are given the following information relative to the inventory accounts of the XYZ Corporation. Assume that beginning and ending inventories were purchased when the general price index was 124 and 136.4, respectively.

	Historical Cost	Replacement Cost	General Price Index
Beginning Inventory	$ 37,500	$44,300	124
Purchases	114,850	*	130.2 (average)
Ending Inventory	43,250	52,400	136.4

*Replacement Cost of Goods Sold = $122,100

a. Compute the historical cost of goods sold.

b. Compute realizable, realized and unrealized cost savings.

c. Compute the fictional and real components of realizable, realized and unrealized cost savings in end-of-period dollars.

11.8. The ABC Corporation purchased some office equipment for $50,000 on January 1, when the price level was 100. The equipment is to be depreciated over ten years on the straight-line basis, with no salvage value. At year end, replacement of this equipment would require an outlay of $60,000. During the year, the price level gradually rose to 112. The average price level was 106.

a. Give the journal entries necessary under replacement cost accounting relative to the equipment (depreciation, cost savings, etc.). Show all computations.

b. Compute the real and fictional components of realizable, realized and unrealized cost savings in end-of-period dollars.

c. Assuming the facts as given in the problem, suppose that the equipment has a historical salvage value of $1,000 (i.e., the total cost was $51,000). Management estimates the salvage value to be $1,500 at year end (i.e., total replacement cost is $61,500). How should the salvage value be treated to reflect the relevant changes in general and specific prices in end-of-period dollars?

11.9. You are given the following information for the RRC Corporation.

RRC CORPORATION
Statement of Financial Position at December 31, 19x5

ASSETS		LIABILITIES AND STOCKHOLDERS' EQUITY	
Cash	$12,000	Current Liabilities	$15,000
Inventory	20,000	Capital Stock	27,000
Land	10,000	Retained Earnings	—
		Total Liabilities and	
Total Assets	$42,000	Stockholders' Equity .	$42,000

Other Data:

(1) The land and inventory were purchased toward the end of 19x5, when the company was organized.

(2) Relevant general price index figures are:

End of 19x5	95
Middle of 19x6	100
End of 19x6	105

(3) Cash sales in 19x6 were $48,000.

(4) Merchandise purchased for cash, $35,000.

(5) Ending inventory = $18,000 (historical cost), $24,000 (replacement cost); the LIFO cost flow assumption is used.

(6) Cost to replace the land was $12,500 at 12/31/x6.

(7) Replacement cost of goods sold = $42,000.

Required:

a. Compute real realizable and real realized and real unrealized cost savings for 19x6 in end-of-19x6 dollars.

b. Prepare a statement of real income for the year ended December 31, 19x6, in end-of-19x6 dollars.

c. Prepare replacement cost statements of financial position and changes in financial position adjusted for changes in the general price level for 19x6.

11.10. The following data pertain to the RC Corporation.

RC CORPORATION
Statement of Financial Position, December 31, 19x5

	Historical Cost	Replacement Cost
ASSETS		
Cash	$ 1,000	$ 1,000
Accounts Receivable	1,500	1,500
Marketable Securities	2,000	1,900
Inventories	3,200	3,400
Total Current Assets	$ 7,700	$ 7,800
Plant and Equipment	$12,000	$15,000
Less: Accumulated Depreciation	3,000	3,750
	$ 9,000	$11,250
Land	4,000	9,000
Total Fixed Assets	$13,000	$20,250
Total Assets	$20,700	$28,050

LIABILITIES

Accounts Payable.	$ 4,000	$ 4,000
Long-Term Debt.	3,000	3,000
Total Liabilities.	$ 7,000	$ 7,000

STOCKHOLDERS' EQUITY

Capital Stock.	$10,000	$10,000
Retained (Realized) Earnings	3,700	3,700
Unrealized Cost Savings/Holding Gains. . . .	——	7,350
Total Stockholders' Equity	$13,700	$21,050
Total Liabilities and Stockholders' Equity	$20,700	$28,050

19x6 Transaction Data:

Cash Sales	$40,000
Merchandise Purchases, Cash.	28,000
Ending Inventory, Historical Cost	3,800
Interest Expense, Cash	270
Replacement Cost of Goods Sold	29,700
Cash Operating Expenses, Excluding Depreciation	5,200
Ending Inventory, Replacement Cost.	4,650

Additional Data:

(1) The firm's prior years' realized income amounts and related general price-level index values are as follows.

Realized Income		General Price Level	
Year	Amount	End of Year	Average for Year
19x0	——	100.	——
19x1	$ 500	104.	102
19x2	600	106.	105
19x3	800	110.	108
19x4	975	116.	113
19x5	825	128.	122
19x6	——	136.	132
	$3,700		

(2) The marketable securities were purchased in June, 19x5; cost to replace them at 12/31/x6 was $2,100.

(3) The inventory at 12/31/x5 was purchased late in 19x5, when the general price level was 125. Inventories are accounted for under the FIFO cost flow assumption. The ending inventory at 12/31/x6 was purchased when the price level was 134.

(4) On June 30, 19x6, a patent was purchased for $8,000 cash. The patent has an eight-year life; its cost is to be amortized on the straight-

line basis. At year end, the patent was estimated to be worth $8,800. One-half year of amortization is to be taken in 19x6.

(5) Plant and equipment is being depreciated over twenty years on the straight-line basis, no salvage value. It was acquired on 1/5/x1. Its replacement cost "new" rose to $15,000 at the end of 19x5 and to $18,000 at the end of 19x6.

(6) The land was purchased during 19x4 when the price level was 112; its replacement cost rose to $9,000 at the end of 19x5. On June 20, 19x6, one-fifth of the land was sold for $2,000. The remaining land has a replacement cost of $7,500 at year end.

(7) The long-term debt carries a coupon rate of 9 percent and matures on 12/31/x9. During 19x6, interest rates gradually declined to 7 percent. Interest is paid annually at year end.

(8) The capital stock was issued on 1/1/x1.

Required:

a. Prepare a complete set of replacement cost financial statements for 19x6. (NOTE: These are the same as for problem 9.2.)

b. Prepare the journal entry necessary to adjust the 12/31/x5 replacement cost equity section for changes in the general price level since 1/1/x1. Show all computations in proper form.

c. Compute real realizable, real realized and real unrealized gains for 19x6 in 12/31/x6 dollars.

d. Prepare a statement of real income for 19x6 in 12/31/x6 dollars.

e. Prepare adjusted replacement cost statements of financial position for 12/31/x6 and 12/31/x5 in 12/31/x6 dollars.

f. Prepare the 19x6 adjusted replacement cost statement of changes in financial position in 12/31/x6 dollars.

12 Summary and Conclusions

The purpose of this chapter is to summarize where we have been, and to pull together the threads. We need to do this in order to gain a clear understanding of each of the alternative methods of accounting for inflation. When one has spent a long time looking at detailed techniques, it is sometimes easy to lose sight of the more basic, underlying aspects. Therefore, this chapter summarizes and reemphasizes the essential features of the alternative accounting systems discussed in this book and evaluates the positive and negative aspects of each.

Illustrative Example 12.1 provides a numerical illustration of how some simple transactions would be treated under four alternative accounting systems: historical cost accounting, general price-level accounting, replacement cost accounting and real replacement cost accounting. Careful study of the numerical calculations and results will highlight the basic differences between the systems and, we hope, will place the preceding chapters in a more useful perspective.

We now turn to an analysis of the major problems of historical cost accounting and see to what extent these problems are resolved by the three systems proposed to account for the effects of changing prices. Then we shall conclude the book with an overall evaluation of the four alternative accounting systems.

Illustrative Example 12.1

Numerical Illustration Contrasting
the Alternative Accounting Systems*

There are essentially two different kinds of accounting for changing prices: current value accounting and constant dollar accounting. In the following description, three methods are presented: current value accounting, general price level adjusted (constant dollar) accounting, and (a synthesis of these two kinds) current value accounting combined with general price level adjustments.

---

*Sidney Davidson and Roman L. Weil, "Inflation Accounting," *Financial Analysts Journal* (January-February 1975).

The first and the last of these [illustrated in colums (2) and (4) of Tables A and B] are similar methods because the balance sheet totals are identical. Reported net income differs, however, and the balance sheet items are classified in different ways.

Revenues, Inventory, Cost of Goods Sold and Holding Gains or Losses

Table A shows transactions for a hypothetical company for a year in which the general price level increased by 32 percent (20 percent in the first six months and 10 percent in the second six months—$1.20 \times 1.10 = 1.32$). The fair market value of inventory units (widules) was $50 per unit on January 1, $80 on June 30, and $90 on December 31. (It is not at all unusual, of course, for some specific price changes to differ substantially from the change in the general price level. Realistic cases of even more substantial differences than those used in the example are easily found.)

The company starts the year with $100 cash and $100 of contributed capital, as shown in the January 1 balance sheet. The company buys two widules on January 1 for $50 each and sells one on June 30 for $120.

Historical Dollar Generally Accepted Accounting Principles: Column (1) shows how these transactions are accounted for under generally accepted accounting principles (GAAP). Revenues are $120, cost of goods sold is $50, and net income is $70.

Current Value Accounting: Column (2) shows how the transactions would be accounted for under current value or replacement cost accounting. Revenues are still $120. The cost of the unit sold, at the time it was sold, is $80, so the operating income is $40. In addition, there is a realized holding gain on the item sold of $30 (equal to current value at time of sale of $80 less acquisition cost of $50). Furthermore, there is an unrealized holding gain of $40 (equal to current value of $90 at end of year less acquisition cost of $50). Thus net income is $110 (equals $40 − $30 + $40). The December 31 balance sheet shows all assets and liabilities at current values as of December 31.

General Price Level Adjusted Accounting Based on Historical Costs: Column (3) shows general price level adjusted accounting as described in APB Statement No. 3 and in this article. All costs are historical, but financial statement data are restated to dollars of constant purchasing power. In the illustration, the dollars of constant purchasing power are December 31 dollars.

Revenues of $120 realized on June 30 are the equivalent of $132 of December 31 purchasing power; prices increased by 10 percent between June 30 and December 31 so that it takes $132 in December to buy the same general market basket (as represented by the GNP Deflator) that could have been bought on June 30 for $120.

The cost of goods sold of $50 in historical dollars is reported as $66 (equals $1.32 \times 50) in terms of December 31 purchasing power.

Since the company held cash ($120) from June 30 through December 31, when the purchasing power of the dollar declined by 10 percent, there is a loss on holdings of monetary items of $12 (equals $0.10 \times 120).

The balance sheet shows the historical cost of inventory restated to dollars dated December 31. The amount of capital contributed by owners was $100 in terms of January 1 purchasing power. This amount is equivalent to $132 of December 31 purchasing power since prices increased by 32 percent during the year. Hence contributed capital is shown on the balance sheet in terms of December 31 purchasing power as $132. The retained earnings amount shown on the balance sheet is transferred from the income statement.

Table A.

Traditional Accounting Compared with Current Value and Constant-Dollar Accounting

Balance Sheet as of January 1, 19xx
Cash: $100   Contributed Capital: $100

Date	January 1, 19xx	June 30, 19xx	December 31, 19xx
GNP Deflator	100 — (20% increase)⟶	120 — (10% increase)⟶	132
Cost of one Widule	$50	$80	$90
Transaction	Buy 2 widules at $50 each, $100.	Sell 1 widule for $120.	Close books and prepare statements.

	Historical Dollars		Constant Dollars Dated 12/31/xx	
Cost Basis Usual Name	Acquisition GAAP	Replacement Current Value	Acquisition GPLA	Replacement Cur. Val. & GPLA
Income Statement	(1)	(2)	(3)	(4)
Revenues	$120	$120	$132[a]	$132[a]
Cost of Goods Sold	50	80	66[b]	88[c]
Operating Income	$ 70	$ 40	$ 66	$ 44
Realized Holding Gains	—	30[d]	—	22[e]
Gain (Loss) on Monetary Items	—	—	(12)[f]	(12)[f]
Realized Income	$ 70	$ 70	$ 54	$ 54
Unrealized Holding Gains	—	40[g]	—	24[h]
Net Income	$ 70	$110	$ 54	$ 78
Balance Sheet				
Assets				
Cash	$120	$120	$120	$120
Inventory	50	90	66[b]	90
Total Assets	$170	$210	$186	$210
Equities				
Contributed Capital	$100	$100	$132	$132
Retained Earnings	70	70	54	54
Unrealized Holding Gains	—	40	—	24
Total Equities	$170	$210	$186	$210

(1) Traditional (2) Easy to Explain/Hard to Audit (3) Hard to Explain/Easy to Audit (4) Hard to Explain/Hard to Audit

[a]$120 × 1.10 [b]$50 × 1.32 [c]$80 × 1.10 [d]$80 — $50 [e]($80 — 1.20 × $50) × 1.10 [f]$120 × (−10%) [g]$90 — $50 [h]$90 — ($50 × 1.32)

Current Values Adjusted for General Price Level Changes: Column (4) of Table A shows the accounting when the principles of current value accounting are combined with the principles of stating all amounts in constant dollars. This approach has received acceptance among many theorists as the best possible approach, but is not likely to be required in the forseeable future.

Revenues are translated to end of year dollars as in Column (3). Cost of goods sold in current values is $80 as of June 30. But these are dollars of June 30 purchasing power. Translated to dollars of December 31 purchasing power, cost of goods sold is 10 percent more than $80, or $88.

The realized holding gain is measured as follows. In terms of June 30 purchasing power, the holding gain is current value on June 30 less acquisition cost translated into dollars of June 30 purchasing power. The acquisition cost of $50 on January 1 is the equivalent of $60 (equals $1.20 \times \$50$) of June 30 purchasing power. Hence the realized holding gain is $80 (current value as of June 30) less $60 (cost in June 30 dollars), or $20. This holding gain of $20 is measured in dollars of June 30 purchasing power and represents $22 (equals $1.10 \times \$20$) of December 31 purchasing power.

The unrealized holding gain is somewhat easier to compute: The current value of one widule on December 31 is $90. It cost $50 on January 1, which is equivalent to $66 (equals $1.32 \times \$50$) of December 31 purchasing power. The unrealized holding gain is $24 (equals $90 - \$66$).

Cash was held during the second half of the year when prices declined by 10 percent so there is a loss on holdings of monetary items of $12, calculated as before.

The balance sheet shows inventory at current values as of December 31 and the amount of contributed capital in terms of December 31 purchasing power. Notice that the balance sheet totals in Column (4) are the same as in Column (2). This is no coincidence. The only basic difference between the two approaches to current value accounting is that net income is reported differently. When the effects of changing prices are incorporated into current value accounting, we get a separation of real holding gains from nominal holding gains. The $32 difference between the net incomes reported in Columns (2) and (4) reflects the fact that the contributed capital in December 31 dollars is exactly $32 more than contributed capital in January 1 purchasing power. That $32 is not reported as income in price level adjusted current value accounting but is in historical dollar current value accounting.

Long-Lived Assets and Accounting for Changing Prices
Accounting for long-lived assets and depreciation in schemes designed to reflect changing prices requires some special techniques. These are explained in this section and in Table B. The assumptions for the illustration are spelled out at the head of Table B.

Current Value Accounting: At the start of 19x4, the current value of the asset is $20,000 and it is 30 percent "gone," so accumulated depreciation must be $6,000 and the book value must be $14,000. During the year 10 percent of the asset's cost is allocated to depreciation charges for the year. The asset's average cost during the year is $22,500 equals ($20,000 + $25,000)/2. Thus the depreciation charge for the year, based on 10 percent of "cost," is $2,250.

During the year, however, the current value of a similar, but new, asset increased from $20,000 to $25,000. Thus the owner of the asset has a holding gain. The gain on an unused asset would have been $5,000 but, on average, our asset was only 65 percent new during the year. (It was 70 percent new at the start of the year and 60 percent new at the end of the year.) Thus our holding gain is only 65 percent of $5,000, or $3,250.

General Price Level Adjustments for Long-lived Assets: Column (3) of Table B shows the accounting for the long-lived asset with general price level adjustments. During the four years since the asset was acquired, the general price level increased by 40 percent. The December 31 balance sheet would show the asset's cost at $14,000, which is equal to the original cost of $10,000 restated to December 31, 19x4, dollars. At the start of the year the asset of 30 percent is gone so the book value at the start of the year is $0.70 \times \$14,000$ equals $9,800 of December 31, 19x4, purchasing power.

Depreciation charges for the year are 10 percent of cost stated in December 31 dollars, or $1,400. As of the end of the year, the asset is 60 percent gone.

Of all the adjustments in generally price level accounting, the depreciation adjustment is likely to show the largest change from the traditional statements. Furthermore, it is likely to be the least meaningful. Only when the current value, or replacement cost, of assets similar to the ones being depreciated have changed as the GNP Deflator has changed will the adjustment reflect relevant information.

Current Value Adjusted for General Price Level Changes: Column (4) of Table B shows the accounting when the techniques of Column (2) for current values and Column (3) for general price level adjustments are combined.

The current value of the asset at the beginning of 19x4 was $20,000 but that amount is equal to $22,000 of December 13, 19x4, purchasing power. Since the asset is 30 percent gone at the start of 19x4, its book value is $15,400, or 70 percent of $22,000, in December 31 purchasing power.

The depreciation charge for the year is 10 percent of the average value of the new asset expressed in December 31, 19x4, dollars. The average value during 19x4 is $23,500 [equals $(1.10 \times \$20,000 + \$25,000)/2$]. Hence the depreciation charge for the year is $2,350.

The holding gain for the year is computed as follows. An unused asset increased in value by $3,000 (equals $\$25,000 - 1.10 \times \$20,000$) of December 31 purchasing power. On average our asset was 65 percent unused during 19x4, so the holding gain is 65 percent of $3,000, or $1,950.0. It is not coincidence that the net book values of the asset to be shown on the December 31 balance sheet is the same in Columns (2) and (4).

Summary

Columns (1) of Tables A and B show generally accepted accounting principles. Columns (2) show current value accounting. Current value accounting is easy to explain but hard to audit. It requires estimates of the current values of all assets

Table B.

Illustration of Depreciation Computations, General Price Level Adjustments and Related Holding Gains for Long-Lived Assets

ASSUMPTIONS

1. Machine purchased new on 1/1/X1 for $10,000.
2. Machine lasts 10 years and has zero salvage value at retirement.
3. Depreciation computed on a straight-line basis at 10 percent of cost per year.
4. GNP Deflator increased by 40 percent between 1/1/X1 and 12/31/X4.
5. GNP Deflator increased by 10 percent between 1/1/X4 and 12/31/X4.
6. New Machine of exactly the same type as the one purchased in (1) costs $20,000 on 1/1/X4 and $25,000 on 12/31/X4.
7. Used machine just like the one purchased in (1) costs $14,000 on 1/1/X4 and $15,000 on 12/31/X4.

	Historical Dollars		Constant Dollars Dated 12/31/X4	
	GAAP	Current Value	GPLA	Current Value & GPLA
	(1)	(2)	(3)	(4)
Balance Sheet, 1/1/x4				
Asset "Cost"	$10,000	$20,000	$14,000[a]	$22,000[b]
Less Accumulated Depreciation[c]	(3,000)	(6,000)	(4,200)	(6,600)
Book Value (30% gone)	$ 7,000	$14,000	$ 9,800	$15,400
Income Statement for 19x4				
Depreciation (10% of Average "Cost" During Year)	(1,000)	(2,250)[d]	(1,400)[e]	(2,350)[f]
Holding Gain	——	3,250[g]	——	1,950[h]
Balance Sheet, 12/31/x4				
Book Value (40% gone)	$ 6,000	$15,000	$ 8,400	$15,000
Asset "Cost"[i]	$10,000	$25,000	$14,000	$25,000

Footnotes for Table B

[a] $10,000 × 1.40.

[b] $20,000 × 1.10.

[c] Asset is 30 percent gone at January 1; 30 percent of "Cost."

[d] 10 percent of average cost of new asset during year; 0.10 × ($20,000 + $25,000)/2 = $2,250.

[e] 10 percent of adjusted cost of $14,000.

[f] 10 percent of average cost [=0.5 × ($22,000 + $25,000)] of new asset expressed in dollars dated December 31, 19X4.

[g] Gain on "unused" asset during year is $5,000. On average, our asset was 65 percent new during the year; 0.65 × 5,000 = $3,250.

[h] Gain on "unused" asset during year in constant dollars dated December 31, 19x4, is $3,000 = $25,000 − 1.10 × $20,000. On average, our asset was 65 percent new during the year; 0.65 × $3,000 = $1,950.

[i] Note that 40 percent of "cost" is the book value shown just above.

and liabilities. More often than not, prices for "used" assets are hard to get. Auditors would be required to make substantial judgmental decisions in implementing current value accounting. But we live in a litigious age and auditors are reluctant to exercise judgment in such situations because, occasionally, judgments would have to be published that could not be well documented and might lead to lawsuits if the judgment was proved wrong by subsequent events.

Other problems of current value accounting have not yet been settled by theorists. When there is a "bid-asked" spread for an asset—the replacement cost is higher than the current selling price (or net realizable value)—which of these numbers should be used? Those who believe in replacement costs are called "entry value" theorists and those who believe in net realizable values are called "exit value" theorists.

Columns (3) show historical costs adjusted for general price level changes. This is the treatment that is likely to be required. It is in many ways a meaningless, and sometimes misleading, treatment. But it is easy to audit and is objective. Two auditors given the same historical records and the same data for the GNP Deflator are likely to derive the same general price level adjusted statements.

The accounting shown in Columns (4) is, in our opinion, the best solution to the problem of accounting for changing prices. It incorporates both current values and holding gains and losses on all assets including the recognition of gain or loss on holdings of monetary items.

The Major Problems of Historical Cost Accounting

Historical cost accounting has many deficiencies which surface during periods of inflation. Perhaps the most common criticism of historical cost accounting is that it uses a rubber ruler. In other words, dollars of varying purchasing power get mixed together in historical cost accounts. As a result, current revenues are not matched by current costs. The costs charged against current revenues are a mixture of this period's expense, last period's expense and, in the case of items such as depreciation, expense expressed in dollars of various vintages that may go back quite a larger number of years. While accounting is rightly concerned with dollars, dealing only with the number of dollars may not be relevant information. For instance, confederate dollars are not the same as greenbacks. People are usually interested in knowing not simply the number of dollars, but command over goods or purchasing power. In order to reflect purchasing power properly, an adjustment has to be made to take into account the changing purchasing power of the dollar. Without such an adjustment one is using mixed dollars or, if you like, a rubber ruler.

Second, certain holding gains or cost savings get confused with regular operating income—inventory profits, for example, get lumped in with operating income. The result blurs the meaning of reported net income and rate of return, and the predictive power of the income figure is weakened. Items such as inventory profits are caused by changing inventory prices and are not a true reflection of operating profitability.

Third, on the statement of financial position, in periods of inflation, asset values tend to become rapidly outdated. Therefore the historical cost asset values on the statement of financial position lose their meaning.

Fourth, the effect of inflation on the firm tends to be overlooked. For instance, there is no indication of the effective income tax rate being paid. We refer to the percentage of the inflation-adjusted net income that is being paid out as income taxes. Similarly, there is a failure to indicate the effective dividend payout ratio, and the ability of the firm to replace its assets.

We will concentrate on these four major criticisms of historical cost accounting and summarize the possible solutions for dealing with them.

One possible solution is general price-level adjusted accounting, or purchasing-power accounting as currently proposed by the Financial Accounting Standards Board. We have also reviewed replacement cost accounting and real replacement cost accounting—that is, replacement cost accounting adjusted for general price- level changes. Let us consider each of these methods in relation to the criticisms that have been made of historical cost accounting. Through this comparison, we will be able to get some idea of the relative advantages and disadvantages of each of the proposed methods in overcoming the criticisms.

Mixing dollars of different purchasing power causes a distortion of the measurement unit, the dollar. Clearly, general price-level accounting is addressed to this particular criticism, for that method converts mixed dollars of different purchasing power to common dollars of constant purchasing power. Therefore the major advantage of general price-level accounting is that it tends to standardize the monetary unit. However, we must point out that many people do not agree that either the GNP Deflator or the Consumer Price Index provides an appropriate standard. But general price-level adjusted accounting does make a strong attempt to avoid the rubber-ruler problem and thus reduce the measurement error caused by fluctuations in the purchasing power of the dollar.

The Rubber Ruler

Replacement cost accounting also overcomes to some extent the problem of the rubber ruler. Although current costs are matched against current revenues, the correction for changes in purchasing power is incomplete. Holding gains, for instance, compare beginning-of-period and end-of-period changes in the replacement cost of assets—beginning and end-of-period (i.e., mixed) dollars. Therefore, if purchasing power has changed over the period, this change is not reflected in the calculation of holding gains under replacement cost accounting. In other words, under replacement cost accounting holding gains, whether realized or unrealized, do not allow for general purchasing-power changes in the interim. So replacement cost accounting represents a significant improvement over historical cost accounting with respect to the rubber-ruler problem. On the other hand, it does not solve this problem as well as general price-level adjusted accounting does. The real replacement cost accounting system matches current costs against current revenues and standardizes the monetary unit in terms of purchasing power and therefore does take into account the rubber-ruler problem. We believe that real replacement cost accounting is most effective in overcoming the purchasing-power problem, followed by general price-level accounting and replacement cost accounting.

Holding Gains and Operating Results Confused

Let us consider the second criticism of historical cost accounting namely, the confusing of holding gains with operating results. The concept of holding gains versus operating income does not exist in the general price-level accounting system. This particular concept, a major strength of replacement cost accounting, carefully separates current operating income and holding gains. Therefore, the two versions of replacement cost accounting are superior in this respect to general price-level accounting.

Another way of stating this conclusion is to point out that general price-level accounting is no different from historical cost accounting in terms of recognizing the effects of specific item price changes. General price-level accounting, like historical cost accounting, applies the realization principle of not recognizing any gain until the evidence of a completed transaction is available. Therefore, *un*realized holding gains are not taken into account under either historical cost accounting or under general price-level accounting. Since the *un*realized holding gains are not taken into account, the effects of replacement cost changes for assets such as inventories and plant do not enter the income statement. Hence current costs are not matched against current revenues under general price-level adjusted accounting.

Outdated Asset Values

The third criticism of historical cost accounting, that asset values are outdated and therefore not meaningful, clearly applies with equal force to general price-level adjusted accounting statements. The same asset values are reflected, except that general price-level accounting statements express these values in terms of dollars of constant purchasing power, rather than in dollars of mixed purchasing power (as in historical cost accounting). However, asset values are no more updated under general price-level adjusted accounting than under historical cost accounting.

Many items undergo price changes that have no relationship whatsoever to the general movement of prices. As a simple example, consider the price of hand-held electronic calculators, which has been rapidly dropping for the past several years. The total amount of this change in the last three or four years has been large. Over the same time period, the general price level has increased significantly. Therefore, a general price-level adjustment on such assets would be misleading indeed. The movements of many specific prices have no relation to the general price level. One must question the relevance of making a general price-level adjustment for items whose specific prices have changed in a different fashion.

Under either method of replacement cost accounting, however, asset values are updated and a more meaningful position statement is produced. The position statement is restored to its original importance and usefulness, and the updating of asset values permits the calculation of a meaningful rate of return on investment. Such a calculation expresses current operating income as a percentage of stockholders' equity and provides a useful indicator of current cost profitability. With respect to this important standard of comparison, replacement cost accounting is superior to general price-level accounting.

We now turn to the fourth criticism of historical cost accounting, that it does not disclose the impact of inflation on the firm. Historical cost accounting does not, for instance, indicate the effective tax rate or the effective dividend payout ratio. This criticism applies almost as strongly to general price-level adjusted accounting statements, where the income reported does not result from matching current costs against current revenues. Rather, it is historical cost accounting that has been adjusted for changes in the purchasing power of the dollar. Therefore, it is not a completely current income figure; it cannot be used to compute a proper effective tax rate or effective dividend payout ratio. While general price-level adjusted statements do provide some improvement over historical cost accounting statements in this respect, the degree of improvement is slight. A much greater improvement is gained from the use of replacement cost accounting and, in particular, by the use of real replacement cost accounting, which allows an effective tax rate and an effective dividend payout ratio to be computed.

Showing the Impact of Inflation on the Firm

With respect to financial statements released outside the firm, the property of *objectivity*, of great importance to accountants, is a major strength of historical cost accounting and, to a lesser but still significant degree, of general price-level accounting as well. It is true that some important areas of disagreement must be resolved with respect to general price-level accounting in order for it to reach the degree of objectivity which applies to historical cost accounting. For instance, serious controversy still surrounds the treatment of purchasing-power gains on long-term monetary obligations. Also, in order for objectivity to be maximized, it is necessary to agree on which version of the GNP Implicit Price Deflator should be used when

Other Factors

producing general price-level adjusted accounting statements. Presumably, it could be agreed that the latest version of that GNP Implicit Price Deflator available as of statement date should always be used. In fact, such a rule would certainly improve the objectivity of general price-level adjusted accounting statements.

Because replacement cost figures involve a higher degree of subjectivity and estimation, a certain amount of objectivity is necessarily lost. In terms of objectivity, historical cost accounting is the superior system, followed by general price-level adjusted accounting. Lagging significantly behind are both versions of replacement cost accounting.

Let us now consider the question of *relevance* to the user. Historical cost accounting does not take into consideration the rubber-ruler problem, nor does it separate holding gains from operating results. For this and other reasons, the degree of relevance of historical cost accounting statements seems rather low. General price-level adjusted accounting statements offer a higher degree of relevance than historical cost accounting, because they provide the purchasing-power (rubber-ruler) correction. They also contain information unavailable under historical cost accounting, that is, the purchasing-power gain or loss on net monetary items.

The relevance of replacement cost accounting statements appears to be much higher than that of general price-level adjusted accounting statements, because the major effects of inflation, namely, changes in the specific prices of particular assets, are taken into account, even though those assets may remain on hand. The greatest degree of relevance appears to be attached to real replacement cost accounting statements, which not only allow for unrealized effects of price changes but also are expressed in terms of dollars of standardized purchasing power.

The basic and important question that needs to be asked when comparing different accounting systems concerns the meaning of the resulting income figure. Under historical cost accounting, the net income figure represents *realized* profit. However, this implies nothing about the ability of the firm to replace assets that have been used up in the production process. Since replacement costs tend to rise, the problem of ability to replace consumed assets becomes important. Historical cost accounting reports only profits based on past costs; it is not concerned in any way with present replacement costs.

General price-level accounting presents a net income figure that is somewhat confusing. This figure does not represent conventional realized profit alone, since it includes purchasing-power gains or losses on monetary items. Therefore, the meaning attached to net income under general price-level adjusted accounting certainly is not conventional realized profit. In fact, it is not quite clear what the precise meaning of this profit concept actually is.

The replacement cost accounting net income figure does directly address the problem of increased replacement cost of resources consumed in the production process. Current operating income represents the earnings in excess of what the firm would presently require to maintain intact its physical operating capacity. This is important information for managerial purposes.

Of course, the income figure resulting from replacement cost accounting requires correction for changes in purchasing power. This refinement is provided by real replacement cost accounting. In the short run, the appeal of general price-level accounting with its high degree of objectivity and its simplicity in application is likely to influence the authoritative accounting bodies. We believe, however, that in the long term, real replacement cost accounting is likely to be introduced as a preferred alternative, given its significant superiority in providing relevant information during inflationary periods.*

The Final Choice

Exhibit 12.2 summarizes the discussion in tabular form. It is our conclusion that, all things considered, real replacement cost accounting offers the greatest net advantage to users of financial statements. It is appropriate to point out that users of financial statements can be divided into two broad groups. On the one hand, there are many users of published financial statements who are outside the firm. The other significant user group is the management of the firm. With respect to outside users, objectivity is an important attribute. For managerial use, however, relevance usually takes first place over objectivity. Replacement cost accounting clearly seems the superior method for managerial use. This may not be quite as clearly the case for published financial statements, where there is more room for debate. We believe, however, that real replacement cost accounting provides the most useful information not only for managerial use but also for published financial statements.

Exhibit 12.2

Relative Merits of the Alternative Accounting Systems

System of Accounting	Constant Purchasing Power	Separation of Operating and Holding Results	Current Values	Showing Impact of Inflation	Objectivity	Relevance
Historical Cost	Poor	Poor	Poor	Poor	Best	Poor
General Price Level	Best	Poor	Poor	Poor	Good	Poor
Replacement Cost	Good	Good	Good	Good	Poor	Good
Real Replacement Cost	Best	Good	Good	Best	Poor	Best

*For more on the issues of *relevance* and *interpretability* of the accounting information being provided by these alternative systems, see Robert R. Sterling, "Relevant Financial Reporting in an Age of Price Changes," *Journal of Accountancy* (February 1975): 42–51.

Index

Accounting Principles Board:
  Opinion No. 11, *Accounting for Income Taxes*, 78, 205
  Statement No. 3, *Financial Statements Restated for General Price-Level Changes*, 8
Alcoa, 92
Alexander, Michael, 222
Allied Chemical, 92
American Appraisal Company, 222
American Brands, 92
American Can, 92
American Institute of Certified Public Accountants:
  Accounting Research Study No. 6, *Reporting the Financial Effects of Price-Level Changes*, 12
  Accounting Research Study No. 12, *Reporting Foreign Operations of U.S. Companies in U.S. Dollars*, 79n
Anaconda, 92
Appraisal Considerations, current value and replacement cost accounting, 253–256
Assets:
  form, 135
  markets for, 135
  service potentials and replacement cost, 135, 136
  valuation date, 135
AT&T, 92
Avon, 93
Backer, Morton, 218n, 219
Barber-Ellis of Canada, Limited:
  auditor's report (Touche Ross & Co.), 223
  current replacement cost financial statements, 222–227
Baxter Labs, 93
Bell, Philip W., 114n, 264n
Bethlehem Steel, 92
Bowater Paper Corporation Limited, 218
Broken Hill Proprietary Company Limited, 218
Brunswick, 93
Burton, John C., 213

Canadian Institute of Chartered Accountants, 7
Chemetron, 93
Chrysler, 92
Clark, David, 53
Coca Cola, 93
Compania Minera Aguilar, S.A., 218
Consumer Price Index:
  discussion of, 22, 83
  table of, 3
Contribution margin, 126
Cost savings (*see also* Holding gains):
  defined, 114
  in replacement cost accounting, 114
Creole Petroleum Corporation, 218
Current operating income, replacement cost accounting:
  defined, 117
  usefulness of, 132, 141
Currently attainable standard costs, 167
Davidson, Sidney, 87, 88, 91, 109, 288n
Debit-credit equality, general price level accounting, 46
Deferred income taxes:
  on unrealized cost savings in replacement cost accounting, 204–209
  treatment in general price level accounting, 78–79
Depreciating accounting:
  double-declining balance:
    general price level estimation procedure, 97–99
    replacement cost accounting, 181–183
  general price level accounting, 14–15, 33
  replacement cost accounting, 174
  sum-of-the-years' digits:
    general price level estimation procedure, 97–99
    replacement cost accounting, 180–181
Dow Chemical, 93
du Pont, 92
Eastman Kodak, 92
Edwards, Edgar O., 114n, 141n, 264n

Electric and Musical Industries Limited, 218
English Institute of Chartered Accountants, 7
Entry price:
  defined, 135
  historical cost, 135, 136
  present cost, 135, 136, 137
  replacement cost, 135, 136, 137
  reproduction cost, 135, 136
Esmark, 92
Exit price:
  current value, 135, 138
  defined, 135
  expected value, 135, 138
  opportunity value, 135, 138–139
Exxon, 92
Fictional gains:
  defined, 262
  measurement of, 262–263, 264–268, 270
FIFO (*see* inventory cost flow assumptions)
Financial Accounting Standards Board:
  exposure draft, "Accounting for the Translation of
    Foreign Currency Transactions and Foreign
    Currency Financial Statements", 79n
  exposure draft, "Financial Reporting in Units of
    General Purchasing Power", 8
FISH (first-in, still-here), 146n
Fixed manufacturing overhead, replacement cost
  accounting, 184–186
Flow chart, replacement cost accounting, 121
Foreign currency balances and general price level
  accounting, 79–81
Foreign exchange rate, defined, 7, 79
General Electric Company:
  estimation of general price-level adjusted financial
    statements illustrated, 92, 101–105
  sales compared with N.V. Philips' Gloeilampen-
    fabrieken, 114
General Foods, 92
General Motors, 92
General price-level adjusted financial statements, esti-
  mation procedures, 97–110
Genesco, 93
Goodyear, 92
Gould, 93
Gross National Product Implicit Price Deflator:
  discussion of, 22, 84
  table of, 28, 85
Gulf Oil, 93

Gulf & Western, 93
Handy-Whitman Index of Public Utility Construction
  Costs, 221
Hanna, John R., 214
Haskins and Sells, 90
Heineken's Bierbrouwerij Maatschappij NV, 219
Hicks, John R., 131n
Hicksian income:
  defined, 131
  importance to accounting, 260, 313
Hilton Hotels, 93
Holding gains (*also see* cost savings):
  defined, 113
  in replacement cost accounting, 113
  on securities, 190
Holiday Inns, 93
IBM, 93
Imasco Limited (*see* Imperial Tobacco Company of
  Canada, Limited)
Imperial Tobacco Company of Canada, Limited;
  inventory valuation problems, 214–215
  replacement cost financial statements, 216–217
Income tax accounting:
  deferred income taxes:
    general price level accounting, 76–79
    historical cost accounting, 76–79
    replacement cost accounting, 204–209
  permanent differences, 76, 204
  timing differences, 76, 204
Income tax expense,
  general price level restatement, 76–79
Indiana Telephone Corporation:
  auditors' report (Arthur Andersen & Co.), 64, 69
  corporate comparative data, 66–67
  historical and general price level financial state-
    ments, 60–64
  treatment of purchasing power gain or loss on
    monetary items, 68–69
Inland Steel, 93
International Harvester, 92
International Nickel, 92
International Paper, 92
Inventory cost flow assumptions:
  FIFO (first-in, first-out):
    general price level accounting, 14
    general price level accounting estimation proce-
      dure, 96
    historical cost accounting, 146

Inventory cost flow assumptions: (continued)
  FIFO (first-in, first-out): (continued)
    replacement cost accounting, 150–160
  LIFO (last-in, first-out):
    effect on earnings of firms switching to, 168–169
    general price level accounting estimation procedure, 96–97
    historical cost accounting, 146–147
    replacement cost accounting, 150–160
    NIFO (next-in, first-out), replacement cost accounting, 164
  Weighted average:
    general price level accounting estimation procedure, 97
    historical cost accounting, 147
    replacement cost accounting, 150–160
"Inventory profits," 163
Inventory systems:
  periodic, 145
  perpetual, 162
Inventory valuation:
  lower of cost or market:
    general price level accounting, 24
    lower of restated cost or market, general price level accounting, 81
    replacement cost accounting, 162–163
IT&T, 93
Johns-Manville, 92
Kelly, James N., 86, 87
Knol, A. W., 218n
Koninklijke Nederlandsche Hoogovens en Staalfabrieken NV, 219
Koppers Company, Inc., 93, 215n
Latent income taxes:
  N.V. Philips' Gloeilampenfabrieken, 206
  on unrealized cost savings/holding gains, 206–209
LIFO (see inventory cost flow assumptions)
LISH (last-in, still-here), 146n
Livingstone, J. Leslie, 221
Loews, 93
Lower cost of market (see inventory valuation)
Manufactored inventories, replacement cost accounting, 166–167
Marshall and Stevens, 222
Martin Marietta, 93
MCA, 93
Measurement problem, in accounting, 259–261
Merck, 93

Monetary assets, defined, 9
Monetary items:
  defined, 9
  list of common monetary items, 48–51
Monetary liabilities, defined, 9
Money gains, 262
N.V. Philips' Gloeilampenfabrieken:
  auditors' report (Klynveld Kraayenhof & Co.), 233
  replacement cost financial statements (Philips Lamp), 234–244
  sales compared with General Electric Company, 114
Net monetary items, defined, 10
Net realizable value, 138
NIFO (see inventory cost flow assumptions)
Nonmonetary items:
  defined, 10
  formula for restatement in general price level accounting, 11
  list of common nonmonetary items, 48–51
Objectivity, of accounting information, 297–299
Operating income, defined, 113, 131
Opportunity cost, 135 (see also opportunity value)
Opportunity value, defined, 138
Owens-Illinois, 92
Petersen, Russel J., 109, 110
Pfizer, 93
Philip Morris, 93
Philips Lamp (see N.V. Philips' Gloeilampenfabrieken)
Pillsbury, 93
Prices, individual commodities, table of, 3
Procter & Gamble, 92
Public Telephone Corporation, purchase by Indiana Telephone Corporation, 59, 70
Purchasing power, defined, 1
Purchasing-power gain or loss on monetary items:
  computation of illustrated, 30, 31
  defined, 9
  disclosure in financial statements, 68–69, 74–75
  formula for computation of in general price level accounting, 10
  general price level accounting estimation procedure, 99–100
Ratio to restate, general price level accounting, 9
Real gains:
  defined, 262
  measurement of 262–263, 268–270
Real income (loss):

defined, 260
measurement of, 271–272
Real rate of return on equity, 281–282
Realizable cost savings:
    defined, 117
    fictional, 264–265
    real, 268
Realizable income, 131
Realization criterion, historical cost accounting,
        89, 111
Realized cost savings:
    defined, 119
    fictional, 265–268
    real, 268
Realized income, replacement cost accounting:
    defined, 117, 132
    equivalence with historical cost net income, 117
Relevance, of accounting information 298–299
Replacement cost income, defined, 117
Restatement factor, general price level accounting, 9
Restatement process in general price level accounting,
        steps for, 23–24
"Revalorization" problem, 177–179
Rockwell International, 93
Rosenfield, Paul, 110
"Rubber ruler" problem, in accounting, 294, 295–296
Salvage value, replacement cost accounting, 183
Sandilands Commission, 112, 113
Schedule of sources and applications of monetary
        items, 23
Schindler, James S., 109
Sea Pines Corporation, illustrative schedules and
        notes dealing with current value accounting,
        246–252
Sears, Roebuck, 92
Securities and Exchange Commission:
    "Notice of Proposed Amendments to Regulation
        S-X to Require Disclosure of Certain Replace-
        ment Cost Data in Notes to Financial State-
        ments (S7-579)", 112
Selfridges Limited, 218
Shank, John K., 53
Shell Oil Company:
    auditors' report (Price Waterhouse & Co.), 72, 75
    estimate of general price level adjusted income, 93

supplementary price level adjusted financial infor-
        mation, 73
Shieneman, Gary S., 168n
Sorter, George H., 146n
Speculative gains and replacement cost of goods
        sold, 166n
Standard Oil of California, 92
Sterling, Robert R., 299n
Sunbeam, 93
"Swarm of bees" analogy, 2, 261
Sweeney, Henry W., 7n
Technological change:
    and replacement cost, 220–221
    and reproduction cost, 220–221
Temporal method of foreign currency translation, 79n
Texaco, 92
The Theory and Measurement of Business Income,
        114n, 264n
Toledo Edison Company, "General Price Level
        Financial Statement Study", 74–75
Touche Ross & Co., 90, 222
Trans Union, 93
U.S. Steel, 92
Union Carbide, 92
United Aircraft, 92
Unrealized cost savings:
    change in, 127–128
    defined, 120
    real, 269
Valuation problem, in accounting, 259–261
Value added, defined, 136, 137
Value in exchange, 141
Value in use, 141
Van Bruinessen, Dr. Wessel, 213
Vancil, Richard F., 86, 87
Walgreen, 93
Weighted average (*see* inventory cost flow
        assumptions)
Weil, Roman L., 87, 88, 91, 109, 166n, 288n
Westinghouse Electric, 92
Weyerhaeuser, 93
Wholesale price index, discussion of, 83
Woolworth, 92
Yield to maturity, bonds, 191
Zenith, 93